*Music
Reference and Research
Materials*

Music
Reference and Research
Materials

AN ANNOTATED BIBLIOGRAPHY

THIRD EDITION

COMPILED BY

Vincent Duckles

THE FREE PRESS
A Division of Macmillan Publishing Co., Inc.
NEW YORK

Collier Macmillan Publishers
LONDON

The Free Press
A Division of Macmillan Publishing Co., Inc.
866 Third Avenue, New York, N.Y. 10022

Collier-Macmillan Canada Ltd.

Library of Congress Catalog Card Number: 73–10697

Printed in the United States of America

printing number
1 2 3 4 5 6 7 8 9 10

Library of Congress Cataloging in Publication Data

Duckles, Vincent Harris, 1913–
    Music reference and research materials.

    1. Music—Bibliography. 2. Bibliography—
Bibliography—Music. I. Title.
ML113.D83   1974   016.78   73–10697
ISBN 0–02–907700–1

Contents

Contents

GUIDES TO SYSTEMATIC AND HISTORICAL MUSICOLOGY 121

BIBLIOGRAPHIES OF MUSIC LITERATURE 128

BIBLIOGRAPHIES OF MUSIC 188

Introduction to
the Third Edition

SINCE THE SECOND EDITION of this work appeared in 1967, there have been substantial gains in the area of music reference and research materials, both in quantity and in quality. Quantity is indicated by the fact that this third edition incorporates more than 600 new entries; quality is represented in a number of distinguished new works that have come into existence during the past five years—for example, Barry Brook's *Thematic catalogues in music* (no. 1826); Rita Benton's *Directory of music research libraries*, volumes 2 and 3 (no. 1127); and several important additions to the series issued under the auspices of the International Inventory of Musical Sources (nos. 1079 ff.). The reprint publishers have been increasingly active during the past few years, and their work has restored a great many valuable music reference books to the shelves. A special effort has been made to call these titles to the attention of our readers.

No significant changes have been made in the organization of the work. A new section covering *Music History in Pictures* has been added. New categories treating *Individual Composers* and *Music of Individual Composers* have also been introduced. These sections are far from comprehensive, however; they are intended to call attention to useful types of reference tools that might otherwise be overlooked by the student. In spite of the increased size and scope of this volume, selectivity has remained the rule. Those who look for complete or comprehensive coverage in any category will be disappointed. In some cases the selection has been involuntary, based as it is upon the resources of a particular music research library here at Berkeley. But more often than not the selection has been deliberate, intended to highlight the kinds of questions raised by graduate students in music and to suggest approaches to the solution of their research problems. Over the years I have accumulated an increasing debt to those generous users who have both called my attention to errors and omissions in the text and suggested improvements. They are too numerous to mention individually, but their collective impact on this new edition of *Music Reference and Research Materials* has been considerable.

Berkeley, California   *Vincent Duckles*
1974

Introduction to
the Second Edition

THE PLEA FOR CORRECTIONS and additions that concluded the *Introduction* to the first edition of this work has not gone unheeded. Responses have come from a wide group of music students, teachers, and librarians. The chagrin at having one's oversights pointed out has been more than balanced by the pleasure at finding that this bibliography has been extensively and searchingly used. I am particularly grateful for suggestions made by my own students at the University of California, and to my colleague Daniel Heartz. John Davies, Music Librarian of the British Broadcasting Corporation, London, made many helpful comments, as did Jan La Rue, New York University, Frederick Crane, Lousiana State University, and George Skapski of San Fernando Valley State College. For assistance in the preparation of the manuscript of this edition, I am indebted to Lee Rosen.

Apart from the correction of old entries and the addition of new, no major changes have been introduced in this edition. A few minor revisions in organization should be noted, however. These include (1) an added section on *Jazz and Popular Music* under *Bibliographies of Music*; (2) the printed and manuscript sources of early music have been combined under one alphabet rather than two; and (3) *Catalogs of Private Collections* have been extracted from the general list of music library catalogs and entered in a section of their own. A substantial number of new book reviews have been added, and much attention has been given to making the *Index* more usable from a subject point of view.

The bibliography of music is an actively growing field. This is reflected not only in the fact that more than 200 new entries have been added to this edition, but also in the high quality of the work that is being done. The International Inventory of Musical Sources has been progressing slowly but surely toward its goal. The publication of the catalogs of major Italian music libraries has been moving ahead under the direction of Claudio Sartori in the series Bibliotheca Musicae. In this country we have the exemplary bibliography of *Instrumental music printed before 1600* by Howard Brown and the long-awaited *Index of Festschriften* by Walter Gerboth. Our control over the materials of popular song has been greatly enhanced by the appearance of Richard Wolfe's bibliography of *Secular music in America, 1801–25* and by the work of James Fuld and Nat. Shapiro. Two new series devoted exclusively to music bibliography are off to a promising start: the Detroit Studies in Music Bibliography and the Music Library Association Index Series.

Vincent Duckles

1966

Introduction to the First Edition

A BIBLIOGRAPHY can be regarded as the relatively inert by-product of scholarly activity, or it can be treated as an active ingredient in the learning process. The latter perspective has been adopted in this guide to *Music Reference and Research Materials*. While no one but a professional bibliographer may be expected to come for his leisure reading to a list of books, most of us can respond with interest to an organized survey of the literature of a particular field. A bibliography, in fact, offers one of the best means of gaining an over-all impression of a subject area. It throws the essential patterns of a discipline into relief, casting light on what has been accomplished and drawing attention to the shadows where work still needs to be done. This guide has been designed to illuminate the bibliographical resources for musical scholarship. It is, above all, intended to serve a teaching purpose. Implicit in its organization is the concept that bibliography is an approach to knowledge, a way in which the student can progress toward mastery in his chosen field of specialization within the larger dimensions of the field of music. The guide was developed, through a series of editions beginning in 1949, as a text for a graduate seminar entitled "An Introduction to Musical Scholarship" given in the Music Department of the University of California at Berkeley. If its pattern has been determined to some extent by the way in which music bibliography is taught in a specific institution, its structure is still flexible enough to permit other teachers to use it in their own way.

The work is actually intended to fulfill the requirements of two groups: graduate students who need to become acquainted with the resources for musical research, and music reference librarians whose job it is to help others find the information they want. While the needs of the two have much in common, there are points at which their interests diverge. Much more is listed here than will be required for reference services in any but a large music research library, and there is material included which the scholar would rarely need to consult unless he moved outside of the traditional framework of historical musicology.

The present volume is much larger than any of its predecessors, yet it remains a selective list. One limitation in coverage, strictly enforced, is the selection of titles that pertain directly or exclusively to *music*. This criterion eliminates a great deal of valuable reference material, particularly important in areas that lie on the borderline between musicology and other disciplines: liturgics, the theater arts, literature, the dance, etc. No musicologist can afford to neglect such general reference tools as the *Encyclopedia of Religion and Ethics*, or Cabrol's *Dictionnaire d'archéologie chrétienne et de liturgie*, or, in another area, the *Census of Medieval and Renaissance Manuscripts in the U.S. and Canada*, by Semour de Ricci, or Paul O. Kristeller's valuable survey of the catalogs of *Latin Manuscript Books before 1600*. The fact that these tools are indispensable only serves to demonstrate that musicology is far from being a self-sufficient and self-contained discipline. But an attempt to list all of the peripheral resources would inflate the present work and destroy its focus. There are excellent bibliographies of general reference works currently available. Perhaps the best service to be offered to the young musicologist here is to direct him to Constance M. Winchell's *Guide to Reference Books* (7th ed., 1951, and later supplements) or to Theodore Besterman's *World Bibliography of Bibliographies* (3rd ed., 1955–56). If all else fails, he should be urged to rely on that universal repository of fact and resource, *the reference librarian*, who sits behind a desk in every large library, prepared to guide the inquiring student through the complex paths of information retrieval. But there is a distinct advantage to be gained in approaching the general reference tools from the musician's point of view. Recently Keith E. Mixter has furnished such an approach in his manual on *General Bibliography for Music Research* (1962), published as Number 4 in the Detroit Studies in Music Bibliography. It is a pleasure to be able to point to that work as a useful complement to this one.

A few further statements should be added to make clear what ground this guide is, and is not, intended to cover. It does not represent the well-rounded library of musical literature; it contains no entries for biography, no local histories, no monographs or studies devoted to most of the subject areas into which the field of music can be subdivided. It is certainly not a basic list of titles which every music library should acquire; but it does provide a list from which the essential materials for a music reference collection can be selected. It can best be described as a bibliography of music bibliographies, its emphasis being on those works which themselves serve as points of departure for further investigations: lists, inventories, alphabetized compilations of facts about music. The one section which falls most conspicuously outside of this pattern of bibliographical emphasis is the section on "Histories and Chronologies." This is the only category in which books are listed for what they contain intrinsically rather than for their function as guides to further information.

In its preliminary forms this book has been put to use in a number of courses in music bibliography throughout the country, and as a result has benefited from the suggestions of several generous-minded critics. I am particularly indebted to Professor Albert T. Luper of the State University of Iowa, and to Professor Otto Albrecht of the University of Pennsylvania for their help in this respect. The form of the annotations owes much to Richard Angell of the Library of Congress, who placed his notes at my disposal. My colleagues in the Music Library of the University of California at Berkeley, Harriet Nicewonger and Minnie Elmer, have made their influence felt on nearly every page in matters that have to do with the selection of titles, the framing of the annotations, and the reading of proof.

One feature which has been introduced for the first time in the current edition is the citation of book reviews. These are offered as practical aids to the evaluation of the items. No effort has been made to achieve complete coverage: reviews are cited only for the more recent items, and are confined largely to those published in the English-language journals.

The entries are numbered throughout this book, and for the most part, each title is entered once. There are some instances of duplicate entries, however, when the content of the item calls for its listing in more than one category. Eitner's *Quellen-Lexikon* is a case in point. This title is entered once as a dictionary of biography, and again as a bibliography of early music.

Abbreviations are used sparingly. What they save in space in a work of this kind is rarely commensurate to the inconvenience caused to the user. They are confined to the standard symbols for the dictionaries and journals most frequently cited in reviews: *Grove* for *Grove's Dictionary of Music and Musicians,* 5th edition; *MGG* for *Die Musik in Geschichte und Gegenwart; Acta M* for *Acta musicologica; JAMS* for *Journal of the American Musicological Society; MQ* for *The Musical Quarterly;* and *Notes* for *Music Library Association Notes,* 2nd series.

A bibliographer's work is never done. Even as this edition goes to press, I am troubled by the submerged voices of would-be entries which may have been overlooked, and entries which may have been misplaced or misrepresented. Other music bibliographers proceed, unconcerned, with their work, the results of which will eventually call for supplements, or even substantial revisions in our present pattern of organization. But if one were too attentive to such considerations a work of this kind would never reach the point of publication. Now that it has made its appearance, I hope that it will attract collaboration, in the form of corrections, additions, or suggestions for improvement, from all who have occasion to use it.

Vincent Duckles

1964

*Music
Reference and Research
Materials*

Dictionaries and Encyclopedias

THE MOST COMPREHENSIVE bibliography of music dictionaries and encyclopedias is James B. Coover's *Music lexicography*, 3rd edition, 1971 (see no. 1846), which offers some 1,800 titles. Other convenient listings appear in the article "Lexika der Musik," by Hans Heinrich Eggebrecht, in *MGG*, vol. 8, and in the "Sachteil" of the Riemann Musik Lexikon, 12th edition, 1967. See also A. Hyatt King's survey in *Grove*, 5th ed., vol. 2, and the article "Dictionaries of music" in the *Harvard dictionary*, 2nd ed., 1969. A useful, chronological approach is found in a list by Richard Schaal printed in the *Jahrbuch der Musikwelt* (no. 1823), 1949, p. 105–11, and also in *Hinrichsen's music book* (no. 1820), vol. 7, p. 594–601, under the title, "The fore-runners of the *Grove-Blom*."

A growing recognition of the value of early dictionaries as historical documents has brought many out-of-print titles into current availability through the efforts of such reprint publishers as the Da Capo Press, Frits A. M. Knuf of Hilversum, Georg Olms of Hildesheim, Dover Publications in New York, and the Akademische Druck und Verlagsanstalt of Graz.

The present list includes the most important music dictionaries and encyclopedias in current use, in modern languages, cited as far as is

1

possible under their latest editions. It also includes a selection of titles of those early works available in modern reprints or of continuing value for reference purposes.

GENERAL

Those works in which both terms and biography are treated in a single alphabet are cited as "general" dictionaries and encyclopedias. The prototype for such reference tools is Johann Walther's *Musikalisches Lexicon*, published in 1732 (no. 62). From this important work two lines of descent may be traced, one leading through a series of concise dictionaries—usually in one volume and intended for quick reference, the other moving in the direction of multivolume, large-scale works with extended articles, more properly described as encyclopedias.

1 / **Abert, Hermann J.,** ed.   Illustriertes Musik-Lexikon. Stuttgart, J. Engelhorns Nachf., 1927. 542 p.

A popular general dictionary, based on *Riemann* (no. 46) and *Das neue Musiklexikon* (no. 95). 503 pictures on 72 plates and numerous short musical examples. Contributing editors: Hermann Abert, Friedrich Blume, Rudolf Gerber, Hans Hoffmann, and Theodor Schwartzkopff.

2 / **Algemene Muziekencyclopedie,** onder leiding van A. Corbet en Wouter Paap.   Redactiesecretaris: J. Robijns. Antwerpen, Zuid-Nederlandse Uitg. [1957–63] 6 v.

Comprehensive coverage of all aspects of music, including ethnomusicology, popular music, jazz. Brief biographies include performers, musicologists, composers, dancers. Major articles signed by contributors from England, Israel, United States, U.S.S.R., etc. Subject bibliographies and discographies and brief lists of works for composers and musicologists. Valuable for its wide biographical range. Illustrated.

3 / **Allorto, Riccardo e Alberto Ferrari.**   Dizionario di musica. Milano, Casa Editrice Ceschina [1959], 576 p.

A popular dictionary of terms and biography. Brief biographical entries mentioning representative works of minor composers and giving full tabulations of works of major composers. Well printed and illustrated, 8 plates in color. No bibliographical references.

4 / **Arma, Paul et Yvonne Tiénot.** Nouveau dictionnaire de musique. Paris, Éditions Ouvrières [1947], 285 p.

A "pocket" dictionary comprising some 2,000 biographical entries and 6,000 terms. 365 illustrations and short musical examples. Brief articles and summary listings of composers' works. Table of abbreviations.

5 / **Blom, Eric.** Everyman's dictionary of music. 5th edition. Revised by Jack Westrup, John Caldwell, Edward Ollison, and R. T. Beck. London, Dent; New York, St. Martin's Press, 1971. 397 p.

First pub. in 1946; U.S. ed., 1948; rev. ed., 1965; further rev. ed., 1968.

A popular quick-reference book of terms and biography. Small in size but exceedingly rich in information. Excludes living performers. Summary listings of composers' works.

Review of the 1954 ed. by Vincent Duckles in *Notes*, 13 (1955), p. 70–72.

6 / **Bonaccorsi, Alfredo.** Nuovo dizionario musicale Curci. Milano, Curci [1954], 557 p.

Emphasis on terms and forms, but with essential biographies. Brief bibliographies for most articles, including references to modern republications for composers.

Review in *Rassegna musicale*, 24 (1954), p. 389–91.

7 / **Borba, Tómas [e] Fernando Lopes Graça.** Dicionário de música ilustrado. Lisboa, Edições, 1956, 2v.

8 / **Bottenheim, S. A. M.** Prisma encyclopedie der muziek. Bewerkt en ingeleid door Wouter Paap. [2. druk], Utrecht, Het Spectrum, 1957. 2 v.

9 / **Coeuroy, André.** Dictionnaire critique de la musique ancienne et moderne. Paris, Payot, 1956. 413 p.

Primarily biographical, its chief value is in the section "Écoles moderne" (p. 92–191): chronological lists by country, giving brief stylistic characteristics and one or two works for each composer. Important modern composers are entered in the main alphabet. Appropriate cross references.

Collins Music Encyclopedia.
   See **Westrup, Jack A., and F. L. Harrison.**
     The new college encyclopedia of music . . . , no. 63.

10 / **Cooper, Martin,** ed. The concise encyclopedia of music and musicians. New York, Hawthorn Books [1958], 516 p.
   English edition: London, Hutchinson, 1958.

It is [the] "average music lover" for whom the present work is designed. The expert and connoisseur are already well catered for with twelve-volume dictionaries and detailed studies of particular musical fields, but my task has been to present in a concise, easily digestible form the history and technical rudiments of an art which plays an increasing part in our life. [Foreword]

Biographical entries are brief. Longer discussions of major terms and forms. No bibliographies. Well illustrated with 16 color plates and more than 100 in monochrome. 17 contributors apart from the editor.

11 / **Corte, Andrea Della e G. M. Gatti.** Dizionario di musica. 6. ed. Torino, G. B. Paravia [1959], 724 p.
   First published in 1925.
   Includes personal names, subjects, instruments, and cities covering all countries and periods, but with emphasis on Italian names and topics. Brief biographies list major works, with fair coverage of republications of old music, especially for Italian composers.

DBG-Musiklexikon.
   See **Herzfeld, Friedrich.** Ullstein Musiklexikon,
     no. 24.

12 / **Diccionario Enciclopédico de la Música.** [Dirección general: A. Albert Torrellas] Barcelona, Central Catalana de Publicaciones [1947]–52. 4 v.

Supersedes *Diccianario de la música ilustrado*, 1927–29. 2 v.

Contributors include composers and musicologists from Spain, Portugal, and Latin America.

Vol. 1: "Terminología, tecnología, morfología, instrumentos." Technical terms in all languages, including Greek and Oriental (transliterated). No bibliography or documentation.

Vols. 2–3: "Biografías, bibliografía, monografías, historia, argumentos de operas." Biographies of composers, performers, musicologists, with emphasis on Spanish and South American musicians. Lists of works for major composers, classified listing for minor figures. Historical articles under names of countries. Extended articles for Spanish provinces, covering folk music, history, composers, institutions, etc. No bibliographical references.

Vol. 4 "Apéndice, por A. Albert Torrellas . . ."

13 / **Dizionario Ricordi della Musica e dei Musicisti.** [Direttore: Claudio Sartori; redattori, Fausto Broussard *et al.*, Milano] Ricordi, 1959. 1,155 p.

Wide biographical coverage, including living performers, important composers of light music, musicologists. Concise articles, excellent bibliographies and lists of compositions.

Review by Jack A. Westrup in *Music and letters*, 41 (1960), p. 80–81; by James B. Coover in *Notes*, 17 (1960), p. 564–66.

14 / **Dunstan, Ralph.** A cyclopaedic dictionary of music . . . 4th ed., greatly enl. and rev. London/Philadelphia, Curwen [1925], 632 p.

First published in 1908. Reprint by Da Capo Press, New York, 1973.

Terms and biography. Very brief entries, numerous short musical illustrations. Intended for amateurs. Suffers from an excess of misleading and useless information. Numerous appendices of vocabulary, pronunciation, music theory, etc. The "Musical bibliography" (p. 618–31) is chiefly of 19th-century works in English.

15 / **Enciclopedia Salvat de la Música.** Barcelona–Madrid–Buenos Aires–Mexico–Caracas–Bogotá–Rio de Janeiro, Salvá, 1967. 4 v.

This is a Spanish adaptation of the *Encyclopédie de la musique* published by Fasquelle. See no. 16.

5

Review by Daniel Devoto in *Revue de musicologie*, 57 (1971), p. 87–88.

16 / Encyclopédie de la Musique. [Publié sous la direction de François Michel en collaboration avec François Lesure et Vladimir Fédorov, et un comité de rédaction composé de Nadia Boulanger *et al.*] Paris, Fasquelle [1958–61], 3 v.

Preceding the dictionary proper is a series of essays (vol. 1, p. 1–238) devoted to general information about music in society: festivals, concerts, radio, the music press, education in France, copyright laws, institutions and associations. A "Livre d'Or," p. 35–76, gives portraits and facsimile pages from the manuscripts of leading contemporary composers. Chronological table of music history, p. 203–38.

Much emphasis on ideas and principles rather than on individuals and works. Biographical articles are short. Bibliographical references, many to *MGG*. Lists of works for major composers; fuller treatment of subjects. Many signed articles. Excellent illustrative material, musical and pictorial. Especially valuable for its coverage of modern music.

Review by James B. Coover in *Notes*, 16 (1959), p. 381–83.

17 / Encyclopédie de la Musique et dictionnaire du conservatoire. Fondateur, Albert Lavignac; Directeur, Lionel de La Laurencie. Paris, C. Delagrave, 1913–31. 2 parts in 11 v.

Originally published in fascicles.

Part I: "Histoire de la musique." Part II: "Technique, esthétique, pédagogie."

The work was designed, in the tradition of the French encyclopedists, as a universal repository of musical knowledge. It is international in scope, although most of the contributors are French. Many of the studies are full-scale monographs and still rank among the most important surveys of their fields. History is treated by country. Among the chief contributors are Maurice Emmanuel, Amédée Gastoué, Oscar Chilesotti, Romain Rolland, Henry Expert, and Rafael Mitjana. Part II deals with music theory, instruction, and aesthetics in all aspects, including acoustics, notation, instrument making, choreography, institutions. Major articles by Charles Koechlin, Paul Rougnon, and Vincent d'Indy. Illustrated; numerous musical examples.

The *Encyclopédie* lacks an index, and for this reason the detailed tables of contents at the end of each part are most useful as a guide to its contents. A partial index, compiled by Robert Bruce in *Notes*, ser. 1 (May 1936), is not generally available.

18 / **Encyclopédie methodique,** ou par ordre de matières; par une société de gens de lettres, de savans et d'artites . . . *Musique,* publiée par MM. Framery et Ginguené. Paris, Chez Panckoucke, 1791–1818. 2 v.

Vol. 1: A–G, 760 p. Vol. 2 H–Z, 558 p.

Publisher varies. Tome II, Paris, Chez Mme. veuve Agasse. In this volume the name of De Momigny is added to that of the two other compilers. Vol. 1 contains a musical appendex of 74 p.; vol. 2, of 114 p.

The *Encyclopédie methodique* is a large general reference work of which the two volumes cited are concerned with music. These volumes are of considerable historical importance since they incorporate articles from Rousseau's *Dictionnaire de musique* (no. 298) and from the Diderot-d'Alembert *Encyclopédie* along with more recent commentary. Articles are signed.

19 / **Encyclopedie van de Muziek.** Hoofdredactio: Louis M. G. Arntzenius *et al.* Met bijzondere medwerking van J. Kunst *et al.* Amsterdam, Elsevier, 1956–57. 2 v.

Vol. 1: A–H. Vol. 2 I–Z.

20 / **Entsiklopedicheskiĭ Muzykal'nyĭ Slovar'.** Otvetstvennyi redaktor G. V. Vsevolodovich sostaviteli B. S. Shteinpress i I. M. IAmpol'skii. Moskva, Gos. Nauk. Izd. "Bol'shaia sovetskaia entsiklopediia" 1959. 326 p.

A second edition appeared in 1966. 631 p.

One of the standard Russian encyclopedias of music.

Everyman's Dictionary of Music.
See **Blom, Eric,** no. 5.

21 / **Grove, Sir George,** ed. Grove's dictionary of music and musicians. 5th ed., edited by Eric Blom. London, Macmillan; New York, St. Martin's Press, 1970.

The set has been issued in an unabridged paperback reprint by St. Martin, New York, 1970.

A 6th edition, completely rewritten, is in process as of spring, 1973.
Supplementary volume, ed. by Eric Blom; assoc. ed., Denis Stevens, 1961. 493 p.

First published in 1879–89; 2nd ed., 1904–10, ed. by J. A. Fuller-Maitland 3rd ed., 1927–28, ed. by H. C. Colles; 4th ed., 1940, ed. by H. C. Colles. A supplementary volume to the 3rd edition appeared in 1940, covering the period from 1928 to 1940, with new information pertaining to earlier entries. An American supplement, edited by W. S. Pratt, containing material on the U.S., Canada, and Spanish America, was published in 1920 and again in 1928.

Grove's dictionary is the standard comprehensive music encyclopedia in English. It includes information on music history, theory and practice, instruments, terms, and biographies in one alphabet. Signed articles, bibliographies, and useful lists of works for composers since Bach.

Although the 5th edition was completely reset, expanded, and brought up to date, it falls short of *MGG* as a tool for scholarship; however, it holds an undisputed place as the major music reference work in English.

Review of 5th ed. by Richard S. Hill in *Notes*, 12 (1954), p. 85–92; by William Glock in *The score*, no. 11 (Mar. 1955), p. 53–56; by Paul Henry Lang in MQ, 41 (1955), p. 215–22; in *The Times literary supplement*, Dec. 3, 1954, p. 778 (anon). See also A. Hyatt King, "Grove V and MGG," in *The monthly musical record*, 85 (1955), p. 115–19, p. 152–57, p. 183–85; also corrections and additions in the *Musical times*, 96 (1955), p. 591–96, p. 643–51. Review of *Supplementary volume* by Vincent Duckles in *Notes*, 19 (1962), p. 246–47.

22 / **Gurvin, Olav og Ø. Anker,** eds. Musikkleksikon. Ny revidert utg. Oslo, Dreyer [1959], 902 columns.

First published in 1949.

Biography, including jazz musicians, performers, and composers. Title entries for dramatic works, familiar art songs, and folk songs. Terms, short articles, partial lists of works, occasional bibliographical references. Popular.

23 / **Hamburger, Povl.** Aschehougs musikleksikon. København, Aschehoug, 1957–58. 2v.

Supersedes the *Illustreret musikleksikon* (no. 41), edited by Hortense Panum and William Behrend, published in 1940.

24 / **Herzfeld, Friedrich.** Ullstein Musiklexikon. Mit 4500 Stichwörtern, 600 Notenbeispielen, 1000 Abbildungen, und 32 Tafelseiten. Berlin/Frankfurt/Wien, Verlag Ullstein, 1965. 631 p.

Also published under the title *DBG-Musiklexikon* by the Deutsche Buch-Gemeinschaft, Berlin.

A one-volume music dictionary for ready reference. Profusely illustrated with small-scale portraits and musical examples. References to recordings.

25 / **Honegger, Marc.** Dictionnaire de la musique. I: Les hommes et leurs œuvres. Bordas, 1970. 2 v.

Part 1, A–K. Part 2, L–Z.

A third volume devoted to terms is projected under the title *Science de la musique: technique, esthétique et sociologie.*

A handsome, well-illustrated work, produced with the collaboration of some 186 authorities; international in scope.

26 / **Hughes, Rupert.** Music lovers' encyclopedia, containing a pronouncing and defining dictionary of terms, instruments, etc. . . . including a key to the pronunciation of sixteen languages, many charts, an explanation of the construction of music for the uninitiated, a pronouncing biographical dictionary, the stories of the operas, and numerous biographical and critical essays by distinguished authorities. Completely revised and newly edited by Deems Taylor and Russell Kerr. Garden City, N.Y., Garden City Books [1954], 897 p.

A popular general music dictionary. First published in 1903 under the title *The musical guide*; subsequent editions in 1912 and 1939.

27 / **Hyōjun Ongaku Jiten.** [Standard music dictionary, ed. by Sansaku Meguro] Tokyo, 1966.

For a Japanese multivolume encyclopedia of music, see no. 55.

28 / **Jacobs, Arthur.** A new dictionary of music. 2nd ed., Harmondsworth, Penguin, 1967. 425 p.

First published in 1958, followed by a hardcover edition with new introduction and corrections in London and Chicago, 1961.

9

A pocket dictionary for the inquiring music-lover, with brief identifications of people (mostly composers and performers), terms, operatic and other specific titles, and all sorts of musical topics. [*Notes*, 16 (1958), p. 68.]

Review of the 1961 ed. by Harold Samuel in *Notes*, 20 (1963), p. 657–58.

29 / **Keller, Gerard en P. Kruseman.** Geïllustreerd muzieklexicon, onder redactie van G. Keller en Philip Kruseman, met medewerking van Sam Dresden, Wouter Hutschenruijter, Willem Landré . . . 's-Gravenhage, J. P. Kruseman, 1932. 966 p.

Supplement of 319 p. published in 1949; then reissued in two volumes (vol. 1, p. 1–664; vol. 2, p. 665–966).

Brief articles, bibliographical references, and lists of major works for composers. Similar to *Abert* (no. 1) in form and content, but useful in connection with contemporary Dutch names.

30 / **Larousse de la musique.** [Dictionnaire encyclopédique] en 2 volumes. Publié sous la direction de Norbert Dufourcq, avec la collaboration de Félix Raugel, Armand Machabey. Paris, Larousse [1957], 2 v.

Also issued in an Italian edition: *Dizionario musicale Larousse.* A cura di Delfino Nava. Milona, Edizioni Paoline, 1961. 3 v.

A handsome, beautifully illustrated dictionary. Brief but authoritative articles by international contributors. Biographies (composers, performers, musicologists, choreographers); title entries (operas, ballets, manuscripts); subjects (terms, places). Some emphasis on ethnomusicology. Bibliographies given in an appendix to each volume under the same headings as the articles.

Special features: Discography and analysis (vol. 1, p. 587–626; vol. 2, p. 537–640). Musical examples in analytical section. Two phonorecords, "Illustrations sonores," issued with the encyclopedia: (1) Les instruments de musique (with vol. 1 and (2) Principaux termes du langage technique (with vol. 2).

Review by Paul Henry Lang in *MQ*, 45 (1959), p. 120–23; by James B. Coover in *Notes*, 16 (1959), p. 381–83.

31 / **Malá Encyklopédia Hudby.** Spracoval kolektiv autorov. Vedúci autorského kolektívu Marián Jurík. Vedecký redaktor Dr. Ladislav Mokrý, CSc. Bratislava, Obzor, 1969. 642 p.

A Slovak dictionary of music and bio-bibliography. P. 629–42: bibliography. Illustrated. No bibliographical references with the articles.

32 / **Mendel, Hermann.** Musikalisches Conversations-Lexikon. Eine Encyklopädie der gesammten musikalischen Wissenschaften. Für Gebildete aller Stände, unter Mitwirkung der Literarischen Commission des Berliner Tonkünstlervereins . . . Berlin, L. Heimann; New York, J. Schuberth, 1870–79. 11 v.

Reprint of the 2nd ed., 12 vols., by Georg Olms, Hildesheim.

2nd ed. with supplementary volume, "Ergänzungsband," Berlin, R. Oppenheim, 1880–83. 3rd ed., "Neue wohlfeile Stereotyp-Ausgabe," Leipzig, List & Francke [1890–91].

Founded by Mendel, continued (vols. 7–11) by August Reissmann. One of the major 19th-century general music encyclopedias. Superseded in most respects, but still useful for obscure names and earlier concepts and criticism. Partial lists of works; few bibliographical references.

33 / **Meyers Handbuch über die Musik.** Herausgegeben und bearbeitet von der Fachredaktion Musik des Bibliographisches Instituts. 2nd ed., Mannheim, Bibliographisches Institut, 1961. 1,062 p.

A miscellaneous assemblage of facts about music, musicians, and musical institutions. Lists of libraries, societies, research institutes, performers, etc. Wide in scope but superficial in coverage. The emphasis is on European musical activities and persons.

P. 493–993: a biographical dictionary of musicians. Combined index of subjects and persons.

34 / **Moore, John W.** Complete encyclopaedia of music, elementary, technical, historical, biographical, vocal and instrumental. Boston, J. P. Jewett, 1854 [copyright notice, 1852], 1,004 p.

Appendix . . . containing events and information occurring since the main work was issued. Boston, Oliver Ditson, 1875. 45 p.

Reprinted by Ditson in 1880.

The first comprehensive American musical dictionary, containing more than 5,000 terms, 4,000 biographical citations, 200 articles, many of which are drawn from Gerber, Choron and Fayolle, Burney,

Hawkins, Hogarth, Calcott, Gardiner, Busby, Hamilton, Schilling, and Fétis. Substantial additional material from *Dwight's musical journal* and the *New York musical times*. Especially rich in notices of 18th- and 19th-century musicians, although somewhat weak in early Americana.

35 / **Moser, Hans J.** Musik Lexikon. Vierte, stark erweiterte Aufl. Hamburg, H. Sikorski, 1955. 2 v.

First published in 1932–35; 2nd ed., 1943; 3rd ed., 1951. Ergän-zungsband A–Z. 287 p. (1963).

Brief, authoritative articles, with special emphasis on bibliographies and lists of early music in new editions. Addressed to German readers, but increasingly international in scope with the later editions. The 4th edition, first to appear in two volumes, is extensively revised, with many new articles and bibliographical additions.

36 / **La Musica,** sotto la direzione di Guido M. Gatti, a cura di Alberto Basso. Torino, Unione Tipografico-editrice Torinese, 1966–68. 6 v.

Parte prima: *Enciclopedia storica*, v. 1–4 (1966).

Parte seconda *Dizionario*, v. 5–6 (1968).

A large-scale, handsomely illustrated reference tool. There are only 196 entries in the *parte prima*, of which 81 are biographies. All of the articles are extended, averaging 16 to 18 pages each. Useful tabulations of composers' works. The contributors are chiefly Italian but include a number of international authorities.

The dictionary, *parte seconda*, serves as an index to the *Enciclopedia*, articulating with it and offering brief entries for terms and the biographies of minor musicians.

Review of the *Enciclopedia storica* by Vincent Duckles in *Notes*, 24 (1947), p. 263–64; of the *Dizionario* by Hans Lenneberg in *Notes*, 27 (1970), p. 51–52, and by Georg Karstädt in *Die Musikforschung*, 24 (1971), p. 458–61.

37 / **Musiikin Tietokirja.** Toimituskunta: Tiovo Haapanen *et al.* Helsingissä, Kustannusoskeyhtiö Otava [1948], 573 p.

Terms, subjects, operas, biographies (including performers, publishers, musicologists, many contemporary composers). Emphasis on Scandinavian musicians. Partial lists of works.

38 / **Die Musik in Geschichte und Gegenwart.** Allgemeine Enzyklopädie der Musik . . . Edited by Friedrich Blume. Kassel u. Basel, Bärenreiter Verlag, 1949–1967. 14 v.

Published in fascicles, the last being nos. 136/137.

The work continues in a *Supplement*, of which four issues have appeared (as of Jan. 1973). A final index volume is projected.

MGG is a comprehensive music reference work of the highest scholarly merit. In German, but international in scope and coverage. Articles contributed by specialists throughout the world. Gives complete listings of composers' works and detailed bibliographical references. Many of the articles are full-scale monographs, and all attempt to embody the latest research. Many illustrations.

Reviewed by Willi Apel in *JAMS*, 3 (1950), p. 142–45; 5 (1952), p. 56–57, and p. 138–39; by Charles Warren Fox in *Notes*, 7 (1950), p. 466–67, 10 (1953), p. 451–52, 12 (1954), p. 92–93; by Paul Henry Lang in *MQ*, 36 (1950), p. 141–43, 38 (1952), p. 477–79. Reviewed in *Die Musikforschung* by Rudolph Steglich, 6 (1953), p. 260–64; by Hans Ehinger, 8 (1955), p. 92–96; by Kurt von Fischer, 9 (1956), p. 331–36, and 10 (1957), p. 423–28; by Hellmut Federhofer in 12 (1959), p. 338–41.

Publication of the 5th edition of *Grove* in 1954 provided the occasion for some critical comparisons between *Grove* and *MGG*. See Richard S. Hill in *Notes*, 12 (1954), p. 85–92, and A. Hyatt King, "Grove V and MGG" in *The monthly musical record*, 85 (1955), p. 115–19, p. 152–57, and p. 183–85. For a fascinating discussion of the genesis, organization, and production of a great music reference work, see "*Die Musik in Geschichte und Gegenwart:* a postlude," by Friedrich Blume in *Notes*, 24 (1967), p. 217–44.

See also Jack Westrup, "Kritische Anmerkungen zu *Die Musik in Geschichte und Gegenwart*, volumes 9–14," trans. by Ludwig Finscher in *Die Musikforschung*, 22 (1969), p. 217–25.

Two of Blume's major survey articles have been translated by M. D. Herter Norton and published separately by W. W. Norton: 1. *Renaissance and baroque music, a comprehensive survey* (1967), 180 p. 2. *Classic and romantic music, a comprehensive survey* (1970), 213 p. The former is reviewed by Vernon Gotwals in *Notes*, 24 (1968), p. 488–89.

39 / **Muzička Enciklopedija.** [Glavni redaktor: Josip Andreis] Zagreb, Izdanje i naklada leksikografskog zavoda, 1958–63. 2 v.

13

Vol. 1: A–J, 760 p. Vol. 2: K–Z, 855 p.

Contributors: Yugoslavian musicologists. Major articles signed.

Condensed biographical, extended subject entries. Well-organized bibliographies and lists of works. Living performers excluded. International coverage, with emphasis on Slavic composers. Excellent in content and appearance.

Review by Josef Brozek in *Notes*, 21 (1963–64), p. 128–29.

40 / **Norlind, Tobias.** Allmånt musiklexikon. 2. omarbetade uppl. Stockholm, Wahlström & Widstrand, 1927–28. 2 v.

First published in parts, 1912–16.

Many biographies, with full lists of compositions, including information as to dates and publishers.

41 / **Panum, Hortense, and William Behrend.** Illustreret musikleksikon. Nyudgave under redaktion af Povl Hamburger, under medvirken af William Behrend, O. M. Sandvik, Jürgen Balzer. København, Aschehoug, 1940. 735 p.

First issued in parts, 1924–26. Superseded by *Aschehougs musikleksikon*, ed. by Povl Hamburger, 1957.

Designed for popular use. International in coverage, but with emphasis on Scandinavian names and subjects. Based on the first edition of *Norland* (no. 40) and the Schytte translation of *Riemann*.

42 / **Pena, Joaquín.** Diccionario de la música Labor; iniciado por Joaquín Pena, continuado por Higinio Anglés, con la colaboración de Miguel Querol y otros distinguidos musicólogos españoles y extranjeros. Barcelona, Labor, 1954. 2 v.

Begun in 1940 as an adaptation of *Riemann*, but developed as a new dictionary of music for Spanish-speaking countries. Contributors are Spanish and Spanish-American. Foreign biographies drawn from *Riemann*, *Grove*, *Baker*, *Schmidl*, etc. Covers bio-bibliography, technique, and history. Designed for professional musicians and for general use.

43 / **Pratt, Waldo S.** The new encyclopedia of music and musicians. New and rev. ed., New York, Macmillan, 1929. 969 p.

First published in 1924.

Originally planned as an abridgement of the second edition of *Grove*, but developed as an independent work. Arranged in three main alphabets: terms, biography, institutions and organizations. Appendices for bibliography, musicians before 1700, and operas and oratorios produced since 1900. Covers primarily the 18th to 20th centuries, with emphasis on living musicians aand the American scene. Excellent definitions of musical terms.

44 / **Reiss, Jósef Władysław.** Mala encyklopedia muzyki. [Redaktor naczelny Stefan Sledzinski Wyd. 1] Warszawa, Państwowe Wydawn. Naukowe, 1968. 1,269 p.

First issued in 1924; later edition, 1960.

Popular dictionary, international coverage, with definitions of terms, fairly extended articles on topics, brief biographies of composers, performers, critics, etc. Short bibliographies for major subjects. Illustrated. An interesting feature is the biographical index, which assembles all references to individuals.

45 / **Ricordi Enciclopedia della Musica.** Direttore: Claudio Sartori. Vice-direttore, Riccardo Allorto. Milano, Ricordi, 1963–64. 4 v.

The major modern Italian encyclopedia of music. Well printed and illustrated, including color plates. Contributions by some 232 international specialists. Long articles signed. Good bibliographical coverage.

46 / **Riemann, Hugo.** Musik-Lexikon. 12. völlig neubearbeitete Auflage in drei Bänden. Hrsg. von Wilibald Gurlitt. Mainz, B. Schott's Söhne, 1959–1967. 3 v.

Vol. 1: *Personenteil*, A–K, 1959. 986 p. Vol. 2: *Personenteil*, L–Z, 1961. 976 p. Vol. 3: *Sachteil*, 1967. 1,087 p. (Vol. 3 ed. by Hans Heinrich Eggebrecht.) Two supplementary volumes, *Ergänzungsbände*, are projected. The first, A-K, appeared in 1972, edited by Carl Dahlhaus.

The 12th edition is the latest in the series based on Reimann's work, first published in 1882. The present edition is the first in which terms and biography are treated in separate alphabets. Alfred Einstein was editor of the 9th, 10th, and 11th editions and added much to the scope and authority of the work.

Riemann's *Musik-Lexikon* is a universal dictionary of music covering all times and places and incorporating the achievements of German musical scholarship. Superior to *Moser* (no. 35) in typography and organization and to *Baker* (no. 65) in bibliographical coverage. Lists of works are included within the bodies of the articles; modern editions of early works and bibliographical references in separate paragraphs.

Riemann has been widely translated, and most of the translations have incorporated new materials of national interest. The principal translations are as follows:

Dictionnaire de musique. Traduit d'après la 4me édition par Georges Humbert. Paris, Perrin, 1895–1902. 2me éd., Paris, Perrin, 1913. 3me éd., entièrement refondue et augm. sous la direction de A. Schaeffner, avec la collaboration de M. Pincherle, Y. Rosketh, A. Tessier. Paris, 1931.

Dictionary of music. New edition, with many additions by the author. Trans. by J. S. Shedlock. London, Augener, 1893. Also 1897 as *Encyclopedic dictionary of music.* Later editions in 1902 and 1908. Reprint of the 1908 edition by Da Capo Press, 1970.

Muzykal'nyi slovar' . . . Moskva, P. Iurgenson, 1901–1904, a Russian translation from the 5th German edition.

Nordisk musik-lexikon, udarbeidet af H. V. Schytte, København, 1888–92, 2 v. with a *Supplement* (c. 1906).

Reviews of the 12th ed. *Personenteil* by Vincent Duckles in *Notes,* 16 (1959), p. 240–42, and 18 (1961), p. 572–74; by Paul Henry Lang in *MQ,* 45 (1959), p. 563–66; by Hans H. Eggebrecht in *Die Musikforschung,* 12 (1959), p. 221–23; and by Charles van den Borren in *Revue belge de musicologie,* 14 (1960), p. 137–38.

Reviews of the 12th ed. *Sachteil* by Jack Alan Westrup in *Music and letters,* 49 (1968), p. 256–57; by François Lesure in *Revue de musicologie,* 54 (1968), p. 115–16; by Hans Oesch in *Melos* (1969), p. 15; and by Vincent Duckles in *Notes,* 27 (1970), p. 256–58. See also the review-article by Walter Wiora, "Hugo Riemann und 'der neue Riemann,'" in *Die Musikforschung,* 22 (1969), p. 348–55.

47 / Rubertis, Victor de. Pequeño diccionario musical, tecnológico y biográfico, 6. ed., corregida y aumentada. Buenos Aires, Ricordi Americana, 1962. 349 p.

48 / **Sandved, Kjell Bloch.** Musikkens verden. Musik fra A–Z. Udg. ved Kjell B. Sandved. [Overs. fra norsk] Gennemset og revideret af Vagn Kappel. Redaktionssekretaer: K. Claussen. [Ny udg.] Hovedred.: Sverre Hagerup Bull. København, Musikkens Verden, 1964. 2,272 columns.

A Danish general dictionary of music.

49 / **Schilling, Gustav.** Encyclopädie der gesammten musikalischen Wissenschaften, oder, Universal-Lexikon der Tonkunst . . . Stuttgart, F. H. Köhler, 1835–37. 6 v.

Supplement-Band, hrsg. von Gustav Schilling, 1842.

Reprint announced by Georg Olms, Hildesheim, including the supplement.

One of the leading 19th-century repositories of musical knowledge. A comprehensive work with emphasis on the subject aspects, but including numerous biographies displaced or reduced in later reference works.

50 / **Schilling, Gustav.** Universal-Lexikon der Tonkunst. Neue Hand-Ausgabe in einem Bande. Mit Zugrundlegung des grösseren Werkes neu bearbeitet, ergänzt und theilweise vermehrt von Dr. F. S. Gassner . . . Stuttgart, F. Köhler, 1849. 918 p.

A one-volume condensation of the preceding six-volume work. Remarkably full of information. In many instances the entries are more comprehensive and up to date than in the original printing.

51 / **Scholes, Percy A.** The concise Oxford dictionary of music. 2nd edition. London/New York, Oxford Univ. Press, 1964. 636 p.

First published in 1952. Issued as a paperback, 1968.

Primarily a reduction of the *Oxford companion* (no. 52). Includes "some hundreds of short biographical entries for vocal and instrumental performers and conductors . . . and some hundreds of entries concerning individual compositions." About 10,000 entries, 3,500 biographical.

Review of the 1st ed. by Charles Warren Fox in *Notes*, 9 (1952), p. 605–06.

52 / **Scholes, Percy A.** The Oxford companion to music. Edited by John Owen Ward. 10th ed., completely rev. and reset and with many

17

additions to text and illustrations. London/New York, Oxford Univ. Press, 1970. 1,189 p.

First published in 1938.

Intended for the general reader. The *Companion* is a unique one-man encyclopedia, unified by the compiler's opinions, tastes, and interests, which are always stimulating but occasionally provincial. Especially strong in articles on the sociology of music and in a number of entries overlooked in most music reference works (e.g., "Misattributed compositions," "Nick-named compositions"). Detailed cross references, but no bibliographies. A bibliographical supplement issued with the 1940 edition has not been reprinted. See no. 562.

Review of the 8th ed. by Charles Warren Fox in *Notes*, 8 (1950), p. 177–78; of the 9th ed. by Vincent Duckles in *Notes*, 13 (1955), p. 70–72. For a further evaluation of this work, see the article "Music lexicography" by Vincent Duckles in *College music symposium*, 11 (1971), p. 121 ff.

53 / **Scholes, Percy A.** The Oxford junior companion to music. London/New York, Oxford Univ. Press, 1966. 435 p.

54 / **Seeger, Horst.** Musiklexikon in zwei Bänden, Leipzig, Deutscher Verlag für Musik, 1966. 2 v.

Vol. 1, A–K. Vol. 2, L–Z.

Represents the Marxist (East German) approach to music lexicography. Articles by 44 East European contributors. Summary listings of composers' works; no bibliographies for articles on major topics. Illustrated.

55 / **Shimonaka, Yasazuro,** ed. Ongaku jiten. Tokyo, Heibonsha, 1954–57. 12 v.

The major Japanese encyclopedia of music.

Vol. 12 is an index in Japanese and English.

56 / **Sohlmans Musiklexikon.** Nordiskt och allmänt uppslagsverk för tonkonst, musikliv och dans. Redaktion: Gösta Morin, Carl-Allan Moberg, Einar Sunström. Stockholm, Sohlmans Förlag [1948–52], 4 v.

A second edition is scheduled for publication in 1973 by the Gummesson Graphic Group Ltd. It is projected in five volumes, of approximately 700 pages each, containing some 17,000 entries.

The major modern Swedish music encyclopedia. Contributions by leading Scandinavian musicologists. Biography, title entries for operas, ballets, etc., subject entries for persons, places, institutions. Good lists of works; bibliographies somewhat uneven. Wide biographical coverage, especially for living performers. Many portraits.

57 / **Svensson, Sven E. E.** Bonniers illustrerade musiklexikon. Under medverkan av Erik Noreen. Stockholm, A. Bonnier [1946], 1,379 p.

Popular, well-illustrated, universal in coverage, but with emphasis on Scandinavian names, especially performers. Bibliographical references.

58 / **Thompson, Oscar,** ed. The international cyclopedia of music and musicians. 9th ed., edited by Robert Sabin. New York, Dodd, Mead, 1964. 2,476 p.

First published in 1939. 8th ed. (1958), ed. by Nicolas Slonimsky.

The best one-volume general dictionary of music in English. Strong list of contributors, with extended signed articles for major persons and subjects. Large number of title entries. Particularly valuable for detailed lists, given in tabulated form, of works by major composers. Through the 8th edition the work carried an appendix of opera plots and an extensive bibliography of music literature.

Review of the 5th ed. by Charles Warren Fox in *Notes*, 7 (1950), p. 291–92; of the 9th ed. by Irene Millen in *Notes*, 22 (1965), p. 733–35.

59 / **Tonkonsten,** Internationellt musiklexikon. Stockholm, Nordiska Uppslagsböcker [1955–57] 2 v.

Popular, illustrated dictionary giving pronunciations of foreign names, lists of works and bibliographies for major composers, bibliographical references on important topics. Covers popular music. Signed articles by Scandinavian contributors.

60 / **Tschierpe, Rudolf.** Kleines Musiklexikon, mit systematischen Übersichten und zahlreichen Notenbeispielen. [6. ergänzte-Auflage] Hamburg, Hoffmann und Campe, 1959. 414 p.

First published in 1946; 2. Aufl., 1948; 3. Aufl., 1949; 4. Aufl., 1951; 5. Aufl., 1955.

19

Excellent small general dictionary. Brief but inclusive. Representative works listed for major composers. Bibliographical references. Tables illustrating dance forms, theory and history. Appendix lists major writers on music with their fields of specialization; another lists titles of operas, operattas, oratorios, choral and orchestra works.

Ullstein Musiklexikon.
See **Herzfeld, Friedrich,** no. 24.

61 / **Viotta, Henri Anastase.** Lexicon der toonkunst. Met medewerking van de heeren Peter Benoit, Frans Coenen, F. Gernsheim, L. van Gheluwe, G. A. Heinze, Richard Hol, Dan. de Lange, W.f.g. Nicolai, etc. Amsterdam, P. N. van Kampen, 1883–85. 3 v.

First printed in 1881–85.

The standard 19th century Dutch encyclopedia of music. The emphasis is on biography.

62 / **Walther, Johann G.** Musikalisches Lexicon, oder musikalische Bibliothek. Leipzig, Wolffgang Deer, 1732. 659 p., 22 fold. plates.

Facsimile reprint edited by Richard Schaal (1953) and published by Bärenreiter in the series *Documenta musicologica*, Erste Reihe, 3.

Walther's *Lexicon* established the pattern for modern dictionaries that combine terms and biography, as in *Riemann* and *Moser*. It also constitutes a primary source of information about late baroque musical knowledge and practice.

63 / **Westrup, Jack A., and F. L. Harrison.** The new college encyclopedia of music. New York, Norton [1960], 739 p.

Published in England, 1959, under the title *Collins music encyclopedia*.

A "popular" student dictionary. Detailed summaries of works for major composers, fields of activity for minor ones. References to early works published in the standard historical editions or anthologies.

Technical articles with musical illustrations. Title entries for repertory works. Selective bibliographies, primarily English. British pronunciations.

Review by James B. Coover in *Notes*, 17 (1960), p. 564–66.

64 / **Zenei Lexikon.** [írtak] Szabolcsí Bence [és] Tóth Aladár. Átdolgozott új loadás, föszerkesztö: Bartha Dénes, szerkesztö: Tóth Margit. Budapest, Zenemükiadó Vallalat, 1965. 3 v.

This is a revision and expansion of a work that was first issued in 1930–31.

A general music encyclopedia of high quality. Major articles signed by outstanding musicologists, Hungarian and foreign. Long articles on national music, forms, music for various instruments. Biographical articles discuss major works and list others by category. Short bibliographies.

Revue by J. Gerely in *Revue de musicologie*, 53 (1967), p. 185–87.

BIOGRAPHY, INTERNATIONAL

Listed here are dictionaries and encyclopedias, international in coverage, in which the emphasis is exclusively or mainly on persons engaged in activities related to music: composers, performers, scholars, critics, impresarios, etc. The line that separates biographical dictionaries from volumes of collected biography is a rather arbitrary one. The distinction is essentially between works that contain numerous brief entries, alphabetically arranged, and works that consist of collections of essays on a fairly limited group of musicians. Works in the latter category have been excluded, and for this reason the user should not expect to find entries for such titles as Donald Brook's *Masters of the keyboard* (London, 1947) or his *Singers of today* (London, 1949), David Ewen's *Dictators of the baton* (New York, 1943), or Madeleine Goss's *Modern music-makers* (New York, 1952).

65 / **Baker, Theodore.** Baker's biographical dictionary of musicians. 5th ed. Completely revised by Nicolas Slonimsky. New York, G. Schirmer [1958], 1,855 p.

First published in 1900; subsequent editions in 1905, 1919, and 1940. Reprinted in 1965, with a 143-page *Supplement* providing biographical information on some 700 new names as well as updating numerous old entries. Also a 1971 *Supplement*. 262 p.

Baker's is by far the best biographical dictionary in English; a standard work from its beginning. Through the 3rd edition early figures were treated briefly, with references to *Grove* and *Eitner*. For the 4th edition, these biographies were rewritten as independent articles (by Gustave Reese, Gilbert Chase, and Robert Geiger). The 5th edition was greatly enlarged and checked carefully for accuracy. Treats musicians in all categories. Long lists of works. Outstanding bibliographical coverage.

Review of 5th ed. by Brooks Shepard, Jr., in *Notes*, 16 (1959), p. 239–40; by Philip L. Miller in *MQ*, 45 (1959), p. 255–58.

Review of the 1971 *Supplement* by Gloria Rose in *Notes*, 29 (1972), p. 253-54.

66 / **Bertini, Giuseppe.** Dizionario storico-critico degli scrittori di musica, e de'piu celebri artisti di tutte le nazioni si'antiche che moderne. Palermo, Dalla Tipografia reale di Guerrà. 1814–15. 4 v. in 2.

> Tomo primo: Discorso preliminare, p. i–lvi, AA–BU. 167 p.
> Tomo secondo: C–KU. 234 p.
> Tomo terzo: LA–RU. 245 p.
> Tomo quarto: SA–Z. 145 p.

An early Italian dictionary of musical biography. Bertini leans heavily on *Choron and Fayolle* (see no. 70) for his information but adds much new material. His "Discorso preliminare" is a perceptive discussion of the role of bibliography in enhancing musical knowledge.

67 / **Bingley, William.** Musical biography; memoirs of the lives and writings of the most eminent musical composers and writers who have flourished in the different countries of Europe during the last three centuries. London, H. Colburn, 1814. 2 v.

2nd ed., 1834. Reprint of the 2nd ed. by Da Capo Press, New York, 1971.

Brief, anecdotal accounts grouped chronologically and by national schools.

68 / **Brown, James Duff.** Biographical dictionary of musicians, with a bibliography of English writings on music. Paisley and London, A. Gardner, 1886. 637 p.

Reprint by Georg Olms, Hildesheim, 1970.

International in coverage but with pronounced British slant.

69 / **Carlson, Effie B.** A bio-bibliographical dictionary of twelve-tone and serial composers. Metuchen, N.J., Scarecrow Press, 1970. 233 p.

Entries for 80 twelve-tone and serial composers, from Gilbert Amy to Bernd Alois Zimmerman.

70 / **Choron, Alexandre É., et F. J. M. Fayolle.** Dictionnaire historique des musiciens, artistes et amateurs, morts ou vivans, qui se sont illustrés en une partie quelconque de la musique et des arts qui y sont relatifs. . . . Paris, Valade, 1810–11. 2 v.

Another printing, 1817. Reprint by Olms, Hildesheim, 1970.

The first French biographical dictionary of importance. International in scope. Partial lists of works for major composers. A valuable guide to early 19th-century musical opinion. The dictionary proper is preceded by an 81-page "Sommaire de l'histoire de la musique" by Choron.

Translated and expanded in the English *A dictionary of musicians,* 1824. See no. 73.

A Critical Dictionary of Composers and Their Music.
See **Young, Percy M.,** no. 102.

71 / **Cross, Milton, J.** The Milton Cross new encyclopedia of the great composers and their music, by Milton Cross and David Ewen. Rev. and expanded. Garden City, N.Y., Doubleday, 1969. 2 v.

A popular biographical dictionary.

72 / **A Dictionary of Modern Music and Musicians.** Ed. by Arthur Eaglefield-Hull. London, J. M. Dent, 1924; New York, E. P. Dutton, 1924. 543 p.

Reprint of the 1924 ed. by Da Capo Press, New York, 1971, and by the Scholarly Press, 1972.

Primarily biographical, although there are entries for terms related to modern music. For the period c. 1880–1820, the best international coverage of any dictionary of its time. Written with the aid of numerous foreign collaborators. Also includes publishers, musicologists, organizations, new instruments, etc. (See also no. 95.)

73 / **A Dictionary of Musicians,** from the earliest ages to the present time, comprising the most important biographical contents of the works of Gerber, Choron and Fayolle, Count Orloff, Dr. Burney, Sir John Hawkins, etc. Together with more than 100 original memoirs of the most eminent living musicians and a summary of the history of music. London, Sainsbury, 1824. 2v.

Reprinted in 1827.

Reprint of the original edition by Da Capo Press, New York, 1966. The reprint incorporates an essay on the work by H. G. Farmer, originally printed in *Music and Letters*, 12 (1931), p. 384–92.

Largely a translation of Choron and Fayolle (no. 70), including the "Summary of the history of music," but with substantial additions of English musicians. The first major biographical dictionary of musicians in English. Its tone is popular and anecdotal, but the work furnishes an excellent picture of contemporary taste and opinion. The compiler is not identified, but the work has been attributed to its publisher, John Sainsbury.

Review of the reprint edition by Vincent Duckles in *Notes*, 23 (1967), p. 737–39.

74 / **Eitner, Robert.** Biographisch-bibliographisches Quellen-Lexikon der Musiker und Musikgelehrten der christlichen Zeitrechnung bis zur Mitte des 19. Jahrhunderts . . . Leipzig, Breitkopf & Härtel, 1898–1904. 10 v.

Eitner's *Quellen-Lexikon* is mainly a bibliography of primary sources, but it does contain much useful biographical information, often helpful with respect to obscure names.

For fuller information on this important reference work, see under *Bibliographies of music* (no. 1065).

75 / **The Etude Music Magazine.** Portraits of the world's best-known musicians, an alphabetical collection of notable musical personalities of the world covering the entire history of music. Compiled and edited by Guy McCoy. Philadelphia, Theodore Presser [1946], 251 p.

Portraits and brief identifications of 4,748 composers, performers, and other musicians, largely reprinted from *Etude*, 1932–40. Geographical index of American names.

One of the few dictionaries of its kind. Of limited value, however, since the portraits are reproduced at little more than postage-stamp size.

76 / **Ewen, David.** Composers of today, a comprehensive biographical and critical guide to modern composers of all nations. 2nd ed. New York, H. W. Wilson, 1936. 332 p.

First published in 1934. The work has been superseded by nos. 78 and 79.

Brief biographies, critical discussion, and classified lists of the principal works for about 200 living composers. Portraits. Lists of recordings.

77 / **Ewen, David.** Composers of yesterday, a biographical and critical guide to the most important composers of the past. New York, H. W. Wilson, 1937. 488 p.

Biographies, lists of works, bibliographies, lists of recordings, and portraits of about 200 composers from Dunstable to the end of the 19th century. Selected on the basis of current acceptance or importance in music history.

78 / **Ewen, David.** Composers since 1900: a bibliographical and critical guide. New York, H. W. Wilson, 1969. 639 p.

Supersedes *Composers of today* (1934 and 1936), *American composers today* (1949), and *European composers today* (1954).

Portraits; listing of major works, and short bibliographies of writings about the composers under consideration.

Reviewed in *The Booklist*, 66 (July 1970), p. 1290–91.

79 / **Ewen, David.** European composers today; a biographical and critical guide. New York, H. W. Wilson, 1954. 200 p.

A companion volume to the previously published *American composers of today* (no. 178). Together, these two volumes replace *Composers of today* (no. 76), above, and have been replaced in turn by no. 78.
Review by Frank C. Campbell in *Notes*, 11 (1954), p. 476.

80 / **Ewen, David.** Living musicians. New York, H. W. Wilson, 1940. 390 p.
First supplement . . . , 1957.
A dictionary of performers, especially American or active in America. Portraits. The supplement contains biographies of 147 musicians who have come into prominence since 1940.

      Ewen, David. Popular American composers . . .
        See no. 198 under "Jazz, Popular, and Folk Musicians."

81 / **Fétis, François J.** Biographie universelle des musiciens et bibliographie générale de la musique. 2me éd. Paris, Firmin Didot Fréres, 1866–70. 8 v.
First published in 1835–44. *Supplément et complément*, pub. sous la direction de M. Arthur Pougin. Paris, 1878–80. 2 v.
A reprint of the second edition, with the supplements by Arthur Pougin, has been announced for publication (1972) by Editions Culture et Civilisation, Brussels, with a critical introduction by L. Weemaels, P. Huyskens, and G. Thinès. 10 v.
Fétis's work set the standard for modern biographical research in music. A tremendous scholarly achievement for its time, it contains a vast amount of biographical and bibliographical information, complete lists of works, and—occasionally—annotated lists of books about composers. Although outdated and marred by the author's personal critical bias, it remains a useful starting point for research and serves as a record of the earlier stages of musicology.

82 / **Gerber, Ernst Ludwig.** Historisch-biographisches Lexikon der Tonkünstler, welches Nachrichten von dem Leben und Werken

musikalischer Schriftsteller, berühmter Componisten, Sänger, usw. . . .
enthält. Leipzig, J. G. I. Breitkopf, 1790–92. 2 v.

See annotation under no. 83 below.

83 / **Gerber, Ernst Ludwig.** Neues historisch-biographisches Lexikon der Tonkünstler . . . , Leipzig, A. Kühnel, 1812–13. 4 v.

The Gerber *lexika* are early biographical dictionaries of great historical importance. The compiler expanded the biographical content of Walther's *Lexikon* (no. 62) and produced the first major self-contained dictionary of musical biography. The four-volume edition of 1812–14 supplements but does not supersede the earlier two-volume edition (no. 82 above). Both compilations must be used for complete coverage.

The two Gerber *lexica* have been reprinted by Akademische Druck- u. Verlagsanstalt, Graz, under the editorship of Othmar Wessely. Wessely has also edited a supplementary volume containing additions and corrections made by Gerber's contemporaries and published in the Leipzig *Allgemeine musikalische Zeitung* and other journals. Also included are the author's manuscript revisions. A full transcription of the title of the reprint edition is given as follows:

Historisch-Biographisches Lexikon der Tonkünstler (1790–92) und Neues historisch-biographisches Lexikon der Tonkünstler (1812–14). Mit den in den Jahren 1792 bis 1834 veröffentlichten Ergänzungen sowie der Erstveröffentlichung handschriftlicher Berichtigungen und Nachträge. Hrsg. von Othmar Wessely. Graz. Akademische Druck- u. Verlagsanstalt, 1966–69. 4 v.

84 / **Le Grandi Voci.** Dizionario critico-biografico dei cantanti, con discografia operistica. Roma, Istituto per la Collaborazione Culturale, 1964. 1,044 columns.

Published under the direction of Rodolfo Celletti; consultants for the discographies, Raffaele Vegeto and John B. Richards; editor, Luisa Pavolini.

An illustrated dictionary of opera singers, historical and contemporary, with discographies of the major artists.

85 / **Hughes, Rupert.** The biographical dictionary of musicians. Originally compiled by Rupert Hughes, completely revised and newly

edited by Deems Taylor and Russell Kerr. Over 8,500 entries, together with a pronouncing dictionary of given names and titles and a key to the pronunciation of sixteen languages. New York, Blue Ribbon Books, 1940. 481 p.

Reprint by Scholarly Press, 1972.

A popular reference work. Brief entries with representative works for composers mentioned. Useful for the abundance of obscure performers entered.

86 / **The International Who Is Who in Music.** Fifth (mid-century) edition. J. T. H. Mize, editor-in-chief. Chicago, Who is Who in Music [1951], 576 p.

Biographies, with portraits, of persons active in music, including educators, musicologists, private teachers, performers. Not strictly international, since the emphasis is on musicians active or well known in the U.S. Contains a number of supplementary lists and directories, e.g., the principal symphony orchestras in the U.S., Canada, and other countries. Strongly directed toward the commercial aspects of music.

87 / **International Who's Who in Music and Musical Gazetteer,** a contemporary biographical dictionary and a record of the world's musical activity, edited by César Saerchinger. New York, Current Literature Pub. Co., 1918. 861 p.

The geographical index and directory of schools and organizations are now only of historical interest, but the biographical section is still useful for minor figures of the first two decades of the century. Composers, performers, critics, musicologists, teachers—their education, activity, principal works, addresses.

88 / **Kutsch, K. J.** A concise biographical dictionary of singers, from the beginning of recorded sound to the present, by K. J. Kutsch and Leo Riemens. Translated from German, expanded and annotated by Harry Earl Jones. Philadelphia, Chilton Book Co., 1969. 487 p.

First printed in German under the title *Unvergängliche Stimmen,* Bern u. München, Francke Verlag, 1962.

Brief biographies of great singers who have flourished since the invention of sound recording. Entries include information on the singers' principal roles, the character of the voice, and the labels under which recordings were made. No detailed discographies.

Review by Phillip L. Miller in *Library Journal* (Oct. 15, 1969). See also "Discographies."

89 / **MacKenzie, Barbara, and Findlay MacKenzie.** Singers of Australia from Melba to Sutherland. Melbourne, Lansdowne Press, 1967. 309 p.

Biographies, with a liberal selection of portraits. Bibliography and index; data on results of vocal competitions in Australia.

90 / **Mattheson, Johann.** Grundlage einer Ehren-Pforte, woran der tüchtigsten Capellmeister, Componisten, Musikgelehrten, Tonkünstler, etc. erscheinen sollen. Zum fernern Ausbau angegeben von Mattheson, Hamburg, 1740. Vollständiger, originalgetreuer Neudruck mit gelegentlichen bibliographischen Hinweisen und Matthesons Nachträgen, hrsg. von Max Schneider. Berlin, Leo Liepmannssohn, 1910. 428 p., with *Anhang* of 51 p.

A 1969 reprint of the 1910 ed., issued by Bärenreiter, Kassel.

Mattheson's work is, strictly speaking, a volume of collected biography rather than a biographical dictionary. But the volume stands first, chronologically, among all self-contained works of musical biography, establishing the precedent for Gerber's *Lexikon* (no. 82) and subsequent dictionaries of musical biography. Most of the essays were contributed by the subjects themselves.

91 / **Merseburger, Carl W.** Kurzgefasstes Tonkünstler-lexikon für Musiker und Freunde der Musik. Begründet von Paul Frank [pseud.]. Neu bearbeitet und ergänzt von Wilhelm Altmann. 14. stark erweierte Auflage. Regensburg, G. Bosse, 1936. 730 p.

First published in 1860 as P. Frank's *Kleines Tonkünstler-lexikon*. Title varies slightly in subsequent editions.

Heinrichshofen's Verlag, Wilhelmshaven, have announced a 15th edition of this work consisting of a reprint of the 1936 edition as volume 1 and a second volume covering the period from 1937 to 1972. The editor is Helmut Roesner.

One of the most popular of the prewar German dictionaries of

29

musical biography. Extremely wide coverage, but with minimum data. Over 18,000 entries, including composers, librettists, performers, musicologists. Many minor figures. No lists of works or bibliographical references. Useful for quick reference.

Review of the 15th edition by Nyal Williams in *Notes*, 29 (1973), p. 448.

92 / **Mirkin, Mikhail Iur'evich.** Kratkii biograficheskii slovar' zarubezhnykh kompozitorov. (Brief biographical dictionary of foreign composers.) Moskva, Sovetskii kompozitor, 1969. 265 p.

A biographical dictionary covering some 2,500 musicians excluding Russian and Soviet composers.

93 / **Les Musiciens Célèbres.** [Publié sous la direction de Jean Lacroix . . .] [Genève] L. Mazenod, 1946. 385 p.

Also published in German under the title *Die berühmten Musiker.* Genève, 1946.

An "art" publication, chiefly valuable for its fine full-page portraits of musicians. 66 individual biographies and several group articles, chronologically arranged. P. 293–349: brief identifications of other composers.

94 / **Musikens Hven-Hvad-Hvor.** Udarbejdet af Nelly Back-hausen og Axel Kjerulf. København, Politikens Forlag, 1950. 3 v.

Vol. 1: "Musikhistorie." Chronology from antiquity to 1900, with composer index. Vols. 2–3: Biographies (composers, performers, musicologists) indicating field of activity and principal works. Vol. 3: p. 141–414. Title list of 15,000 entries, including operas, repertory works, popular and musical comedy songs, folk songs. For each, identification, composer, and date if known.

A new edition of vols. 2–3, the biographies section, appeared in 1961, edited by Ludvig Ernst Bramsen, Jr.

95 / **Das Neue Musiklexikon,** nach dem *Dictionary of modern music and musicians,* hrsg. von A. Eaglefield-Hull, übersetzt und bearb. von Alfred Einstein. Berlin, M. Hesse, 1926. 729 p.

A German translation of no. 72, with many additions and corrections by Einstein. Most of the information in this revision is incorporated in the 11th edition of the Riemann *Musik-Lexikon*.

96 / Prieberg, Fred K. Lexikon der neuen Musik. Freiburg & München, K. Alber, 1958. 495 p.

Primarily biographical, but with a few articles on aspects of and trends in contemporary music (film music, radio operas, polytonality, 12-tone music, *musique concrète*, etc.) Factual rather than critical, covering education, activities, and principal works of 20th-century composers.

97 / Sakka, Keisei. Meikyoku jiten. Tokyo, Ongaku no Tomosha, 1969. 702 p.

Title: Dictionary of famous music and musicians.

A general bio-bibliography in Japanese.

98 / Schäffer, Boguslaw. Leksykon kompozytorów XX wieku. v. 1– Kraków, Polskie Wydawnictwo Muzyczne, 1963–65. Vol. 1: A–L. Vol. 2: M–Z.

A Polish-language dictionary of 20th-century composers. International in coverage but particularly strong in Slavic musicians. Portraits, bibliographies.

99 / Schmidl, Carlo. Dizionario universale dei musicisti. Milano, Sonzogno [1928?–29], 2 v.

Supplemento, 1938. 806 p. First pub. 1887–89 in 1 vol.

The major bio-bibliography in Italian and best general biographical source for Italian musicians. Emphasis on native composers, librettists, and performers, with full articles on well-known persons and brief accounts of minor ones. Dates of first productions of dramatic works. Lists of works, including modern republications. Particularly valuable for articles on Italian literary figures and their relations to music. All forenames are Italianized.

100 / Schnoor, Hans. Oper, Operette, Konzert. Ein praktisches Nachschlagebuch für Theater- und Konzertbesucher, für Rundfunkhörer, Fernsehteilnehmer und Schallplattenfreunde. Gütersloh, C. Bertelsmann, 1963. 575 p.

First printed in 1955.

A handbook for the musical amateur and concertgoer. Organized biographically, but with emphasis on the composers' works in the current repertory. Some 347 musical examples and numerous illustrations. With an appended glossary and indexes of persons and subjects.

101 / **Thomson, Ronald W.** Who's who of hymn writers. London Epworth Press, 1967. 104 p.

Brief biographies of the principal Protestant hymn text writers with a representative selection of their hymns.

Unvergängliche Stimmen
See **Kutsch, K. J.** (no. 88).

Who's Who in Music . . . See no. 135.

102 / **Young, Percy M.** Biographical dictionary of composers, with classified list of music for performance and study. New York, Crowell, 1954, 381 p.

Published in England under the title *A critical dictionary of composers and their music*. London, Dobson, 1954.

Selective list of 500 composers. Brief critical surveys of each, titles of representative works, and references to further sources of information, usually in English. Intended for the general student rather than the specialist.

BIOGRAPHY, NATIONAL

Any dictionary of musical biography may be expected to be strong in names within its own language group. There are numerous specialized dictionaries of biography devoted specifically to the musicians of particular countries. Only the most important of such dictionaries are listed here, with the emphasis on recent, currently available publications. They are tabulated in the following list for quick reference.

ARGENTINA

103 / **Arizaga, Rodolfo.** Enciclopedia de la música Argentina. Buenos Aires, Fondo Nacional de las Artes, 1971. 371 p.

Chiefly a biographical dictionary of Argentine musicians but including some terms for dance forms, musical institutions, and the like. Partial lists of composers' works. Chronological tables covering the history of Argentine music from 1901 to 1970.

AUSTRALIA

104 / **McCredie, Andrew D.** Catalogue of 46 Australian composers and selected works. . . . Canberra, Advisory Board. Commonwealth Assistance to Australian Composers, 1969. 20 p. (Music by Australian Composers, survey no. 1.)

AUSTRIA

105 / **Knaus, Herwig.** Die Musiker im Archivbestand des Kaiserlichen Obersthofmeisteramts (1637–1705). Wien, Hermann Böhlaus Nachf., 1967. 2 v. (Österreichische Akademie der Wissenschaften . . . Veröff. der Kommission für Musikforschung, Heft 7 u. 8.)

An archive study of early Austrian musicians, made up of transcriptions of documents pertaining to musical activity in Austrian courts, chapels, and municipalities. Each volume has an index of names. For a similar study based on French archives, see no. 1418.

106 / **Suppan, Wolfgang.** Steirisches Musiklexikon. Im Auftrage des Steirischen Tonkünstlerbundes unter Benützung der "Sammlung Wamlek" bearb. . . . Graz, Akademische Druck- und Verlagsanstalt, 1962–1966. 676 p. 56 plates.
Issued serially between 1962 and 1966.
A biographical dictionary of musicians associated with Graz and other parts of Steiermark. Comprehensive for pre-1800 names, selective for post-1800. Good bibliographical coverage for composers' works and for writings on the musicians.
Review by Fritz Racek in *Die Musikforschung*, 22 (1969), p. 388–89.

BELGIUM

107 / **Centre Belge de Documentation Musicale.** Music in Belgium: contemporary Belgian composers. Brussels, Published in cooperation with the CeBeDeM, by A. Manteau, 1964. 158 p.
A publication designed to stimulate interest in contemporary Belgian music. Biographical sketches of 48 modern Belgian composers, with lists of their major works. Portraits. Index of names and brief lists of recordings.

108 / **Hemel, Victor van.** Voorname belgische toonkunstenaars uit de 18de, 19de, en 20ste eeuw. Beknopt overzicht van hun leven en oeuvre. Derde bijgewerkte druk. Antwerpen, Cupidouitgave, 1958, 84p.
Brief biographies of 101 Belgian musicians, covering the period from Loeillet to the present.

109 / **Vannes, René.** Dictionnaire des musiciens (compositeurs) . . . avec la collaboration de André Souris. Bruxelles, Maison Larcier, 1947, 443 p.
Belgian composers from the 15th century to 1830, with comprehensive lists of works, published or in manuscript, and references to other sources of information.
Comments by Richard S. Hill in *Notes*, 6 (1949), p. 607–608.

BULGARIA

110 / **Entsiklopediĩa na Bŭlgarskata Muzikalna Kultura.** Ed. by Venelin Krŭstev. Sofia Bŭlgarska Akademiia na Naukite, 1967, 465 p.

A Bulgarian bio-bibliographical dictionary of musicians. Illustrated. Contains much information on Bulgarian instruments and musical institutions.

CANADA

111 / **Canadian Broadcasting Corporation.** Catalogue of Canadian composers; edited by Helmut Kallmann. Rev. and enl. ed. Ottawa, 1952? 254 p.

Reprint by The Scholarly Press, 1972.

356 brief biographical sketches, giving activities, education, addresses. Listings of works as complete as possible, giving titles, dates of publication, medium, duration, publisher. Unpublished works included. Lists of Canadian publishers and composers' organizations.

112 / **Canadian Broadcasting Corporation.** Thirty-four biographies of Canadian composers. Prepared and distributed by the International Service of the Canadian Broadcasting Corp., English and French texts. Montreal, Canadian Broadcasting Corp., 1964. 110 p.

CZECHOSLOVAKIA

113 / **Československý Hudebni Slovník,** osob a institucí. Praha, Státní hudební vydavatelství, 1963–65. 2 v.

Editors: Gracian Černušák, Bohumír Štedroň, Zdenko Nováček.

A Czech bio-bibliographical dictionary. Also includes entries under names of places and institutions.

Review by Camillo Schoenbaum in *Die Musikforschung,* 18 (1965), p. 347–49.

114 / **Dlabač, Jan Bohumir.** Allgemeines historisch Künstlerlexikon für Böhmen und zum Theil auch für Mähren und Schlesien. Auf Kosten der hochlöblichen Herrenstände Böhmens hrsg. Prag, Gedruckt bei G. Hasse, 1815. 3 v.

An early dictionary of Czech (Bohemian and Moravian musicians. Reprint by Frits A. M. Knuf, Hilversum, Holland.

115 / **Gardavský, Čeněk, ed.** Contemporary Czechoslovak composers. Prague, 1965. 562 p.

Biographies and bibliographical information on more than 300 Czech composers. English text. Also published in French.

FRANCE

116 / **Brossard, Yolande de.** Musiciens de Paris, 1535–1792; actes d'État civil d'après le Fichier Laborde de la Bibliothèque Nationale. Préf. de Norbert Dufourcq. Paris, A. et J. Picard, 1965. 302 p. (Vie musicale en France sous les rois Bourbons, 11.)

A directory of early Parisian musicians based on a card file compiled by Léon de Laborde (d. 1869). Comprises some 6,624 cards listing musicians of all kinds active in Paris during the period covered. Index of musicians arranged chronologically under their specialties.

117 / **Dictionnaire des musiciens Français.** Paris, Seghers, 1961. 379 p. (Dictionnaires Seghers, 3.)

A pocket, illustrated dictionary of French musicians. Coverage is selective, particularly for contemporary figures. Brief summaries of the major works of composers; no full listings or bibliographical references.

118 / **Favati, Guido.** Le biografie trovadorische, testi provenzali dei secc. XIII e XIV, edizione critica . . . Bologna, Libreria Antiquaria Palmaverdi, 1961. 523 p. (Biblioteca degli „studi mediolatine e volgari," 3.)

Not a French biographical dictionary in the ordinary sense, but a critical edition of the original 13th- and 14th-century biographical descriptions of the troubadour composers.

For specialists in Romance philology and Medieval music; to be used in connection with *Gennrich* (no. 1072) and *Pillet* (no. 1093).

> **Jurgens, Madeleine.** Documents du Minutier Central . . .
> See "Catalogs of Music Libraries," no. 1418.

119 / **Muller, René.** Anthologie des compositeurs de musique d'Alsace. Strasbourg, Fédération de sociétés catholiques de chant et de musique d'Alsace, 1970. 190 p.

GERMANY

120 / **Fellerer, Karl G.,** ed. Rheinische Musiker. Köln, Arno Volk-Verlag, 1960– (Beiträge zur rheinischen Musikgeschichte, 43, 53, 58, 64, 69, 80–).

A series of volumes giving biographical and bibliographical information on musicians of the Rhineland. Issued serially. Each volume is alphabetically complete in itself, but the indexing is cumulative. Numerous contributors. Beginning with Folge 6 (1969), the editor is Dietrich Kämper. The work follows the pattern of Mattheson's *Grundlage einer Ehren-Pforte* (1740) in that many of the biographies of living musicians are self-compiled.

121 / **Fey, Hermann.** Schleswig-Holsteinische Musiker, von den ältesten Zeiten bis zur Gegenwart; ein Heimatbuch. Hamburg, C. Holler, 1922. 126 p.

Dictionary arrangement. Full bibliographies of compositions, with authority references. "Quellennachweis," p. 125–26.

122 / **Kossmaly, Karl und C. H. Herzel.** Schlesisches Tonkünstler-Lexikon, enthaltend die Biographieen aller schlesischen Tonkünstler, Componisten, Cantoren, Organisten, Tongelehrten, Textdichter, Orgelbauer, Instrumentenmacher . . . hrsg. von Kossmaly und Carlo (pseud.) Breslau, E. Trewendt, 1846–47. 332 p.

Issued in four parts, each in a separate alphabet. Long articles giving classified lists of compositions, roles for performers, concert programs.

123 / **Kürschners Deutscher Musiker-Kalender 1954.** Zweite Ausgabe des *Deutschen Musiker-Lexikons.* Herausgeber: Hedwig und E. H. Mueller von Asow. Berlin, Walter de Gruyter, 1954. 1,702 columns.

First published in 1929 under the title, *Deutsches Musiker-Lexikon.* Ed. by Erich H. Müller.

Biographies of living German, Austrian, and Swiss musicians in all categories and German-born musicians in foreign countries. Entries give essential biographical information and detailed lists of works. Excessive use of abbreviations. Indexes of names by date of birth (1854–1939) and date of death (1929–1954).

124 / **Ledebur, Carl F. H. W. P. J., Freiherr von.** Tonkünstler-Lexikon Berlins von den ältesten Zeiten bis auf die Gegenwart. Berlin, L. Rauh, 1861. 704 p.

Reprint by Frits Knuf, Hilversum, Holland.

An important early dictionary of Berlin musicians. Entries for composers, publishers, performers, amateurs, born or active in Berlin, with detailed bibliographies of compositions.

125 / **Lipowsky, Felix J.** Baierisches Musik-Lexikon. München, Giel, 1811. 338 (438) p.

Reprint of the original edition by Frits A. M. Knuf, Amsterdam, 1971.

An early dictionary of some historical importance. Covers Bavarian composers and performers, listing major compositions. Occasional title-page transcriptions.

126 / **Verband Deutscher Komponisten und Musikwissenschaftlicher.** Komponisten und Musikwissenschaftlicher der Deutschen Demokratischen Republik. Kurzbiographien und Werkverzeichnisse. Berlin, Verlag Neue Musik, 1959. 199 p.

2nd expanded edition, Berlin, 1967. 239 p.

Brief biographical sketches of East German composers and musicologists, with listings of their major works. Preceded by a group of essays on musical life and institutions in the Eastern zone. Portraits.

GREAT BRITAIN (INCLUDING IRELAND AND SCOTLAND)

127 / **Baptie, David.** Musical Scotland, past and present. Being a dictionary of Scottish musicians from about 1400 till the present time, to which is added a bibliography of musical publications connected with Scotland from 1611. Paisley, J. and R. Parlane, 1894. 53 p.

Reprint by Georg Olms, Hildesheim, 1972.

128 / **Composers' Guild of Great Britain.** I. Chamber music by living British composers. Catalogue published by the British Music Information Centre, 1969. 42 p. II. Orchestral music by living British

composers. Catalogue published by the British Music Information Centre, 1970. 82 p.

The first list is confined to chamber music for three or more instruments. Composers listed alphabetically. Information includes instrumentation, duration, publisher or agent, and availability of material.

The orchestral music list is classified in three major headings: (1) works for full, small, or chamber orchestra; (2) works for string orchestra; and (3) works for brass or military bands. Data is similar to that of the chamber music catalogue above.

129 / **Brown, James D., and Stephen S. Stratton.** British musical biography: a dictionary of musical artists, authors, and composers born in Britain and its colonies. Birmingham, Stratton, 1897. 462 p.

Reprint by Da Capo Press, New York, 1971.

The emphasis is on composers living at the time of publication. Great masters treated briefly to afford room for the obscure. Includes a large number of English names that cannot be found elsewhere, with excellent bibliographies.

130 / **Dublin. Music Association of Ireland.** A catalogue of contemporary Irish composers. Dublin, Music Association of Ireland, 1968. (74 p.)

Data on the works of 23 contemporary Irish composers, including brief biographical information, addresses, full descriptions of works: titles, media, timing, instrumentation, availability. List of publishers and list of abbreviations.

131 / **Huntley, John.** British film music. London, Skelton Robinson, 1947. 247 p.

P. 189–229: biographical index of British film composers. Lists many names not to be found in other reference sources together with a listing of film scores.

132 / **Highfill, Philip H., Jr.** A bibliographical dictionary of actors, actresses, musicians, dancers, managers, and other stage personnel in London, 1660–1800. Carbondale, Southern Illinois University Press, 1973–.

When completed this work will comprise some six volumes. The first two contain approximately 1800 biographical entries detailing all the facts that exhaustive research has been able to recover about the performers and other stage personnel listed.

133 / Palmer, Russell. British music. London, Skelton Robinson, 1948. 283 p.

Biographical index of contemporary British musicians and musical organizations. Portraits.

134 / Pulver, Jeffrey. A biographical dictionary of old English music. London, Kegan Paul; New York, Dutton, 1927. 537 p.

Reprints by the Da Capo Press, New York, 1973, with a new introduction by Gilbert Blount and by Bert Franklin, New York, 1969.

English musicians active from about 1200 to the death of Purcell (1695). Cites manuscript sources, contemporary publications, and occasionally modern editions. Somewhat discursive in style, with lists of works scattered through the bodies of the articles, but useful as a starting point for the study of early English musicians. See also the author's companion volume covering old English musical terms (no. 297).

135 / Who's Who in Music, and musicians' international directory. 5th edition. New York, Hafner Publishing Co., 1969. 432 p.

Editorial director: W. J. Potterton.

First published in 1935, with subsequent edition in 1937, 1950, and 1962.

Primarily devoted to British musicians and musical institutions. Includes articles on various British musical organizations and many helpful lists (publishers, periodicals, festivals, music schools and colleges) in the "directory" section. The largest section, 353 p., is devoted to biographies of living musicians, in which a fair number of Americans and other foreigners are included. The directory contains an "overseas section" giving international listings of music publishers, retailers and wholesalers, orchestras and opera companies.

Review of the 1962 ed. by Fred Blum in *Notes*, 19 (1962), p. 442–43.

HOLLAND

136 / Gregoir, G. J. Biographie des artistes-musiciens néerlandais des XVIIIe et XIXe siècles, et des artistes étrangers résidant ou ayant résidé en Néerlands à la même époque. Anvers, L. de La Montagne, 1864. 238 p.

Brief biographies of Netherland musicians. Careers summarized, major works mentioned for composers, but no full listings.

137 / **Het Toonkunstenaarsboek van Nederland 1956.** Amsterdam Nederlandse Toonkunstenaarsraad, 1956. 240 p.
Edited by Dr. Jos. Smits van Waesberghe.
A source book of information on Dutch organizations, institutions, and persons connected with music. Members of the Dutch society of composers are listed alphabetically, with addresses and a key to their activities and affiliations. They are also listed by place.

138 / **Letzer, J. H.** Muzikaal Nederland, 1850–1910. Bio-bibliographisch woordenboek... 2. uitgaff met aanvulligen en verbeteringen. Utrecht, J. L. Beijers, 1913. 201 p., with 10 p. of additions.
Composers, musicologists, performers, etc., active in Holland 1850–1910. Biographies, lists of works, occasional dates of first performances.

139 / **Straeten, Edmond vander.** La musique aux pays-bas avant le XIXe siècle. Documents inédits et annotés. Compositeurs, virtuoses, théoriciens, luthiers, opéras, motets, airs nationaux, académies, maîtrises, livres, portraits, etc. Bruxelles, C. Muquardt, 1867–88. 8 v.
Vols. 2–7 published by G. A. Van Trigt; vol. 8 by Schott. Reprint by Dover, New York, 1968. 4 v.
Not strictly a biographical dictionary but an invaluable collection of documents, transcripts of records, biographical and bibliographical notes related to the activities of Flemish musicians (Dutch and Belgian). Vol. 6 is devoted to Flemish musicians in Italy; vols. 7–8, to Flemish musicians in Spain. Rich in information of the greatest interest to students of early European music.

HUNGARY

140 / **Contemporary Hungarian Composers.** Budapest, Editio Musica, 1970. 156 p.
Brief biographies, lists of works, portraits of 73 contemporary Hungarian composers, including such recently deceased musicians as Bartok and Kodaly. P. 144–56: discography.

141 / **Molnár, Imre.** A magyar muzsika könyve, szerkesztette Molnár Imre. . . . Budapest, Merkantil-Nyomda, 1936. 632 p.

Institutions, organizations, and biographical entries for composers, performers, and other musicians.

INDIA

142 / **Sambamoorthy, P.** A dictionary of South Indian music and musicians. Madras, The Indian Music Publishing House, 1952–.
In progress. Vol. 1: A–F. Vol. 2 (1959): G–K.
Portraits of composers and performers.

143 / **Who's Who of Indian Musicians.** New Delhi, Sangeet Natak Akademi, 1968. 100 p.
Brief biographical data on living Indian musicians, giving date of birth, area of specialization, addresses.

ISRAEL (AND JEWISH MUSICIANS IN GENERAL)

144 / **Gradenwitz, Peter.** Music and musicians in Israel: a comprehensive guide to modern Israeli music. Tel Aviv, Israeli Music Publications, 1959. 226 p.
Biographies, varying in length, of about 60 composers, grouped by school. Appendix, p. 133–63, contains an alphabetical listing of composers and their works, but without reference to the biography section. Also given is a list of publishers and a group of publishers' catalogs.

145 / **Saleski, Gdal.** Famous musicians of Jewish origin. New York, Bloch, 1949. 716 p.
First published in 1927 under the title, *Famous musicians of a wandering race.* 463 p.
Informal biographies, classified according to type of musical activity: composers, conductors, violinists, etc. About 400 entries. No bibliographies, but major works are mentioned in the articles. Portraits. P. 679–716: Israeli musicians.

146 / **Shalita, Israel, and Hanan Steinitz.** Encyclopedia of music. Vol. 1: a biographical dictionary of Jewish and world musicians; vol. 2: dictionary of terms, theory, instruments, forms and history of Jewish and world music. Tel-Aviv, Joshua Chachik, 1965. 2 v.
In Hebrew with indexes of Hebrew equivalents for English names and terms. International in scope, but entered here among national works because of its language.

147 / **Stengel, Theophil und Herbert Gerigk.** Lexikon der Juden in der Musik, mit einem Titelverzeichnis jüdischer Werke. Berlin, B. Hahnefeld, 1943. 404 columns. (Veröffentlichungen des Instituts der NSDAP zur Erforschung der Judenfrage . . . 2.)

First published in 1940. 380 p.

Among the more shameful products of German National Socialism were dictionaries of Jewish musicians compiled to further the purposes of anti-semitism. This and the item following may be cited as examples of their kind.

148 / **Girschner, Otto.** Repetitorium der Musikgeschichte. Elfte Auflage. Köln, P. J. Tonger, 1941. 438 p.

A question-answer survey of music history.

P. 350–411: "Juden in der Musik," a biographical supplement first introduced in the 9th edition, 1936.

149 / **Who Is Who in Acum.** Authors, composers, and music publishers. Biographical notes and principal works. Compiled and edited by Menashe Ravina and Shlomo Skolsky. Israel, ACUM Ltd., Société d'auteurs, compositeurs et éditeurs de musique en Israel, 1965. 95 p.

Brief biographies, with lists of works, of authors, composers, and publishers affiliated with ACUM, a performing rights organization in Israel.

ITALY

150 / **Alcari, C.** Parma nella musica. Parma, M. Fresching, 1931. 259 p.

A biographical dictionary of musicians born in Parma. Emphasis is placed on 19th-century figures. Extended bibliographies for the most important musicians (e.g., Verdi, Pizzetti).

151 / **Angelis, Alberto de.** L'Italia musicale d'oggi. Dizionario dei musicisti: compositori, direttori d'orchestra, concertisti, insegnanti, liutae, cantanti, scrittori musicali, librettisti, editori musicali, ecc. 3rd ed., corredate di una appendice. Roma, Ausonia, 1928. 523, 211 p.

First published in 1918; 2nd edition, 1922.

Living Italian musicians, with comprehensive lists of works.

152 / **Damerini, Adelmo.** Musicisti toscani; scritti di G. Barblan *et al.*, settembre 1955, a cura di Adelmo Damerini e Franco Schlitzer. Siena, Ticci, 1955. 81 p.

A publication of the *Accademia musicale chigiana*.
Musicians of Tuscany.

153 / **Masutto, Giovanni.** I maestri di musica italiani del secolo XIX. Notizie biografiche . . . Terza edizione, corretta ed aumentata. Venezia, G. Cecchini, 1882. 226 p.
First printed in 1880 by Fontana, Venice.

LATIN AMERICA

154 / **Mariz, Vasco.** Dicionário bio-bibliográfico musical (brasileiro e internacional). Pref. de Renato Almeida. Rio de Janeiro, Livraria Kosmos, 1948. 246 p.
Brief biographies of the best-known figures in music since the Renaissance, including performers. Useful chiefly for Brazilian musicians.

155 / **Mayer-Serra, Otto.** Música y músicos de Latinoamérica. México, Editorial Atlante, 1947. 2 v.
Primarily biographical, although some terms, dance forms, and instruments are included. Listings of composers' works vary from brief resumes to full tabulations for major composers. Portraits.

156 / **Pan American Union. Music Section.** Composers of the Americas, biographical data and catalogs of their works. Washington, D.C., Pan American Union, 1955–.
Each issue contains from 4 to 16 names, alphabetically arranged, with brief biographies in English and Spanish. Portraits. Dates from scores, sometimes autographs. Works are given chronologically within principal media, with dates of composition, timing, publisher, and recordings if any. Also lists unpublished works.

POLAND

157 / **Chybiński, Adolf.** Słownik muzyków dawnej Polski do roku 1800. Krakow, Polskie Wydawnictwo Muzyczne, 1949. 163 p.
Biographical dictionary of musicians (composers and performers) active in Poland in 1800. Brief articles mentioning principal works. List of references for each entry. Preface discusses sources of information such as *Fétis*, *Eitner*, and many Polish publications and archives.

158 / **Chybiński, Józef.** Słownik muzyków polskich. Ed. Józef Chominski. Warsaw, Polskie Wydawnictwo Muzyczne, 1962. 2 v.

At head of title: Instytut Sztuki Polskiej Akademii Nauk. Vol. 1: A–L. Vol. 2: M–Z.

159 / **Sowinski, Wojciech.** Les musiciens polonais et slaves, anciens et modernes; dictionnaire biographique . . . Précédé d'un résumé de l'histoire de la musique en Pologne . . . Paris, A. Le Clerc, 1857. 599 p.

Another edition, in Polish, published in 1874. Reprint by the Da Capo Press, New York, 1971.

"Résumé de l'histoire de la musique en Pologne," p. 1–44. "Anciens instruments de musique chez les polonais et les slaves," p. 45–58. Long biographical articles, with full bibliographies for major composers.

PORTUGAL

160 / **Amorim, Eugénio.** Dicionário biográfico de musicos do norte de Portugal. Porto, Edições Maranus, 1935. 110 p.

Chiefly 19th-century and living musicians. Some extended articles, with compositions listed in the body of the text.

161 / **Mazza, José.** Dicionário biográfico de musicos portugueses, com prefácio e notas do José Augusto Alegria . . . Lisboa, 1945? 103 p.

"Extraido de revista, *Ocidente*, 1944/45."

A dictionary compiled around 1790 and preserved in a manuscript in the Biblioteca Publica de Évora. Entries arranged by Christian names; many names of members of religious orders. The dictionary occupies p. 13–40; additional biographical information supplied by the editor from other sources, p. 41–103.

162 / **Vasconcellos, Joaquim A. da Fonseca E.** Os musicos portuguezes. Biographia-bibliographia. Porto, Imprensa Portugueza, 1870. 2 v.

Long biographical articles, lists and discussions of compositions. Useful for early names, library locations of manuscripts, etc. Discussions of operas include dates and places of first performances.

163 / **Vieira, Ernesto.** Diccionario biographico de musicos portuguezes; historia e bibliographia da musica em Portugal. Lisboa, Moreira e Pinheiro, 1900–1904. 2 v.

More inclusive than *Vasconcellos*, above. Comprehensive lists of works for major composers. Vol. 2 includes much supplementary material and a chronological index.

RUMANIA

164 / **Cosma, Viorel.** Muzicieni români. Compozitori si muzicologi. Lexicon. (Rumanian musicians, composers and musicologists. A dictionary.) Bucuresti, Uniunii Compozitorilor, 1970. 475 p.

Expansion of a work first issued in 1965.

Biographical data and information on the works of the most prominent Rumanian composers and musicologists. Includes musicians of earlier times, but stresses the contemporary scene. Portraits and discographies.

SCANDINAVIA

165 / **Kappel, Vagn.** Contemporary Danish composers against the background of Danish musical life and history. 2nd rev. ed. Copenhagen, Det Danske Selskab, 1950. 116 p.

A public relations document, first issued in 1948.

Biographical sketches of 14 contemporary Danish composers. Representative works cited but no full lists. Discography of Danish music, p. 97–113.

166 / **Sundelin, Torsten.** Norrländskt musikliv. Uppsala, Almqvist u. Wiksell, 1946. 358 p.

SOUTH AFRICA

167 / **Huskisson, Yvonne.** The Bantu composers of southern Africa. A publication of the South African Broadcasting Corporation, 1969. 335 p.

Text in English and Afrikans.

Portraits of musicians, index of composers, and a study of the traditional instruments of the Bantu.

SPAIN

168 / **Alcahali y de Mosquera, José Maria Ruiz de Lihori y Pardines, Baron de.** La música en Valencia. Diccionario biográfico y crítico ... Valencia, Domenech, 1903. 445 p.

Biographies of widely varying length, with summary lists of works for major composers. Under "Anónimos," p. 39–170, the compiler introduces long literary digressions concerning liturgical drama, dance music, military music, etc., with musical examples.

SWITZERLAND

169 / **Refardt, Edgar.** Historisch-biographisches Musikerlexikon der Schweiz. Leipzig/Zürich, Hug u. Co., 1928. 355 p.

Comprehensive biographical coverage for names connected with Swiss music from the Middle Ages to the end of the 16th century. Musicians and instrument makers of the 17th and 18th centuries; composers only for the 19th and 20th centuries. Lists of works.

170 / **Schweizer Musiker-Lexikon.** Dictionnaire des musiciens suisses. . . . Im Auftrag des Schweizerischen Tonkünstlervereins bearbeitet von rédigé a la demande de l'Association des Musiciens Suisses, par Willi Schuh *et al.* Zürich, Atlantis Verlag, 1964. 421 p.

The expansion of a biographical dictionary of Swiss musicians that appeared originally as vol. 2 of the *Schweizer Musikbuch* (Zürich, 1939). Treats Swiss musicians of all periods as well as foreign musicians resident in Switzerland or associated with the music of that country. Articles in French and German. Excellent bibliographical coverage.

171 / **Swiss Composers' League.** 40 contemporary Swiss composers. Amriswil, Bodensee Verlag, 1956. 222 p.

Brief biographies and critical comment. A few representative works are described and a larger selection listed, with imprints and instrumentation given. Recordings. Portraits. Text in English.

TURKEY

172 / **Öztuna, T. Yilmaz.** Türk musikisi ansiklopedisi. Istanbul, Milli Egitim Basimevi, 1969–   .

Vol. 1: A–L. 368 p.

Turkish dictionary of musical terms and biography. The terms cover general concepts, the biographies are confined to Turkish musicians. Bibliographical references.

U.S.S.R.

173 / **Bélza, Igor' Fedorovich.** Handbook of Soviet musicians. Edited by Alan Bush. London, Pilot Press, 1944. 101 p.

First printing, 1943. Reprints by the Greenwood Press, Westport, Conn., 1971, and by the Scholarly Press, St. Clair Shores, Michigan, 1972.

40 short biographies. Portraits. Separate bibliographical section giving a list of each composer's works. English titles, dates given when known.

174 / **Sovetskie Kompozitory,** kratkiĭ biograficheskiĭ spravochnik. Sostaviteli: G. Bernandt e A. Dolzhanskii. Moskva, Sovetskiĭ Kompozitor, 1957. 695 p.

Biographical sketches of 1,072 composers, with a full listing of their compositions arranged by medium, with dates of first performance for large works. Literary works by the musicians are also listed.

Review by Fred K. Prieberg in *Musical America*, 78 (July 1958), p. 28–29.

175 / **Vodarsky-Shiraeff, Alexandria.** Russian composers and musicians, a biographical dictionary. New York, H. W. Wilson, 1940. 158 p.

Reprint by the Greenwood Press, New York, 1969.

Brief biographies of outstanding figures: composers, performers, teachers, critics. Classified lists of major works, bibliographical references. Cross references to variant spellings of Russian names.

UNITED STATES

176 / **American Society of Composers, Authors, and Publishers.** The ASCAP biographical dictionary of composers, authors and publishers. 3rd ed. Compiled and edited by the Lynn Farnol Group, Inc. New York, American Society of Composers, Authors and Publishers, 1966. 845 p.

First published in 1948. 2nd ed., 1952.

Brief biographies of some 5,238 members, including writers of lyrics, composers of popular and serious music. Major works listed. Separate listing of publisher members, p. 815–45.

Review by Ruth Hilton in *Notes*, 24 (1967), p. 46.

177 / **The College Music Society.** Directory of music faculties in American colleges and universities 1968–1970). Compiled and edited by Harry B. Lincoln. Binghamton, N.Y., College Music Society, 1970.
Began publication with the volume for 1967–1968.
A directory of 11,800 teachers of music in 1,100 institutions. Part I: departmental listing by state and school. Part II: Listings by areas of specialization. Part III: national alphabetical listings.
Review of the 1967–68 edition by R. M. Longyear in *Journal of research in music education*, 16 (1968), p. 220–21.

178 / **Ewen, David.** American composers today, a biographical and periodicals. Superseded by *Composers since 1900*, no. 78.
Composers active in the U.S. and Latin America, 1900–1946. Principal works and recordings listed. Bibliographical references to books and periodicals. Superseded by *Composers since 1900*, no. 78.
Review by Lee Fairley in *Notes*, 6 (1949), p. 615–16.

Ewen, David. Popular American composers . . .
See under "Biography (Jazz, popular, and folk musicians)."

179 / **Historical Records Survey. District of Columbia.** Bio-bibliographical index of musicians in the United States of America from colonial times . . . sponsored by the Board of Commissioners of the District of Columbia. 2nd ed. Washington, D.C., Music Section, Pan American Union, 1956. 439 p.
First printed in 1941. Unaltered reprint, 1970, by the AMS Press, New York, and the Scholarly Press, St. Clair Shores, Michigan, 1972.
An index to biographical information contained in 66 works (dictionaries, histories, etc.) on American music, with page references to the volumes indexed.

180 / **McCarty, Clifford.** Film composers in America: a checklist of their work. Foreword by Lawrence Morton. Glendale, Calif., John Valentine, 1953. 193 p.
Reprint by Da Capo Press, New York, 1972.
163 names, with film scores listed by date. Index of film titles; index of orchestrators.
Review by F. W. Sternfeld in *Notes*, 11 (1953), p. 105.
Also entered as no. 812.

181 / **Mangler, Joyce Ellen.** Rhode Island music and musicians, 1733–1850. Detroit, Information Service, 1965. 90 p. (Detroit studies in music bibliography, 7.)

Primarily a directory of early Rhode Island musicians; indexed by profession and by chronology.

Supplement I: organ builders and installations in Rhode Island churches. Supplement II: membership in the Psallonian Society 1816–32. Bibliography of primary and secondary sources.

Review by Donald W. Krummel in *Notes*, 23 (1966), p. 265.

182 / **Music and Dance in California and the West.** Richard D. Saunders, editor. Hollywood, Bureau of Musical Research, 1948. 311 p.

Earlier editions with slightly varying titles in 1933 and 1940.

This and the following six titles (nos. 182–189) are a series of regional reference works covering different sections of the United States. Long articles on the development of musical and dance activities. Biographical sketches of composers, performers, conductors, educators, etc. Portraits. Pronounced emphasis on the commercial aspects of music.

183 / **Music and Dance in the Central States.** Edited by Richard D. Saunders; compiled by William J. Perlman. Hollywood, Bureau of Musical Research, 1952. 173 p.

184 / **Music and Dance in the New England States.** Sigmund Spaeth, editor-in-chief; William J. Perlman, director and managing editor. New York, Bureau of Musical Research, 1953. 347 p.

185 / **Music and Dance in New York State.** Sigmund Spaeth, editor-in-chief; William J. Perlman, director and associate editor . . . 1952 ed. New York, Bureau of Musical Research, 1951. 435 p.

186 / **Music and Dance in Pennsylvania, New Jersey and Delaware.** Sigmund Spaeth, editor-in-chief; William J. Perlman, director and managing editor. New York, Bureau of Musical Research, 1954. 339 p.

187 / **Music and Dance in the Southeastern States.** Sigmund Spaeth, editor-in-chief; William J. Perlman, director and managing editor. New York, Bureau of Musical Research, 1952. 331 p.

188 / **Music and Dance in Texas, Oklahoma and the Southwest.** Edited by E. Clyde Whitlock and Richard D. Saunders. Hollywood, Bureau of Musical Research, 1950. 256 p.

189 / **North Carolina Federation of Music Clubs.** North Carolina musicians, a selective handbook. Chapel Hill, University of North Carolina Library, 1956. 82 p. (Univ. of North Carolina Library Extension pubn., v. 21, no. 4.)

190 / **Reis, Claire R.** Composers in America; biographical sketches of contemporary composers with a record of their works. Rev. and enl. ed. New York, Macmillan, 1947. 399 p.

First published in 1930 under the title *American composers . . .*

A survey of music written by American serious composers, 1915 to 1947. Biographies of 332 composers, with a classified listing of their works, manuscripts included (date, publisher, duration). Supplementary list of 424 names without further biographical data.

Review by Lee Fairley in *Notes*, 4 (1947), p. 458–59.

191 / **Smith, Julia,** ed. Directory of American women composers, with selected music for senior and junior clubs. First edition. Chicago, National Federation of Music Clubs, 1970. 51 p.

Here is a first *Directory of American women composers*. . . . The *Directory* contains the names of over 600 composers who have written, or are now writing music that ranges from very easy to the most difficult and experimental, including electronic music. [Editor's *Foreword*]

No work lists, but type of music composed is indicated for each composer as well as for the publishers who have issued their works. Key to music publishers and distributors (p. 48–51).

192 / **Thomson, Virgil.** American music since 1910. With an introduction by Nicolas Nabokov. New York, Holt, Rinehart and Winston, 1970. 204 p. (Twentieth-century composers, 1.)

Primarily a collection of critical essays, but contains a biographical dictionary of 106 American composers, p. 118–185. Brief biographies with stimulating commentary. Principal works cited.

193 / **Works Projects Administration. Northern California.** Celebrities in El Dorado, 1850–1906. Cornel Lengyel, editor. San Francisco, prepared with the assistance of the Works Project Administration of California; sponsored by the City and County of San Francisco, 1940. 270 leaves (typescript). (The history of music in San Francisco, 4.)

A biographic record of 111 prominent musicians who have visited San Francisco and performed here from the earliest days of the gold rush era to the time of the great fire, with additional lists of visiting celebrities (1909–1940), chamber music ensembles, bands, orchestras, and other music making bodies. [Editor's Note]

YUGOSLAVIA

194 / **Kovačević, Krešimir.** Hrvatski kompozitori i njihova djela. Zagreb, Naprijed, 1960. 553 p.

Biographies of 50 Croatian composers, for the most part contemporary, with descriptive accounts of their principal works. Summaries in English. Classified index of works analyzed; general index.

195 / **Savez Kompozitora Jugoslavije.** Kompozitori i muzicki pisci Jugoslavije. Članovi Saveza kompozitora Jugoslavije 1945–1967. Katalog. (Yugoslav composers and music writers. Members of the Union of Yugoslav Composers 1945–1967. Catalogue.) Sastavila Milena Milosavljević-Pěsić. . . . Beograd, Savez kompozitora Jugoslaviue, 1968. 663 p.

Contemporary Yugoslav composers and writers on music. Brief biographies; full bibliographies of works. Portraits. Addresses. Preceded by "An introduction to contemporary Yugoslav musical creation," by Krešimir Kovačević, p. 45–75.

BIOGRAPHY, JAZZ, POPULAR, AND FOLK MUSICIANS

Considerable attention has been directed in recent years to the musicians active in the folk and popular strata of our culture, whose names rarely find their way into the traditional music lexica. The titles given here are representative of the growing resources in this area. The works cited are primarily biographical in emphasis. Related information will be found in the section *Jazz and popular music* under "Bibliographies of Music."

196 / **Charters, Samuel B.** Jazz: New Orleans. Rev. ed., New York, Oak Publications, 1963. 173 p.
First published in 1958 by Walter C. Allen.
Brief descriptions of musicians and groups, under chronological periods. Appendix of discography; index to names of musicians and bands, to halls, cabarets, and tune titles. Illustrated.

197 / **Chilton, John.** Who's who of jazz: Storyville to Swing Street. Philadelphia, Chilton Book Co., 1972. 419 p.
First published in London by The Bloomsbury Book Shop, 1970. 447 p.
Brief biographies of more than 1,000 jazz musicians tracing their affiliations with various groups. Portraits. A partial listing of bandleaders mentioned in the text (p. 416–18).

198 / **Ewen, David.** Popular American composers, from revolutionary times to the present. New York, H. W. Wilson, 1962. 217 p.
First supplement, 1972. 121 p.
A bibliographical reference guide to 130 of the most important American composers of popular music, from William Billings to Andre Previn. Portraits. Chronological list of the composers, with an index to some 3,500 songs. The *First supplement* updates the information in the 1962 volume and adds 31 new biographies.

199 / **Feather, Leonard.** The encyclopedia of jazz. Completely revised, enlarged and brought up to date. New York, Horizon Press, 1960. 527 p.
First published in 1955. *Supplement*, 1956.
P. 13–90: introductory essays on the history, sociology, and structure of jazz. P. 96–473: biographies of jazz musicians, outlining their careers and summarizing their recording activities. Addresses given.

200 / **Feather, Leonard.** The encyclopedia of jazz in the sixties. Foreword by John Lewis. New York, Horizon Press, 1966. 312 p.
Similar in content and organization to the preceding. Numerous

portraits. Biographies stress affiliations with recording companies. Short essays on the state of jazz, the results of jazz polls, etc.

201 / **Gammond, Peter and Peter Clayton.** Dictionary of popular music. New York, Philosophical Library, 1961. 274 p.

A dictionary of names, terms, titles of major popular songs. Listings of works and recordings for the principal composers of popular music. Pronounced British slant.

202 / **Gentry, Linnell.** A history and encyclopedia of country, western, and gospel music. 2nd ed., completely revised. Nashville, Tenn., Claimon Corp., 1969. 598 p.

First published in 1961 by the McQuiddy Press, Nashville.

A major reference work in its field. Part II is an anthology of magazine articles on country, western, and gospel music since 1904. Part III: country musical shows since 1924. Part IV: biographies of country, western, and gospel singers, musicians, and comedians.

203 / **Lawless, Ray McKinley.** Folksingers and folksongs in America; a handbook of biography, bibliography, and discography. Illustrated from paintings by Thomas Hart Benton and others and from designs in Steuben glass. New revised ed. with special supplement. New York, Duell, Sloan and Pearce, 1965. 750 p.

First published in 1960.

A general book of knowledge for folk song enthusiasts, with information pertaining to singers, song collecting, sources and recordings. The largest part of the work is devoted to biographical information on American folk singers.

Review of the first edition by Rae Korson in *Notes*, 18 (1960), p. 62.

204 / **Panassie, Hughes, and Madeleine Gautier.** Dictionnaire du jazz. Préface de Louis Armstrong. Nouvelle édition revue et augmenté. Paris, Albin Michel, 1971. 360 p.

First published by Robert Laffont, Paris, 1954. English translation under the title: *Guide to jazz.* Trans. by Desmond Flower. New York, Houghton Mifflin, 1956.

The *Dictionnaire* is a standard source book on jazz; it is chiefly biographical but with some terms included. Portraits.

205 / **Rice, Edward le Roy.** Monarchs of minstrelsy, from "Daddy" Rice to date. New York, Kenny Publishing Co., 1911. 366 p.

Colorful biographical sketches of the leading performers in American minstrel shows of the late 19th century. Illustrated. The information is arranged roughly in chronological order.

206 / **Rose, Al, and Edmond Souchen.** New Orleans jazz family album. Baton Rouge, Louisiana State University Press, 1967. 304 p.

Copiously illustrated with many early photographs. Special sections devoted to the musicians, the ensembles, and the places where they performed.

207 / **Roxon, Lillian.** Rock encyclopedia. New York, The Universal Library, Grosset and Dunlap, 1971. 611 p.

Brief, vividly written biographical sketches of individuals and groups connected with rock. Discographies of albums and of singles. Review by Gilbert Chase in *Notes*, 28 (1972), p. 196–97.

208 / **Stambler, Irwin.** Encyclopedia of popular music. New York, St. Martin's Press, 1965. 359 p.

Terms, biography, and titles in one alphabet. Special articles: "Tape recorder tips" by Vern Bushway (p. 259–64); "Stereophonic sound" by W. P. Hopper, Jr. (p. 265–68); "The popular song" by Hal Levy (p. 269–71). An appendix lists recipients of awards issued by radio, TV, and motion picture industries. Discography. Bibliography.

209 / **Stambler, Irwin, and Grulun Landon.** Encyclopedia of folk, country, and western music. New York, St. Martin's Press, 1969. 396 p.

A source book made up chiefly of biographical entries to performers and groups. Appendices include special articles on "Changing attitudes toward folk music" by Sam Hinton; "The rise and fall of country music" by Bill Anderson, and "Country and pop music: development and relationship" by Ed Kahn. Also award listings and a selective discography and bibliography.

210 / **Ténot, Frank.** Dictionnaire du jazz. Paris, Larousse, 1967. 256 p. (Les dictionnaires de l'home du XXe siècle).

One of the Larousse popular, subject-oriented, dictionaries. Good, brief discussions, chiefly biographical but with some jazz terms. Illustrated.

211 / **Vernillat, France, and Jacques Charpentreau.** Dictionnaire de la chanson française. Paris, Larousse, 1968. 256 p.

A dictionary of French popular song. Coverage extends from the 13th century to the present day, but with emphasis on singers of the 19th and 20th centuries. The dictionary is preceded by a "petite histoire de la chanson française." Illustrated.

MUSICAL INSTRUMENTS, MAKERS AND PERFORMERS

There is a substantial group of reference books concerned with the construction, performance, and iconography of musical instruments. A great deal of work has been done with respect to the violin, and there is an increasing number of reference tools devoted to keyboard and to wind instruments.

For specific descriptions, prices, and illustrations of individual instruments, particularly those of the string family, the student should not neglect the catalogs of various dealers: Hamma, Herrmann, Hill, Lyon & Healy, Wurlitzer, etc. These are not included in our listing.

For the iconography of musical instruments, see *Buchner* (no. 221), *Besseler* (no. 478), *Kinsky* (no. 493), and *Komma* (no. 494).

See also "Bibliographies of Music Literature" (no. 698ff.) and "Catalogs of Musical Instrument Collections" (no. 1564ff.).

212 / **Avgerinos, Gerassimos.** Lexikon der Pauke. Frankfurt am M., Verlag Das Musikinstrument [1964], 105 p. (Das Musikinstrument, 12.)

A dictionary of terms, chiefly German, connected with drums and drum playing.

213 / **Bachman, Alberto A.** An encyclopedia of the violin. Translated by Frederick H. Martens, edited by Albert E. Wier, New York, D. Appleton, 1925. 470 p.

Reprinted, with a new preface by Stuart Canin, by Da Capo Press, New York, 1966.

A source book on the violin, its history, construction, literature, and performers. Organized by chapters, many of which contain lexicons and bibliographies: for example, Chap. II, "Violin makers in Europe"; Chap. III, "Violin makers in America"; Chap. XXI, "Glossary of musical terms"; Chap. XXII, "Biographical dictionary of violinists"; Chap.

XXIII, "Literature relating to the violin"; Chap. XXV, "A list of music for the violin." Portraits and illustrations.

214 / **Bachman, Alberto A.** Les grands violinistes du passé. . . . Paris, Fischbacher, 1913. 468 p.

Biographies of 40 violinist-composers, varying in length but with lists of works and a number of full or partial thematic catalogs (i.e. Corelli, Kreutzer, Leclair, Rode, Sarasate, Tartini, Viotti, Vivaldi, etc.).

215 / **Baines, Anthony.** European and American musical instruments. London, Batsford, 1966. 174 p. 824 plates.

A "pictorial museum" of musical instruments selected from American and European collections. Instruments are grouped by families: stringed, woodwind, brass, and percussion. Much precise technical information along with historical background. All instruments are identified as to present location.

Review by Albert Protz in *Die Musikforschung*, 21 (1968), p. 388–89.

216 / **Bechler, Leo, und Bernhardt Rahm.** Die Oboe und die ihr verwandten Instrumente, nebst biographischen Skizzen der bedeutendsten ihrer Meister. Anhang: Musikliteratur für Oboe und englisch Horn, zusammengestellt von Dr. Philipp Losch. Leipzig, C. Merseburger, 1914, 98 p., 32 p. (Anhang). Reprint of the 1914 edition by Saendig, Wiesbaden, 1972.

A history of the oboe and related instruments, with brief biographical sketches of famous players. Supplementary list of works for oboe and English horn, solo and with other instruments.

217 / **Boalch, Donald H.** Makers of the harpsichord and clavichord, 1440 to 1840. London, G. Ronald [1956], 169 p.

Lists 820 makers of early keyboard instruments and describes more than 1,000 of their instruments, giving dates, registers, compasses, histories, and present ownership. 32 photo plates.

Review by Frank Hubbard in *Notes*, 14 (1957), p. 572–73. Review in *The Times literary supplement*, Dec. 21, 1956.

218 / **Bone, Philip James.** The guitar and mandolin: biographies of celebrated players and composers [2nd ed., enl.]. London, New York, Schott, 1954. 388 p.

First published in 1914. Reprint by Schott, London, 1972.

Performers and composers, including "standard" composers who have written for guitar or mandolin. Major works are mentioned, but there are no complete listings. Portraits.

Review by Richard Capell in *Music and letters*, 35 (1954), p. 254.

219 / **Bowers, Q. David.** Encyclopedia of automatic musical instruments. Cylinder music boxes, disc music boxes, piano players and player pianos, coin-operated pianos, orchestrions, photoplayers, organettes, fairground organs, calliopes, and other self-playing instruments mainly of the 1750–1940 era. Including a dictionary of automatic musical instrument terms. New York, The Vestal Press, 1972. 1,008 p.

Profusely illustrated. Much documentary information. A book for collectors of automatic musical instruments.

220 / **Bragard, Roger, and Ferdinand J. de Hen.** Musical instruments in art and history. Preface by G. Thibault. Trans. by Bill Hopkins. New York, Viking Press (n.d.), 281 p., 119 plates.

Originally published in French. German translation by Dieter Krickeberg, Stuttgart, Belser Verlag, 1968.

An attractive "picture book" of early instruments, with popular commentary.

Review of the German edition by J. H. van der Meer in *Die Musikforschung*, 24 (1971), p. 481–83; of the English edition by Edmund A. Bowles in *Notes*, 25 (1969), p. 735–36, and by Mary Remnant in *Music and letters*, 50 (1969), p. 301–303.

221 / **Buchner, Alexander.** Musical instruments through the ages. Trans. by Iris Urwin. London, Spring Books [1956].

First published, with the text in Czech, by Artia, Prague. German edition: *Musikinstrumente im Wandel der Zeiten.*

Not a dictionary or encyclopedia, but important as a collection of beautifully reproduced plates, some 323 in number, of musical instruments and representations of musical performance in painting, engraving, and sculpture.

222 / **Buchner, Alexander.** Musikinstrumente der Völker. [Ins Deutsche übers. von O. Guth. Grafische Gestaltung von M. Houska. Notenbeispiele gezeichnet von J. Milota. Hanau/Main] Dausien [c1968], 295 p.

223 / **Burks, Aldine K.** Follow the pipers; a guide to contemporary flute artists and teachers. Westfield, N.Y., 1969. 181 p.

A directory of flute players. Alphabetical listing of flutists with addresses and brief biographical details; list of music schools and their flute faculty members; orchestras and ensembles with their flute personnel; discography of flute music and list of recording companies.

224 / **Carfagna, Carlo, [e] Mario Gangi.** Dizionario chitarristico italiano. (Chitarristi, liutisti, tiorbisti, compositori, liutai ed editori.) Ancona, Bèrben, 1968. 97 p.

In two alphabets, the first devoted to guitarists, lutenists, theorbo players and composers, the second to instrument makers and editors.

225 / **Clarke, A. Mason.** A biographical dictionary of fiddlers, including performers on the violoncello and double bass, past and present, containing sketches of their artistic careers. Together with notes of their compositions. London, W. Reeves, 1895. 360 p.

Reprint of the original edition by Scholarly Press, St. Clair Shores, Michigan, 1972.

Anecdotal accounts.

226 / **Crane, Frederick.** Extant medieval musical instruments: a provisional catalogue by types. Iowa City, University of Iowa Press, 1972. 105 p.

Brief descriptions of the surviving medieval musical instruments in art and archaeological museums throughout the world. The instruments are classified according to the Hornbostel-Sachs system (idiophones, chordophones, and aerophones). 30 of the instruments are illustrated in rather crude pen sketches.

P. 91–105: bibliography.

227 / **Fairfield, John H.** Known violin makers. [New York, Bradford Press, 1942] 192 p.

Separate listings of European makers from the 16th century and American makers. For each, a brief biography, description of works, and the current price range of the instruments.

228 / **Gorgerat, Gérald.** Encyclopédie de la musique pour instruments à vent. Lausanne, Éditions Rencontre [1955], 3 v.

A pretentious work which attempts to cover all information pertaining to the making and performance of wind instruments and much more that has no particular relevance. Useful fingering charts for all winds. Several special lists, as follows:

Vol. 3, p. 243–83: Principal works for wind instruments, solo and ensemble. Vol. 3, p. 285–340: Dictionary of composers cited in the text. Brief identifications; no page references. Vol. 3, p. 341–524: Table of French terms with their equivalents in Italian, German, English, and Spanish.

229 / Hamma, Fridolin. German violin makers; a critical dictionary . . . translated by Walter Stewart. London, W. Reeves [1961], 49 p., 80 pl.

Translated from the 1948 German edition, *Meister deutscher Geigenbaukunst*. Stuttgart, 1948.

Alphabetical listing of 550 names of important German makers, with plates illustrating their work.

Review by Cynthia L. Adams in *Notes*, 19 (1962), p. 261–62.

230 / Hamma, Walter. Meister italienischer Geigenbaukunst. (Zum 100 jähr. Bestehen der Firma Hamma & Co., Stuttgart, im Jahre 1964. Engl. Übers.: Walter J. Stewart. Franz. Übers.: Aristide Wirsta.) Stuttgart, Schuler, 1965. 728 p.

Revision and expansion of a work first published in 1931.

Describes more than 300 instruments made by Italian masters. Descriptions arranged alphabetically by makers, with biographical information and photographic plates of details.

231 / Haupt, Helga. "Wiener Instrumentenbauer von 1791 bis 1815," in *Studien zur Musikwissenschaft, Beihefte der Denkmäler der Tonkunst in Oesterreich*. Bd. 24. Graz, Hermann Böhlaus, 1960. p. 120–84.

Alphabetical listing of Viennese instrument makers in all categories. Addresses, dates of activity. A well-documented study.

232 / Henley, William. Universal dictionary of violin and bow makers. [Managing ed., Cyril Woodcock. Brighton, Sussex, Amati Pub. Co., 1959–60] 5 v.

The series continues as vol. 6: *Dictionary of contemporary violin and bow makers*, by Cyril Woodcock. Brighton, 1965. 96 p. 132 plates.

Vol. 7: *Price guide and appendix*, by Henley & Woodcock, 1969. 101 p. 16 plates.

Biographies in the *Universal dictionary* are of varying length. Long accounts of important figures with descriptions of famous instruments. Maintains a rather subjective and literary tone.

The *Price guide* gives listings for English and for American dealers.

233 / **Herzog, Hans Kurt.** Piano-Nummern deutscher, europäischer und überseeischer Instrument. Piano-numbers of German, European and foreign pianos, grands, harpsichords, harmoniums . . . 2. erw. Aufl. Frankfurt/M., Verlag Das Musikinstrument, 1967. 51 p. (Schriftenreihe Das Musikinstrument, 2.)

First edition published under title *Taschenbuch der Piano-Nummern deutscher, europäischer und überseeischer Instrumente*. Text in English, French, German, and Swedish.

234 / **Hirt, Franz Josef.** Meisterwerke des Klavierbaus. Geschichte der Saitenklaviers von 1440 bis 1880. Olten, Ure Graf Verlag, 1955. 521 p.

Beautifully illustrated book with information about the history, design, construction, makers, etc., of keyboard instruments. Full-page photographic plates, useful sections of biography and bibliography.

235 / **International Council of Museums.** Ethnic musical instruments: identification-conservation. . . . Edited by Jean Jenkins. London, H. Evelyn for the International Council of Museums, 1970. 59 p.

Parallel English and French texts.

236 / **Irwin, Stevens.** Dictionary of electronic organ stops: a guide to the understanding of the stops on all electronic organs with instructions on how to use and how to combine them and a listing of substitute stops. New York, G. Schirmer, 1968. 207 p.

237 / **Irwin, Stevens.** Dictionary of Hammond organ stops: a translation of pipe-organ stops into Hammond organ number arrangements; an introduction to playing the Hammond organ. Rev. 4th ed. containing an appendix: how to use the two new Hammond drawbars, number arrangements for all stops using the two new drawbars, and special theatre-organ number arrangements. New York, G. Schirmer, 1970. 172 p.

238 / **Irwin, Stevens.** Dictionary of pipe organ stops. Detailed descriptions of more than 600 stops together with definitions of many other terms connected with the organ and an examination of the acoustical properties of many types of pipes and the various divisions of the organ. New York, G. Schirmer [1962], 264 p.

Illustrated. Includes a short bibliography.

239 / **Jacquot, Albert.** Dictionnaire pratique et raisonné des instruments de musique anciens et modernes. 2nd ed. Paris. Fischbacher, 1886. 280 p.

Many names of Eastern instruments included. Some illustrations. Brief definitions. No bibliography.

240 / **Jahnel, Franz.** Die Gitarre und ihr Bau. Technologie von Gitarre, Laute, Mandoline, Sistern, Tanbur und Saite. Frankfurt am Main, Verlag Das Musikinstrument, 1963. 250 p.

A compendium of information on the construction of the guitar and other fretted instruments. Bibliography, numerous tables and lists, detailed plans and technical data. A handsomely designed and printed volume, invaluable for the musical instrument maker or interested performer.

241 / **Jalovec, Karel.** Enzyklopädie des Geigenbaues. Leiden, E. J. Brill, 1965. 2 v.

Vol. 1: 940 p., 51 colored illustrations on 24 plates. Vol. 2: 405 illustrations on 595 plates; 3,000 reproductions of violin makers' labels.

English translation by J. B. Kozak, published by Hamlyn, London, 1968.

242 / **Jalovec, Karel.** German and Austrian violin makers. Translated from the Czech by George Theiner, edited by Patrick Hanks. London, Hamlyn, 1967. 439 p.

243 / **Jalovec, Karel.** Italian violin makers. Rev. ed. London, P. Hamlyn, 1964. 445 p.

First published in Prague, 1952; published in London, 1958, with text in Czech and English.

Accounts of Italian violin makers, with descriptions and dimensions of important instruments. Many illustrations, some in color. Index by place; scale plans, facsimiles of labels.

244 / **Jalovec, Karel.** The violin makers of Bohemia; including craftsmen of Moravia and Slovakia. London, Anglo-Italian Publication [1959], 129 p., 392 plates.

Originally published in Czech under the title *Cesti houslari.* Prague, 1959. German ed., 1959.

Covers the work of some 1,200 Czech violin makers. Photographs of instruments, and a section of makers' labels in facsimile.

245 / **Langwill, Lyndesay Graham.** An index of musical wind-instrument makers. 3rd ed., rev., enl., and illustrated. Edinburgh, Lyndesay G. Langwill, 1972. 232 p.

First published in 1960. 2nd edition, 1962.

P. 1–175: alphabetical index of musical wind-instrument makers with accompanying bibliographical references and locations of examples of early instruments in museums and private collections. P. 176–81: bibliography with occasional annotations. P. 182–88: collections. A short selection of makers' marks. Index of makers by place.

Review of first edition by Josef Marx in *Notes*, 18 (1961), p. 234–36; of the second edition by Georg Karstädt in *Die Musikforschung*, 18 (1965), p. 90–91; of the third edition by Anthony Baines in *Galpin Society journal*, 25 (July 1972), p. 134–35.

246 / **Lütgendorff, Willibald Leo, Freiherr von.** Die Geigen- und Lautenmacher vom Mittelalter bis zur Gegenwart, nach den besten Quellen bearbeitet. . . . 4. mit der 3. übereinstimmende Aufl., Frankfurt am Main, Frankfurter Verlags-Anstalt, 1922. 2 v.

First published in 1904, in 1 volume.

Vol. 1: History of the making of stringed instruments by country. Index of manufacturers by city, with dates of birth and death. Bibliography, p. 403–20. Many illustrations.

Vol. 2: Biographical dictionary of makers of stringed instruments. P. 583–668: facsimiles of trademarks and labels.

247 / **Marcuse, Sibyl.** Musical instruments; a comprehensive dictionary. New York, Doubleday, 1964. 608 p.

Reprinted by Country Life, London, 1966.

Intended to serve English readers as Sachs *Real-Lexikon* (No. 260) does German. World coverage, although the author acknowledges incompleteness with respect to non-European and folk instruments.

P. 603–08: listing of 206 sources of information about instruments.

248 / **Michel, Norman E.** Historical pianos, harpsichords and clavichords. Pico Rivera, Calif. [1963], 209 p.

Reprinted in 1970. 236 p.

A volume of photographs of pianos. P. 1–46: photos of pianos, birthplaces, family homes, and historical societies related to 35 presidents of the U.S. P. 47–86: pianos and homes of statesmen, actors, etc. P. 87–135: photos from libraries, historical societies, museums, and other institutions. P. 136–209: photos of musical instruments from all over the world. A curious exercise in bibliographical namedropping.

249 / **Michel, Norman E.** Michel's piano atlas. Contains names of pianos, dates of manufacture, and serial numbers. Pico Rivera, Calif. [1961], 272 p.

First published as *Pierce piano atlas*, 1947– .

6,580 names of pianos. For some of these, there is no information other than name; for others, complete lists of serial numbers.

250 / **Möller, Max.** The violin-makers of the low countries (Belgium and Holland). Amsterdam, M. Möller, 1955. 165 p.

A historical survey of violin making in Belgium and Holland.

P. 23–129: photographic plates, chiefly of instruments in detail. P. 131–53: "Alphabetical Register," brief critical comments on the makers and their work. Glossary of terms in English, French, German, and Flemish.

251 / **Morris, W. Meredith.** British violin makers, a biographical dictionary of British makers of stringed instruments and bows and a critical description of their work. 2nd ed., rev. and enl. London, R. Scott, 1920. 318 p.

First published in 1904.

P. 87–259: alphabetical dictionary of violin and bow makers. Some labels in facsimile. P. 261–94: "A list of present-day makers, and a few old makers recently discovered."

252 / **Niemann, Walter.** Klavier-lexikon: Elementarlehre für Klavierspieler, Anleitung zur Aussprache des italienischen, Tabelle der Abkürzungen in Wort und Notenschrift, Literaturverzeichnis, ausführliches Fremdwörter-, Sach- und Personal-lexikon. 4. völlig umgearb. und reich verm. Aufl. . . . Leipzig, C. F. Kahnt, 1918. 365 p.

First published in 1912 as *Taschen-Lexikon für Klavierspieler*.

253 / **Norlind, Tobias.** Systematik der Saiteninstrumente. Stockholm [Emil Kihlströms Tryckeri], 1936–39. 2 v.

At head of title: Musikhistorisches Museum, Stockholm.

Vol. 1: *Geschichte der Zither* (1936). Vol. 2: *Geschichte des Klaviers* (1939).

Detailed classification and description of stringed instruments based on the archive in the Musikhistorisches Museum in Stockholm, where records of some 40,000 instruments are maintained. Illustrated. Bibliographical references and locations given for specific instruments in European and American collections. The work was projected in four parts, only two of which were completed.

254 / **Poidras, Henri.** Critical and documentary dictionary of violin makers old and modern, translated by Arnold Sewell. . . . Rouen, Imprimerie de la Vicomté, 1928–30. 2 v.

Originally published in French, 1924, with a 2nd ed. in 1930. There is also a one-volume English edition, 1928.

Brief biographical notices with critical comments, arranged alphabetically under national schools: Italian, French, German, etc. Photographic plates of instruments; facsimiles of labels.

255 / **Prat, Marsal Domingo.** Diccionario biográfico, bibliográfico, histórico, crítico de guitarras (instrumentos afines), guittaristas (profesores, compositores, concertistas, lahudistas, amateurs), guitarreros (luthiers), danzas y cantos, terminología. Buenos Aires, Casa Romero y Fernández [1934], 468 p.

The main alphabet contains biographies and lists of compositions. P. 423–52: dance forms. P. 453–64: terminology.

256 / **Profeta, Rosario.** Storia e letteratura degli strumenti musicali. Firenze, Marzocco, 1942. 659 p.

A history of instrumental music, its composers and performers, consisting chiefly of a recital of names of musicians grouped under their instruments and respective national schools. Minimal biographical and bibliographical information given.

257 / **"Provisional Index of Present-day Makers of Historical Musical Instruments (Non-keyboard)."** In the *Galpin Society journal*, 13 (July 1960), p. 70–97.

A useful guide to sources of modern replicas of historical instruments. Makers of historical keyboard instruments are listed in an appendix, p. 86287.

258 / **Roda, Joseph.** Bows for musical instruments of the violin family. Chicago, W. Lewis & Son, 1959. 335 p.

Brief history and description of the bow, including statistics as to dimensions and weight.

P. 119–325: biographical list of bow makers, with 47 excellent plates of their work.

259 / **Sachs, Curt.** Handbuch der Musikinstrumentenkunde. (Reprografischer Nachdruck der 2. Aufl., Leipzig, 1930). Hildesheim, Olms; Wiesbaden, Breitkopf u. Härtel, 1967. 419 p. (Kleine Handbücher der Musikgeschichte nach Gattungen, 12.)

First published in 1920.

Not precisely a dictionary but a systematic and historical description of musical instruments classified according to their methods of sound production: idiophones, membranophones, chordaphones, aerophones, etc. Much of the same ground is covered in Sachs' *The History of musical instruments* (New York, Norton, 1940), in which the approach is chronological and by cultural areas.

260 / **Sachs, Curt.** Real-Lexikon der Musikinstrumente, zugleich ein Polyglossar für das gesamte Instrumentengebiet. [Rev. and enl. ed.] New York, Dover Publications [1964], 451 p.

First published in Berlin, 1913; unaltered reprint of the original edition issued by G. Olms, Hildesheim, 1962.

A technical and historical dictionary of instruments of all periods and countries. Names of instruments and parts of instruments in some 120 languages and dialects—European, African, and Asian. Locations of examples in instrument collection. Illustrations; some bibliographies. This is Sachs's great work in this field and one of the best sources of information on instruments.

For a recent English-language dictionary inspired by the *Real-Lexikon*, see no. 247.

Review by Guy Oldham in *Musical times*, v. 107 (Dec. 1966), p. 1064–65.

Review by J. A. Westrup in *Music and letters*, v. 4:3 (July 1966), p. 277–78.

261 / **Samoyault-Verlet, Colombe.** Les facteurs de clavecins Parisiens, notices biographiques et documents, 1550–1793. Paris, Société Française de Musicologie, 1966. 189 p. (Publications de la Société Française de Musicologie Sér. 2, Tome 11.)

Biographies of some 140 Parisian makers of keyboard instruments, based largely on archival documents.

Review by Maurice A. Byrne in *Galpin Society journal*, 25 (July 1972), p. 136–37.

262 / **Sárosi, Bálint.** Die Volksmusikinstrumente Ungarns. Leipzig, Deutscher Verlag für Musik, 1968. 147 p. (Handbuch der europäischen Volksmusikinstrumente. Serie I, Band I.)

Sárosi's work is the first of a series projected to cover folk instruments in Czechoslovakia, Bulgaria, the Soviet Union, Greece, Portugal, Turkey, and Norway.

The Hungarian folk instruments are grouped according to type, with detailed commentary, illustrations, and transcriptions of music. Bibliography, and glossary of Hungarian instrument names.

Review by Fritz Bose in *Literature, music, fine arts*, 1 (1968), p. 230–31.

263 / **Stainer, Cecilia.** A dictionary of violin makers, compiled from the best authorities. London, Novello, 1896. 102 p.

A useful biographical dictionary of violin makers with critical evaluations of their work. Still in print. Contains a bibliography of literature on violin making.

264 / **Straeten, Edmund S. J. vander.** The history of the violin, its ancestors and collateral instruments from [the] earliest times to the present day; with 48 plates and numerous illustrations in [the] text. London, Cassell [1933], 2 v.

Vol. 1, p. 55–416, and the whole of vol. 2 consist primarily of biographies of violinists grouped by period, and under period by country. Biographical index, vol. 2, p. 443–73. Information on many obscure violinist-composers not elsewhere readily accessible, with lists of works by category.

265 / **Thornsby, Frederick, W.,** ed. Dictionary of organs and organists. Bournemouth, H. Logan [1912], 364 p.

Chiefly concerned with 19th-century British organs and organists.
P. 111–231: "Brief specifications of the principal organs in the
British Isles." P. 239–352: "The organist's *who's who*: Brief bio-
graphical notes of the leading British organists."

266 / **Tintori, Giampiero.** Gli strumenti musicali. Ricera icono-
grafia di Alberto Basso. Turin, 1972. 2 v. 138 plates.

The main organization is geographical, with subdivisions covering
the various types of instruments. Numerous musical examples, a comprehensive bibliography and glossary; general index.

267 / **Valdrighi, Luigi Francesco.** Nomocheliurgografia antica e
moderna, ossia Elenco di fabbricatori di strumenti armonici con note
esplicative e documenti estratti dall'Archivio di Stato in Modena.
Bologna, Forni, 1967. 327 p. (Bibliotheca musica Bononiensia. Sezione
1, n. 3.)

Reprint of the Modena 1884 edition, with supplements originally
published 1888–1894.

P. 2–106: an alphabetical listing of 3,516 instrument makers, giving
name, nationality, dates of birth and death, name of special instrument, and the school, style, or system. Many of these names are given
fuller biographical treatment in the section following, p. 107 to end.

268 / **Vannes, René.** Dictionnaire universel des luthiers. 2nd éd.
revue et augmentée. Bruxelles, Les Amis de la Musique, 1951. 408
[163] p.

Tome second. Tome additif et correctif. Bruxelles, 1959. 198, lviii p.

First published in 1932, Paris, Fischbacher, under the title *Essai d'un
dictionnaire universel.* . . .

Most comprehensive of all dictionaries of violin makers. Each
volume has its own alphabet of biographical entries. Bibliographical
references. Both volumes combined give 3,400 facsimiles of makers'
labels. Vol. 2, p. 67–198: index of makers by place of birth or center
of activity.

Review by Doris Commander in *Violins and violinists*, 12 (Nov.,
1951), p. 326; review of *Tome second* by Albert Van der Linden in
Revue belge de musicologie, 14 (1960), p. 144, and by William Lichtenwanger in *Notes*, 17 (1960), p. 577.

269 / **Vercheval, Henri.** Dictionnaire du violiniste. . . . Paris, Fischbacher, 1923. 192 p.

Part I, p. 9–141, includes terms of interest to violinists, history of stringed instruments, etc. Part II, p. 143–92, is a biographical dictionary of violinists, composers, teachers, violin and bow makers, giving dates and nationalities.

270 / **Winternitz, Emanuel.** Musical instruments of the Western world. Photographs by Lilly Stunzi. New York and Toronto, McGraw-Hill Book Co. (n.d.), 259 p. 60 plates.

This work was published in German under the title, *Die schönsten Musikinstrumente des Abendlandes.*

A magnificent picture book of music iconography.

Review by Howard Mayer Brown in *Notes,* 25 (1968), p. 223–25.

271 / **Wörthmüller, Willi.** "Die Nürnberger Trompeten- und Posaunenmacher des 17. und 18. Jahrhunderts." In *Mitteilungen des Vereins für Geschichte der Stadt Nürnberg.* Bd. 46 (1955), p. 372–480.

Also published separately.

A musicological study the major portion of which is a dictionary of 40 Nuremberg brass instrument makers of the baroque period with a listing of their surviving instruments. Tracing of monograms and other makers' devices. 5 plates.

272 / **Wright, Rowland.** Dictionnaire des instruments de musique; étude de lexicologie. London, Battley Bros., 1941. 192 p.

An etymological dictionary of names for musical instruments mentioned in French writings from ancient times to the end of the 19th century. Extremely well documented; precise bibliographical references. One of the few dictionaries of terms to employ a thoroughly etymological approach.

273 / **Zuth, Josef.** Handbuch der Laute und Gitarre. Wien, Verlag der Zeitschrift für die Gitarre, 1926. 297 p.

Terms; biographies of performers, instrument makers, and composers giving titles of compositions, publishers, and dates. International coverage for all periods, including many early names. A scholarly work with supported statements and bibliographical references.

TERMS

Dictionaries of terms have a longer history than any other form of music lexicography. Their prototype is Johannes Tinctoris' *Terminorum musicae diffinitorium* (no. 310), a work compiled in the late 15th century. Almost equally significant is Sébastien de Brossard's *Dictionnaire de musique*, 1701 (no. 280), one of the first in the long line of "modern" dictionaries of music.

A few specialized dictionaries of terms will be found under other headings in this volume. See no. 238 (pipe organ stops); no. 272 (names of musical instruments); no. 317 (liturgical music terms).

274 / **Albina, Diāna.** Mūzikas terminu vardnica. Redigejis J. Licitis. Riga, Latvijas valsts izdevnieciba, 1962. 303 p.

A Latvian dictionary of musical terms.

275 / **Apel, Willi.** Harvard dictionary of music. 2d ed., rev. and enl. Cambridge, Mass., Belknap Press of Harvard University Press, 1969. 935 p.

First printed in 1944. The fifth printing, 1947, contains a section of "addenda and corrigenda to the original entries." The second edition, 1969, has been completely reset.

The standard reference work in English for nonbiographical information, designed to provide accurate and pertinent information on all musical topics. The emphasis is on the historical approach. Good bibliographies; excellent brief historical articles.

Review of the second edition by Charles Rosen in *The New York Review of Books*, 14 (Feb. 1970), p. 11–15; in *The Booklist*, 66 (May, 1970), p. 1055–1061); by Vincent Duckles in *Notes*, 27 (1970), p. 256–58.

276 / **Apel, Willi, and Ralph T. Daniel.** The Harvard brief dictionary of music. Cambridge, Mass., Harvard Univ. Press, 1960. 341 p.

Paperback edition: New York, Washington Square Press, 1961.

Reprinted in folio, with text in 4 columns, by Amsco Music Publishers, New York, 1971. 132 p.

Review by James B. Coover in *Notes*, 18 (1961), p. 239–40.

277 / **Baker, Theodore.** Dictionary of musical terms . . . with a supplement containing an English-Italian vocabulary for composers. New York, G. Schirmer [1923], 257 p.

First published in 1895.

Reprint of the 1923 edition. New York, AMS Press, 1970.

Useful small manual, with brief definitions of English and foreign words, especially those used in performance. More extended articles on topics such as pitch, notation, instruments. More than 9,000 terms treated.

278 / **Bobillier, Marie** (Michael Brenet, pseud.). Dictionnaire pratique et historique de la musique. Paris, A. Colin, 1926. 487 p.

2nd edition appeared in 1930.

The standard French dictionary of terms, including terms from Greek and medieval music theory, historical sketches of musical forms. Fairly long articles, excellent small illustrations. No bibliographies.

279 / **Bobillier, Marie** (Michael Brenet, pseud.). Diccionario de la música, histórico y técnico. Tradducción de la última edición francesa, revisada y notablemente ampliada con multitud de artículos nuevos . . . por José B. Humbert, J. Ricart Matas & Aurelio Capmany. Barcelona, Iberia, J. Gil [1964], 548 p.

Translation of the 2nd edition of the preceding, revised and with special emphasis on Spanish terms, Latin and South American terminology and folklore. Profusely illustrated.

280 / **Brossard, Sébastien de.** Dictionnaire de musique, contenant une explication des termes grecs, latins, italiens & françois les plus usitez dans la musique . . . Paris, Christophe Ballard, 1703.

A preliminary edition appeared in 1701, in octavo format. The first folio edition (1703 above) has been reprinted in facsimile by Antiqua, Amsterdam, 1964. An octavo edition, Paris 1705, has been reprinted, with an introduction by Harald Heckmann, by Frits A. M. Knuf, Hilversum 1965.

Brossard's *Dictionnaire* is the prototype for all modern dictionaries of musical terms. It is also a pioneer work in music bibliography, since it contains a listing of more than 900 authors who have written about music from antiquity to Brossard's time.

For an early English musical dictionary based on *Brossard*, see no. 289.

Review of the 1964 (Amsterdam) reprint by Vincent Duckles in *Notes*, 24 (1968), p. 700–01.

281 / **Carter, Henry H.** A dictionary of Middle English musical terms. Bloomington, Indiana, Indiana Univ. Press [1961], 655 p. (Indiana University humanities series, 45.)

Reprint by Kraus, New York, 1968.

Terms are not only defined but quoted in their original contexts with citation of their sources. P. 569–604: bibliography of works quoted; p. 605–49: works consulted but not quoted.

Review by Leonard Ellinwood in *Notes*, 19 (1962), p. 262–63.

282 / **Chetrikov, Svetoslav.** Muzikalen terminologischen rechnik. Sofiia, Nauka i izkustvo, 1969. 463 p.

A Bulgarian dictionary of musical terms.

283 / **Dolzhanskii, A.** Kratkii muzkalnyi slovar. 3rd ed. Moskva, 1959. 517 p.

First published Leningrad, 1952.

284 / **Eggebrecht, Hans Heinrich.** Handwörterbuch der musikalischen Terminologie. Im Auftrag der Kommission für Musikwissenschaften und der Literatur zu Mainz . . . Wiesbaden, F. Steiner, c. 1972– .

A work that promises to be the most thorough and scientific treatment of musical terms ever projected. An exhaustive historical and etymological analysis of term families, showing their changes in meaning and citing quotations from the literature. The dictionary is compiled in looseleaf format, with dividers and indexes. About four issues are projected for publication, two per year.

For a preliminary notice and discussion, see *Archiv für Musikwissenschaft*, 25 (1968), p. 241–77, and 27 (1970), p. 214–22.

285 / **Elsevier's Dictionary of Cinema, Sound and Music,** in six languages: English/American, French, Spanish, Italian, Dutch, and German. Compiled and arranged on an English alphabetical base by W. E. Clason. Amsterdam/New York, Elsevier Publishing Co., 1956. 948 p.

One of a series of poylglot technical dictionaries relating to special fields of science and industry. 3,213 terms, with brief definitions and the equivalent phrases in French, Spanish, Italian, Dutch, and German. Indexes in each of the five languages.

286 / **Gerigk, Herbert.** Fachwörterbuch der Musik. [Münchberg i. Bayern] B. Hahnefeld [1954], 206 p.

A small, useful dictionary of German definitions of the most common musical terms in French, Italian, and Latin, with some in English. Review by Richard Schaal in *Die Musikforschung*, 8 (1955), p. 245.

287 / **Gold, Robert S.** A jazz lexicon. New York, Knopf, 1964. 363 p.

A dictionary of terms from the world of jazz. Both musical and sociological interest. Date of usage is specified where possible. Informative introduction and bibliography.

288 / **Grant, Parks.** Handbook of music terms. Metuchen, N.J., The Scarecrow Press, 1967. 476 p.

The availability of several excellent music dictionaries and encyclopedias intended for the scholar, the music professor, and the musicologist points up the need for a book less advanced (though not too brief) intended for persons who make only a modest claim to musical knowledge. [Author's *Preface*]

Review by James W. Pruett in *Notes*, 24 (1968), p. 720–21.

289 / **Grassineau, James.** A musical dictionary; being a collection of terms and characters, as well ancient as modern; including the historical, theoretical, and practical parts of music. . . . London, printed for J. Wilcox, 1740. 347 p.

Reprint by Broude Brothers, New York, 1967 (Monuments of music and music literature in facsimile. Ser. 2, vol. 40).

Grassineau can be described as the first important dictionary of music in English. It is largely an adaptation of *Brossard* (no. 280), but with some important additions. A later edition, 1769, has an appendix containing additional terms from Rousseau's *Dictionnaire* (no. 298).

290 / **Janovka, Tomas Baltazar.** Clavis ad thesaurum magnae artis musicae, seu eluciadarium omnium ferè rerum av verborum, in musica figurali tam vocali, quàm instrumentali obvenietum. Consistens

potissimum in definitionibus & divisionibus; quibusdam recentioribus de scala, tono, cantu, & genere musicae & c. sententijs, variísque exqvisitis observationibus . . . alphabetico ordine compositum à Thoma Balthasare Janovka. Vetero-Pragae, in Magno collegio Carolino typis Georgij Labaun, 1701. 324 p.

Scheduled for reprint publication by Frits A. M. Knuf, Hilversum, Holland, as vol. 3 of the series *Facsimile reprints of early music dictionaries.*

This work shares with *Brossard* (no. 280) the distinction of being one of the first modern dictionaries of musical terms. The two compilers worked simultaneously but independently of each other.

291 / **Katayen, Leila and Val Telberg.** Russian-English dictionary of musical terms. New York, Telberg Book Corp., 1965. 125 leaves (Typescript).

Russian-English equivalents in musical terminology. No definitions. Short bibliography.

292 / **Koch, Heinrich Christoph.** Musikalisches Lexikon, welches die theoretische und praktische Tonkunst, enecyclopädisch bearbeitet, alle alten und neuen Kunstwörter erklärt, und die alten und neuen Instrumente beschrieben, enthält. . . . Frankfurt am Main, A. Hermann dem Jüngern, 1802. 2 v.

One of the first of a long line of German dictionaries of terms. Particularly important for definitions and concepts pertaining to late baroque and classic music and instruments.

A revised edition, by Arrey von Dommer, printed in Heidelberg, 1865, has very little resemblance to the original.

Reprint publication by Georg Olms, Hildesheim, 1964.

293 / **Leuchtmann, Horst, u. Philippine Schick.** Langenscheidts Fachwörterbuch, Musik. Berlin, Langenscheidt, 1964.

An English-German, German-English dictionary of terms. No definitions, merely verbal equivalents.

294 / **Lichtenthal, Pietro.** Dizionario e bibliografia della musica. Milano, A. Fontana, 1826. 4 v.

The first two volumes of this work are a dictionary of terms, the last two, a bibliography of music literature based on Forkel's *All-*

gemeine Literatur der Musik (see no. 549). A French edition of the dictionary of terms, "traduit et augmenté par Dominique Mondo," appeared in Paris in 1839.

295 / **Limenta, Fernando.** Dizionario lessicografico musicale italiano-tedesco-italiano. Milano, Hoepli, 1940. 391 p.

Designed to provide precise Italian equivalents for German technical terms not adequately treated in most dictionaries.

296 / **Padelford, Frederick M.** Old English musical terms. Bonn, P. Hanstein, 1899. 112 p. (Bonner Beiträge zur Anglistik, 4.)

297 / **Pulver, Jeffrey.** A dictionary of old English music and musical instruments. London, Kegan Paul; New York, E. P. Dutton, 1923. 247 p.

Terms used by Tudor and early Stuart musicians. Fairly long articles, with references to early literary and musical sources for the terms. 10 plates of early English instruments.

298 / **Rousseau, Jean J.** Dictionnaire de musique. Paris, Duchesne, 1768. 548 [i.e., 556] p., 13 folded plates.

Reprint by G. Olms, Hildesheim, and by Johnson Reprint Corp., New York, 1969.

Several editions published in Paris and Amsterdam during the 18th century. An English edition, translated by William Waring, published under the title *A complete dictionary of music*, 2nd edition, London, 1779.

Based on articles written by Rousseau for the Diderot and d'Alembert *Encyclopédie* but not included in that work. Reflects the stimulating and highly personal views of an 18th-century man of letters. Wide influence and considerable historical importance.

299 / **Sacher, Jack, ed.** Music A to Z. Based on the work of Rudolf Stephan. [Translators: Mieczyslaw Kolinski and others] New York, Grosset & Dunlap, 1963. 432 p.

A translation, with additions and corrections, of Rudolf Stephan's music dictionary in the Fischer Lexikon series, see no. 307.

Review by Theodore Karp in *JAMS*, 17 (1964), p. 394–95; by Harold Samuel in *Notes*, 20 (1963), p. 658–59.

300 / **Schaal, Richard.** Abürzungen in der Musik-Terminologie. Eine Übersicht. Wilhelmshaven, Heinrichshofen's Verlag, 1969. 165 p. (Taschenbücher zur Musikwissenschaft, 1.)

A dictionary of the abbreviations most frequently used to refer to musical practice, bibliography, institutions. Intended primarily for German music students, but of general utility.

301 / **Schaal, Richard.** Fremdwörterlexikon Musik. Englisch-Französisch-Italienisch. Wilhelmshaven, Heinrichshofen's Verlag, 1970. 2 v. (Taschenbücher zur Musikwissenschaft, 2, 3.)

Vol. 1: A–Ist. Vol. 2: Jac–Zur.

A polyglot dictionary of English, French, and Italian terms with their German equivalents. Contains more than 15,000 foreign terms.

302 / **Seagrave, Barbara G., and Joel Berman.** The A.S.T.A. dictionary of bowing terms for string instruments. Urbana, American String Teachers Association, 1968. 53 p.

303 / **Siliakus, H. J.** 500 German musical terms and their English translations together with 500 useful phrases. Adelaide, South Australia, University of Adelaide, 1968. 113 p. (German word lists, 1: Musicology.)

> This booklet is not a dictionary, but a special word list for musicologists who need a reading knowledge of German. It will only be useful for those who have mastered the elements of the German language, since we assume a knowledge of basic grammar and familiarity with about 1,000 basic words. [Author's *Preface*]

304 / **Sinzig, Pedro.** Dicionário músical. Rio de Janeiro, Kosmos, 1947. 613 p.

A modern Portuguese-language dictionary of terms. Based largely on Apel and Riemann. Bibliographical references.

305 / **Smith, W. J.** A dictionary of musical terms in four languages. London, Hutchinson [1961], 195 p.

English terms with equivalents in French, Italian, and German. Pronunciations given in phonetic symbols. No definitions.

306 / **Stainer, Sir John, and W. A. Barrett.** Dictionary of musical terms. Hildesheim, Olms, 1970. 456 p.

Reprint of the 2nd ed., Novello, 1898.

Terms in Italian, French, Latin, German, Hebrew, Greek, Russian, Spanish, and Arabic, with brief English definitions.

307 / **Shephan, Rudolf.** Musik. [Frankfurt am Main] Fischer Verlag [1957], 382 p. (Das Fischer Lexikon, Enzyklopädie des Wissens, 5.)

This work has been translated and expanded in Sacher's *Music A to Z*; see no. 299.

General articles cover major topics, with more detailed information approached through an index. Topical bibliographies, p. 355–64. 10 plates. A scholarly summation of musical knowledge for the general reader.

308 / **Terminorum Musicae Index.** Part I– International Musicological Society, 1970– .

A polyglot dictionary of musical terms in English, German, French, Italian, Spanish, Russian, and Hungarian.

309 / **Thiel, Eberhard.** Sachwörterbuch der Musik. Stuttgart, Alfred Kröner Verlag, 1962. 602 p. (Kröners Taschenausgabe, 210.)

Review by Harold Samuel in *Notes*, 20 (1963), p. 658.

310 / **Tinctoris, Johannes (Jean).** Dictionary of musical terms. An English translation of *Terminorum musicae diffinitorium* together with the Latin text. Translated and annotated by Carl Parrish [with a bibliographical essay by James B. Coover], New York, Free Press [1963], 108 p.

A 15th-century dictionary of musical terms, and one of the first books on music to be printed. 291 terms defined. Important for an understanding of Renaissance music theory and practice. The Latin text was reprinted in Coussemaker's Scriptorum (1867), in Forkel's *Allgemeine Literatur der Musik* (1792), and with a German translation in Chrysander's *Jahrbuch der Musikwissenschaft*, I (1963). It appeared in a French translation with introduction and commentary by Armand Machabey (Paris, 1951), and in an Italian translation by Lionello Cammarota (Rome, 1965).

311 / **Tovey, Donald F.** Musical articles from the *Encyclopaedia britannica*. London, New York, Oxford Univ. Press, 1944. 256 p.

Paperback edition: New York, Meridian Books, 1956, as *The forms of music.*

28 articles on the larger aspects of music. Shorter ones (madrigal, sonata, etc.) are briefly historical; others (harmony, sonata forms, etc.) are comprehensive and analytical. Reprinted from Tovey's contributions to the 11th edition of the *Britannica.*

312 / **Vannes, René.** . . . Essai de terminologie musicale. Dictionnaire universel comprenant plus de 15,000 termes de musique en italien-espagnol-portugais-français-anglais-allemand-latin et grec. . . . Thann, "Alsatia," ca. 1925. 230 p.

Reprint by Da Capo Press, New York, 1970.

Most extensive manual of its kind, containing 15,000 entries in eight languages. Includes forms, terms, instruments in current use. Brief definitions given under the original or characteristic language, with equivalents in other languages. No explanatory or historical material.

313 / **Wotton, Tom S.** A dictionary of foreign musical terms and handbook of orchestral instruments. Leipzig, Breitkopf & Härtel, 1907. 226 p.

Reprint by Scholarly Press, 1972.

Less comprehensive than Vannes (no. 312). Designed as an aid to score reading, including orchestral terms, instruments, tempo indications, etc. Primarily in French, German, and Italian.

CHURCH MUSIC

This section begins with a list of several general dictionaries relating to church music. This is followed by a list of handbooks on the hymnology of various Protestant groups, with citations under the denominations represented. Such handbooks are essentially bibliographies of sacred music, but most of them contain enough biographical and factual information to justify listing them among the encyclopedias and dictionaries of church music.

314 / **Carroll, J. Robert.** Compendium of liturgical music terms. Toledo, Ohio, Gregorian Institute of America, 1964. 86 p.

An attempt to provide a single source for information most frequently requested by students and working church musicians. [Preface]

315 / **Encyclopédie des Musiques Sacrées.** Publiée sous la direction de Jacques Porte. Paris, Éditions Lagergerie, 1968–1970. 4 v. [vol. 4 consists of sixteen 7-in. phonodiscs.]

Vol. I: "L'expression du sacré en Orient, Afrique, Amérique du Sud."

Vol. II: "Traditions chrétiennes—des premiers siècle aux cultes révolutionnaires."

Vol. III: "Traditions chrétiennes (suite et fin)—essence, nature et moyens de la musique chrétienne."

A handsomely designed publication. Numerous full-page color plates. The editor is assisted by a large group of authorities, chiefly French. The contributions are all extended articles; no definitions of terms.

316 / **Handbuch zum evangelischen Kirchengesangbuch.** Hrsg. von Christhard Mahrenholz und Oskar Söhngen, unter Mitarbeit von Otto Schlisske. Band I—Göttingen, Vanderhoeck & Ruprecht, 1956– .

Supplementary volume: *Die Lieder unserer Kirche*, by Johannes Kulp. Göttingen, 1958.

A compendium of information related to the German Lutheran hymnal, projected in five volumes.

Summary of contents: Vol. I: 1: Word and subject concordance (2nd ed., 1956). Vol. I: 2 (1965): The biblical sources of the songs. Vol. II: 1 (1957): Biographical sketches of the poets and the composers. Vol. II: 2: History of the Lieder. Vol. III: 1 (1970): Studies of the individual songs and their melodies.

317 / **Hughes, Anselm.** Liturgical terms for music students; a dictionary. Boston, McLaughlin & Reilly [1940], 40 p.

Reprint (1971) by the Scholarly Press, St. Clair Shores, Michigan.

Concise definitions of terms likely to occur in the literature of ancient ecclesiastical music of the West. Tables give structure of mass and office. Includes terms from the church calendar, terms referring to notation, texts with explanations of their places in the liturgy.

318 / **Julian, John.** A dictionary of hymnology, setting forth the origin and history of Christian hymns of all ages and nations. Rev. ed. with new suppl. London, J. Murray, 1907. 1,768 p.

Unaltered reprint in two valumes, New York, Dover, 1957.

First published in 1892.

Entries under authors, titles, and subjects of hymn texts. Brief but adequate biographical notices. Long articles on American, English, Latin, etc., hymnody. For individual hymns gives original publication and location in other hymnals. Contains a vast amount of information on musical and literary aspects of Christian hymnody.

319 / **Kornmüller, P. Utto. Lexikon der kirchlichen Tonkunst.** . . . 2. verb. und verm. Aufl. Regensburg, A. Coppenrath, 1891–95. 2 v. in 1.

First published in 1870.

Vol. 1: Dictionary of subjects, terms, and instruments connected with Catholic church music, with a subject index of topics discussed in extended articles.

Vol. 2: Biographical dictionary of church musicians. Published works cited for early names, categories of compositions for recent ones.

320 / **Kümmerle, Salomon.** Encyklopädie der evangelischen Kirchenmusik. Gütersloh, E. Bertelsmann, 1888–95. 4 v.

Originally published in Lieferungen, 1883-95.

Terms and biographies related to Protestant church music. Entries for chorale titles, with full musical quotations of the melodies. The author was responsible for basic research on the melodies of the Lutheran chorale.

Review by Friedrich Spitta in *Vierteljahrschrift für Musikwissenschaft*, 1 (1885), p. 235–38.

321 / **McCutchan, Robert G.** Hymn tune names, their sources and significance. Nashville, Abingdon Press [1957], 206 p.

Alphabetical listing of tunes, giving their metrical structures and thematic incipits in letter notation. Commentary related to authors, composers, and sources. Numerous cross references. Melodic index. First line index of texts, with author, translator, and tune name.

322 / **Mizgalski, Gerard.** Podreczna encyklopedia muzyki kościelnej. Poznan—Warszawa—Lublin, Ksiegarnia sw. wojciecha, 1959. 566 p.

A Polish dictionary of sacred music. Biographical articles all stress contributions to church music. Illustrated.

323 / **Ortigue, Joseph Louis d'.** Dictionnaire liturgique, historique et théorique de plain-chant et de musique d'église, au moyen âge et dans les temps modernes. Paris, J. P. Migne, 1853. 1,563 p. (Nouvelle encylopédie théologique, Tome 29.)

A pioneer reference work on liturgical music, of considerable historical importance. Documented with frequent references to the works of the leading 18th- and early 19th-century specialists in church music.

324 / **Stubbins, George W.** A dictionary of church music. London, Epworth Press [1949], 128 p.

A practical reference book for the use of church organists and choir directors. Short explanations of technical terms and concise information on topics related to church music.

325 / **Weissenbäck, Andreas.** Sacra musica; Lexikon der katholischen Kirchenmusik. Klosterneuburg, Augustinus Druckerei [1937], 419 p.

Biography, terms, and subjects in one alphabet. Articles on religious organizations and music publishing houses. More comprehensive in coverage than Kornmüller (no. 319), but the articles are briefer.

Congregational

326 / **Companion to Congregational Praise.** Edited by K. L. Parry, with notes on the music by Erik Routley. London, Independent Press [1953], 580 p.

P. 1–336: notes on the words and music for 884 hymns and chants. P. 337–550: biographical notes on hymn writers and composers.

Chronological listing of 396 musical sources. Index of tune names and first-line index of hymns.

Episcopal

327 / **Protestant Episcopal Church in the U.S.A.** The Hymnal 1940 companion. [3rd ed. rev.] New York, Church Pension Fund, 1956. 741 p.

First published in 1949.

Contains historical essays on texts and tunes; biographies of authors, composers, translators, and arrangers. List of organ works based on hymn tunes, with publishers. Index of scriptural texts; general index; melodic index; index of tunes; first-line index.

328 / **Protestant Episcopal Church of England.** Historical companion to hymns, ancient and modern. Edited by Maurice Frost. London, Printed for the Proprietors by William Clowes & Sons [1962], 716 p.

The latest revision of a work compiled in 1909 by W. H. Frere under the title *Historical edition of hymns ancient and modern*; revised in 1950.

P.1-124: Introduction, with contributions by Egon Wellesz, Ruth Massenger, C. E. Pocknee, and Lowther Clarke covering the history of hymnody and of the Anglican hymnal. P. 125–478: Texts and commentary for 636 hymns, including the language of the original if translated. Index of first lines, brief biographies of hymn writers, chronological list of authors and translators, alphabetical index of tunes, index of plainsong, notes on the composers, with chronology, list of publications and tunes, metrical index.

Evangelical and Reformed

329 / **Haeussler, Armin.** The story of our hymns: the handbook to the hymnal of the Evangelical and Reformed Church. St. Louis, Eden Publishing House, 1952. 1,088 p.

Commentary on 561 hymns and other liturgical pieces. Biographies of hymn writers and notes on sources. Bibliography. Index of scriptural texts, topical index, metrical index, indexes of tune names, composers, arrangers, and sources. First-line index.

Lutheran

330 / **Polack, William G.** The handbook of the Lutheran hymnal. 2nd and rev. ed. St. Louis, Concordia [1942], 681 p.

Texts of and commentary on 660 Lutheran hymns. Biographical and historical notes on the authors and composers. Index of biblical references, table of hymns for feasts and festivals, first-line index, including stanzas of hymns; index of tunes, metrical index, topical index, index of authors and translators.

Mennonite

331 / **Hostetler, Lester.** Handbook to the Mennonite hymnary. Newton, Kansas, General Conference of the Mennonite Church of North America, Board of Publications, 1949. 425 p.

Commentary on 623 Mennonite hymns and other liturgical pieces. Bibliography. Indexes.

Methodist

332 / **Gealy, Fred Daniel.** Companion to the hymnal; a handbook to the 1964 Methodist hymnal. Nashville, Abingdon Press [1970], 766 p.

333 / **McCutchan, Robert C.** Our hymnody, a manual of the Methodist hymnal. 2nd ed. New York, Abingdon Press [1942], 619 p.

First published in 1937.

Commentary on 664 hymns and other liturgical pieces. Hymn calendar, bibliography, and nine special indexes.

Mormon

334 / **Cornwall, J. Spencer.** Stories of our Mormon hymns. 2nd edition, revised and enlarged. Salt Lake City, Utah, Deseret Book Co., 1963. 302 p.

A popular companion to the Mormon hymnal, giving information on composers and writers of texts for approximately 311 hymns used in the Mormon church.

Presbyterian

335 / **Handbook to the Hymnal.** Philadelphia, Presbyterian Board of Christian Education, 1935. 566 p.

Unitarian

336 / **Foote, Henry W.** American Unitarian hymn writers and hymns. Compiled for the Hymn Society of America for publication in the Society's proposed *Dictionary of American hymnology.* Cambridge, Mass. [Author], 1959. 270 leaves (typescript).

Contains an historical sketch of American Unitarian hymnody, a catalog of American Unitarian hymn books, alphabetical list of hymn writers, biographical sketches, and first-line index of published hymns.

OPERA AND THEATER MUSIC

Dictionaries of opera and theater music are of two principal kinds: (1) compilations of facts related to the history or to the production of musical dramatic works, in which case they can be cited as dictionaries or handbooks of opera, or (2) listings of operatic works, often in chronological order, associated with a particular place: city, country, or opera house. Works of the latter kind can properly be described as "Bibliographies of Music," and will be found cited under that heading in the subdivision "Local Opera Repertoires."

Listeners' guides to opera and collections of opera plots have been excluded.

One encyclopedia of theater arts demands mention at this point, although its coverage extends far beyond the realm of music. This is the *Enciclopedia dello spettacolo*, Roma, Casa Editrice le Maschere, 1954–62. 9 v. This great illustrated reference work was published under the auspices of the Cini Foundation and covers all aspects of the theater, with contributions by outstanding authorities in the field.

Other reference works related to opera will be found cited under the entries **Kutch** (no. 88), **Le Grandi Voci** (no. 84), and **Highfill** (no. 132).

84

337 / **Altmann, Wilhelm.** Katalog der seit 1861 in den Händel gekommenen theatralischen Musik (Opern, Operetten, Possen, Musik zu Schauspielen, usw.) Ein musikbibliographischer Versuch . . . Wolfenbüttel, Verlag für musikalische Kultur and Wissenschaft, 1935. 384 p. (incomplete)

This work was published in *Lieferungen*, of which four appeared carrying the entries through "Siegmund, Josef."

Operas, ballets, and incidental music since 1861, arranged under composer with references from librettist, etc. Gives brief titles of works, type, librettist, date of first performance if known, type of score, language of text, and publisher. There is no key to the abbreviations of publishers' names, but most of these can be readily identified.

338 / **Bernandt, Grigoriĭ B.** Slovar' oper. Vpervye postavlennykh ili izdannykh v dorevoliutsionnoi Rossii i v SSSR. Moskva, Sovetskiĭ Kompozitor, 1962. 554 p.

A dictionary of operas first performed or first published in Russia during the period 1736–1959. Entries are alphabetical by title. Information includes genre of the work, composer, first performance, librettist, literary source, and many details that relate to production. Indexed by composer, librettist, and author of the original literary source.

339 / **Brockpähler, Renate.** Handbuch zur Geschichte der Barockoper in Deutschland. Emsdetten, Verlag Lechte, 1964. 394 p.

A handbook of historical information related to German Baroque opera. Organized by place (47 municipalities), each entry includes a bibliography of relevant literature, sections devoted to the history of music or opera in particular in the place, and a listing of the works performed. Indexed by place, musicians, poets, and dancing masters.

340 / **Burton, Jack.** The blue book of Broadway musicals. Watkins Glen, N.Y., Century House [1952], 320 p.

Lists title, date, composer, author, principals, and musical numbers for more than 1,500 operettas, musical comedies, and revues from the 1890s to 1951. Arranged by decades, with a general introduction to each period.

Reprint with additions by Larry Freeman. Watkins Glen, N.Y., Century House, 1969. 327 p.

The second book in a trilogy on popular music, the first of which was *The blue book of Tin Pan Alley* (see no. 955) and the third *The blue book of Hollywood musicals* (see no. 341).

341 / **Burton, Jack.** The blue book of Hollywood musicals; songs from the sound tracks and the stars who sang them since the birth of the talkies a quarter-century ago. Watkins Glen, N.Y., Century House [1953], 296 p.

> Complementing *The blue book of Tin Pan Alley* (1951) and *The blue book of Broadway musicals* (1952), this present anthology completes a trilogy on popular music. [*Introduction*]

See also *The blue book of Tin Pan Alley* (1962), entered under "Bibliographies of Music: Jazz and Popular" (see no. 955) and *The index of American popular music* (see no. 944).

342 / **Caselli, Aldo.** Catalogo delle opere liriche pubblicate in Italia. Firenze, Leo S. Olschki, 1969. 891 p.

An ambitious attempt to cover all operas produced in Italy from 1600 to the present. Organized to permit approaches through the composer, city and theater, title, librettist. The effort to achieve comprehensiveness leads to some sacrifice in accuracy.

Review by Thomas Walker in *Notes*, 26 (1970), p. 758–59.

343 / **Clemént, Félix, et Pierre Larousse.** Dictionnaire des opéras (Dictionnaire lyrique) contenant l'analyse et la nomenclature de tous les opéras, opéras-comiques, opérettes et drames lyrique représentés en France et à l'étranger depuis l'origine de ces genres d'ouvrages jusqu'à nos jours. . . . Rev. et mis à jour par Arthur Pougin. Paris, Librairie Larousse [1905], 1,203 p.

First published in 1869 under the title *Dictionnaire lyrique*. Reprint by Da Capo Press, New York, 1969. 2 v.

Title entries (frequently under the French form, with references to other forms) for operas and comic operas presented in France and elsewhere from the beginnings to the date of publication. For each entry: language of text, number of acts, authors of words and music, place and date of first performance, brief sketch of plot, occasional criticism. Index of composers. A comprehensive work.

344 / **Dassori, Carlo.** Opere e operisti (dizionario lirico 1541– 1902). . . . Genova, Tipografia editrice R. Istituto Sordomuti, 1903. 977 p.

Includes 15,406 operas by 3,628 composers. Author and title lists only, no descriptive and critical matter.

Part I: Alphabetical list of composers, with dates of birth and death, chronological list—under composer—of operas, with dates and places of first performances.

Part II: Title list of all operas that have been performed in Italy.

345 / **Directory of American Contemporary Operas.** Central Opera Service Bulletin, vol. 10, no. 2 (Dec. 1967). 79 p.

A listing of operas by American composers premiered since 1930; arranged alphabetically by composer with information as to place of first performance, librettist, cast and number of acts, availability (from composer, publisher, etc.).

A special issue of the Central Opera Service Bulletin; editor, Mrs. Maria F. Rich.

346 / **Eaton, Quaintance.** Opera production: a handbook. Minneapolis, University of Minnesota Press, 1961. 266 p.

Contains useful information on 224 "long" and 148 "short" operas, including timings, difficulty of leading roles, instrumentation, source and cost of scores and parts, photographs of productions, lists of performing groups.

347 / **Ewen, David.** New complete book of the American musical theater. New York, Holt, Rinehart, and Winston, 1970. 800 p.

A sourcebook of information about American musical comedies and revues.

348 / **Ewen, David.** The new encyclopedia of opera. New York, Hill and Wang, 1971. 759 p.

First published in 1955; reissued with a supplement in 1963.

Composers, text incipits, terms, plots, singers, librettists, theatres, all in one alphabet.

Review by Piero Weiss in *Notes*, 28 (1972), p. 679–80.

349 / **Johnson, H. Earle.** Operas on American subjects. New York, Coleman-Ross Co., 1964. 125 p.

An alphabetical listing, by composer, of operas from the 17th century to the present based on American subject matter or involving American characters. The entries supply much interesting information related to plot, performance, and estimates by contemporary critics. Topical, title, and general indexes.

87

See also Julius Mattfeld's *A handbook of American operatic premieres*, no. 355.

350 / **Kürschners Biographisches Theater-Handbuch.** Schauspiel, Oper, Film, Rundfunk: Deutschland, Österreich, Schweiz. Hrsg. von Herbert A. Frenzel und Hans J. Moser. Berlin, W. de Gruyter, 1956. 840 p.

Names, addresses, activities of singers, music directors, actors, critics, dancers, choreographers, composers, librarians of theater collections, etc. Entries are for persons living as of 1956.

351 / **Lessing, G. E.** Handbuch des Opern-Repertoires. [Neubearbeitung] London, New York, Boosey & Hawkes, 1952. 393 p.

An organized compilation of facts related to the performance of 392 operas in the current repertoire, including casts of characters, locales of action, instrumentation, duration of acts, dates of first performance, and publishers of the music.

> A work of reference intended for the use of theatrical managers, conductors, dramatists and in libraries. [Author's *Preface*]

352 / **Lewine, Richard, and Alfred Simon.** Encyclopedia of theater music: a comprehensive listing of more than 4,000 songs from Broadway and Hollywood, 1900–60. New York, Random House [1961], 248 p.

A guide to the song repertory of the American musical theater.

Part I: Theater songs, 1900–24. Part II: Theater songs, 1925–60. Part III: Motion picture songs. Part IV: Show chronology, 1925–60.

Songs are listed alphabetically by title, with composer, lyricist, show, and year given. List of published vocal scores and index of shows.

353 / **Loewenberg, Alfred.** Annals of opera, 1597–1940, compiled from the original sources; with an introduction by Edward J. Dent. 2nd ed., rev. and corrected. Genève, Societas Bibliographica [1955], 2 v.

First published in 1943 by W. Heffer, Cambridge. 879 p. Reprint by Scholarly Press, 1972.

Vol. 1: chronological listing of operas by dates of first performance, including (with a few exceptions) only works known to have been produced. The list is limited to older operas that are extant and modern ones that have created interest outside their countries of origin. Each entry includes composer's name, original title of the work, English translation for all languages except German, French, and Italian. Librettist identified; place and date of first performance given.

Vol. 2: indexes by title, composer, librettist, and a general index for other names, places, and subjects.

A work of distinguished scholarship; essential for the historical study of opera.

Review of 2nd ed. by Edward N. Waters, in *Notes*, 13 (1956), p. 285–86.

354 / **Manferrari, Umberto.** Dizionario universale delle opere melodramatiche. Firenze, Sansoni, 1954–55. 3 v. (Contributi alla biblioteca bibliografica italica, 4, 8, 10.)

One of the most comprehensive of all listings of opera. Entries under composer, giving title, librettist, place and date of first performances in other opera houses.

355 / **Mattfeld, Julius.** A handbook of American operatic premieres, 1731–1962. Detroit, Information Service, Inc., 1963. 142 p. (Detroit studies in music bibliography, 5.)

This guide to operatic performances in the United States attempts to present a record of the premieres of nearly 2,000 operas and related works from 1731 to the end of 1962. . . . Included are operas by native and naturalized composers, which have been performed outside the country. [*Preface*]

Works listed alphabetically by title, with a composer index.

356 / **Moore, Frank L.** Crowell's handbook of world opera. New York, Thomas Y. Crowell, 1961. 683 p.

Pub. in England under title: *The handbook of world opera*, London, Arthur Baker [1962], with intro. by Darius Milhaud.

Rich accumulation of facts under headings such as the operas, the people in opera, the characters in opera, first lines and titles of famous musical numbers, chronology of opera, glossary, themes of most famous musical numbers, recordings of complete operas. Numerous special indexes.

357 / **Opera Manual:** a handbook of practical operatic information. Edited by Mrs. Charles A. Matz and Marguerite Wickersham. New York, Central Opera Service, 1956.

Contains lists of operas in modern translation; chamber operas, citing voices and instruments needed, sets, duration, source of music. Information on costume and scenery rentals. Bibliography of stagecraft materials; lists of awards for singers; opera activity in the U.S., 1955–56; addresses of publishers, opera groups; unpublished translations, sources of chamber operas, etc.

358 / **Richard Rodgers Fact Book.** New York, the Lynn Farnol Group, Inc., 1965. 582 p.

A compendium of facts related to the career of Richard Rodgers. Largest section devoted to his stage, film, and television scores; works entered chronologically from 1920 to 1965, with production information, story, cast, musical numbers, and excerpts from contemporary reviews. General bibliography and discography; indexes of musical compositions and productions.

359 / **Rieck, Waldemar.** Opera plots, an index to the stories of operas, operettas, etc., from the sixteenth to the twentieth century. New York, The New York Public Library, 1927. 102 p.

Over 200 books and editions published in English, French, German, and Danish during the past 80 years have been indexed; 998 composers are represented by more than 2,775 works in operator form. [*Introduction*]

360 / **Riemann, Hugo.** Opern-Handbuch. Repertorium der dramatisch-musikalischen Litteratur (Opern, Operetten, Ballette, Melodramen, Pantomimen, Oratorien, dramatische Kantaten, usw.). Leipzig, H. Seemann Nachfolger [n.d.], 862 p.

Originally published by C A. Koch, Leipzig, 1887. Intended as an opera supplement to Riemann's *Lexikon.*

Title articles give genre, number of acts, composer, librettist, first performance. Composer articles give dates, chronological list of operas. Librettist entries give dates and chief activity.

361 / **Rosenthal, Harold, and John Warrack.** Concise Oxford dictionary of opera. London, Oxford Univ. Press, 1964. 446 p.

A richly informative pocket dictionary of opera. Special emphasis laid on the growth of opera in Eastern Europe, on literary backgrounds and relationships, and on singers. Includes a brief bibliography for further study.

Reissued as an Oxford Univ. Press paperback.

Review by David Z. Kushner in *Notes*, 22 (1965–66), p. 906.

362 / **Ross, Anne.** The opera directory. London, John Calder; New York, Sterling Pub. Co. [1961], 566 p.

A source book of current opera facts and figures. Introductions and headings in six languages (English, French, German, Italian, Spanish, Russian). Material organized under 13 headings, the most important of which are opera singers, conductors, producers and designers, technical staff, theaters and producing organizations, festivals, living composers, works by living composers, librettist, colleges and schools of music, casting index, glossary.

The identical volume is issued with various foreign title pages under the imprints of publishers in Paris, Geneva, Berlin, London, New York, etc.

363 / **Smith, William C.** The Italian opera and contemporary ballet in London, 1789–1820; a record of performances and players with reports from the journals of the time. London, The Society for Theatre Research, 1955. 191 p.

Cites 618 works produced in the London theaters during the period under consideration, with commentary by the author and quotations from contemporary sources. Indexes of operas, burlettas, cantatas; of ballets and divertissements; of singers, ballet personnel, composers, and instrumentalists.

364 / **Towers, John.** Dictionary-catalogue of operas and operettas which have been performed on the public stage. Morgantown, W. Va., Acme Pub. Co. [1910], 1,045 p.

Reprint by Da Capo Press, New York, 1967. 2 v.

Title list of 28,015 operas, giving for each composer his nationality and birth and death dates. Alternative or translated titles included. Composer index. No information on librettists, no historical or descriptive material.

Review by Donald Krummel in *Notes*, 24 (1968), p. 502–03.

365 / **Westerman, Gerhart von.** Knaurs Opernführer. Von Gerhart von Westerman und Karl Schumann. (München, Zürich) Dromer/Knaur, 1969. 511 p.

MISCELLANEOUS

366 / **Barlow, Harold, and S. Morgenstern.** A dictionary of musical themes. New York, Crown, 1948. 642 p.

Contains 10,000 themes from instrumental works, arranged alphabetically by composer. Indexed by scale degrees in letter notation with all themes transposed to C major or minor. Title index.

367 / **Barlow, Harold, and S. Morgenstern.** A dictionary of vocal themes. New York, Crown, 1950. 547 p.

Reissued, 1966, under the title *A dictionary of opera and song themes.*

Contains themes from operas, cantatas, oratorios, art songs, and miscellaneous vocal works, arranged alphabetically by composer. Indexed by scale degrees as in the preceding work. Title and first-line index.

Review by Harold Spivacke in *Notes*, 8 (1951), p. 334–35.

368 / **Berger, Kenneth W.** Band encyclopedia. Evansville, Indiana, Distributed by Band Associates, 1960. 604 p.

A compendium of information useful to band directors. Includes revisions of the author's earlier publications: *Band bibliography; Band discography;* and *Bandmen*, a biographical dictionary of band musicians.

Review by Keith Polk in *Notes*, 18 (1961), p. 424–26; by J. M. Lundahl in *Journal of research in music education*, 10 (1962), p. 81–82.

369 / **Burrows, Raymond M., and Bessie C. Redmond.** Concerto themes. New York, Simon and Schuster, 1951. 296 p.

More inclusive than *Barlow and Morgenstern* (no. 367) for concertos. Alphabetical arrangement by composer. Indexed by concerto titles, keys, and solo instruments.

370 / **Burrows, Raymond M., and Bessie C. Redmond.** Symphony themes. New York, Simon and Schuster, 1942. 295 p.

371 / **Cobbett, Walter W.** ed. Cyclopedic survey of chamber music. 2nd ed. London, Oxford Univ. Press, 1963. 3 v.

First published in 2 volumes, 1929–1930.

Cobbett's *Cyclopedia* is a biographical and subject dictionary of chamber music, giving full lists of works in this category under composer. Solo works and piano compositions excluded. The main emphasis is critical and analytical. Excellent critical and bibliographical material, with signed articles by outstanding authorities.

The second edition is a reissue of the original two volumes with minor corrections, plus a third volume which brings the information up to date.

Volume 3 of the 1963 edition is made up of extended articles surveying chamber music since 1929 in Europe, Great Britain, Russia, and America. Editor and principal contributor is Colin Mason. The chapter on "Chamber music in America" is by Nicolas Slonimsky; on "Soviet chamber music" by I. I. Martinov. Classified bibliography on chamber music; index of composers.

Review of the second edition by Homer Ulrich in *Notes*, 21 (1963–64), p. 124–26.

372 / **Heinzel, Erwin.** Lexikon historischer Ereignisse und Personen in Kunst, Literatur und Musik. Wien, Verlag Brüder Hollinek, 1956. 782 p.

A dictionary treating the artistic, literary, and musical works based on the lives of historical persons or events. Entries arranged alphabetically with persons and events interfiled. The information includes a summary of the historical details followed by a classified listing of the art works in which the person or event is represented.

373 / **Read, Gardner.** Thesaurus of orchestral devices. New York, Pitman, 1953. 631 p.

Reprint by the Greenwood Press, New York, 1969.

Intended to be a lexicon of instrumentation which will serve the student and/or professional orchestrator in the same manner and to the same degree that Bartlett's *Familiar quotations* or Roget's *Thesaurus* aid both the student of literature and the established writer. [*Preface*]

Nomenclature in English, Italian, French, and German, with ranges of instruments, lists of devices, with reference to the page and measure number of the score. List of music publishers and their U.S. agents. Index of nomenclature and terminology.

374 / **Slonimsky, Nicolas.** Thesaurus of scales and melodic patterns. New York, Coleman-Ross, 1947. 243 p.

Described by the author as "a reference book for composers in search of new materials." Contains nearly 1,000 scales, both traditional and contrived.

375 / **Vernillat, France, and Jacques Charpentreau.** Dictionnaire de la chanson française. Paris, Librairie Larousse, 1968. 256 p.

A dictionary of French popular song. Full historical coverage, but with emphasis on the early 19th and 20th centuries. Includes both terms and biography. Illustrated. No bibliographical references.

Also entered as no. 211.

Histories and Chronologies

WE HAVE BEEN particularly selective in this area. The titles include only the standard general histories of music in the major European languages together with some of the more recent outline histories. Excluded are all histories devoted to the music of a particular national group and most early histories (pre-1850) unless—as in the case of Burney, Hawkins, Forkel, or Martini—they are of extraordinary interest and are currently available. Also excluded are histories of special periods, or forms except as they occur as part of a comprehensive series. Music histories come and go, and few of those designed for the general reader, or for the music student, may be expected to outlive their time. This will account for the fact that some of the familiar occupants of library shelves—such as Dommer, Naumann, Rowbotham, and Rockstro—are missing from this list.

It is true of the early histories as it was of the early dictionaries that a number of titles have been restored to availability through modern reprint publication. Mention of this fact will be made in the annotations that follow, even though publication may still be in the projected stage as of 1973.

Those who want a comprehensive, chronological listing of music histories will find one in the appendix to Warren Allen's *Philosophies of music history* (no. 1834), under the title "Bibliography of literature concerning the general history of music in chronological order." See also the article "Histories" by S. T. Worsthorne in *Grove's* 5th edition, vol. 4, p. 296–306, for both a chronological and a systematic listing.

HISTORIES

376 / **Abbiati, Franco.** Storia della musica. 2nd ed. Milano, Garzanti, 1944–53. 5 v.

A general history of music for Italian readers. Numerous pictorial and musical illustrations. Each major section is followed by an anthology of excerpts from the writings of modern authorities on the period under consideration.

Contents: Vol. I: Roma, Medio Evo, Rinascimento. Vol. 2: Seicento. Vol. 3: Settecento. Vol. 4: Ottocento. Vol. 5: Novecento.

In 1967 a new revision of the work began publication with a somewhat different organization of the matterial. Vol. 1: Dalle origini al Cinquecento. Vol. 2: Il Seicento e il Settecento. Vol. 3: L'Ottecento.

377 / **Adler, Guido,** ed. Handbuch der Musikgeschichte. . . . 2. vollständig durchgesehene und stark ergänzte Aufl. Berlin-Wilmersdorf, H. Keller, 1930. 2 v.

Unaltered reprint of the 2nd ed., Schneider, Tutzing, 1962.

First printed in 1924 in one volume. Adler's *Handbuch* is the standard compendium of music history, representing the fruits of German scholarship in its most flourishing and influential period. Major articles contributed by such authorities as Alfred Einstein, Wilhelm Fischer, Robert Haas, Friedrich Ludwig, Curt Sachs, Arnold Schering, Peter Wagner, and Egon Wellesz.

378 / **Ambros, August Wilhelm.** Geschichte der Musik. . . . 3. gänzlich umbearb. Aufl. Leipzig, Leuckart, 1887–1911. 5 v.

Republication by Georg Olms, Hildesheim, 1968.

One of the last major one-man histories of music. The author did not live to carry the fourth volume past the beginning of the 17th century. Based on original research, the work is particularly important for its coverage of the sources of Medieval and Renaissance music.

Bd. I: Ancient music. 1862. 2nd ed., 1880. 3rd ed., 1887 (B. v. Sokolowsky, ed.).

Bd. II: Music of the Middle Ages. 1864. 2nd ed., 1880 (Otto Kade). 3rd ed., 1891 (Heinrich Reimann).

Bd. III: The Renaissance to Palestrina. 1868. 2nd ed., 1893 (Otto Kade).

Bd. IV: (not completed by Ambros) Italian music, 1550–1650. 1878 (Gustav Nottebohm). 2nd ed., 1881. 3rd ed., 1909 (Hugo Leichtentritt).

Bd. V: Musical examples for Bd. III, 1882 (Otto Kade). 2nd ed., 1887. 3rd ed., 1911.

The work by Wilhelm Langhans (see no. 432) was intended to complete the Ambros history from the 17th through the 19th century.

379 / **Bernard, Robert.** Histoire de la musique. [Paris] Fernand Nathan, 1961–63. 3 v.

A history of music distinguished for its fine printing and rich illustrative material, including numerous plates in full color. The work lacks bibliography or other documentation. Vol. 1 treats the history of European music to the end of the 18th century; vols. 2 and 3 are concerned with 19th- and 20th-century developments in Europe and the Americas, with brief discussions of Oriental music.

A *Complément à l'histoire de la musique*, containing indexes and glossary, appeared in 1971.

380 / **Bourdelot, Pierre.** Histoire de la musique et des ses effets [par] Pierre Bourdelot [et] Pierre Bonnet. Paris, J. Cochart, 1715. 487 p.

An edition was also printed in Amsterdam, 1725. The Paris edition (1715) has been reprinted by Slatkine. Reprints, Genève, 1969; the Amsterdam edition (1725) has been reprinted by the Akademische Druck- und Verlagsanstalt, Graz, 1966.

This is one of the first general histories of music. It was begun by Pierre Bourdelot, continued by his nephew, Pierre Bonnet, and finally completed and published by the brother of the latter, Jacques Bonnet.

381 / **Bücken, Ernst,** ed. Handbuch der Musikwissenschaft. Wildpark-Potsdam, Akademische Verlagsgesellschaft Athenaion [1927–31], 13 v. in 10.

First issued serially in parts.

A series of monographs on various periods and aspects of music history by the leading German musicologists of the period between World Wars I and II. Well printed and profusely illustrated, including plates in color.

Reprinted by Musurgia, New York, 1949. 13 v. in 9.

382 / [Vol. 1] Besseler, Heinrich. *Die Musik des Mittelalters und der Renaissance* [1931], 337 p.

383 / [Vol. 2] Blume, Friedrich. *Die evangelische Kirchenmusik* [1931], 171 p. Has been reedited under the title, *Geschichte der Evangelischen Kirchenmusik* . . . Herausgegeben unter Mitarbeit von Ludwig Finscher, Georg Feder, Adam Adrio und Walter Blankenburg. Kassel, Bärenreiter, 1965.

Review article by Werner Braun in *Die Musikforschung*, 21 (1968) p. 50–57.

Review of Blume's *Geschichte der evangelischen Kirchenmusik* by U. S. Leupold in *Notes*, 23 (1966), p. 45–46.

384 / [Vol. 3] Bücken, Ernst. *Geist und Form im musikalischen Kunstwerk* [1929], 195 p.

385 / [Vol. 4] Bücken, Ernst. *Die Musik des 19. Jahrhunderts bis zur Moderne* [1929], 319 p.

386 / [Vol. 5] Bücken, Ernst. *Die Musik des Rokokos und der Klassik* [1927], 247 p.

387 / [Vol. 6] Haas, Robert. *Aufführungspraxis der Musik* [1931], 298 p.

388 / [Vol. 7] Haas, Robert. *Die Musik des Barocks* [1929], 290 p.

389 / [Vol. 8] Pt. 1. Heinitz, Wilhelm. *Instrumentenkunde* [1929], 159 p.

390 / [Vol. 8] Pt. 2. Lachmann, Robert. *Die Musik der aussereuropäischen Natur- und Kulturvölker* [1929], 33 p.

391 / [Vol. 8] Pt. 3. Sachs, Curt. *Die Musik der Antike* [1928], 32 p.

392 / [Vol. 8] Pt. 4. Panóff, Peter. *Die Altslavische Volks- und Kirchenmusik* [1930], 31 p.

393 / [Vol. 9] Mersmann, Hans. *Die moderne Musik seit der Romantik* [1928], 225 p.

394 / [Vol. 10] Ursprung, Otto. *Die katholische Kirchenmusik* [1931], 312 p.

395 / **Burney, Charles.** A general history of music, from the earliest times to the present period. London, printed for the author, 1776–1789. 4 v.

Reprinted with critical and historical notes by Frank Mercer. London, Foulis; New York, Harcourt, 1935. 4 v. in 2. Reprint of the Mercer edition by Dover Publications, New York, 1935. Reprint projected by the Akademische Druck- und Verlagsanstalt, Graz, in the series *Die grossen Darstellungen der Musikgeschichte.*

Burney shares with Sir John Hawkins (see no. 412) credit for the emergence of music historiography in the latter part of the 18th century. In addition to its merits as a source of musical information, Burney's work is marked by high literary quality. It set a precedent for generations of music historians to follow.

396 / **Cannon, Beekman C., Alvin H. Johnson, and William G. Waite.** The art of music, a short history of musical styles and ideas. New York, Crowell [1960], 484 p.

Designed as an introduction to the history of music, presupposing little background. The "basic principles of music" are covered in an appendix. No bibliography. Brief musical examples in the text.

Review by Warner Imig in *Journal of research in music education,* 9 (1961), p. 172.

397 / **Chailley, Jacques.** 40,000 years of music. Translated from the French by Rollo Myers, with a preface by Virgil Thomson. London, Macdonald, 1964. 229 p.

Originally published by Librairie Plon, Paris, under the title *40,000 ans de musique* (1961).

99

A provocative if somewhat disorganized approach to music history; treats the subject within the framework of sociology and the history of ideas.

398 / **Combarieu, Jules.** Histoire de la musique des origines au début du XXe siècle. Paris, A. Colin, 1946–60. 5 v.

Vols. 1–3 originally published 1913–19.

I: Des origines à la fin du XVIe siècle. II: Du XVIIe siècle à la mort de Beethoven. III: De la mort de Beethoven au début du XXe siècle. IV: L'aube du XXe siècle (by René Dumesnil, 1958). V: La première moitié du XXe siècle (by René Dumesnil, 1960).

399 / **Confalonieri, Giulio.** Storia della musica. Milano, Nuova accademia editrice [1958], 2 v.

A popular general history, lavishly printed on glossy paper, with 34 plates in full color and hundreds of black and white illustrations. No musical examples. Essential bibliography listed by chapter at the end of the second volume, where there is also a general index and an index of illustrations.

400 / **Corte, Andrea della.** Antologia della storia della musica, dalla Grecia antica all'ottocento. 4. ed., rinnovata in un volume. Torino, G. B. Paravia [1945], 491 p.

First published in 1926 in two volumes.

An anthology of writings on music history, chiefly by modern European scholars but with a few early documents (excerpts from Zarlino, Galilei, Caccini, Peri, etc.). Italian text.

401 / **Corte, Andrea della e Guido Pannain.** Storia della musica. 2. ed. Torino, Unione Tipografico-Editrice Torinese, 1944. 3 v.

First published in 1935; 2nd ed., 1942; reprinted, 1944.

The standard general history of music for Italian readers.

I: Dal medioevo al seicento. II: Il settecento. III: L'ottocento e il novecento.

402 / **Crocker, Richard L.** A history of musical style. New York, McGraw-Hill, 1966. 573 p.

One of the few histories of music to focus attention consistently on musical style.

Crocker's book is also discussed critically by Leo Treitler in "The present as history," an article in *Perspectives of new music* (Spring–Summer, 1969), p. 1–58.

Review by Martin Chusid in *Notes*, 23 (1967), p. 732–33; by Gwynn McPeek in *Journal of research in music education*, 15 (1967), p. 333–36.

Review by Henry Leland Clarke in *JAMS*, 21 (1968), p. 103–5.

403 / **Einstein, Alfred.** A short history of music. 3rd American edition. New York, Knopf, 1947. 438 p.

Also issued as a paperback. Originally published in German, 1934.

One of the most perceptive and authoritative concise histories of music. Published in numerous editions and translations. Most editions incorporate a useful anthology of 39 musical examples, originally issued in 1917 as "Beispielsammlung zur älteren Musikgeschichte." A handsome illustrated edition (London, Cassell, 1953) edited by A. Hyatt King unfortunately does not contain the musical supplement.

404 / **Ferguson, Donald N.** A history of musical thought. 3rd ed. New York, Appleton-Century-Crofts [1959], 675 p.

First published in 1935; 2nd ed., 1948.

An influential one-volume work designed for music history courses at college level. One of the first to propagate the results of German scholarship in America.

405 / **Finney, Theodore M.** A history of music. Rev. ed. New York, Harcourt, 1947. 720 p.

First published in 1935. A well organized student's history.

406 / **Forkel, Johann Nikolaus.** Allgemeine Geschichte der Musik. Leipzig, im Schwikertschen Verlage, 1788–1801. 2 v.

Reprint by the Akademische Druck- und Verlagsanstalt, Graz. Ed. by O. Wesseley in the series *Die grossen Darstellungen der Musikgeschichte.* . . .

The first full-scale history of music in German, by the scholar who has been called "the father of modern musicology." The work is incomplete, covering only as far as the early 16th century.

407 / **Gleason, Harold.** Music literature outlines. Series 1–5. Rochester, N.Y., Levis Music Stores, 1949–55.

Ser. 1: Music in the Middle Ages and Renaissance. 2nd ed., 1951.
Ser. 2: Music in the Baroque.
Ser. 3: American music from 1620–1920.
Ser. 4: Contemporary American music.
Ser. 5: Chamber music from Haydn to Ravel.

Historical outlines, or syllabi, with copious bibliographical references, including discography. The organization of Series 1 and 2 follows closely that of the corresponding works by Reese and Bukofzer in the *Norton history of music series* (see nos. 431, 433).

408 / **Grout, Donald J.** A history of Western music. New York, Norton, 1960. 742 p.

Also published in a shortened edition for use as a text.

Intended for undergraduate college music students or for the general reader. "An elementary knowledge of musical terms and of harmony . . . has been assumed." Based on a stylistic approach. Contains numerous musical and pictorial illustrations. Annotated bibliography for further reading, a chronology of musical and historical events, and a glossary of terms.

Review by Albert T. Luper in *Notes*, 18 (1960); by Warren Allen in *Journal of research in music education*, 8 (1960), p. 124–26; by Alec Harman in *Musical times* (Dec. 1962), p. 845–47.

409 / **Gruber, Roman Il'ich.** Istoriĩa muzykal'noĩ kyl'tury. Moskva, Gosudarstvennoe muzykal'noi izdatel stvo, 1941–1959, 2 v.

A translation into Rumanian by Tatiana Nichitin was issued in Bucarest, 1963– .

A general history of music from antiquity to the beginning of the 17th century, for Russian readers. Vol. 1, part 1 deals with Egypt, Mesopotamia, India, China, etc., as well as Greece and Rome. The final chapter of vol. 2 is concerned with the musical culture of the Western Slavs to the 17th century.

410 / **Handschin, Jacques.** Musikgeschichte in Überblick. 2, ergänzte Auflage. Hrsg. von Franz Brenn. Luzern, Räber, 1964. 442 p.

First published in 1948.

A stimulating short history weighted in the direction of Medieval and Renaissance music. Chronological tables and a classified bibliography.

Review of the 2nd ed. by Joseph Müller-Blattau, in *Die Musik-forschung*, 18 (1965), p. 441.

411 / **Harman, Alec, and Wilfrid Mellers.** Man and his music, the story of musical experience in the West. New York, Oxford Univ. Press, 1962. 1,172 p.

First published in 1957–59 in four volumes: 1, Medieval and early Renaissance music (up to *c.* 1525); 2, late Renaissance and Baroque music (*c.* 1525–*c.* 1750); 3, the sonata principle (from *c.* 1750); 4, Romanticism and the 20th century.

A history designed for the intelligent layman, stressing the social and cultural backgrounds. Comparative chronology and a list of recommended books and music.

Review of vol. 2 by J. Merrill Knapp in *Notes*, 17 (1960), p. 569–70; of vols. 3 and 4 by William S. Newman in *Notes*, 15 (1957), p. 99–101; of the composite volume by Jack A. Westrup in *Music and letters*, 43 (1962), p. 265–66.

412 / **Hawkins, Sir John.** A general history of the science and practice of music. London, Payne and Son, 1776. 5 v.

New edition "with the author's posthumous notes," published by Novello, London, 1853, 3 v. (vol. 3 is an atlas of portraits); reprinted by Novello in 1875. Unabridged republication of the 1853 edition, with a new introduction by Charles Cudworth, New York, Dover, 1963. 2 v. Reprint by the Akademische Druck- und Verlagsanstalt, Graz, 1969. 2 v.

Hawkins's history appeared in the same year that the first volume of Charles Burney's history (no. 395) was published. The two works inevitably invited comparison, largely to Hawkins's disadvantage. His history, however, has much to recommend it. It contains extensive translations of excerpts from early theory works and includes many examples of early music.

Review of the Dover reprint by Bernard E. Wilson in *Notes*, 22 (1966), p. 1026–27.

413 / **Honolka, Kurt,** ed. Knaurs Weltgeschichte der Musik. München/Zürich, Th. Knaur Nachf., 1968. 640 p.

A general history with 500 illustrations and musical examples. 30 color plates.

103

Contributors: Hans Engel, Paul Nettl, Kurt Reinhard, Lukas Richter, Bruno Stäblein.

414 / Keisewetter, Raphael Georg. Geschichte der europäisch-abendländischen oder unserer heutigen Musik. Darstellung ihres Wachsthumes und ihrer stufenweisen Entwicklung von dem ersten Jahrhundert des Christenthums bis auf unsere Zeit. Leipzig, Breitkopf & Härtel, 1834. 116 p.

A second enlarged edition appeared in 1846; this has been reprinted by Sändig, Wiesbaden, 1971. The work appeared in an English translation by Robert Müller, London, Newby, 1848. This, in turn, has been reprinted by the Da Capo Press, New York, 1973, with a new introduction by Frank Harrison.

Kiesewetter's work is the first popular outline history of music in the modern sense. The author organizes his information in 17 different epochs, each characterized by the activity of one or more dominant musical individuals.

415 / Kretzschmar, Hermann, ed. Kleine Handbücher der Musik-geschichte nach Gattungen. Leipzig, Breitkopf & Härtel, 1905–1922. 14 v. in 15.

All the volumes in this set have been reprinted by Olms, Hilde-sheim, 1967–   .

The Kretzschmar *Handbücher* are a series of historical monographs dealing with the development of specific musical forms or disciplines. Although superseded in many respects, these volumes remain basic studies in the areas with which they are concerned.

416 / (1) Arnold Schering: Geschichte des Instrumentalkonzerts ... 1905. 226 p. 2nd Aufl., 1927.

417 / (2) Hugo Leichtentritt: Geschichte der Motette. 1908. 453 p.

418 / (3) Arnold Schering: Geschichte des Oratoriums. 1911. 647 p. Notenanhang, 39 p.

419 / (4) Hermann Kretzschmar: Geschichte des neuen deutschen Liedes. I. Von Albert bis Zelter (all published). 1911. 354 p.

420 / (5) Eugen Schmitz: Geschichte der Kantate und des geistlichen Konzerts. I. Geschichte der weltlichen Solokantate (all published). 1914. 327 p. 2nd Aufl., 1955.

421 / (6) Hermann Kretzschmar: Geschichte der Oper. 1919. 286 p.

422 / (7) Hermann Kretzschmar: Einführung in die Musikgeschichte. 1920. 82 p.

423 / (8) Johannes Wolf: Handbuch der Notationskunde. I. Tonschriften des Altertums und des Mittelalters . . . II. Tonschriften des Neuzeit, Tablaturen, Partitur, Generalbass und Reformversuche. 1913–1919. 2 v.

424 / (9) Hugo Botstiber: Geschichte der Ouvertüre und der freien Orchesterformen. 1913. 274 p.

425 / (10) Georg Schünemann: Geschichte des Dirigierens. 1913. 359 p.

426 / (11) Peter Wagner: Geschichte der Messe. I. Bis 1600 (all published). 1913. 548 p.

427 / (12) Curt Sachs: Handbuch der Musikinstrumentenkunde. 1920. 412 p.

428 / (13) Adolf Aber: Handbuch der Musikliteratur . . . 1922. 696 cols.

429 / (14) Karl Nef: Geschichte der Sinfonie und Suite. 1921. 344 p.

430 / **Laborde, Jean Benjamin de.** Essai sur la musique ancienne et moderne. Paris, Impr. de P. D. Pierres, et se vend chez E. Onfroy, 1780. 4 v.

Reprint by the Akademische Druck- und Verlagsanstalt, Graz.

Laborde's work is the major French contribution to music historiography of the 18th century. The *Essai* is a vast assemblage of information on musical ethnology, organology, history, and biography. Much attention is directed toward French lyric poetry and the chanson.

431 / **Lang, Paul, Henry.** Music in Western civilization. New York, Norton, 1941. 1,107 p.

This work has been widely translated (into German, Spanish, Portuguese, Czech, and Japanese, etc.).

Music in the context of the social, political and cultural currents of Western civilization. One of the most influential of all music histories produced in America, it coincided with, and contributed to, the general acceptance of music history in American higher education. Comprehensive bibliography of literature in all languages in one alphabet, p. 1045–65.

432 / **Langhans, Wilhelm.** Die Geschichte der Musik des 17. 18. und 19. Jahrhunderts in chronologischem Anschlusse an die Musikgeschichte von A. W. Ambros. Leipzig, F. E. C. Leuckart, 1884. 2 v.

Written as a continuation of Ambros's unfinished history, no. 378.

Manuel, Roland.
See **Roland-Manuel,** no. 469.

433 / **Martini, Giovanni Battista.** Storia della musica. Bologna, Lelio dalla Volpe, 1757–81. 3 v.

Reprint by Akademische Druck- und Verlagsanstalt, Graz, 1967. Edited and supplied with an index by Othmar Wessely.

In spite of its archaic methodology, and the fact that Martini did not live to carry his history beyond the music of the ancients, it was an influential work and a source book for later historians.

Review of the reprint edition by Jack Alan Westrup in *Music and letters,* 49 (1968), p. 55–57; and by Werner Kümmel in *Die Musikforschung,* 22 (1969), p. 238–39.

434 / **Nef, Karl.** An outline of the history of music. Trans. by Carl Pfatteicher. New York, Columbia Univ. Press, 1935. 400 p.

Originally published as *Einführung in die Musikgeschichte* in 1920. Many reprintings. An augmented French edition by Yvonne Rokseth appeared in 1931.

An excellent outline history for use in college or university music courses. Brief yet comprehensive, readable yet scholarly. Rich in bibliographical information and musical examples in the text.

435 / **The New Oxford History of Music.** London, New York, Oxford Univ. Press, 1954–   .

Each volume is a composite work made up of contributions by scholars of international repute and edited by a specialist in the period. The set is planned in 10 volumes plus a volume of chronological tables and general index. There is an accompanying set of recordings issued under the title *The history of music in sound* with illustrated booklets designed for teaching purposes. All recordings and pamphlets have appeared.

436 / Vol. 1: Ancient and oriental music, ed. by Egon Wellesz, 1957. 530 p.

Review by Curt Sachs in *Notes*, 16 (1957), p. 97–99; by Roy Jesson in *MQ*, 44 (1958), p. 245–53; by Charles Seeger in *Ethnomusicology*, 3 (1959), p. 96–97.

437 / Vol. 2: Early medieval music up to 1300, ed. by Anselm Hughes, 1951. 434 p.

Review by Charles Warren Fox in *MQ*, 41 (1955), p. 534–47; by Jeremy Noble in *Music and letters*, 36 (1955), p. 65–70.

438 / Vol. 3: Ars Nova and the Renaissance (1300–1540), ed. by Anselm Hughes and Gerald Abraham, 1960. 565 p.

Review by Richard H. Hoppin in *MQ*, 47 (1961), p. 116–25; by Thurston Dart in *Music and letters*, 42 (1961), p. 57–60.

439 / Vol. 4: The age of humanism, 1540–1630. Ed. by Gerald Abraham, 1968. 978 p.

Review by Howard Brown in *Notes*, 26 (1969), p. 133–36; by Paul Doe in *Music and letters*, 51 (1970), p. 66–69; by Claude V. Palisca in *JAMS*, 23 (1970), p. 133–36.

The following volumes are in preparation:

5. Opera and church music (1630–1750)
6. The growth of instrumental music (1630–1750)
7. The symphonic outlook (1745–1790)

8. The age of Beethoven (1790–1830)
9. Romanticism (1830–1890)
10. Modern music (1890–1950)
11. Chronological tables and general index

440 / The Norton History of Music Series. New York, Norton, 1940– .

A publisher's series consisting of independent works on different periods in the history of music. At one time it was announced that the volumes would be reissued as a set. In that case, some of the titles listed below may not be included.

The volumes by Reese and Bukofzer are particularly rich in bibliographical content.

441 / Curt Sachs: The rise of music in the ancient world, East and West. 1943. 324 p.

442 / Gustave Reese: Music in the Middle Ages. 1940. 502 p.

Also published in an Italian edition under the title *La musica nel medioeve*. Florence, Sansoni, 1964. 642 p. Much new illustrative material has been added to this edition.

443 / Gustave Reese: Music in the Renaissance. 1954. 1,022 p. Revised edition, 1959.

Review by Denis Stevens in *Music and letters*, 36 (1955), p. 70–73; by Edgar H. Sparks in *Notes*, 17 (1960), p. 569.

444 / Manfred Bukofzer: Music in the Baroque era, from Montiverdi to Bach. 1947. 489 p.

445 / Alfred Einstein: Music in the romantic era. 1947. 371 p.

446 / William W. Austin: Music in the 20th century from Debussy through Stravinsky. 1966. 708 p.

Also printed by Dent, London, 1967.

Review by Peter Evans in *Music and letters*, 49 (1968), p. 43–47; by Henry Leland Clarke in *Journal of research in music education*, 15 (1967), p. 174–76.

447 / The Oxford History of Music. 2nd ed. London, Oxford Univ. Press, 1929–38. 7 v. (plus an introductory volume.)

First printed in 1901–1905 in six volumes. Vols. 4–6 of the 2nd edition are reprints of the original volumes.

448 / Introductory volume, edited by Percy C. Buck, 1929. 239 p.

A symposium by nine scholars covering Greek and Hebrew music, notation, musical instruments, theory to 1400, plainsong, folk song, social aspects of music in the Middle Ages. Chapter bibliographies, p. 233–39.

449 / Vols. 1–2: H. E. Wooldridge. The polyphonic period. 2nd rev. ed. by Percy C. Buck, 1928–32.

450 / Vol. 3: Hubert Parry. The music of the 17th century. 1938. 486 p.

451 / Vol. 4: J. A. Fuller-Maitland. The age of Bach and Handel. 2nd ed. 1931. 362 p.

452 / Vol. 5: W. H. Hadow. The Viennese period. 1931. 350 p.

453 / Vol. 6: Edward Dannreuther. The romantic period. 1931. 374 p.

454 / Vol. 7: H. C. Colles. Symphony and drama, 1850–1900. 1934. 504 p.

455 / **The Pelican History of Music.** Edited by Alec Robertson and Denis Stevens. Harmondsworth, Middlesex, Penguin Books, 1960–1969. 3 v.

Reissued by Barnes and Noble, New York, under the title *A history of music.*

Vol. 1: Ancient forms to polyphony. Vol. 2: Renaissance and baroque. Vol. 3: Classical and romantic.

A popular history of music with contributions from leading authorities, including the editors; e.g., Alec Robertson, "Plainchant"; Denis Stevens, "Ars antique"; Gilbert Reaney, "Ars nove." Peter Crossley-Holland, "Non-Western music"; Hugh Ottaway, "The Enlightenment and the Revolution"; A. J. B. Hutchings, "The 19th century"; etc.

Review of vol. 3 by William S. Newman in *Notes,* 26 (1970), p. 504–06.

456 / **The Prentice-Hall History of Music Series.** Englewood Cliffs, N.J., Prentice-Hall, 1965– .

A publisher's series for which H. Wiley Hitchcock serves as general editor. Short one-volume surveys by leading American scholars covering the major historical periods as well as folk and non-Western music. (The numbering of the volumes is arbitrary.)

457 / (1) Bruno Nettl: Folk and traditional music of the Western continents. 1965. 213 p.

Review by Alfred W. Humphreys in *Journal of research in music education*, 13 (1965), p. 259–60; by Fritz Bose in *Die Musikforschung*, 21 (1968), p. 107–08; by Wolfgang Suppan in *Jahrbuch für Volkslied-forschung*, 12 (1967), p. 217–18.

458 / (2) William P. Malm: Music cultures of the Pacific, the Near East, and Asia. 1967. 169 p.

459 / (3) Albert Seay: Music in the medieval world. 1965. 182 p.

Review by Leo Treitler in *Journal of research in music education*, 14 (1966), p. 235–36; by Peter Gülke in *Die Musikforschung*, 21 (1968), p. 108–09.

460 / (4) Claude V. Palisca: Baroque music. 1968. 230 p.

Review by David Burrows in *Notes*, 25 (1969), p. 717–18.

461 / (5) Reinhard G. Pauly: Music in the classic period. 1965. 214 p.

Review by Eugene Helm in *Notes*, 25 (1968), p. 40–41.

462 / (6) Rey. M. Longyear: Nineteenth-century romanticism in music. 1969. 220 p.

463 / (7) Eric Salzman: Twentieth-century music: an introduction. 1967. 196 p.

464 / (8) Wiley H. Hitchcock: Music in the United States: a historical introduction. 1969. 270 p.

Review by Ross Lee Finney in *Notes*, 26 (1969), p. 271–72.

465 / **Printz, Wolfgang Caspar.** Historische Beschreibung der edelen Sing- und Kling-kunst ... Dresden, J. C. Mieth, 1690. 240 p.

Reprint by the Akademische Druck- und Verlaganstalt, Graz, 1964. Edited and indexed by Othmar Wessely.

This work has been described as the first history of music. Printz's observations are based largely on Biblical authority and legend, but his work exercised considerable influence on 18th-century music lexicographers and historians.

466 / **Prunières, Henry.** A new history of music; the Middle Ages to Mozart. Trans. and ed. by Edward Lockspeiser. New York, Macmillan, 1943. 413 p.

Originally published as *Nouvelle histoire de la musique*, Paris, 1934–36. 2 v.

Valuable for its emphasis on the earlier peroids.

467 / **Renner, Hans.** Geschichte der Musik. Stuttgart, Deutsche Verlags-Anstalt, 1965. 704 p.

A well-illustrated student's history. Traditional chronological arrangement with useful appendices devoted to notation, voice ranges, the composition of orchestras, musical instruments, and glossary. Index of names and subjects.

468 / **Riemann, Hugo.** Handbuch der Musikgeschichte. 2nd ed. [edited by Alfred Einstein.] Leipzig, Breitkopf & Härtel, 1920–23. 2 v. in 4.

First published in 1904–1913. Reprint by Johnson Reprint Corporation, New York.

A product of one of the most vigorous and stimulating minds in German musicology, always provocative, frequently misleading. Extensive chapter bibliographies and sections devoted to brief biographies of musicians; the emphasis, however, is on musical styles and forms. Numerous transcriptions of early music, all of which must be viewed in the light of Riemann's unorthodox editorial methods.

469 / **Roland-Manuel, ed.** Histoire de la musique. Paris, Gallimard, 1960–1963. 2 v. (Encyclopédie de la Pléiade, 9 and 16.)

Vol. 1: "Des origines à Jean-Sébastien Bach." 2,238 p. Vol. 2: "Du XVIIIe siècle à nos jours." 1,878 p.

111

An important work. The language is French but the approach is international, consisting of contributions by specialists from many different countries. Vol. 1 begins with a chapter on "Elements et geneses," followed by surveys of the music of non-Western cultures, of ancient and oriental music, and of the music of the Moslem world. Thereafter the organization is chronological within individual countries. At the end of vol. 2 there are chapters devoted to contemporary music and to the history of musicology and of criticism. Each volume has a chronological table and index, plus an analytical table of contents.

470 / **Sachs, Curt.** Our musical heritage, a short history of music. 2nd edition. Englewood Cliffs, New Jersey, Prentice-Hall, 1955. 351 p.
First published in 1948.
Designed as a textbook for introductory courses in music history. References to essential bibliography.

471 / **Salazar, Adolfo.** La música en la sociedad europea. (México) El Colegio di México, 1942–46. 9 parts in 4 v.
A general history for Spanish readers, from antiquity to the end of the 19th century.

472 / **Smijers, Albert,** ed. Algemeene muziekgeschiedenis; geïlustreerd overzicht der Europeesche muziek van de oudheid tot heden. 4. bijgewerkte druk. Utrecht, W. de Haan, 1947. 518 p.
1st edition, 1938; 2nd edition, 1940.
A composite history in eight books, each written by a different Dutch or Flemish scholar. Short bibliographies after each book. Plates and numerous musical illustrations.

473 / **Strunk, W. Oliver.** Source readings in music history from classical antiquity through the romantic era. New York, Norton, 1950. 919 p.
Reissued in a paperback edition, 5 vols., 1965.
87 items extracted from the writings of theorists, composers, teachers, critics, and practical musicians, arranged chronologically under topics. Each item is introduced with a few concise and illuminating comments by the editor. The translations are excellent, the editorial work exemplary. An indispensable volume in any library of music history.

Review by Manfred Bukofzer in *Notes*, 8 (1951), p. 517–18; by Erich Hertzmann in *MQ*, 37 (1951), p. 430–32; by Leo Schrade in *JAMS*, 4 (1951), p. 249–51.

474 / **Subirá, José.** Historia de la música. 3. ed., reformada, ampliada, y puesta al dia. Barcelona, Editorial Salvat, 1958. 4 v.

First published in 1947; 2nd edition, 1951.

Handsomely printed and illustrated, musically and pictorially. Some emphasis on ethnomusicology. The approach is generally chronological, but with chapters on the development of notation, 17th-century theory, and performance practice.

475 / **Ulrich, Homer, and Paul Pisk.** A history of music and musical style. New York, Harcourt, 1963. 696 p.

The authors' purpose in writing this history of music has been to offer a clear, straightforward presentation of historical developments in musical style. [*Preface*]

Review by Susan Thiemann in *Notes*, 20 (1963), p. 638–42.

476 / **Wiora, Walter.** The four ages of music. Translated by M. D. Herter Norton. New York, Norton, 1965. 233 p.

Originally issued by W. Kohlhammer Verlag, Stuttgart, 1961, under the title *Die vier Weltalter der Musik* (Urban-Bücher, 56).

An original approach to music history and its periodization, treating the subject in the context of universal history and anthropology.

Review by Johannes Riedel in *Journal of research in music education*, 13 (1965), p. 260–61; by Rose Brandel in *Notes*, 24 (1968), p. 695–97.

477 / **Wörner, Karl H.** Geschichte der Musik. Ein Studien- und Nachschlagebuch. Fünfte, durchgesehene und erweiterte Auflage. Göttingen, Vandenhoeck u. Ruprecht, 1972. 598 p.

First published in 1954; 2nd ed., 1956; 3rd ed., 1961; 4th ed., 1965.

A well-organized outline history of music with excellent bibliographical information. Utilizes a variety of approaches: stylistic, national, biographical. Paragraphs are numbered for easy reference.

A 5th edition, in English translation, has been issued by the Free Press, New York, 1973.

MUSIC HISTORY IN PICTURES

When Georg Kinsky produced his *Geschichte der Musik in Bildern* in 1929 (see no. 493), he established a tradition in music history writing that has remained very much alive to the present day. The distinction between illustrated histories of music and histories that tell their story primarily through the use of visual materials is somewhat arbitrary. Increasing attention is being paid to the iconography of music, not merely as the source of attractive "picture books" but as a branch of serious musicological research. There are efforts under way to establish an international inventory of music iconography and to standardize methods of description and cataloging (see no. 1840). Much material of iconographical interest will be found under the heading "Dictionaries and encyclopedias: musical instruments."

478 / **Besseler, Heinrich, and Max Schneider,** eds. Musikgeschichte in Bildern. v. 1– . Leipzig, Deutscher Verlag für Musik, 1961– .

A multivolume work projected to cover all periods in the history of music as well as some of the systematic branches. Publication of the volumes and their respective subsections (Lieferungen) will not necessarily follow in chronological order. Each issue contains numerous plates, with commentary, a bibliography, chronological tables, and indexes. The following issues have been released to date:

BAND I: MUSIKETHNOLOGIE

479 / Lief. 1: Paul Collaer. *Ozeanien* (1965), 234 p.
Review by Dieter Christensen in *Die Musikforschung*, 20 (1967), p. 339–41; by Bruno Nettl in *Notes*, 23 (1966), p. 276; by Wolfgang Suppan in *Jahrbuch für Volksliedforschung*, 16 (1971), p. 262–64.

480 / Lief. 2: Paul Collaer. *Amerika. Eskimo und indianische Bevölkerung.* (1967), 211 p.
Review by Fritz Bose in *Die Musikforschung*, 22 (1969), p. 522-23; by Bruno Nettl in *Notes*, 24 (1968), p. 717–17.

BAND II: MUSIK DES ALTERTUMS

481 / Lief. 1: Hans Hickmann. *Ägypten* (1961), 187 p.
Review by Caldwell Titcomb in *JAMS*, 17 (1964), p. 386–91; by Fritz Bose in *Die Musikforschung*, 17 (1964), p. 184–85.

482 / Lief. 4: Max Wegner. *Griechenland* (1964), 143 p.
Review by Emanuel Winternitz in *JAMS*, 19 (1966), p. 412–15.

483 / Lief. 5: Günter Fleischhauer. *Eturien und Rom* (1965), 195 p.

484 / Lief. 7: Samuel Martí. *Alt-Amerika; Musik der Indianer in präkolumbischer Zeit* (1970), 195 p.
Review by Wolfgang Suppan in *Jahrbuch für Volksliedforschung*, 16 (1971), p. 262–64.

BAND III: MUSIK DES MITTELALTERS UND DER RENAISSANCE

485 / Lief. 2: Henry George Farmer. *Islam* (1966), 206 p.
Review by Emmy Wellesz in *Music and letters*, 49 (1968), p. 73–74; by Essa Zonis in *JAMS*, 22 (1969), p. 293–96.

486 / Lief. 3: Joseph Smits van Waesberghe. *Musikerziehung* (1969), 214 p.
Review by Hans Oesch in *Literature, Music, Fine Arts*, 5 (1972, p. 232–33.

BAND IV: NEUZEIT

487 / Lief. 1: Hellmuth Christian Wolff. *Oper, Szene und Darstellung von 1600 bis 1900* (1968), 214 p.
Review by Karl Michael Komma in *Literature, music, fine arts*, 1 (1968), p. 220–22; by Christoph-Hellmut Mahling in *Die Musikforschung*, 23 (1970), p. 97–99.

488 / Lief. 2: Heinrich W. Schwab. *Konzert. Öffentliche Musikdarbietung vom 17. bis 19. Jahrhundert* (1971), 230 p.

489 / Lief. 3: Walter Salmen. *Haus- und Kammermusik zwischen 1600 und 1900* (1969), 203 p.

490 / **Collaer, Paul, and Albert van der Linden.** Historical atlas of music: a comprehensive study of the world's music, past and present . . . with the collaboration of F. van den Bremt. Pref. by Charles van den Borren. Trans. by Allan Miller. Cleveland, World Pub. Co., 1968. 175 p.

Also published by Harrap, London and Toronto, 1968. Originally published as *Atlas historique de la musique* by Elsevier, Paris, 1960.

An illustrated survey of music history, with 15 full-page maps and more than 700 illustrations.

Review by Robert E. Wolf in *MQ*, 47 (1961), p. 413–16.

491 / **Dufourcq, Norbert,** ed. La musique des origines à nos jours. Préface de Claude Delvincourt. Nouv. éd., rev., augm. Paris, Larousse, 1954. 591 p.

The reprinting of a work first published in 1946 and carried through seven editions.

Richly illustrated compendium of music history and related fields, the work of 44 scholars, chiefly French. Organized in 5 books, of which the third (p. 83–431) deals with the history of Western music. Other books treat of the voice and instruments, ancient and Near Eastern music, non-European music, and musical aesthetics. A series of 17 appendices cover special topics such as notation, theory, criticism, libraries and other institutions. 6 colored plates and numerous black-and-white illustrations.

492 / **Dufourcq, Norbert.** La musique, les hommes, les instruments, les œuvres. Paris, Larousse, 1965. 2 v.

Tome 1: "La musique, des origines à la mort de Rameau." Tome 2: "La musique, de l'aube du classicisme à la periode contemporaine."

This work is an expansion of the preceding. The articles are contributed by leading authorities, chiefly French. A fine, visually oriented history of music. It also serves as the basis for another Larousse publication: *Larousse encyclopedia of music*, ed. by Jeoffrey Hindley, New York, World Publishing Co., 1971.

493 / **Kinsky, Georg.** A history of music in pictures. New York, Dutton, 1937. 363 p.

Originally published in German in 1929; first English edition, 1930. Reprint, New York, Dover, 1951. There is also a French edition.

Pictures include musicians' portraits, music in painting, drawing and sculpture; facsimile pages of early musical and theoretical works. Pictures of early instruments. Arranged chronologically from antiquity to the early 20th century. Index to instruments, place names, and personal names.

494 / **Komma, Karl Michael.** Musikgeschichte in Bildern. Stuttgart, Alfred Kröner, 1961. 332 p.

743 well-reproduced illustrations covering the history of music from ancient times to the present; detailed commentary on each illustration.

Review by Hans Engel in *Die Musikforschung*, 18 (1965), p. 440–41.

495 / **Lang, Paul Henry, and Otto Bettmann.** A pictorial history of music. New York, Norton, 1960. 242 p.

The text is based on Lang's *Music in Western civilization*, no. 431, with selected illustrations. Inferior reproduction technique.

496 / **Lesure, François.** Musik und Gesellschaft im Bild. Zeugnisse der Malerei aus sechs Jahrhunderten. . . . Aus dem Französischen von Anna Martina Gottshick. Kassel, Bärenreiter, 1966. 245 p. 105 plates, 24 in color.

Skillful use of pictorial materials to illuminate the musical-social structure of European culture from the 14th through the 19th centuries.

Review by Steven J. Ledbetter in *Notes*, 24 (1968), p. 702–04.

497 / **Pincherle, Marc.** An illustrated history of music. Ed. by Georges and Rosamond Bernier. Trans. by Rollo Myers. New York, Reynal, 1959. 221 p.

Published in France under the title *Histoire illustrée de la musique*. Paris, Gallimard, 1959.

A beautifully designed volume, with 200 illustrations in black and white, 40 in full color. The text is planned as an introduction to music history but maintains a high standard of accuracy and critical comment. The work lacks a bibliography or any other documentation apart from the illustrations.

Review by Denis Stevens in *The musical times*, 101 (Aug. 1960), p. 493; by Emanuel Winternitz in *Notes*, 18 (1960), p. 48–50; by Jack A. Westrup in *Music and letters*, 41 (1960), p. 388.

CHRONOLOGIES

498 / **Chailley, Jacques.** Chronologie musicale en tableaux synoptiques. Paris, Centre de Documentation Universitaire et S.E.D.E.S. réunis, 1955– . 140 p.
Part I: 310 to 1600.
A workbook of musical chronology, with parallel tables of political, literary, and artistic events. Most detailed for the period prior to the 15th century.

499 / **Detheridge, Joseph.** Chronology of music composers. Birmingham, J. Detheridge, 1936–1937. 2 v.
Vol. I: 820–1810. Vol. 2: 1810–1913.
More than 2,500 names of composers arranged chronologically by date of birth. Brief comments on their activity, fields of composition, nationality. Numerous inaccuracies and misleading statements, but valuable for its comprehensive coverage. Alphabetical list of names.
Reprint, 1972, by Scholarly Press, St. Clair Shores, Michigan.

500 / **Dufourcq, Norbert, Marcelle Benoit, et Bernard Gagnepain.** Les grandes dates de l'histoire de la musique. Paris, Presses Universitaires de France, 1969. 127 p. (Que sais-je? 1,333.)
Dates of events, with historical commentary, from the first century to 1960. Organized according to periods: Middle Ages, Renaissance, 17th, 18th, 19th and 20th centuries.

501 / **Eisler, Paul E.** World chronology of music history. Vol. 1– . Dobbs Ferry, New York, Oceana Publication, 1972–
An ambitious multivolume survey of the chronology of music, projected in eight to ten volumes. According to the publisher it will contain, when completed, over 100,000 entries covering all significant dates in music history: composers, compositions, performers, premieres, and other pertinent dates. Vol. I covers the period from *c.* 30,000 through the late 16th century.

502 / **Lahee, Henry Charles.** Annals of music in America; a chronological record of significant musical events from 1640 to the present day, with comments on the various periods into which the work is divided. Freeport, New York, Books for Libraries Press, 1970. 298 p.

Reprint of a work first published in 1922.

503 / **Mattfeld, Julius.** Variety music cavalcade, 1620–1961; a chronology of vocal and instrumental music popular in the United States. With an introduction by Abel Green. 3rd edition. Englewood Cliffs, N.J., Prentice-Hall, 1971. 766 p.

Originally appeared in a modified form as *Variety radio directory 1938–39*, supplemented in weekly issues of the periodical *Variety*. First issued as *Variety music cavalcade 1620–1650* in 1952. A revised edition appeared in 1962.

A chronological bibliography of American popular music, with parallel social and historical events listed for each year. Index of musical works by title, with dates of first publication.

Review by Irving Lowens in *Notes*, 20 (1963), p. 233–34.

Also entered as no. 962.

504 / **Mies, Paul, und N. Schneider.** Musik im Umkreis der Kulturgeschichte. Ein Tabellenwerk aus der Geschichte der Musik, Literatur, bildenden Künste, Philosophie und Politik Europas. Köln, P. J. Tonger, 1953. 2 v.

Vol. 1: chronological tables of musical periods and events. Vol. 2: parallel tables of history, philosophy, literature, art, and architecture.

505 / **Schering, Arnold.** Tabellen zur Musikgeschichte, ein Hilfsbuch beim Studium der Musikgeschichte. Fünfte Auflage bis zur Gegenwart ergänzt von Hans Joachim Moser. Wiesbaden, Breitkopf & Härtel, 1962. 175 p.

First published in 1914; 3rd edition, 1921; 4th edition, 1934.

Chronological tables outlining the important events in music history from antiquity to 1962, including birth and death dates of musicians, the principal events of their lives, significant publications and performances, dates marking the activity of important music centers, and stylistic developments. Parallel historical and cultural events given. The 4th edition contained a 30-page supplement giving the contents of the major *Denkmäler* and *Gesamtausgaben* published by Breitkopf & Härtel. The 5th edition deletes this but offers an index of names and subjects.

506 / **Slonimsky, Nicolas.** Music since 1900. 4th edition. New York, Charles Scribners's Sons, 1971. 1,595 p.

First published by Norton, N.Y., 1937; 2nd edition, 1938; 3rd edition, 1949.

Contains a "Tabular view of stylistic trends in music, 1900–1969." "Descriptive chronology: 1900–1969." Letters and documents. There is an index to the descriptive chronology. The first two editions contained a "Concise biographical dictionary of 20th-century musicians," omitted in later editions.

The chronology records significant events in the development of contemporary music: dates of composition and first performance, the founding of institutions and societies, births and death of contemporary musicians. International in scope, but with increased emphasis on American music for the past two decades. An appendix quotes many of the major documents in the history of contemporary music.

The 4th edition includes a dictionary of terms (p. 1421–1502).

Review by Jack Alan Westrup in *Music and letters*, 53 (1972), p. 447–48.

507 / **Thompson, Oscar.** Tabulated biographical history of music. New York, Harcourt, Brace, 1936.

13 folding charts tracing the major events in the careers of more than 100 musicians from Guido d'Arezzo (*c.* 995) through 1936.

120

Guides to Systematic and Historical Musicology

THIS SECTION lists a group of works designed to introduce the student to the methods, materials, and philosophy of musical research. These works vary widely in pattern and approach, some concerned with the content, others with the method of the discipline. Some emphasize the historical aspects of research, others the systematic. The present list is not intended to be exhaustive. The reader will find useful bibliographies of writings on musicology in Lincoln Spiess's *Historical musicology, Appendix I*, by Ernst C. Krohn (see no. 530 below) and in *Perspectives in musicology*, compiled by Barry S. Brook (see no. 511).

More than a century has passed since the term "Musikwissenschaft" was introduced by Friedrich Chrysander (*Jahrbücher für musikalische Wissenschaft*, 1863), and ever since that time musicologists have been attempting to define their field, to plot its structure and clarify its relationships to other areas in the humanities. For a general discussion of the history of musical scholarship and a comprehensive bibliography on the subject, see the article "Musikwissenschaft" by Walter Wiora and Hans Albrecht in *MGG*, vol. 9, col. 1192–1220.

121

508 / **Adler, Guido.** Methode der Musikgeschichte. Leipzig, Breitkopf & Härtel, 1919. 222 p.

Reprint by Gregg International, 1971.

This, along with the author's *Der Stil in der Musik* (1929), is a basic study of the content and method of historical musicology. Contains a bibliographical supplement, "Verzeichnis von bibliographischen Hilfswerken für musikhistorische Arbeiten," now outdated but of interest as a listing of music references prior to World War I.

509 / **Barbag, Seweryn.** Systematyka muzykologji. Lwów, "Lwowskie Wiadomości Muzyczne i Literackie," 1928. 111 p.

A Polish manual of musicological method, with bibliographical supplements: p. 56–91, general works of musicological interest; p. 91–98, Poilsh works of musicological interest.

510 / **Broeckx, Jan L.** Methode van de muziekgeschiedenis, met een inleiding door Prof. Dr. F. Van der Mueren. Antwerpen, Metropolis, 1959. 368 p.

A comprehensive survey of the methods and content of historical musicology. The three major divisions of the work treat (1) basic concepts, (2) working procedures, and (3) terminology. Numerous bibliographical references in the text and in a bibliographical appendix, p. 329–39.

511 / **Brook, Barry S., Edward O. D. Downes, and Sherman Van Solkema.** Perspectives in musicology. The inaugural lectures of the Ph.D. program in music at the City University of New York. New York, W. W. Norton, 1972. 363 p.

15 scholars, American and European, assess the position of their discipline and project its future.

P. 335–46: "Musicology as a discipline: a selected bibliography."

512 / **Chailley, Jacques,** ed. Précis de musicologie. Paris, Presses Universitaires de France, 1958. 431 p.

A syllabus published under the auspices of the Institute of Musicology of the University of Paris. Contributions by 25 French musicologists covering varied aspects of musical research. The emphasis is historical. Main approach is chronological, but there are chapters devoted to music bibliography, ethnomusicology, instruments, dance, philosophy, and aesthetics. Bibliography is stressed throughout.

513 / **Erdely, Stephen.** Methods and principles of Hungarian ethnomusicology. Bloomington, Indiana, Indiana University and Mouton and Co., The Hague, 1965. 150 p. (Indiana University Publications, Uralic and Altaic Series 52.)

Review by Benjamin Rajaczky in *Jahrbuch für Volksliedforschung*, 12 (1967), p. 233–34. By John S. Weissmann in *Ethnomusicology*, 11 (1967), p. 129–31.

514 / **Fellerer, Karl G.** Einführung in die Musikwissenschaft. 2. neubearb. und erweiterte Aufl. Münchberg, B. Hahnefeld, 1953. 190 p.

First published in 1942.

Historical musicology plays a comparatively minor role in this survey of the content of musical knowledge. Emphasis is on the systematic areas: acoustics, aesthetics, psychology, sociology, and pedagogy. Extensive bibliographies for each chapter.

Review by Glen Haydon in *Notes*, 11 (1953), p. 111–12; *anon* in *Die Musikforschung*, 8 (1955), p. 96–97.

515 / **Garrett, Allen M.** An introduction to research in music. Washington, Catholic University of America Press, 1958. 169 p.

A rather superficial attempt to survey the content and methods of musicology in a course intended for first year graduate students in music.

Review by Donald J. Grout in *Notes*, 16 (1959), p. 247–49.

516 / **Harrison, Frank Ll., Mantle Hood, and Claude V. Palisca.** Musicology. Englewood Cliffs, N.J., Prentice-Hall, 1963. 337 p. (The Princeton studies: humanistic scholarship in America.)

Harrison writes on "American musicology and the European tradition," Palisca on "American scholarship in Western music." and Hood on "Music, the unknown." Stimulating, throughtful statements on the place of musicology in the world of learning. The work has already exercised a wide influence on discussions of the nature and purposes of musical scholarship in America. See Joseph Kerman's paper on "A profile for American musicology," in *JAMS*, 18 (1965), p. 61–69, and the reply by Edward Lowinsky, "Character and purposes of American musicology," in the same journal, p. 222–34.

Review by Jan La Rue in *JAMS*, 17 (1964), p. 209–14; by Vincent Duckles in *Notes*, 21 (1964), p. 368–69; by Paul Henry Lang in a review editorial in *MQ*, 50 (1964), p. 215–26. Joint review by Charles

Seeger, Lincoln B. Spiess, and David McAllester in *Anuario, inter-American institute for musical research*, 1 (1965), p. 112–18.

517 / **Haydon, Glen.** Introduction to musicology: a survey of the fields, systematic and historical, of musical knowledge and research. New York. Prentice-Hall. 1941. 329 p.

Unaltered reprint by the Univ. of North Carolina Press, Chapel Hill, 1969.

Systematic musicology (acoustics, psychology, aesthetics, theory and pedagogy) occupies the major emphasis of this work. Historical musicology is treated only in the last 54 pages. Chapter bibliographies, with a general bibliography at the end, p. 301–13.

518 / **Helm, Eugene, and Albert T. Luper.** Words and music: form and procedure in theses, dissertations, research papers, book reports, programs, and theses in composition. Hackensack, N.J., Joseph Boonin, 1971. 78 p.

A manual emphasizing the technical and mechanical aspects of academic literature.

519 / **Hood, Mantle.** The ethnomusicologist. New York, Mc-Graw-Hill, 1971. 386 p.

A stimulating and practical exposition of what ethnomusicologists are and do. Illustrated.

Review by Willard Rhodes in *MQ*, 58 (1972), p. 136–41.

520 / **Husmann, Heinrich.** Einführung in die Musikwissenschaft. Heidelberg, Quelle und Meyer, 1958. 268 p.

An introduction to systematic musicology. Much attention is given to the acoustical and psychological aspects of the subject. The approach embraces all musical phenomena in all cultures. Extensive bibliography organized by chapter headings, p. 235–55.

Review by Werner Korte in *Die Musikforschung*, 13 (1960), p. 340–42.

521 / **Irvine, Demar B.** Methods of research in music. Part I: Methods. Seattle, Washington, 1945. 69 p. (typescript)

A syllabus for music research students at the college level. Emphasis on methodology, with chapters covering "the field," "the problem," "the sources," "the facts," "the report." No bibliography.

522 / **Irvine, Demar. B.** Writing about music, a style book for reports and theses. Section edition, revised and enlarged. Seattle and London, Univ. of Washington Press, 1968. 211 p.

A much enlarged edition of a work first published in 1956.

A guide to the preparation of the research report in music, with detailed instructions regarding the preparation of the manuscript, documentation, use of illustrations, abbreviations, and the improvement of literary style.

523 / **Kretzschmar, Hermann.** Einführung in die Musikgeschichte. Leipzig, Breitkopf & Härtel, 1920. 82 p. (Kleine Handbücher der Musikgeschichte, 7.)

A brief, narrative account of the content of and sources for the historical study of music. Relevant literature is mentioned in context. Chapter I traces the development of music historiography through the 19th century.

Also cited as no. 422.

524 / **Lissa, Zofia.** Wstep do muzykologii. Warszawa, Państwowe Wyda Wnictwo Naukowe, 1970. 228 p.

A Polish guide to musicological method by one of the leading musicologists of that nation. Covers both the historical and the systematic aspects of the disciple. Extensive chapter bibliographies.

525 / **Machabey, Armand.** La musicologie. Paris, Presses Universitaires de France, 1962. 128 p. (Que sais-je, 978.)

Brief, popular survey of the scope, content, and methods of musicology treated under five headings: "Sources," "Les élements," "Les formes," "Les instruments," "Diffusion." Highly selective bibliography.

526 / **Madsen, Clifford K., and Charles H. Madsen, Jr.** Experimental research in music. Englewood Cliffs, New Jersey, Prentice-Hall, 1970. 116 p.

A research manual emphasizing the quantitative and descriptive aspects of musical scholarship.

527 / **Morgan, Hazel B.** Music research handbook, for: music education, music theory, music history, music literature, musicology . . . in collaboration with Clifton A. Burmeister, Evanston, Ill., The Instrumentalist, 1962. 110 p.

A compendium of devices and methods intended to assist students in the preparation of "research" papers. What is implied by the term rarely extends beyond the requirements of a student's term report.

528 / **Riemann, Hugo.** Grundriss der Musikwissenschaft. 4. Aufl. durchgesehen von Johannes Wolf. Leipzig, Quelle und Meyer, 1928. 160 p. (Wissenschaft und Bildung, 34.)

529 / **Schiedermair, Ludwig.** Einführung in das Studium der Musikgeschichte: Leitsätze, Quellen, Übersichten und Ratschläge. 4. umbearb. und erweiterte Aufl. Bonn, F. Drümmlers Verlag, 1947, 167 p.

First published in 1918.

Brief surveys, with bibliographies, of the major historical periods. Concluding chapters deal with methodology, institutions, advice to students, etc. A useful appendix lists major *Gesamtausgaben* and the contents of publishers' series devoted to early music.

530 / **Spiess, Lincoln B.** Historical musicology, a reference manual for research in music . . . with articles by Ernst C. Krohn, Lloyd Hibberd, Luther A. Dittmer, Tsang-Houei Shu, Tatsuo Minagawa, Zdenek Novacek. Brooklyn, Institute of Medieval Music, 1963. 294 p.

A text and reference book of musical research, includes lists of suggested topics for class and seminar reports, term papers, and dissertations; with a copious bibliography, index of publishers, etc. [*Publishers' preface*]

The bibliography consists of 1,980 numbered items, in all categories, distributed throughout the text. Ernst C. Krohn's essay, "The development of modern musicology," p. 153–172, provides a useful bibliography of the history of the discipline.

Review by Vincent Duckles in *Notes*, 20 (1963), p. 469–71.

531 / **Watanabe, Ruth T.** Introduction to music research. Englewood Cliffs, N.J., Prentice-Hall, 1967. 237 p.

A useful discussion of the procedures, resources, and techniques preliminary to research activity in music. The main subdivisions are as follows: Part I, library orientation. Part II, the research paper. Part III, survey of research materials.

Review by Donald W. Krummel in *Notes*, 24 (1968), p. 481–82.

532 / **Westrup, Sir Jack Alan.** An introduction to musical history. New York, Harper and Row, 1964. 174 p.

First published in London, 1955, as a volume in the Hutchinson University Library.

This is not a history of music. It is simply an attempt to outline some of the problems which historians and students have to face, and to give some idea of the conditions in which music has come into existence. [Author's *Preface*]

Although intended as a layman's guide to music history, this little book is one of the few clear treatments of the problems of music historiography in English.

Review by Allen P. Britton in *Journal of research in music education*, 3 (1955), p. 154.

Bibliographies of
Music Literature

THE TERM "MUSIC LITERATURE" as applied here refers to writings on music as opposed to musical scores. Such writings may appear as periodical articles or monographs; they may be cited in complete, self-contained bibliographical works or in serial publications; and they can be organized in terms of a variety of subject fields. Nearly every dissertation or research study will have its appended bibliography of relevant literature, and most of the authoritative dictionaries or encyclopedias have subject bibliographies connected with their articles. It would be impossible to cite all of these resources, but the titles selected are numerous enough to form a substantial section of the present book. Following is an outline of the subdivisions employed:

Bibliographies of Music Literature
General
Current or Annual
Lists of Music Periodicals
Special and Subject Bibliographies
Contemporary Music
Dissertations

Ethnomusicology
Musical Instruments
Jazz
Medieval and Renaissance Music
Baroque and Classic Music
Music Education
National Music
Opera and Theater Music
Primary Sources: Early Music Literature
Sacred Music
Writings on Individual Composers

See also "Catalogs of Music Libraries and Collections." Many of the published catalogs of major libraries contain separate volumes or sections devoted to holdings in books on music.

GENERAL

533 / **Aber, Adolf.** Handbuch der Musikliteratur in systematisch-chronologischer Anordnung. Leipzig, Breitkopf & Härtel, 1922. 696 cols. (Kleine Handbücher der Musikgeschichte, 13.)

Reprints by Olms, Hildesheim, and Breitkopf & Härtel, Wiesbaden, 1967.

A classified bibliography for students of music history. International coverage, although strongest in German materials. Entries from at least 13 important musicological journals are included. Subject and author indexes.

Also listed as part of the *Kretzschmar* series of music history, no 428.

534 / **Adlung, Jacob.** Anleitung zu der musikalischen Gelahrtheit, 1758. Faksimile-Nachdruck hrsg. von H. J. Moser. Kassel, Bärenreiter, 1953. 814 p. (Documenta Musicologica, Erste Reihe, 4.)

2nd ed., revised by J. A. Hiller, 1783.

Chronologically one of the first important critical bibliographies of music literature. The author proposed to list all works on musical subjects necessary to "educated music lovers, and particularly to lovers

129

of keyboard music," as well as to builders of organs and other instruments.

See the description of this work in Gustav Reese's *Fourscore classics of music literature* (no. 782) New York, Liberal Arts Press, 1957. P. 74–75.

535 / **Azhderian, Helen Wentworth.** Reference works in music and music literature in five libraries of Los Angeles County. Los Angeles, Published for the Southern Calif. Chapter of the Music Library Association by the University of Southern Calif., 1953. 313 p.

A partial supplement of holdings in the USC Library, January 1952– June 1962. Prepared by Joan M. Meggett. 1962. 13 p.

A bibliography of musicological literature, approx. 4,500 entries. International coverage. Full bibliographical citations. Classified listing with author index. The libraries represented are The Henry E. Huntington Library, The William Andrews Clark Memorial Library, The Los Angeles Public Library, and the libraries of the University of Southern California and the University of California at Los Angeles.

Review by Otto Albrecht in *Notes*, 11 (1954), p. 468–69; by Vincent Duckles in *JAMS*, 7 (1954), p. 242–43.

536 / **Becker, Carl F.** Systematisch-chronologische Darstellung der musikalischen Literatur von der frühesten bis auf die neueste Zeit. . . . Leipzig, R. Friese, 1836. 571 cols. and 34 p.

Nachtrag, 1839.

Reprint by Frits A. M. Knuf, Hilversum, 1966.

Becker presents a classified bibliography of many now obscure works. His work fills the gap, chronologically, between *Lichtenthal* (no. 554) and Eitner's *Bücherverzeichniss*, 1885, (no. 548). Includes newspaper and periodical articles. Gives place of publication, date, pagination, with brief annotations; 33-page index by subject, author, etc.

537 / **Belknap, Sara Y.** Guide to the musical arts. New York, Scarecrow Press, 1957. (not paginated)

Indexes 11 English-language and 2 foreign music and theater journals for the period 1953–56. Two major sections: I: Articles; II: Illustrations. The *Guide* has serious shortcomings as a reference tool: unnumbered pages, confused entries, much space devoted to ephemera. Its chief value lies in the section on illustrations.

See also the author's *Guide to the performing arts*, no. 569.

538 / **Besterman, Theodore.** Music and drama: a bibliography of bibliographies. Totowa, N.J., Rowman and Littlefield, 1971. 365 p.

A listing extracted by the publisher from the 4th edition of the author's *World bibliography of bibliographies* (1965).

539 / **Bibliographia Hungarica, 1945–1960.** Catalogus systematicus notarum musicarum in Hungaria editarum. (ed. by I. Pethes, *et al.*) Budapest, Orszagos Szechenyi Konyvtar, 1969.

540 / **Blechschmidt, Renate.** "Bibliographie der Schriften über Musik aus der Deutschen Demokratischen Republik, 1945–59." In *Beiträge zur Musikwissenschaft*, Jahrg. 1 (1959), Heft 3, p. 51–75; Jahrg. 2 (1960), Heft 1, p. 50–68; Heft 2, p. 64–78.

Classified list covering the writings on music produced in Germany (East zone) for the 15-year period.

541 / **Blom, Eric.** A general index to modern musical literature in the English language, including periodicals for the years 1915–26. London, Philadelphia, Curwen [1927], 159 p.

Reprint of the 1927 edition by Da Capo, New York, 1970.

Entries for books by author and for parts of books by catchword subject in one alphabet.

542 / **Blum, Fred.** Music monographs in series; a bibliography of numbered monograph series in the field of music current since 1945. New York, Scarecrow Press, 1964. 197 p.

Gives contents of more than 259 monographic series in the music field originating in some 30 countries.

> Over one-third of them may best be described as broadly musicological in content, many issued under the auspices of universities or scholarly societies; others, ranging in tone from the academic to the popular, cover the gamut of musical subject matter. . . . [*Preface*]

Review by Thomas Watkins in *Current Musicology* (Fall, 1965), p. 227–29; by Richard Schaal in *Die Musikforschung*, 22 (1969), p. 521.

543 / **Breitkopf & Härtel** (Publishers). Das Musikbuch, eine nach Gruppen und Gattungen geordnete Zusammenstellung von Büchern über Musiker, die Musik und Instrumente, mit erläuternden Ein-

führungen . . . aus dem Verlage von Breitkopf & Härtel. Leipzig, Breitkopf & Härtel, 1913. 390 p.

Nachtragsband, 1926. 149 p.

A trade catalog of Breitkopf & Härtel books on music. Illustrated. Gives detailed descriptions of the works and their content. The book provides a useful survey of German music literature as issued by the leading music publisher of the first third of the 20th century.

544 / **Briquet, Marie.** La musique dans les congrès internationaux (1835–1939). Paris, Heugel, 1961. 124 p. (Publications de la Société Francaise de Musicologie, 2ème sér. Tome X.)

A bibliographical survey of the contributions on music made at international congresses from 1835 to 1939. Classified listing of 164 congress reports with the papers on music itemized. Indexed by place of meeting, by chronology, by author, and by subject.

Review by Richard Schaal in *Die Musikforschung,* 17 (1964), p. 183.

545 / **Büchting, Adolf.** Bibliotheca musica. Verzeichnis aller in Bezug auf die Musik . . . 1847–66, im deutschen Buchhandel erschienenen Bücher und Zeitschriften. Nebst Fortsetzung 1: die Jahre 1867–71 umfassend. Nordhausen, A. Büchting, 1867–72. 2 v.

A bibliography of music literature covering German publications from 1847 to 1871. The work takes its place chronologically after that of Becker (no 536) in the history of music bibliography. The gap of eight years in coverage between *Becker* and *Büchting* has been filled by Robert Eitner. See no. 548.

546 / **Carl Gregor, Duke of Mecklenburg.** Bibliographie einiger Grenzgebiete der Musikwissenschaft. Baden-Baden, Librairie Heitz, 1962. 200 p. (Bibliotheca bibliographica Aureliana, 6.)

A bibliography devoted to areas peripheral to the traditional emphasis of historical musicology. Includes books and periodical articles on aesthetics; psychology; sociology of music; relations between music and the other arts; musical interests of poets, writers, philosophers, etc. 3,519 entries, alphabetical by author, with indexes of subjects and of persons as subjects.

Review by Wolfgang Schmieder in *Die Musikforschung,* 20 (1967), p. 461–62.

547 / **Darrell, Robert D.** Schirmer's guide to books on music and musicians; a practical bibliography. New York, G. Schirmer, 1951. 402 p.

A bibliography of currently available (in 1951) books in English. Detailed subject classifications, numerous annotations. Full bibliographical information, including publisher's prices.

Appendix I, p. 346–77: selected books in French, German, Italian, and Spanish. Appendix II, p. 378–84: juvenile literature. Key to publishers, chiefly American.

Review by Raymond Kendall in *Notes*, 9 (1951), p. 119–20; by Richard S. Angell in *JAMS*, 5 (1952), p. 60–61.

548 / **Eitner, Robert.** Bücherverzeichnis der Musikliteratur aus den Jahren 1839 bis 1846 im Anschluss an Becker und Büchting . . . Leipzig, Breitkopf & Härtel, 1885. 89 p. (Monatshefte für Musikgeschichte. Beilage. 17. Jahrgang.)

Intended to bridge the gap between Becker's bibliography, no. 536 and Büchting's, no 545.

549 / **Forkel, Johann N.** Allgemeine Literatur der Musik, oder Anleitung zur Kenntniss musikalischer Bücher, welche von den ältesten bis auf die neusten Zeiten bey den Griechen, Römern und den meisten neuern europäischen Nationen sind geschrieben worden. Leipzig, Schwickert, 1792. 540 p.

Reprint of the original edition by Georg Olms, Hildesheim, 1962.

The first comprehensive bibliography of music literature and still a work of great utility. Classified listing of some 3,000 works on all aspects of musical knowledge, with brief biographical notices of the authors and descriptive annotations. Complete tables of contents are given for the most important books.

Forkel's classification system has served as the model for many subsequent bibliographies. See Scott Goldthwaite, "Classification problems, bibliographies of literature about music," in *Library Quarterly* Oct., 1948), p. 255 ff.

Forkel's work was expanded and translated into Italian by Pietro Lichtenthal in 1826. See no 554.

550 / **Gerboth, Walter.** An index to musical Festschriften and similar publications. New York, W. W. Norton, 1969. 188 p.

Expanded publication of a bibliographical work that first appeared in *Aspects of Medieval and Renaissance music, a birthday offering to Gustave Reese*, New York, W. W. Norton, 1966, p. 183–307.

The most comprehensive treatment of music Festschriften available. In three parts: A. List of Festschriften under the name of the individual or institution honored; B. Subject listing of more than 2,700 articles; C. Author and secondary-subject index.

Review by Donald Seibert in *Notes*, 26 (1970), p. 760–61.

551 / **Kahl, Willi, und Wilhelm-Martin Luther.** Repertorium der Musikwissenschaft. Musikschrifttum, Denkmäler und Gesamtausgaben in Auswahl (1800–1950) mit Besitzvermerken deutscher Bibliotheken und musikwissenschaftlicher Institute. Kassel, Bärenreiter, 1951. 271 p.

A comprehensive bibliography of music literature, broadly classified, including useful lists of Festschriften, conference reports, and critical editions. International in scope. Prepared as a union list of musicological holdings in postwar German libraries. Some 2,795 items. Indexed by persons, subjects, and geographical locations.

Review by Otto E. Albrecht in *Notes*, 11 (1954), p. 468–69; by Vincent Duckles in *JAMS*, 7 (1954), p. 242–45.

552 / **Krohn, Ernst C.** The history of music: an index to the literature available in a selected group of musicological publications. St. Louis, Washington University, 1952. 463 p. (Washington University Library Studies, 3.)

Reissued by Baton Music Co., St. Louis, 1958.

Classified index of articles on music history in 39 leading musicological publications—chiefly German and English periodicals. The general arrangement is chronological, with subdivisions by subject. Includes book reviews.

Review by Richard Appel in *Notes*, 10 (1952), p. 105–106; by Scott Goldthwaite in *JAMS*, 6 (1953), p. 250–51; by Wolfgang Schmieder in *Die Musikforschung*, 6 1953), p. 278–80.

553 / **Krohn, Ernst C.** "Musical Festschriften and related publications." In *Notes*, 21 (Winter–Spring, 1963–64), p. 94–108.

A useful listing of *Festschriften*, cited chronologically under four headings: A. works of major musicological interest; B. works compiled in homage to individual musicians, living or of the past; C. commemorative volumes consisting of original music; and D. those celebrating a particular institution, school, society, or performing group.

For a more complete bibliography of *Festschriften*, see under Gerboth, no 550 above.

554 / Lichtenthal, Pietro. Dizionario e bibliografia della musica. Milano, A. Fontana, 1826. 4 v.

Vols. 3 and 4 are a translation of Forkel's *Allgemeine Litteratur der Music* (no. 549) with additions to 1826. Vols. 1 and 2 are the dictionary of musical terms cited as no. 294.

555 / McColvin, Lionel R., and Harold Reeves. Music libraries, including a comprehensive bibliography of music literature and a select bibliography of music scores published since 1957. . . . Completely rewritten, revised, and extended by Jack Dove. London, Andre Deutsch, 1965. 2 v.

First published in 1937–38.

The bibliography of writings on music is found in vol. 2, p. 79–454. Classified according to a modified Dewey schedule; devoted chiefly to works in English. It is somewhat uneven, overdeveloped in topics of particular British interest, incomplete, and inconsistent in citation form.

The work is also cited as no. 813 and 890.

Review by J. P. S. in *Recorded Sound*, 20 (1965), p. 394–95.

556 / Materialy do Bibliografii Muzkyi Polskiej. (Series editor: Tadeusz Strumiłło.) Kraków, Polskie Wydawnictwo Muzyczne, 1954–1964. 4 v.

A series of bibliographies related to Polish music and music literature under the general editorship of Tadeusz Strumiłło.

Vol. I: by Kornel Michałowski; *Opery polskie*, 1954. 227 p. (Polish operas and foreign operas with Polish settings or subjects, listed by title, giving composer, librettist, date and place of first performance.)

Vol. II: Piésni solowe S. Moniuszki, katalog tematyczny. By Erwin Nowaczyk, 1954. 332 p. (Thematic catalog of 304 songs by Moniuszki, giving authors of texts, lists of editions.)

Vol. III: Bibliografia polskiego piśmiennictwa muzycznego. By Kornel Michałowski. 1955. 280 p. (Classified bibliography of books on music in Polish. Lists of theses and dissertations, 1917–54.)

A supplement to vol. III, published as vol. IV, contains classified listings of new Polish books on music published between 1955 and 1963, with some addenda from earlier years.

557 / **Matthew, James E.** The literature of music. London, E. Stock, 1896. 281 p.

Reprint by Da Capo Press, New York, 1969.

Essays on the literature of music in historical sequence to the 18th century, thereafter by topics: histories, biographies, dictionaries, sacred music, opera, instruments, music as a science, bibliography. Narrative style. Matthew, although out of date, provides the only self-contained study of music bibliography available in print. It still presents a useful survey of the earlier literature of music.

558 / **Musikliteratur.** Ein kritischer Führer für Bibliothekare. Berlin, Stadtbibliothek, 1929. 191 p. (Arbeiten der Volksbücherei-Zentrale in der Berliner Stadbibliothek, II..

Compiled by Dr. Karl Th. Bayer.

Classified, annotated bibliography of music literature in German. Designed for users of the Berlin public library. Contains a section in "Sing- und Spielmusik," otherwise restricted to books about music.

559 / **Petermann, Kurt.** Tanzbibliographie. Verzeichnis der in deutscher Sprache veröffentlichten Schriften und Aufsätze zum Bühnen-. Gesellschafts-, Kinder-, Volks-, und Turniertanz sowie zur Tanzwissenschaft, Tanzmusik und zum Jazz. Hrsg. vom Institut für Volkskunstforschung beim Zentralhaus für Kulturarbeit, Leipzig. Leipzig, VEB Bibliographisches Institut, 1966– .

Published in installments, nine of which appeared by 1970, a total of 720 p., covering 4,363 items.

The material is presented according to an organized scheme under 17 headings.

560 / **Refardt, Edgar.** Verzeichnis der Aufsätze zur Musik in den nicht-musikalischen Zeitschriften der Universitätsbibliothek Basel. Leipzig, Breitkopf & Härtel, 1925. 105 p.

A classified list of writings on music in over 500 nonmusical newspapers and peroidicals, arranged alphabetically by author. One of the few efforts to compile a bibliography of musical literature in journals outside of the music field.

561 / **Rösner, Helmut.** Nachdruckverzeichnis des Musikschrifttums. Reprints. Wilhelmshaven, Heinrichshofen's Verlag, 1971. 148 p. (Taschenfücher zur Musikwissenschaft, 5.) Ergänzungsband. Registerband. 1972. 143 p. (Taschenbücher zur Musikwissenschaft, 13.)

136

A bibliography covering reprints of music literature from the period 1960–1970. An alphabetical index of the output of approximately 68 reprint firms. No scores are included.

562 / **Scholes, Percy A.** A list of books about music in the English language prepared as an appendix to the *Oxford companion to music*. London, New York, Oxford University Press, 1940. 64 p.

A subject list which derives chiefly from the compilers' own ilbrary. Bibliographical information is uneven, frequently lacking in place of publication. An informal preface; some annotations.

563 / **Vinquist, Mary, and Neal Zaslaw.** Performance practice: a bibliography. New York, W. W. Norton, 1971. 114 p.

A bibliography of approximately 1200 entries; includes both primary and secondary sources. International in scope. The index brings out writings on major subtopics. P. 6: "a bibliography of performance practice bibliographies" (chiefly unpublished dissertations).

A supplement appears in *Current Musicology*, no. 12 (1971), p. 129–49, under the title "Performance practices bibliography."

564 / **Voorhees, Anna Tipton.** Index to symphonic program notes in books. [Kent, Ohio] School of Library Science, Kent State University, 1970. 136 p. (Keys to music bibliography, 1.)

Indexes 57 books which contain descriptive information on symphonic music. Works are listed alphabetically by composer. The source books are fully and critically annotated.

Review by Richard H. Hunter in *Notes*, 29 (1972), p. 254–55.

CURRENT OR ANNUAL
(Including Periodicals That Offer Regular Listings of
Music Literature)

The only way to keep abreast of publication in the field of music literature is to consul a variety of current listings. Many of these treat special subject areas within the field: ethnomusicology, music theory, sacred music, etc. Periodicals that carry regular listings of music literature are cited in this section by title, with annotations directing attention to the relevant departments. Several of the current bibliographies

of music (scores) are also concerned with music literature; see nos.
823, 829.

565 / **Acta Musicologica.** V. 1– . Internationale Gesellschaft für
Musikwissenchaft, 1928– .

"Index novorum librorum," a department appearing in most issues
of this journal, is one of the best sources of bibliographical information for the period between 1930 and 1950. It gives a classified listing
of books on music in all languages. The department was discontinued
after 1952.

See *An index to Acta Musicologica, Fall 1928–Spring 1967*, by Cecil
Adkins and Alis Dickinson. Basel, Bärenreiter. Author and subject
index.

566 / **African Music.** Journal of the African music society, v.
1– . Roodepoort, Transvaal, Union of South Africa, 1954– .

Each annual issue has a section of "books and pamphlets received"
as well as reviews of current publications in ethnomusicology.

567 / **American Bibliographic Service.** Quarterly checklist of
musicology. An international index of current books, monographs,
brochures, and separates. V. 1– . Darien, Connecticut, American Bibliographic Service, 1959– .

An unclassified numbered listing of current writings on music. The
selection is broad and rather uncritical. Full bibliographical information, including prices. Indexed by authors, editors, and translators in
the last issue of each volume

568 / **"Articles Concerning Music in Non-musical Journals 1949–
64."** In *Current musicology* (Spring, 1965), p. 121–27; (Fall, 1965)
p. 221–26.

The first installment stresses articles on historical subjects; the
second, articles under various systematic headings: acoustics, philosophy and aesthetics, music in literature, psychology, sociology, etc.

569 / **Belknap, Sara Y.** The guide to the performing arts,
1957– . v. 1– . New York, Scarecrow Press, 1960– .

Annual periodical index to the performing arts. Began as a supplement to the compiler's *Guide to the musical arts* (no. 537). Contains
a "general" section and a "television arts" section. References to performing groups and performers as well as general subject headings.

570 / **Bibliographia Musicologica,** a bibliography of musical literature. Vol. 1, 1968. Utrecht, Joachimsthal, 1970– .

An international bibliography of books about music, listed alphabetically by author, with a subject index. Vol. 1 is devoted to literature published in 1968, 2,170 items. Vol. 2, covering literature for 1969, runs to 2,057 items. The listings give publisher, pagination, and price and include current reprints, facsimile editions, and revised editions.

571 / **"Bibliographie der Aufsätze zur Musik in aussermusikalischen Italienischen Zeitschriften."** In *Analecta musicologia,* Veröffentlichungen der Musikabteilung des deutschen historischen Instituts in Rom. Bd. I (1963), p. 90–112. Bd. II (1965), p. 144–228.

A bibliography of writings on music in Italian nonmusical journals. Part 1 by Paul Kast. Part 2 by Ernst-Ludwig Berz. The two installments are organized somewhat differently and indexed independently. The first contains 237 entries, the second, 1,074.

572 / **Bibliographie des Musikschrifttums.** Jahrgang 1936– . Leipzig, Frankfurt a.M., F. Hofmeister, 1936– . (Herausgegeben im Auftrage des Instituts für Musikforschung, Berlin.)

Editors: 1936–37, Kurt Taut; 1938–39, Georg Karstädt; (1940–49, suspended publication) 1950– , Wolfgang Schmieder.

A bibliography of books and an index to periodical literature in all European languages. A large number of nonmusical journals included. Classified by broad subjects, with an index of names (author and subject) and places. The emphasis is on "serious" music.

This bibliography follows in a direct line of descent of the listings in the *Peters Jahrbuch,* no. 585.

Review of *Jahrgang 1950–51* by Richard Schaal in *Die Musikforschung,* 8 (1955), p. 371–72; by Richard S. Hill in *Notes,* 11 (1954), p. 555–57; by Scott Goldthwaite in *JAMS,* 8 (1955), p. 55–57. Review of *Jahrgang 1952–53* by Richard Schaal in *Die Musikforschung,* 10 (1957), p. 440.

573 / **A Bibliography of Periodical Literature in Musicology** . . . Nos. 1–2 1938–39, 1939–40), Washington, D.C., American Council of Learned Societies, 1940–43. 2 v.

Indexes approximately 240 periodicals, all European languages, musical and nonmusical, from Oct. 1938 through Sept. 1940. Signed abstracts or annotations for most of the articles. Vol. 1 contains a list of graduate theses accepted in American colleges, universities, and conservatories, Oct. 1, 1938–Sept. 1, 1939.

Vol. 1 compiled by D. H. Dougherty. Vol. 2, added compilers: Leonard Ellinwood and Richard S. Hill.

574 / **Bollettino Bibliografico Musicale** (Milan) v. 1: 1 (Sept. 1926)– v. 8: 4/5 (April/May 1933). n.s. v. 1: 1 (Jan/Feb. 1952)– v. 1: 7/8 (Aug/Sept. 1952).

A journal devoted to matters of bibliographical interest in music; each issue customarily contains a bibliography of the works of one composer, early or contemporary, chiefly Italian. Regular departments give listings of current music publications, the contents of music journals, music and book reviews.

575 / **Brass Quarterly.** V. 1– . Milford, New Hampshire. The Cabinet Press, 1967– .

Edited by Mary Rasmussen.

Contains in each issue reviews of recordings and scores of brass music as well as a section of "Current publications" classified by instrument or ensemble.

576 / **Brio.** Journal of the United Kingdom Branch of IAML.

"Index of articles published in selected musical periodicals," compiled by Christel Wallbaum. In *Brio,* 1964– .

A biannual subject index to articles in some 23 English-language music periodicals. The listings cover the periods January to June and July to December for each year.

577 / **Bulgarski Muzikalen Knigopis:** trimesechen bibliografski biuletin za novoizliazla literatura po muzika i noti. Soffia, 1958– . (Bulgarski Bibliografski Institut "Elin Pelin.")

Quarterly, classified list of books and periodical articles on music and publications in musical notation issued in Bulgaria. Cumulative index, the October-December issue containing index for the entire year.

578 / **Deutsche Musikbibliographie.** Jahrgang 1– . Leipzig, F. Hofmeister, 1829– .

Title varies: 1829–1942, *Hofmeisters musikalisch-literarischer Monatsbericht.*

Lists German, Swiss, and Austrian publications of music and music literature. Alphabetical by author, giving date and place of publication, pagination, and price. A monthly publication useful chiefly for its listings of music. Indexed by publisher. Entries are cumulated in Hofmeister's *Jahresverzeichnis* . . . (no. 588).

Also cited as no. 827.

579 / **Deutsche Staatsbibliothek (Berlin).** Neuerwerbungen ausländischer Musikliteratur. Vol. 1– . Berlin, Deutsche Staatsbibliothek, 1956– . (Bibliographische Mitteilungen, Nr. 12, 1954–55; Nr. 16, 1956–57; Nr. 19, 1958–60.)

Classified lists of books on music and foreign publications acquired by the Deutsche Staatsbibliothek (East Berlin). Issued at irregular intervals as part of the library's series of *Bibliographische Mitteilungen*. The three volumes appeared in 1956, 1958, and 1962 respectively.

580 / **Deutscher Büchereiverband. Arbeitsstelle für das Büchereiwesen.** Zeitschriftendienst Musik (ZD). 1. Jahrgang—Berlin, Deutscher Büchereiverband, 1966– .

A monthly periodical index of articles from some 50 music periodicals, chiefly German. Approximately 3,000 articles are indexed per year. The editors are Burchard Bulling and Sibylle Schneider. Monthly number 12 is a cumulative volume for the year. Titles are arranged in alphabetical order under subject headings. The listings can also be purchased in card-size format for filing.

581 / **Ethnomusicology.** Journal of the Society for ethnomusicology. Vol. 1– . Middletown, Conn., Wesleyan Univ. Press, 1953– .

Title varies: 1953–57, *Ethno-Musicology Newsletter*.

Imprint varies: after Jan. 1972, "Published by the Society for Ethnomusicology, Inc."

Each issue contains a section of "current bibliography," listing books and periodical articles related to the field. After January 1967 the lists include "discography." Organized by geographical areas and occasional topics, e.g., "dance." The journal also publishes from time to time special bibliographies devoted to the work of leading ethnomusicologists.

582 / **Fontes Artis Musicae.** Review of the International Association of Music Libraries. V. 1– . Paris, International Association of Music Libraries, 1954– .

Each issue contains a "Liste internationale sélective" of music publications classified by country. Music literature appears under the subheading "Ouvrages sur la musique et ouvrages didactiques."

583 / **Hofmeisters Handbuch der Musikliteratur.** Bd. 1– . Leipzig, F. Hofmeister, 1844–

Cumulation of the *Jahresverzeichnis der deutschen Musikalien und Musikschriften.* (no. 588)

Preceded by a similar work compiled by C. F. Whistling and published by Anton Meysel, Leipzig, 1817, listing music and music literature through 1815, with 10 supplements (1 published by Meysel, 2–8 by Hofmeister, 9-10 by Whistling) to 1827. This initial volume, with its 10 supplements, has been reprinted in two volumes by Vienna House, New York, 1972, under the title *Handbuch der musikalischen Litteratur.*

Title varies: Vols. 1–3 (to 1844), C. F. Whistling's *Handbuch der musikalischen Literatur.* Vols. 4–6 (1844–67), *Handbuch der musikalischen Literatur.* Vols. 4–18 (1844–1933), also called *Ergänzungsband 1–15.*

Publication interrupted in Vol. 19 (1943) covering the years 1934–40, through the letter "L" in the alphabet.

The Handbuch is of greatest importance for its music (score) listings, but each volume contains an *Anhang* devoted to books and writings on music. The long life of the series, plus the leading position occupied by German music publishing houses during the period covered, make it one of the major reference tools.

For a detailed description of the organization of this complex trade bibliography, see "A survey of the music catalogues of Whistling and Hofmeister," by Rudolf Elvers and Cecil Hopkinson, in *Fontes artis musicae,* 19 (1972), p. 1–7.

The entry is also cited under *Bibliographies of music,* (no. 830) by virtue of its music listings.

584 / **International Inventory of Music Literature.** RILM abstracts of music literature, 1– . Jan/Apr., 1967– . New York, International RILM Center.

An international quarterly journal devoted to abstracts of current literature on music. Published under the aegis of the International Musicological Society and the International Association of Music Libraries.

Contents in a clear classified arrangement. Abstracts are all given in English. Foreign titles are translated, including those in the Cyrillic alphabet. Each issue contains an author index, and every fourth issue cumulates the entries for the year. The whole is programmed for eventual computer control.

For a full discussion of the RILM project and its implications, see Barry S. Brook, "Music literature and modern communication; revolutionary potential of the ACLS/CUNY/RILM project," in *College Music Symposium*, 9 (1969) p. 48–59.

Review in the *ALA Booklist*, 65 (1969), p. 1239–41.

585 / **Jahrbuch der Musikbibliothek Peters.** V. 1–47. Leipzig, C. F. Peters, 1895–1941.

Most issues contain a section entitled "Verzeichnis der in allen Kulturländern erschienenen Bücher und Schriften über Musik," edited at various times by Rudolf Schwartz, Emil Vogel, Eugen Schmitz, and Kurt Taut. Does not include periodical literature. This section, expanded to include periodical articles, has been continued as the *Bibliographie des Musikschrifttums*, published separately (no 572).

586 / **Jahrbuch für Liturgik und Hymnolgie.** Bd. 1– . Kassel, Johannes Stauda- Verlag, 1955– .

Each volume contains an extensive "Literaturbericht," classified, frequently annotated, and covering all aspects of liturgics and hymnology.

587 / **Jahrbuch für Volksliedforschung.** Im Auftrag des Deutschen Volksliedarchivs. Erster Jahrgang– Berlin & Leipzig, Walter De Gruyter, 1928– .

Editors vary. The yearbook ceased publication between 1951 and 1964.

From 1965 to date it has carried an extensive section devoted to reviews ("Besprechungen") covering the important literature in the field of folksong research.

588 / **Jahresverzeichnis der Deutschen Musikalien und Musikschriften.** Jahrgang 1– . Leipzig, F. Hofmeister, 1852– .

An annual listing which cumulates the material in the *Deutsche Musikbibliographie* (no. 578) and is, in turn, cumulated in *Hofmeisters Handbuch der Musikliteratur* (no. 583).

Title varies: Vols. 1–77 (1852–1928): *Verzeichnis der im Jahre . . . erschienen Musikalien.* Vols. 78–91 (1929–42): *Hofmeisters Jahresverzeichnis.*

Also cited as no. 831.

589 / **Journal of Aesthetics and Art Criticism,** 1941–1964 . . . an index by Peter L. Ciurczak, of articles and book reviews pertaining to music. Emporia, Kansas State Teachers Coll., 1965.

590 / **Journal of the International Folk Music Council.** V. 1– . Published with the assistance of the International Music Council under the auspices of UNESCO, 1949– .

Superseded by the council's *Yearbook,* 1969– . Urbana, Univ. of Illinois Press.

Each volume of this yearly publication contains a section "Publications received," which gives a brief, authoritative survey of a wide range of publications in the field, including periodicals, recordings, and important articles.

591 / **Literature, Music, Fine Arts:** a review of German-language research contributions on literature, music, and fine arts. With bibliographies. Vol. 1– . Tübingen, 1968– . (German studies. Section 3.)

Appears twice a year. A journal devoted to reviews and listings of cultural studies in the German language. All titles and reviews are given in English. The music section provides a useful tool for acquisition purposes.

Some 15 to 20 titles are selected for review, followed by a listing of 75 to 100. Information includes prices.

592 / **Journal of Music Theory.** V. 1– . New Haven, Yale School of Music, 1957– .

Each issue contains a "Bibliography of current periodical literature" covering articles related to music theory.

593 / **Music Article Guide.** A comprehensive quarterly reference guide to significant signed feature articles in American music periodicals. V. 1– . Philadelphia, Pa., Music Article Guide, 1966– .

Indexes (as of 1970) some 158 music periodicals, including many of local or highly specialized interest. Entries are grouped by subject and numbered consecutively within each issue. Indexed by title and author. Brief annotations. Nearly every issue contains a "Dictionary of American music periodicals" listing the journals by title with their addresses.

The *Guide* changed in format after the first volume, from a small loose-leafed volume to full-page typescript.

Published quarterly in 10 categories, one of which is "Musicology."

Review by Bennet Ludden in *Notes*, 24 (1967), p. 719–20, and anon. in *ALA Booklist*, 65 (1969), p. 1239–41.

594 / **The Music Index;** the key to current music periodical literature. V. 1, no. 1– . Detroit, Information Service, Inc., Jan. 1949– .

Currently indexes more than 225 periodicals by subject and author. Published in 12 monthly numbers, with an annual cumulation. Reviews are indexed under "Book reviews."

Review of 1954 annual cumulation by Richard Appel in *Notes*, 14 (1957), p. 364–65; of the 1955 and 1956 cumulations by James B. Coover in *Notes*, 16 (1958), p. 45–46. Review by Richard Schaal in *Die Musikforschung*, 10 (1957), p. 442–43 and anon. in *ALA Booklist*, 65 (1969), p. 123–24.

595 / **Music Library Association Notes,** a magazine devoted to music and its literature. 2nd ser. 1– . The Music Library Association, 1948– .

"Book reviews," a department compiled and edited by a variety of editors and supplemented by a list of current publications on music, is the most comprehensive listing of current music literature available. Since December 1950, the list has been international in scope; classified by language.

596 / **Music Teachers National Association. Committee on Literature about Music.** "Report." 1906– . In its *Proceedings* (annual) 1906– .

Classified lists of books on music in English, giving author, title, publisher, pagination, and price. Includes some translations, new editions, and reprints. Excellent listings of material in English; carefully selected, some annotations. Listed by authors and subjects.

145

597 / **Musica Disciplina.** A yearbook of the history of music. V. 1– . American Institute of Musicology, 1946– .

Title varies: Vol. 1, *Journal of Renaissance and Baroque music.*

Most of the volumes contain a bibliography of books, periodical articles, and editions related to early music, doctoral dissertations included. Compiled since 1958 by Wolfgang Schmieder.

598 / **"Musical Literature."** In *The British catalogue of music.* London, Council of the British National Bibliography, 1957– .

An annual listing, broadly classified, of all books about music published in Great Britain. "Musical literature" appears first in the classified section. Scores, however, occupy the greater part of the volumes. Indexed by author and title.

See also no. 823.

599 / **The Musical Quarterly.** V. 1– . New York, G. Schirmer, 1915– .

The "Quarterly Book-List" in each issue is a selection of books of musicological interest in all languages. Less comprehensive than the current listings in *Notes* (no. 595 above). Compilers, successively, since 1936: Edward N. Waters, Lee Fairley, Frank C. Campbell, Donald W. Krummel, Carroll D. Wade, and Fred Blum.

600 / **The Musical Quarterly. Cumulative Index.** 1915 thru 1959 [v. 1–45]. Compiled by Herbert K. Goodkind. New York, Goodkind Indexes [1960]. 204 p.

Cumulative index supplement, 1960 thru 1962. New York, 1963.

The main volume indexes by author and subject in separate alphabets, the *Supplement* in one alphabet. Indexes book reviews and "Current chronicle" as well as articles.

601 / **Music and Letters.** Index to volumes 1–40, 1920–59. London, Oxford Univ. Press [1962]. 140 p.

An index compiled largely by Eric Blom before his death in 1959 and completed by Jack A. Westrup. Two major sections. 1: articles (filed by author and subject in one alphabet). 2: reviews (similarly treated). Reviews of music are not indexed.

602 / **National Association of Schools of Music.** A list of books on music. Cincinnati, 1935. 57 p.

Supplements 1–10, 1936–57.

Primarily an annotated listing of books in English, with smaller selections of foreign music literature, critical editions, contemporary American scores. Prices given through the eighth supplement. A cumulative index of the original list and the first seven supplements was printed in 1952.

603 / **The Organ.** Index to *The Organ*. A complete index to all articles in *The Organ*, 1921–1970, from the first issue to date. Compiled by Betty Matthews. Bournemouth, K. Mummery, 1970.

604 / **La Rassegna Musicale.** Indice generale delle annate 1928–52 [v. 1–22]. Torino, Roggero & Tortia [1953]. 174 p.

An index, compiled by Riccardo Allorto, of articles, musical performances, reviewed, book reviews, record reviews, and musical subjects.

> **RILM Abstracts of Music Literature**
> See **International Inventory of Music Literature . . .**
>   no. 584.

605 / **Rivista Musicale Italiana.** Indici dei volumi I a XX (1894–1913). Compiled by Luigi Parigi. Torino, Fratelli Bocca, 1917. 256 p.

Indici dei volumi XXI a XXXV (1914–1928). Compiled by A. Salvatori and G. Concina. Torina, 1931. 195 p.

Indici dei volumi XXXVI a LVII (1929–1955). Compiled by Francesco Degrada. Firenze, Leo S. Olschki, 1966. 144 p. (Quaderni della Rivista Italiana di Musicologia a cura della Società Italiana di Musicologie, 1.)

Review of the Degrada index by Ludwig Finscher in *Die Musikforschung*, 21 (1968), p. 365–66.

606 / **Royal Musical Association.** Index to papers read before the members . . . 1874–1944. Leeds, Printed by Whitehead & Miller for the Royal Association, 1948. 56 p.

A subject and an author index to the first 70 volumes of the *Proceedings* of the Association. Compiled by Alfred Lowenberg and Rupert Erlebach.

607 / **[Sovetskaia Literatura o Muzyke]** 1948–53. Compilers S. L. Uspenskaia and B. Yagolim. Moskva, Izdatel'stvo vsesoiuznoi knizhnoi palaty, 1955. 343 p.

A classified list of books and periodical articles in Russian. A bibliograhpical series, issued irregularly; further volumes have appeared as follows:

1958, covering the years 1954–56
1959, covering the year 1957
1963, covering 1958–59
1967, covering 1960–62
1971, covering 1963–65

Title and imprint varies. Name index; list of periodicals.

608 / **Speculum.** An index of musically related articles and book reviews, compiled by Arthur S. Wolf. Ann Arbor, Michigan, Music Library Association Executive Office, 1970. (MLA index series, 9.)

This index appeared originally under the title, *Speculum: a journal of mediaeval studies, 1926–1962 . . . a checklist of articles and book reviews pertaining to music.* Denton, North Texas State Univ., 1965.

This item is also entered as no. 1909.

609 / **Svensk Tidskrift för Musikforskning.** V. 1– . Stockholm, 1919– .

Since 1927 the *Tidskrift* has maintained an annual listing of "Svensk musikhistorisk bibliografi," compiled since 1946 by Åke Davidsson. Broadly classified. Indexes Swedish periodicals.

610 / **Vierteljahrsschrift für Musikwissenschaft.** Ed. by Friedrich Chrysander & Philipp Spitta. V. 1–10. Leipzig, 1885–94.

Each volume contains a section, "Musikalische Bibliographie," compiled by F. Ascherson, which usually includes a listing of scholarly music books, critical editions, and the contents of current scholarly periodicals in all European languages.

611 / **Zeitschrift der Internationalen Musikgesellschaft.** V. 1–15. Leipzig, 1899/1900–13/14.

Most issues contain departments under the headings, "Kritische Bücherschau" and "Zeitschriftenschau." The latter indexes approximately 84 periodicals, chiefly musical, in many languages. Vols. 1–11 by author only. Vols. 12–15 by subject with "see" references from the author.

612 / **Zeitschrift für Musikwissenschaft.** V. 1–17. Leipzig, 1918–35.

Indexes once a year the periodical literature on music in some 200 journals, in many languages. 1914–18 covered retrospectively in the 1918 index, thus articulating with no. 611 above.

LISTS OF MUSIC PERIODICALS

One of the most comprehensive lists of music periodicals is to be found in the article "Zeitschriften" compiled by Imogen Fellinger for *MGG* (see no. 38). Dr. Fellinger's bibliography of 19th-century music periodicals (no. 621) gives virtually complete coverage for the century under her consideration. Still valuable is A. Hyatt King's article, "Periodicals," in the 5th edition of *Grove* (no. 21). The best chronological survey of the early music periodicals is offered by Freystätter (no. 623) but this has been supplemented and expanded in certain respects by the recent historical study by Rohlfs (no. 635).

Musicians should also be aware of the resources of a number of general reference works devoted to periodicals, such as Ulrich's *International periodicals directory* and the *Union List of serials*.

613 / **Blum, Fred.** "East German music journals: a checklist." In *Notes*, 19 (1962), p. 399–410.

100 periodicals listed in alphabetical order (including secondary titles, former titles, and subsequent titles). Gives a critical description of a variety of East German music serials.

614 / **Campbell, Frank C.** A critical annotated bibliography of periodicals. New York, American Choral Foundation, 1962. 14 p. (American choral foundation. Memo 33.)

Evaluates 44 periodicals that treat choral music and materials, giving pertinent details (addresses, price, emphasis, etc.).

615 / **Canadian Library Association.** Union list of music periodicals in Canadian libraries. Compiled by a committee of the Canadian Library Association. Ottawa, 1964. 32 p.

Committee chairman: Jean Lavander.

Gives data on holdings in music periodicals of 66 Canadian libraries. Brief annotations on the nature and content of each periodical listed.

616 / **Clough, F. F., and G. J. Cuming.** "Phonographic periodicals, a survey of some issued outside the United States." In *Notes*, 15 (1958), p. 537–58.

A critical description of some 30 foreign periodicals devoted to recordings, with comments on record coverage in general periodicals.

617 / **Coover, James B.** "A bibliography of East European music periodicals." In *Fontes artis musicae* (1956) p. 219–26; (1957) p. 97–102; (1958) p. 44–45, 93–99; (1959) p. 27–28; (1960) p. 16–21, 69–70; (1961) p. 75–90; (1962) p. 78–80.

This bibliography is an attempt at a comprehensive and authoritative listing of all music periodicals which have been and which are being published in the countries of Bulgaria, Czechoslovakia, Estonia, Finland, Hungary, Latvia, Lithuania, Poland, Rumania, the U.S.S.R., and Yugoslavia. [Compiler's introduction]

618 / **"Directory of American Music Periodicals,"** in *Music article guide*, vol. 1– , Philadelphia, Pa., Music Article Guide, 1966– .

Nearly every issue of the *Guide* carries a list of periodicals, indexed, with the addresses of editors or publishers given. A useful guide to current American music periodicals.

619 / **"Europäische Musikzeitschriften 1945–48."** In *Jahrbuch der Musikwelt*. Bayreuth, J. Steeger, 1949–50. p. 111–23.

A listing useful chiefly as an indication of the periodicals current during the period after World War I. Organized by country. Information brief and inconsistent, with German periodicals given most complete coverage; Russian, Czech, and others very incomplete.

620 / **Fairley, Lee.** "A check-list of recent Latin American music periodicals." In *Notes*, 2 (1945), p. 120–23.

Treats 23 periodicals from the collections of the Library of Congress and the Pan American Union, with brief comments on each. Covers publications between 1940 and 1947.

621 / **Fellinger, Imogen.** Verzeichnis der Musikzeitschriften des 19. Jahrhunderts. Regensburg, Gustav Bosse, 1969. 557 p. (Studien zur Musikgeschichte des 19. Jahrhunderts, 10.)

Locates and lists chronologically more than 2,300 music periodicals, with a rich supply of bibliographical information. Actual coverage extends through journals established as late as 1918.

P. 10–28: historical survey of 19th-century music periodicals. P. 33–37: a bibliography of literature on periodicals. Five indexes: titles, editors, places of publication, printers and publishers, subjects.

Since the initial publication, a series of supplements have appeared in *Fontes artis musicae:* Nachträge, Folge 1, in vol. 17 (1970), p. 2–8. Nachträge, Folge 2, in vol. 18 (1971), p. 59–62. Nachträge, Folge 3, in vol. 19 (1972), p. 41–44.

Review by J. A. Westrup in *Music and letters,* 50 (1969), p. 400–03; by Philip Gossett in *Notes,* 26 (1970), p. 740–41; by Willi Reich in *Literature, music, fine arts,* 2 (1969), p. 200.

622 / **Fredricks, Jessica M.** "Music magazines of Britain and the U.S." In *Notes,* 6 (1949), p. 239–63, 457–59, 7 (1950), p. 372–76.

Lists 200 music periodicals arranged alphabetically by title, with a subject and type index. Brief descriptions of character and contents.

623 / **Freystätter, Wilhelm.** Die musikalischen Zeitschriften seit ihrer Entstehung bis zur Gegenwart. Chronologisches Verzeichnis der periodischen Schriften über Musik. München, T. Riedel, 1884. 139 p.

Unaltered reprint of the original edition by Frits A. M. Knuf, Hilversum, 1963.

Based on E. Gregoir's *Recherches historiques concernant les journaux de musique,* Antwerp, 1872.

A chronological listing, from 1722 to 1844, with extensive annotations as to content, editors, contributors, etc. Still valuable as a convenient source of information on early music periodicals.

624 / **Kallman, Helmut.** "A century of musical periodicals in Canada." In *The Canadian music journal,* 1:1 (1956), p. 37–43; 1:2 (1957), p. 25–35.

The last installment contains a section entitled: "A checklist of Canadian periodicals in the field of music," p. 30–36.

625 / **Malm, William P.** "A bibliography of Japanese magazines and music." In *Ethnomusicology*, 3 (1959), p. 76–80.

Annotated bibliography of 25 Japanese periodicals related to music and the dance. Place, publisher, date of first issue, and price given.

626 / **Michałowski, Kornel.** Bibliografia polskich czasopism muzycznych. Kraków, Polskie Wydawnictwo Muzyczne, 1955– .

A bibliography of Polish music periodicals; classified listings of their contents from 1820 to 1939. 10 vols. to 1964.

627 / **Music Library Association. Northern California Chapter.** A union list of music periodicals in the libraries of Northern California. Edited by C. R. Nicewonger. Published for the Resources Committee, Northern Calif. Chapter, Music Library Association, 1965. 141 leaves (typescript).

Covers the music periodical holdings of 24 Northern California libraries, including both public and academic institutions. A new edition is in preparation, as of 1973.

628 / **"Periodicals and Other Serial Publications."** In *Reference works in music and music literature in five libraries of Los Angeles County.* Edited by Helen W. Azhderian. Los Angeles, 1953. p. 213–39.

629 / **"Music Periodicals, United States."** In *The musician's guide: the directory of the world of music.* 1972 edition. New York, Music Information Service, Inc., 1972. p. 438–457.

Also "Music periodicals foreign." p. 458–500. Grouped alphabetically under countries. Addresses given; editor's name.

630 / **"Periodicals Indexed."** In *The music index annual cumulation.* Detroit, Information Service, Inc.

Regularly indexes some 230 current periodicals. Addresses and subscription prices given. In its first year (1949) the *Index* treated only 81 titles. Since that time there has been a constant increase in the number of periodicals covered.

631 / **"Periodicals."** In *Grove's dictionary of music and musicians,* 5th ed., vol. 6, p. 638–65.

A list, compiled by A. Hyatt King, of over 1,000 music periodicals from all parts of the world, arranged by countries in chronological order of the date of first appearance.

See also the corrections and additions to the above list in the *Supplementary volume* (1961) to *Grove's*, p. 344–47.

632 / **"Periodische Schriften."** In *Jahrbuch der Musikbibliothek Peters*. v. 1–47. Leipzig, C. F. Peters, 1894–1941.

A regular section of the annual "Verzeichnis . . . Bücher und Schriften über Musik," listing new periodicals and other serial publications that have been issued during the year. Compiled by a variety of editors.

633 / **"Revistas Musicales."** In *Diccionario de la música Labor*. Barcelona, Labor, 1954. v. 2, p. 1863–70.

An extensive listing of music periodicals, classified by country, with a short bibliography on musical journalism.

634 / **Riedel, A.** Répertoire des periodiques musicaux belges. Bruxelles, Commission belge de bibliographie, 1954. 48 p. (Bibliographia belgica, S.)

330 items, of which the first 130 are music serials; the remainder are periodicals in the usual sense.

635 / **Rohlfs, Eckart.** Die deutschsprachigen Musikperiodica, 1945–57. Regensburg, G. Bosse, 1961. 108 p. (Forschungsbeiträge zur Musikwissenschaft, 11.)

A source book of information about music periodicals, their history, coverage, distribution, and subject emphasis. Not confined to German journals as the title might suggest. The systematic bibliographic *Anhang*, p. 5–64, lists 589 periodicals in 12 categories. Indexed by chronology, place, title.

Review by Fred Blum in *Notes*, 19 (1961), p. 77–78. By Wolfgang Schmieder in *Die Musikforschung*, 21 (1968), p. 105–107.

636 / **Savig, Norman.** A check-list of music serials in 18 libraries of the Rocky Mountain region. Greely, Colorado, Kastle Kiosk, 1970. 45 p. (typescript)

This list includes music serials in the general sense of the word: periodicals, newspapers, annuals, proceedings, transactions of societies and

and some monograph series and publishers' series [Compiler's introduction]

This work supersedes a *Check-list of music serials in nine libraries of the Rocky Mountain region*, compiled by William M. McClellan in 1963.

The present work lists over 800 title entries and 250 cross references.

637 / Svobodová, Marie. "Music journals in Bohemia and Moravia 1796–1970." In *Fontes artis musicae*, 19 (1972), p. 22–41.

259 journals listed alphabetically by title, with a chronological index. Most of the Czech titles are translated into English, or some indication is given of their content. Items are identified by their number in Fellinger's *Verzeichnis* (no. 621) where applicable.

638 / Thoumin, Jean-Adrien. Bibliographie rétrospective des périodiques français de littérature musicale 1870–1954. Preface de Madame Elizabeth Lebeau. Paris, Éditions documentaires industrielles et techniques, 1957. 179 p.

Alphabetical listing of 594 French music periodicals. Chronological index; indices of persons and places of publication.

639 / Union List of Periodicals in Music in the libraries of the University of London and some other London libraries. London, 1969. 56 p.

Compiled by Dr. M. A. Baird.

Based on the periodical holdings of 23 London libraries, excluding the British Museum.

640 / "Verzeichnis der Zeitschriften und Jahrbücher." In *Hofmeisters Jahresverzeichnis*, v. 100. Leipzig, F. Hofmeister, 1953, p. 334–39.

Lists more than 100 German and Austrian periodicals and yearbooks available in 1951. Since 1953, periodicals are listed in a subsection of the "Anhang: Musikschriften."

See also earlier issues of the *Jahresverzeichnis*.

641 / Weichlein, William J. A checklist of American music periodicals, 1850–1900. Detroit, Information Coordinators, 1970. 103 p. (Detroit studies in music bibliography, 16.)

Review by Dena J. Epstein in *Notes*, 27 (1971), p. 489.

642 / **"Zeitschriften."** In Mendel's *Musikalisches Conversations-Lexikon*, v 11. Berlin, Heimann, 1879. p. 443–62.

An early listing, but still useful for its detailed descriptions of 18th- and 19th-century journals.

643 / **"Zeitschriften."** In *Die Musik in Geschichte und Gegenwart*. Lieferung 135/36. Band 14 (1968), col. 1041–1188.

Compiled by Imogen Fellinger (see also no. 621).

The most comprehensive listing of music periodicals available. Organized by country. Extensive bibliographies of literature on music periodicals.

644 / **"Zeitschriften."** In *Riemann Musiklexikon*. 12th ed. Band 3: *Sachteil*. p. 1073–78.

Historical introduction followed by a selective list, organized by country.

SPECIAL AND SUBJECT BIBLIOGRAPHIES

Contemporary Music

645 / **Basart, Ann Phillips.** Serial music, a classified bibliography of writings on twelve-tone and electronic music. Berkeley and Los Angeles, Univ. of California Press, 1961. 151 p. (University of California Bibliographic Guides.)

A classified bibliography of 823 items treating the literature of 12-tone music, electronic music, the Viennese school (Schönberg, Berg, and Webern) and 20 other contemporary composers using serial techniques. Author and subject indices. Revision currently in progress.

Review by Dika Newlin in *Notes*, 19 (1961), p. 256–57; by James B. Coover in *Journal of music theory*, 6 (1962), p. 316–17; by Donald Mitchell in *Tempo*, 63 (Winter 1962–63), p. 46–48; and by Josef Rufer in *Die Musikforschung*, 17 (1964), p. 315–16.

646 / **Bull, Storm.** Index to biographies of contemporary composers. New York, Scarecrow Press, 1964. 405 p.

Indexes 69 sources of biographical information (dictionaries, who's whos, publishers' lists, etc.) indicating if the composer under consideration is mentioned. No page references given.

647 / **Cross, Lowell M.** A bibliography of electronic music. Toronto, University of Toronto Press, 1967. 126 p.

A bibliography of writings on electronic music. Some 1,562 articles entered.

Review by Otto Luening in *Notes*, 25 (1969), p. 502–503.

648 / **Deliège, Celestin.** "Bibliographie" (of serial and experimental music). In *Revue belge de musicologie*, 13 (1959), p. 132–48.

Broadly classified bibliography of contemporary music with an introduction surveying the literature of the field.

649 / **Edmunds, John, and Gordon Boelzner.** Some twentieth-century American composers, a selective bibliography . . . With an introductory essay by Peter Yates. New York, The New York Public Library, 1959–60. 2 v.

> This bibliography has been made with the purpose of bringing together in a single body separately published writings by and about a representative group of 20th-century American composers . . . conservative, moderate, dodecaphonic, and experimental. *[Preface]*

Vol. 1 includes bibliographies for 15 composers, vol. 2 for 17 (with an introductory essay by Nicolas Slonimsky). There are two appendices, one a listing of composers cited in at least one of 21 standard reference works and the other for composers not cited but who are under 35 and merit some attention.

Both volumes are reprinted with additions from *The bulletin of the New York public library*.

Dissertations

Doctoral dissertations, along with articles in scholarly periodicals, represent the growing edge of research activity in any field. We are currently well supplied with bibliographies of doctoral studies in music for the United States (see no. 650) and for Germany (no. 664), but studies produced in other countries are less easy to locate. Included here are only those reference tools concerned exclusively with studies in music. There are a number of comprehensive national bibliographies of dissertations from which music titles can be extracted. For these, the user should consult Winchell's *Guide to reference books*, latest edition, and its *Supplements*; also Keith Mixter's *General bibliography for music research*.

650 / **Adkins, Cecil.** Doctoral dissertations in musicology. 5th edition. Philadelphia, American Musicological Society, 1971. 203 p.

First published in 1951 in photo-offset from typed copy, issued jointly by a Committee of the Music Teachers' National Association and the American Musicological Society.

2nd edition, 1958; 3rd edition, 1961; 4th edition, 1965, all compiled by Helen Hewitt, who also edited supplements that appeared in *JAMS* and in *The American music teacher*.

Throughout the first four editions, entries are grouped by historical periods under the institutions where the degree was completed. The 5th edition abandons listings under institutions. It contains 1,971 titles, completed or in progress, representing the output of 56 Americans and two Canadian universities. Listings of work in progress are retained for a period of five years, then dropped. Availability in microform is indicated. Indexed by subject and by author.

651 / **De Lerma, Dominique-René.** A selective list of masters' theses in musicology. Compiled for the American Musicological Society. Bloomington, Indiana, Denia Press, 1970. 42 p.

Entries for 257 titles submitted by 36 institutions. Indexes of names, topics, and participating institutions. Entries give information as to availability by photoreproduction or interlibrary loan.

652 / **"Dissertations."** In *Current musicology*, no. 1– . New York, The Music Department, Columbia University, 1965– .

An occasional feature printed in the journal. Offers critical reviews of selected doctoral studies and listings of current dissertations, European as well as American.

653 / **Doe, Paul.** "Register of theses on music." In *R.M.A. research chronicle*, no. 3. Royal Musical Association, 1963. p. 1–25.

The listing is continued in *Research chronicle*, no. 4 (1964), no. 6 (1966), and no. 8 (1970).

Classified bibliography of music research studies, completed or in progress, for a variety of degrees in British universities.

654 / **Gillis, Frank, and Alan P. Merriam.** Ethnomusicology and folk music: an international bibliography of dissertations and theses. Middletown, Conn., Wesleyan University Press, 1966. 148 p.

Cites 873 entries for graduate theses in the field of ethnomusicology, including both master's and doctor's degrees. This bibliography developed from an earlier listing in the journal *Ethnomusicology*, 4 (1960), p. 21–35, with a supplement in the same journal, 6 (1962), p. 191–214.

Review by William Malm in *Notes*, 24 (1968), p. 499–500.

655 / **Hartley, Kenneth R.** Bibliography of theses and dissertations in sacred music. Detroit, Information Coordinators, Inc., 1967. 127 p. (Detroit studies in music bibliography, 9.)

656 / **"Im Jahre . . . Angenommene musikwissenschaftliche Dissertationen."** In *Die Musikforschung*, v. 1– . 1948– .

A listing, annual or at more frequent intervals, of doctoral dissertations completed in German, Austrian, and Swiss institutions during the current year. Beginning with vol. 18 (1965), a special section is devoted to reviews of selected dissertations.

657 / **International Center for Musicological Works in Progress.** "Musicological works in progress." Edited by Cecil Adkins, in *Acta Musicologica*, 44 (1972), p. 146–69.

The first installment of what is expected to be a continuing listing of active research projects, including not only dissertations but postdoctoral studies as well. The entries are classified within major chronological divisions. In many cases the scholar's address is given to encourage communication. Subject index. The list is organized in terms of future automation possibilities.

For a description of the scope of this project and the techniques employed, see Cecil Adkins's report in *Acta Musicologica*, 43 (1971), p. 103–106.

658 / **Music Educators' National Conference.** Bibliography of research studies in music education, 1932–48. Compiled by William S. Larson. Chicago, Music Educators National Conference, 1949. 119 p.

An earlier edition, compiled by Arnold M. Small, appeared in 1944, State Univ. of Iowa Press.

This, and the following five entries, provide continuing documentation for research in music education from 1932 to 1971. From 1957 on the bibliographies have appeared in issues of the *Journal of research in music education.*

659 / **Music Educators' National Conference.** Bibliography of research studies in music education, 1949–56. Compiled by William S. Larson. In *Journal of research in music education*, 5:2 (1957), 225 p.

660 / **Music Educators' National Conference.** Doctoral dissertations in music education, 1957–63. Compiled by Roderick D. Gordon. In *Journal of research in music education*, 12 (Spring 1964), 112 p.

661 / **Music Educators' National Conference.** Doctoral dissertations in music and music education, 1963–67. Compiled by Roderick D. Gordon. In *Journal of research in music education*, 16 (Summer 1968), p. 87–218.

662 / **Music Educators' National Conference.** Doctoral dissertations in music and music education, 1968–71. Compiled by Roderick D. Gordon. In *Journal of research in music education*, 20 (1972), p. 2–185.

In the above, MENC bibliographies coverage includes dissertations submitted for the degree Doctor of Philosophy, Doctor of Education, Doctor of Musical Arts, Doctor of Music Education, and Doctor of Music. No clear distinction is made between research studies in education and those engaging other research areas.

663 / **Northwestern University (Evanston, Illinois) School of Music.** Bibliography of research, School of Music, Northwestern University: theses, projects, dissertations. Ed. by Hazel B. Morgan. Evanston, Ill., 1958. 47 p.

664 / **Schaal, Richard.** Verzeichnis deutschsprachiger musikwissenschaftlicher Dissertationen, 1861–1960. Kassel, Bärenreiter, 1963. 167 p. (Musikwissenschaftliche Arbeiten, hrsg. von der Gesellschaft für Musikforschung, 19.)

An alphabetical listing, by author, of 2,819 music dissertations in the German language. Publication data given for works in print. Subject index.

Review by Erich Schenk in *Die Musikforschung*, 17 (1964), p. 421–23, supplying numerous additional entries.

159

665 / **Texas Music Educators' Association. Research in Music Education Committee.** A bibliography of master's theses and doctoral dissertations in music completed at Texas colleges and universities, 1919–62. Houston, Texas Music Educators Association, 1964. 77 p.

Listings chronological by institution. Research studies in music education completed in 14 Texas colleges or universities. Subject and author indexes.

666 / **"Verzeichnis der im Berichtsjahr . . . bei der Deutschen Bücherei zu Leipzig registrierten musikwissenschaftlichen Dissertationen und Habilitationsschriften."** (Compiled by Ortrun Landmann.) In *Deutsches Jahrbuch der Musikwissenschaft.* Leipzig, Peters, 1957– .

Continues a bibliography of dissertations originally published in the *Peters Jahrbuch.* Primarily those completed in East German institutions.

Ethnomusicology

Vigorous growth in the field of ethnomusicology in recent years has prompted numerous bibliographical studies. No attempt has been made to list the many useful bibliographies appended to monographs, dissertations, and periodical articles in this field. Attention has been called to the listings of current literature and recordings in *Ethnomusicology, journal of the Society for Ethnomusicology* (see no. 581). One of the most comprehensive bibliographies in this area is found in Jaap Kunst's *Ethnomusicology, a study of its nature, its problems . . .* (no. 682).

Additional references will be found under "Bibliographies of Music: Folk song and ballad," and under "Discographies: Ethnic and folk music."

667 / **Aning, B. A.** An annotated bibliography of music and dance in English-speaking Africa. Legon, Institute of African Studies, University of Ghana, 1967. 47 p.

A bibliography of 132 items, including both books and periodical articles. Index of authors. Organized regionally.

Review by Alan P. Merriam in *Ethnomusicology,* 16 (1972), p. 544–45.

160

668 / **Annual Bibliography of European Ethnomusicology.** Vol.
1– . Herausgegeben vom Slowakischen National-Museum in Verbindung mit dem Institut für Musikwissenschaften und dem Institut für deutsche Volkskunde der Deutschen Akademie der Wissenschaften, Berlin, unter Mitwirkung des International Folk Music Council. Bratislava, 1967– .

Vol. 1 (1966) contains 395 items, chiefly periodical articles, listed under country. 1967. 72 p.

Vol. 2 (1967), 1968. 82 p.

Edited by Oskár Elschek, Erich Stockmann, and Ivan Macák. Introduction in German and English.

Vol. 3 (1968), 1969. 108 p.

Vol. 4 (1969), 1970. 85 p.

Review of volume 1 by Rolf Wilh. Brednich in *Jahrbuch für Volksliedforschung*, 15 (1970), p. 182–83. By Frank J. Gillis in *Ethnomusicology*, 16 (1972), p. 138–39.

669 / **Bose, Fritz.** Musikalische Völkerkunde. Freiburg, Atlantis-Verlag, 1953. 197 p. (Atlantis-Musikbücherei.)

"Bibliographie," p. 144–63. 393 items.

670 / **Cavanagh, Beverley.** "Annotated bibliography: Eskimo music." In *Ethnomusicology*, 16 (1972), p. 479–87.

671 / **Colvig, Richard.** "Black music," in *Choice*, a publication of the Association of College and Research Libraries, 6 (Nov. 1969), p. 1169–79.

"A representative selection of English language monographs dealing with the contribution made to music by members of the Negro race on both sides of the Atlantic." 71 items, classified and mostly annotated.

Also published separately by the Oakland Public Library, 1969, 18 p.

672 / **"Current Bibliography and Discography."** . . In *Ethnomusicology*, Journal of the Society for Ethnomusicology. Edited by Joseph C. Kickerson, Neil V. Rosenberg, and Frank J. Gillis.

Editors vary, but the above three names have been active since May 1970.

The best current listing of literature and phonorecords in the field of ethnomusicology.

673 / **De Lerma, Dominique-René, and Michael Phillips.** "Entries of ethnomusicological interest in MGG: a preliminary listing." In *Ethnomusicology*, 13 (1969), p. 129–38.

Attention is directed to eight areas in the German reference work that contain articles of interest to ethnomusicologists: The Americas (7 entries), Africa (13), Asia and Oceania (23), Europe (33), Dance (35), Instruments (47), Miscellaneous (24), and biographies and index of contributors (134).

674 / **Densmore, Frances.** "The study of Indian music in the nineteenth century." In *American Anthropologist*, 29 (1927), p. 77–86.

A survey of early studies in the field of American Indian music; generally valuable, although it contains some errors.

675 / **Emsheimer, Ernst.** "Musikethnographische Bibliographie der nichtslavischen Völker in Russland." In *Acta M*, 15 (1943), p. 34–63.

A bibliography of 433 items concerned with the music of the non-Slavic peoples of Russia. Classified according to ethnic groups. German translations for Slavic titles. Some editions of folk music cited, but chiefly concerned with periodical literature and monographs. Full biblographical information.

676 / **Gaskin, Lionel.** A select biblography of music in Africa; compiled at the International African Institute by L. J. P. Gaskin under the direction of Prof. K. P. Wachsmann. London, International African Institute, 1965. 83 p.

Review by Leonard Vohs in *Die Musikforschung*, 22 (1969), p. 390–91. Review by Douglas Varley and Alan Taylor, in *Ethnomusicology*, 11 (1967), p. 125–28.

677 / **Guèdon, Marie-Françoise.** "Canadian Indian ethnomusicology: selected bibliography and discography." In *Ethnomusicology*, 16 (1972), p. 465–78.

Subdivided by five cultural areas: (1) Eastern woodlands-Great Lakes, (2) Plains, (3) Yukon-Mackenzie basins, (4) Plateau, (5) Northwest coast.

678 / **Haywood, Charles.** A bibliography of North American folklore and folksong. Second rev. ed. New York, Dover Publications [1961], 2 v.

First published in one volume by Greenberg, New York, 1951.

Vol. 1, p. 1–748: concerned with the non-Indian Americans north of Mexico. Vol. 2, p. 749–1,159. With the American Indians north of Mexico. Subdivisions in vol. 1 include general bibliography, regional bibliography, ethnic and occupational bibliography. Vol. 2 is subdivided by cultural areas. Entries for folklore and for folk music are separated under each heading; recordings included. General index. Endpapers are maps of regional and cultural areas.

Review of first ed. by Duncan Emrich in *Notes*, 8 (1951), p. 700–01.

679 / **Henry, Mellinger Edward.** A bibliography for the study of American folk-songs, with many titles of folk-songs (and titles that have to do with folk-songs) from other lands. London, Mitre Press [1937], 142 p.

Studies and collections of music interfiled in one alphabet. The emphasis is on the English-Scottish ballad and its derivatives.

680 / **Herzog, George.** Research in primitive and folk music in the U.S., a survey. Washington, D.C., American Council of Learned Societies, 1936. 97 p.

Surveys U.S. resources for the study of primitive and folk music as of 1936. Record archives are described and their holdings tabulated; collections of primitive musical instruments listed. Bibliographies given for each of the main sections.

681 / **Huerta, Jorge A.,** ed. A bibliography of Chicano and Mexican dance, drama, and music. Oxnard, Calif., Colegio Quetzalcoatl, 1972. 59 p.

P. 36–59: Music Pre-Columbian, Mexican, Aztlan. Includes references to books, journals, and photograph records (for Mexico only).

682 / **Kunst, Jaap.** Ethnomusicology, a study of its nature, its problems, methods and representative personalities, to which is added a bibliography. 3rd ed. enl. The Hague, Nijhoff, 1959. 303 p.

First published in 1950 under the title *Musicologica.* . . . The 2nd edition, 1955, contains a selective bibliography. Reprint of the 3rd ed. and its *Supplement* in 1969.

Bibiliography of the 3rd edition, p. 79–215, lists 4,552 items, most of them with location symbols referring to libraries in Western Europe. Entries which contain extensive bibliographies within themselves are marked with an asterisk. Portraits of ethnomusicologists.

Supplement to the 3rd edition, 1960, 45 p., adds some 500 items to the bibliography; new record listings through 1958, more portraits.

Review of the 3rd ed. by Bruno Nettl in *Notes,* 16 (1959), p. 560–61; of the *Supplement* by William Lichtenwanger in *Notes,* 19 (1961), p. 79.

683 / Laade, Wolfgang. Gegenwartsfragen der Musik in Afrika und Asien. Eine grundlegende Bibliographie. Baden-Baden, Heitz, 1970. 120 p. (Sammlung musikwissenschaftlicher Abhandlungen, 51.)

A regionally organized bibliography of 874 items taken chiefly from current periodical literature. This work also serves as a useful directory of institutions, societies, broadcasting stations involved in the study of Asian-African music.

Lawless, Ray McKinley. Folksingers and folksongs in America . . . See no. 203.

684 / Laws, George M. Native American balladry; a descriptive study and a bibliographical syllabus. Philadelphia, American Folklore Society, 1950. 276 p. (Publications of the American Folklore Society. Bibliographical Series, v. 1.)

685 / League of Nations. International Institute of Intellectual Co-operation. Folklore musical; répertoire international des collections et centres de documentation avec notices sur l'état actuel des recherches dans les différents pays et références bibliographiques. Paris, Département d'Art, d.Archéologie et d'Ethnologie, Institut International de Coopération Intellectuelle [1939], 332 p.

Organization similar to the preceding item. Special section devoted to the international phonorecord archive in Berlin, Paris, and Vienna. P. 307–32: supplement of additions and corrections to the 1934 volume, above.

686 / League of Nations. International Institute of Intellectual Co-operation. Musique et chanson populaires. Paris, Institut International de Coopération Intellectuelle, 1934. 257 p.

A reference book intended to establish an international listing of museums, archives, libraries, and other institutions, public and private, concerned with research or collection in the field of popular music, with descriptions of their facilities. Contributions by leading specialists arranged alphabetically by country. Most of the essays contain bibliographies of studies and editions and a list of names and addresses of specialists.

687 / **Liebermann, Fredric.** Chinese music, an annotated bibliography. New York, Society for Asian Music, 1970. 157 p. (Bibliographies and research aids, Ser. A, No. 1.)

> This bibiliography attempts exhaustive coverage of publications in Western languages as well as critical annotation. [Author's *Preface*]

A bibliography of 1,483 items arranged alphabetically by author. Index of periodicals, of names, and of topics for selected readings. Includes discographies.

688 / **Lomax, Alan, and Sidney R. Cowell.** American folksong and folklore, a regional bibliography. New York, Progressive Education Association, 1942. 59 p.

689 / **Merriam, Alan P.** "An annotated bibliography of African and African-derived music since 1936." In *Africa*, 21 (1951), p. 319–30.

Musikethnologische Jahresbibliographie Europas.
See: **Annual Bibliography of European Ethnomusicology** (no. 668).

690 / **Nettl, Bruno.** Reference materials in ethnomusicology. Second edition, revised, 1967. Detroit, Information Coordinators, 1967. 40 p. (Detroit studies in music bibliography, 1.)
First published in 1961.
A narrative and critical discussion of the leading reference works in the field, organized in terms of the structure of discipline. On p. 37–46 a list of publications is cited, with full bibliographical information.
Review by William Lichtenwanger in *Notes*, 19 (1962), p. 428–30; by Marius Schneider in *Die Musikforschung*, 19 (1964), p. 88–89.

691 / **Nettl, Bruno.** Theory and method in ethnomusicology. New York, The Free Press, 1964. 306 p.
Chapter 2 is a history of the field, focusing on bibliography. Each chapter is followed by a list of publications cited.
Review by David P. McAllester in *MQ*, 51 (1965), p. 425–28.

692 / A Select Bibliography of European Folk Music. Published in cooperation with The International Folk Music Council by the Institute for Ethnography and Folklore of the Czechoslovak Academy of Sciences. Prague, 1966. 144 p.

Editor-in-chief: Karel Vetterl. Co-editors: Erik Dal, Laurence Picken, Erich Stockman.

693 / Song, Bang-Song. An annotated bibliography of Korean music. Providence, Rhode Island, Brown University, 1971. 250 p. (Asian music publications, ser. A, no. 2.)

A bibliography of 1,319 items. Part I cites writings on Korean music in the Korean language; Part II, writings in foreign languages. Indexes of bibliographical sources and of names and subjects. The annotations are brief but informative.

694 / Thieme, Darius L. African music, a briefly annotated bibliography. Washington, D.C., Library of Congress, Reference Department, Music Division, 1964. 55 p. (typescript)

The present work lists sources discussing the music of sub-Saharan Africa. The work is divided into two main sections, the first listing periodicals and serial articles, the second listing books. [*Preface*]

A bibliography of 597 items, with an author and linguistic area index.

695 / Varley, Douglas H. African native music, an annotated bibliography. London, The Royal Empire Soc., 1936. 116 p.

Reprint of the 1st ed.; with additional note, 1970.

Two sections of general bibliography followed by local bibliographies relating to 30 African countries. Special section on "African survivals in the New World." List of museums containing collections of African instruments. Author index. Brief but informative annotations.

696 / Vetterl, Karel. A select bibliography of European folk music. Published in cooperation with the International Folk Music Council by the Institute for Ethnography and Folklore of the Czechoslovak Academy of Sciences. Prague, 1966. 144 p.

166

The bibliography attempts to list the most useful publications, both books and articles, and especially those of a scholarly nature, that bear on the folk music of particular European countries. [*Introduction*]

Organized alphabetically by country. Strong on East European entries, particularly Russian.

Brief review by Rolf Wilh. Brednich in *Jahrbuch für Volksliedforschung*, 14 (1969), p. 175.

Review by Ann Briegleb in *Ethnomusicology*, 12 (1968), p. 161–62.

697 / Waterman, Richard [*et al.*]. "Bibliography of Asiatic musics." In *Notes*, 5:1–8:2 (Dec., 1947–March, 1951) 181 p. in all.

A classified bibliography, published serially, of 3,488 books, monographs, article, sections of larger works, texts, transcriptions and recordings, arranged geographically and ethnologically. All European languages, including Russian and Romanized Turkish.

Musical Instruments

The literature on musical instruments is to be found in a variety of reference books. The reader in search of further information should look under the following additional headings: "Dictionaries of Musical Instrument Makers and Performers" (no. 212 ff.) and "Catalogs of Musical Instrument Collections" (no. 1564 ff.). Many of these reference tools contain appended bibliographies on the subject.

698 / Graaf, G. A. C. de. Literature on the organ, principally in Dutch libraries. Amsterdam, 1957. 71 p.

Lists over 1,250 titles of books, brochures, and reprints concerning the use, the history, and the construction of organs. Does not include books on organ playing.

699 / Heron-Allen, Edward. De fidiculis bibliographia: being an attempt towards a bibliography of the violin . . . London, Griffith Farran and C., 1890–94. 2 v.

Reprint by Holland Press, 1961.

Classified bibliography of literature on the violin in all its aspects. Full bibliographical data with copius annotations. The work was issued in parts, printed on the recto only, and concludes with four supplements.

700 / **Hutschenruyter, Willem.** Bijdrage tot de bibliographie der muziekliteratuur. Een zooveel mogelijk aangevulde samenvatting der boek- en tijdschrift-overzichten, die sedert 1885 zijn opgenomen in het *Vierteljahrschrift für Musikwissenschaft,* het *Zeitschrift der Internationalen Musikgesellschaft,* en het *Jahrbuch der Musikbibliothek Peters.* Vol. 1: Instrumentale muziek, mechanische muziek, electrische muziek, klokken. Zeist, 1941. 513 p (typescript)

An incomplete project, intended to be a comprehensive bibliography of music literature, but progressed only so far as to cover writings on instrumental music, electrical music, and bells.

701 / **Miller, Dayton C.** Catalogue of books and literary material relating to the flute and other musical instruments, with annotations. Cleveland, privately printed, 1935. 120 p.

Catalog of the literary portion of one of the largest collections ever assembled on the flute and related instruments. Now in the Music Division of the Library of Congress (see no. 1634).

Includes material on all wind instruments, in the form of books, pamphlets, periodical articles, newspaper clippings, concert programs, makers' catalogs and price lists, etc. Brief annotations.

702 / **Pohlmann, Ernst von.** Laute, Theorbe, Chitarrone. Die Lauten-Instruments, ihre Musik und Literatur von 1500 bis zur Gegenwart. Zweite Auflage. Bremen, Edition Eres, 1972. 416 p.

First printed in 1968. The 2nd edition is much enlarged.

A source book of information about instruments of the lute family, including sources, composers, literature, descriptions of tablatures, locations of existing instruments, makers.

Review by Stanley Buetens in *Journal of the lute society of America,* 5 (1972), p. 114–16.

703 / **Schlesinger, Kathleen.** A bibliography of musical instruments and archaeology . . . London, W. Reeves, 1912. 100 p.

Only the first 20 plates are devoted to works on musical instruments and the orchestra. Short sections on catalogs of instrument collections and general works on music. The greater part of the volume is concerned with classical and medieval antiquities.

704 / **Torri, Luigi.** La costruzione ed i costruttori degli istrumenti ad arco. Bibliografia liutistica storico-tecnica. 2nd edizione . . . Padova, G. Zanibon, 1920. 43 p.

Brief critical and descriptive annotations. Alphabetically arranged, with a subject index.

705 / **Warner, Thomas E.** An annotated bibliography of woodwind instruction books, 1600–1830. Detroit, Information Coordinators, 1967. 138 p. (Detroit studies in music bibliography, 11.)

Jazz

The literature of jazz is proliferating rapidly at the present time. Readers will find relevant information in several different sections of this book, under "Bibliographies of Music: Jazz and Popular Music" and, above all, under "Discographies: Collectors' Guides to Popular Recordings."

706 / **Carl Gregor, Duke of Mecklenburg.** International jazz bibliography: jazz books from 1919 to 1968. Strasbourg, Heitz, 1969. 198 p. (Sammlung musikwissenschaftlicher Abhandlungen, 49.)

1970 Supplement . . . Graz, Universal Edition, 1971. 109 p. (Beiträge zur Jazzforschung, 3.)

Review of the 1969 edition by Ekkehard Jost in *Die Musikforschung*, 24 (1971), p. 330–31; by Alan P. Merriam in *Ethnomusicology*, 14 (1970), p. 177. Review of the *1970 Supplement* by James Patrick in *Notes*, 29 (1972), p. 236–39.

707 / **Kennington, Donald.** The literature of jazz, a critical guide. Chicago, American Library Association, 1971. 142 p.

Eight short chapters discussing various aspects of jazz documentation, each followed by an annotated bibliography. Title index and general index.

A work first published in England, 1970, by The Library Association.

Review, unfavorable, by Eileen Southern in *Notes*, 29 (1972), p. 35–36.

708 / **Merriam, Alan P.** A bibliography of jazz. With the assistance of Robert J. Benford. Philadelphia, American Folklore Society,

1954. 145 p. (Publications of the American Folklore Society, Bibliographical series, 4.)

Reprint by Da Capo Press, New York, 1970.

3,324 numbered entries, arranged alphabetically by author, with subject emphasis indicated by a code system. Lists 113 jazz periodicals. Subject index.

Review by Marshall W. Stearns in *Notes*, 12 (1955), p. 436–37; of the reprint edition by Eileen Southern in *Notes*, 29 (1972), p. 34–35.

709 / **Reisner, Robert G.** The literature of jazz; a selective bibliography. With an introduction by Marshall W. Stearns. New York, The New York Public Library, 1959. 63 p.

A preliminary edition appeared in the *Bulletin of the New York Public Library*, March–May, 1954.

Cites some 500 books on jazz, 850 periodical articles, and 125 jazz magazines.

Review by William Lichtenwanger in *Notes*, 16 (1959), p. 398.

710 / **Stanley, Lana.** Folk rock: a bibliography on music of the 'sixties. San Jose, Calif., San Jose State College Library, 1970. 80 p. (typescript) (San Jose State College Library, Bibliography series, 3.)

Classified under topical headings and writings on particular groups or individual artists.

Medieval and Renaissance Music

711 / **Gallo, F. Alberto.** "Philological works on musical treatises of the Middle Ages: a bibliographical report." In *Acta Musicologica*, 44 (1972), p. 78–101.

A narrative bibliography treating the work recently accomplished in the editing and description of medieval music treatises. The material is discussed chronologically and by country, with copious notes.

712 / **Gleason, Harold.** Music in the Middle Ages and Renaissance. 2nd ed. Rochester, N.Y., Levis Music Stores, 1951. 158 p. (Music literature outlines, ser. 1.)

The outline follows the organization in Reese's *Music in the Middle Ages*, but each section is accompanied by numerous bibliographical references to books, periodical articles, scores, and recordings.

713 / **Reese, Gustave.** "Bibliography." In his *Music in Middle Ages.* New York, Norton, 1940. p. 425–63.

Lists books, periodical articles, facsimiles, and editions. Difficult to use because the material is grouped by chapter headings. One of the most comprehensive bibliographies available to students of early music.

714 / **Reese, Gustave.** "Bibliography." In his *Music in the Renaissance.* Rev. ed., New York, Norton, 1959. p. 884–946.

A comprehensive bibliography of monographs, editions, and periodical literature related to Renaissance music. Unclassified, alphabetical arrangement.

715 / **Smith, Carleton Sprague and William Dinneen.** "Recent work on music in the Renaissance." In *Modern philology,* 42:1 (Aug. 1944), p. 41–58.

A bibliographical article in narrative style citing and evaluating research and editorial activity in Renaissance music from about 1900 to date of publication.

716 / **Smits van Waesberghe, Joseph.** "Die gegenwärtige Geschichtsbild der mittelalterlichen Musik." In *Kirchenmusikalisches Jahrbuch,* 46– . 1962– .

A narrative survey and discussion, under major topics, of the contributions on medieval music in 19 current musicological and historical journals.

> For 1957–60, in Jahrgang 46 (1962), p. 61–82.
> For 1960–62, in Jahrgang 47 (1963), p. 11–38.
> For 1963, in Jahrgang 48 (1964), p. 1–26.
> For 1964, in Jahrgang 49 (1965), p. 9–33.

717 / **Suñol, Grégorio María.** "Bibliographie générale." In his *Introduction à la paléographie musicale grégorienne.* Paris, Desclée, 1935. p. 511–65.

This bibliography first appeared in 1925 in the original edition of the author's work on Gregorian paleography. Entries are broadly classified and listed in order of publication.

718 / **Velimirovic, Milos.** "Present status of research in Byzantine music." In *Acta musicologica,* 43 (1971), p. 1–20.

A narrative bibliography citing the important work accomplished in this area since 1950.

Baroque and Classic Music

719 / **Gleason, Harold.** Music in the Baroque. Rochester, New York, Levis Music Stores, 1950. (Music literature outlines, ser. 2.)

The outline is based on Bukofzer's *Music in the baroque era* (1947), with much addition documentation.

720 / **Hill, George R.** A preliminary checklist of research on the classic symphony and concerto to the time of Beethoven (excluding Haydn and Mozart.) Hackensack, New Jersey, Joseph Boonin, 1970. 58 p. (Music indexes and bibliographies, 2.)

721 / **Surian, Elvidio.** A checklist of writings on 18th-century French and Italian opera (excluding Mozart). Hackensack, New Jersey, Joseph Boonin, 1970. 121 p. (Music indexes and bibliographies, 3.)

Music Education

722 / **International Society for Music Education.** International listing of teaching aids in music education. Edited by Egon Kraus. Cologne, International Society for Music Education. (Distributing agent: Möseler Verlag, Wolfenbüttel.) 1959. 52 p.

A classified bibliography of materials, since 1945, concerned with music instruction.

Review by Theodore Normann in *Journal of research in music education*, 8 (1960), p. 55–56.

723 / **Modisett, Katherine C.** "Bibliography of sources, 1930–1952, relating to the teaching of choral music in secondary schools." In *Journal of research in music education*, 3 (1955), p. 51–60.

A classified bibliography of 236 items, with a brief introductory survey of the field and its problems.

724 / **Music Educators' National Conference. Committee on Bibliography.** "Music education materials, a selected bibliography."

Published as volume 7, no. 1 of the *Journal of research in music education*, 1959. 146 p.

A classified listing of materials. Major groupings are elementary music education, junior high school, choral materials, instructional materials for instrumental music, music appreciation guides and reference materials, music theory texts and workbooks, audio-visual aids, teacher training.

725 / Music Educators' National Conference. Curriculum Committee. Music education source book (no. 1). Ed. by Hazel N. Morgan. Chicago, M.E.N.C., 1951. 268 p.

First printed in 1947.

Various sections contain brief bibliographies; the 1951 printing has an appendix of revisions and additions. Much of the bibliographical information in the first four printings is now out of date.

726 / Music Educators' National Conference. Music in American Education Committee. Music in American education. Music education source book (no. 2). Ed. by Hazel N. Morgan. Chicago, M.E.N.C., 1955. 365 p.

Brief bibliographies to various chapters and subchapters concerned with aspects of American public school music.

727 / Music Educators' National Conference. Selected bibliography, music education materials. (Prepared for the U.S. Department of State by a special committee of the M.E.N.C.) Chicago, M.E.N.C., 1952. 64 p.

Contains five bibliographies, classified, partially annotated: music education materials for elementary schools, collections for junior high, collections for senior high, instrumental music materials, textbooks on music education. The emphasis is on school music performance materials.

728 / Smits van Waesberghe, Joseph. "Chronologische Übersicht der Musiktraktate, und Literaturverzeichnis." In *Musikerziehung: Lehre und Theorie der Musik im Mittelalter.* Leipzig, 1969. p. 195–202. (Musikeschichte in Bildern, Bd. III, Lfg. 3)

Provides a bibliographical key to the historical study of music education. The "Chronologische Übersicht" cites the most important treatises devoted to music theory and instruction from the 5th to the

173

15th century. The "Verzeichnis" is an extensive bibliography of books and articles on medieval music instruction.

National Music

The first eighteen entries in this section call attention to a series of articles that have appeared in *Acta Musicologica*, the journal of the International Musicological Society, since 1957. These articles survey the bibliographical and research activities in music in various countries since the end of World War II. Most of them cite major scholarly publications, dissertations, and important music reference works.

AUSTRIA

729 / **Wessely, Othmar.** "Die österreichische Musikforschung nach dem zweiten Weltkreig," in *Acta M,* 29 (1957), p. 111–19.

BELGIUM

730 / **Clercx-Lejeune, Suzanne.** "La musicologie en Belgique depuis 1945," in *Act M,* 30 (1958), p. 199–214.

DENMARK

731 / **Schousboe, Torben.** "Dänische musikwissenschaftliche Publikationen seit 1958." In *Acta M,* 44 (1972), p. 1–11.

FINLAND

732 / **Ringbom, Nils-Eric.** "Die Musikforschung in Finnland seit 1940," in *Acta M,* 31 (1959), p. 17–24.

FRANCE

733 / **Lesure, François.** "La musicologie française depuis 1945." In *Act M,* 30 (1958), p. 3–17.

GERMANY

734 / **Heckmann, Harald.** "Musikwissenschaftliche Unternehmungen in Deutschland seit 1945." In *Act M,* 29 (1957), p. 75–94.

HOLLAND

735 / **Reeser, Eduard.** "Musikwissenschaft in Holland." In *Acta M*, 32 (1960), p. 160–74.

ISRAEL

736 / **Gerson-Kiwi, Edith.** "Musicology in Israel," in *Acta M*, 30 (1958), p. 17–26.

ITALY

737 / **Allorto, Riccardo e Claudio Sartori.** "La musicologia italiana dal 1945 a oggi," in *Acta M*, 31 (1959), p. 9–17.

JAPAN

738 / **Nomura, Francesco Yosio.** "Musicology in Japan since 1945," in *Acta M*, 35 (1963), p. 45–53.

LATIN AMERICA

739 / **Devoto, Daniel.** "Panorama de la musicología Latinoamericana," in *Acta M*, 31 (1959), p. 91–109.

NORWAY

740 / **Schjelderup-Ebbe, Dag.** "Neuere norwegische musikwissenschaftliche Arbeiten." In *Acta M*, 44 (1972), p. 25–31.

PORTUGAL

741 / **Kastner, Macario Santiago.** "Veinte años de musicología en Portugal (1940–60), in *Acta M*, 32 (1960), p. 1–11.

SCANDINAVIA

742 / **Rosenberg, Herbert.** "Musikwissenschaftliche Bestrebungen in Dänemark, Norwegen, und Schweden in den letzten ca. 15 Jahren," in *Acta M*, 30 (1958), p. 118–37.

SWEDEN

743 / **Lönn, Anders.** "Trends and tendencies in recent Swedish musicology," in *Acta M*, 44 (1972), p. 11–25.

SWITZERLAND

744 / **Schanzlin, Hans Peter.** "Musikwissenschaft in der Schweiz (1938–58)," in *Acta M*, 30 (1958), p. 214–24.

UNITED STATES

745 / **Goldthwaite, Scott.** "The growth and influence of musicology in the United States," in *Acta M*, 33 (1961), p. 72–79; with a "Codetta: some details of musicology in the United States," by Jan LaRue, p. 79–83.

YUGOSLAVIA

746 / **Cvetko, Dragotin.** "Les formes et les résultats des efforts musicologiques yougoslaves," in *Acta M*, 31 (1958), p. 50–62.

747 / **Beiträge zur Musikwissenschaft.** Sonderreihe: Bibliographien. I. SR Rumanien (1945–1965), 66 p. II. VR Polen (1945–1965), 192 p. 1966.

Rumania and Poland are the first two countries covered in this series of bibliographies devoted to musicological literature in the East-European countries. Printed in a subseries of the leading musicological journal of the German Democratic Republic.

748 / **Bericht über die Musikwissenschaftlichen Arbeiten in der Deutschen Demokratischen Republik 1968.** Herausgegeben vom Zentralinstitut für Musikforschung beim Verband Deutscher Komponisten und Musikwissenschaftler. Berlin, Verlag Neue Musik. 1969. 150 p.

Abstracts of scholarly papers and dissertations by East German musicologists.

749 / **Chase, Gilbert.** A guide to the music of Latin America. A joint publication of the Pan American Union and the Library of Congress. 2nd ed., rev. and enl. Washington, Pan American Union, 1962. 411 p.

First published in 1945 under the title *Guide to Latin American music*. Reprint by AMS Press, New York, 1962.

A general bibliography of Latin American music, followed by listings related to individual composers. Index of authors, names, and subjects.

750 / **Correia de Azevedo, Luís H.** Bibliografia musical brasileira (1820–1950). Rio de Janeiro, 1952. 252 p. (Ministerio da Educaçao e Saúde. Instituto Nacional do Livro, Col. Bl. Bibliografia 9.)

1,639 titles under 13 subject sections. Includes writings by Brazilian authors on non-Brazilian music. Publications containing music only are omitted.

Review by A. Hyatt King in *Music and letters*, 35 (1954), p. 67–68; by Charles Seeger in *Notes*, 11 (1954), p. 551–52.

751 / **Davidsson, Åke.** Bibliografi över Svensk musiklitteratur, 1800–1945. Uppsala, 1948. 215 p.

A classified bibliography of general works, general music histories, histories of music in Sweden, works on musicians of all nationalities, and theoretical works. Restricted to writings by Swedish authors except for subjects connected with Swedish music. 5,432 items in all. Index.

752 / **Dordević, Vladimir R.** Ogled srpske muzichke bibliografije do 1914 godine. (An essay on the Serbian musical bibliography until 1914.)

P. 57–280: a bibliography of 2,350 items, with separate sections for printed music, music literature, and manuscripts. Indexes of authors and titles.

753 / **Ford, Wyn K.** Music in England before 1800: a select bibliography. London, The Library Association, 1967. 128 p.

Classified bibliography in two major divisions: Part I, music and its environment; Part II, persons. Confined to literature published in the 20th century in English, French, and German. The major critical editions of composers' works are cited in Part II.

754 / **Kinscella, Hazel G.** "Americana index to *The musical quarterly*, 1915–57." Published as vol. 6: 2 (1958), of *The journal of research in music education*. 144 p.

Indexes all articles related to American music and musical events.

755 / **Lissa, Zofia.** "Die Musikwissenschaft in Volkspolen (1945–56)." In *Die Musikforschung*, 10 (1957), p. 531–47.

Translated from the Polish by Werner Kaupert.

In narrative style with many titles quoted. Discusses the state and organization of Polish musicology since World War II.

Materiały do Bibliografii Muzyki Polskiej. See no. 556.

756 / **"Music Section."** In *Handbook of Latin American studies*, a guide to the material published in 1935–1948. Nos. 1–14. . . . Cambridge, Mass., Harvard Univ. Press, 1936–51. 14 v.

757 / **Muzíková, Ruzena.** Selective bibliography of literature on Czech and Slovak music. Prague, Czechoslovak Music Information Centre, 1969. 124 p.

A useful bibliography of Czechoslovakian music literature for English readers. Czech titles are given in English translation, with brief descriptions of content and bibliographical features. Classified in nine major sections: bibliography, catalogs, dictionaries, periodical publications, history of Czech and Slovak music, monographs, anthologies, instruments, and notation.

758 / **Nef, Karl.** Schriften über Musik und Volksgesang. Bern, K. J. Wyss, 1908. 151 p. (Bibliographie der schweizerischen Landeskunde, Faszikel V.)

Classified bibliography of literature on Swiss music, its history and practice. Index of names.

759 / **Potúček, Juraj.** Súpis slovenských hudobnín a literatúry o hudobníkoch. (Catalog of Slovak printed music and books on musicians.) Bratislava, Slovenská akademie věd a unmění, 1952. 435 p.

Lists musicians active in Slovakia to 1949 or mentioned in Slovak periodical literature. Bibliographies of works with Slovak texts, 1881 to 1949. Chronological index, classified index, name index.

760 / **Potúček, Juraj.** Súpis slovenskych hudobno-teoretických prác. (Catalog of Slovak musico-theoretical works.) Bratislava, Slovenská akademie věd, 1955. 467 p.

Classified bibliography of literary and theoretical works on Czech music, including periodical articles (p. 15–216). List of theoretical works in chronological order, 1519–1853 (p. 219–25). Biographical section, including, under composers' names, both publications of music and critical articles (p. 223–380). Classified list of music published 1950–52 (p. 383–403).

761 / **Potúček, Juraj.** Výberofá bibliografia zo slovenskej hudobnovednej literatúry 1862–1962. (Selective bibliography of Slovak musicological literature from 1862–1962. Cyclostyled, Bratislava, Slovenská akademie věd, 1963. 116 p.

762 / **Rajeczky, B.** "Musikforschung in Ungarn 1936–1960. (Bibliographischer Bericht.)" In *Studia musicologica*, 1 (1961), p. 225–49.
A brief survey of recent Hungarian musical scholarship, with a classified bibliography of music literature. Hungarian titles given with German translations. Sections on folk music, Hungarian music history, general music history, collective works.

763 / **Rocha da Silva Guimarães, Bertino D.** Primeiro esboco duma bibliografia musical portuguesa, con uma breve notícia histórica de música no nosso país. Porto, 1947. 174 p.
The bibliographical section includes works on music by Portuguese authors, works on music in Portugal by native or foreign authors, old Portuguese pedagogical works, special bibliographies, and music periodicals.

764 / **Schaal, Richard.** Das Schrifttum zur musikalischen Lokalgeschichtsforschung. Kassel, Bärenreiter, 1947. 62 p.
A bibliography of studies of music in various European cities and provinces, arranged alphabetically by place. Includes articles from a few leading periodicals. Very brief citations.

765 / **Sendrey, Alfred.** Bibliography of Jewish music. New York, Columbia Univ. Press, 1951. 404 p.
A classified bibliography of 5,854 items; writings on Jewish music and musicians. Includes periodical articles.
Part II of this work is a bibliography of music, entered as no. 854.
Review by Milton Feist in MQ, 37 (1951), p. 432–35; by Ernst C. Krohn in *JAMS*, 7 (Summer 1954), p. 150–52.

766 / **Urtubey, Pola Suárez.** La música en revistas argentinas. Buenos Aires, Fondo Nacional de las Artes, 1969. 70 p.

179

A bibliography of 652 entries for articles on music in four Argentine periodicals: *La Gaceta musical* (1874-87), *La Moda* (1837–38), Revista de estudios musicales (1949–54), and *La Revista de música* (1927–30). Index of names.

767 / **Vyborny, Zdenek.** "Czech music literature since World War II," in *Notes*, 16 (1959), p. 539–46.
Translated from the German by William Lichtenwanger.
A classified bibliography, each section preceded by a brief descriptive statement. Titles given in Czech and English.

768 / **Weisser, Albert.** Bibliography of publications and other resources on Jewish music. New York, National Jewish Music Council, 1969. 117 p.

Revised and enlarged edition based in part upon *"The bibliography* of books and articles on Jewish music" prepared by Joseph Yasser and published in 1955.

769 / **Woodfill, Walter L.** "Bibliography." In his *Musicians in English society*. Princeton, N.J., Princeton Univ. Press, 1953. p. 315–61.
Unabridged reprint by Da Capo Press, New York, 1959.
A substantial listing of the primary and secondary sources for the study of English music of the late-16th and early-17th centuries. Separated as to works before and after 1700.
The Woodfill bibliography is a fine example of the kind of information to be found in histories of national music or monographs related to the music of a local school or development.

Opera and Theater Music

770 / **Baker, Blanch M.** "Music." In *Theatre and allied arts, a guide to books dealing with the history, criticism, and technic of the drama and theatre and related arts and crafts.* New York, H. W. Wilson, 1952. p. 428–41.
Broadly classified and selective list. Annotated. Few entries have more than an indirect bearing on theater music.

771 / **Bustico, Guido.** Bibliografia della storia e cronistorie dei teatri italiani. Milano, Bollettino bibliografici musicale, 1929. 82 p.

Subtitle: "Il teatro musicale italiano."

Part I (p. 19–27): a general bibliography of the Italian musical theater. Part II (p. 31–83): a bibliography of the musical theater in specific Italian cities, arranged alphabetically by place. Includes periodical articles. Some brief descriptive annotations.

772 / **Grout, Donald J.** "Bibliographies, lexicons, guides, histories, and other works dealing with opera . . ." In his *A short history of opera.* 2nd edition. New York, Columbia Univ. Press, 1965. p. 585–768.

One of the most comprehensive bibliographies of literature on the opera. Includes both books and articles in leading European and American periodicals. Arranged alphabetically by author.

773 / **Surian, Elvidio.** A checklist of writings on 18th-century French and Italian opera (excluding Mozart). Hackensack, J. Boonin, 1970. 121 p. (Music indexes and bibliographies, 3.)

Also entered under no. 721.

Primary Sources: Early Music Literature

The entries in this section are concerned with writings on music that appeared before 1800. For further listings of early music literature, one should consult the general bibliographies compiled before 1840, such as *Becker* (no. 536), *Forkel* (no. 549), and *Lichtenthal* (no. 554). See also the narrative bibliography by James E. Matthew (no. 557) and the catalogs of libraries with noteworthy holdings in early music theory, such as the U.S. Library of Congress (no. 1532), the library of Alfred Cortot (no. 1555), and the Paul Hirsch Library in the British Museum (no. 1559).

774 / **Bukofzer, Manfred F.** "Check-list of baroque books on music." In his *Music in the Baroque era.* New York, Norton, 1947. p. 417–31.

Theory treatises, instruction books, and histories written between c. 1590 and 1770. Modern facsimiles and reprints indicated. Arranged alphabetically by author.

775 / **Coover, James B.** "Music theory in translation; a bibliography." In *Journal of music theory*, 2 (1959), p. 70–95.

Cites only English translations of early theory works. Alphabetical listing, by author, of works from antiquity to the present day.

776 / **Davidsson, Åke.** Bibliographie der musiktheoretischen Drucke des 16. Jahrhunderts. Baden-Baden, Heitz, 1962. 99 p. (Bibliotheca bibliographica aureliana, 9.)

A bibliography of 16th-century theory works; more than 600 titles, arranged alphabetically by author, with bibliographical reference to literature on the sources. Index of persons, including printers, editors, etc. Bibliography, pp. 85–88. 25 facsimile plates.

Review by Fred Blum in *Notes*, 20 (1963), p. 234.

777 / **Davidsson, Åke.** Catalogue critique et descriptif des ouvrages théoriques sur la musique imprimés au XVIe et au XVIIe siècles et conservés dans les bibliothèques suédoises. Upsala, Almquist & Wiksells, 1953. 83 p. (Studia musicologica upsaliensia, 2.)

A union catalog of early works on music theory in Swedish libraries. 108 items, fully described, with locations and references to relevant literature. P. 77–83: bibliography of works cited.

778 / **Farmer, Henry G.** The sources of Arabian music: an annotated bibliography of Arabic manuscripts which deal with the theory, practice, and history of Arabian music from the eighth to the seventeenth century. Leiden, E. J. Brill, 1965. 71 p.

First issued privately by the author in 1940.

Entries arranged chronologically by century, preceded by a brief general discussion of Arabian music and its sources.

Review by Jörg Martin in *Die Musikforschung*, 25 (1972), p. 372–73.

779 / **International Inventory of Musical Sources.** Écrits imprimés concernant la musique. Ouvrage publié sous la direction de François Lesure. München, G. Henle, 1971. 2 v. (RISM ser. B VI, 1/2.) Vol. 1: A–L. Vol. 2: M–Z.

A comprehensive bibliography of writings on music printed before 1800, comprising all theoretical, historical, aesthetic, or technical literature. Location symbols identify copies held in European and American libraries. Brief introduction; listing of the institutions that have contributed information on their holdings.

780 / **International Inventory of Musical Sources.** The theory of music from the Carolingian era up to 1400. Vol. 1– . Edited by Joseph Smits van Waesberghe with the collaboration of Peter Fischer and Christian Maas. Descriptive catalogue of manuscripts. München, G. Henle, 1961– . 155 p. (RISM, ser. B, v. 3:1.)

Offers a description of all manuscripts in which are preserved Latin treatises, however small, dealing with the theory of music which was in use from the Carolingian era to 1400. [*Preface*]

Index of libraries; index of authors and of incipits of anonymous treatises.
Review by James B. Coover in *Journal of music theory*, 6 (1962), p. 314–15.

781 / **Mancyczewski, Eusebius.** "Bücher und Schriften über Musik. Druckwerke und Handschriften aus der Zeit bis zum Jahre 1800." In *Geschichte der K.K. Gesellschaft der Musikfreunde in Wien. . . .* Wien, 1912. Vol. p. 55–84.
An extremely useful listing of the pre-1800 writings on music in the library of the Gesellschaft der Musikfreunde in Vienna.

782 / **Reese, Gustave.** Fourscore classics of music literature; a guide to selected original sources on theory and other writings on music not available in English, with descriptive sketches and bibliographical references. New York, The Liberal Arts Press, 1957. 91 p.
Reprinted by the Da Capo Press, New York, 1970.
80 works presented in chronological order, with illuminating commentary. This bibliography, sponsored by the American Council of Learned Societies, was intended to stimulate new English editions and translations of important early theory works. Index of titles.

783 / **Riley, Maurice W.** "A tentative bibliography of early wind instrument tutors." In *Journal of research in music education*, 6 (1958), p. 3–24.
The listing is chronological under the various instruments: flute, oboe, clarinet, bassoon, horn, trumpet, trombone, tuba, and related instruments. Annotated.

784 / **Warner, Thomas E.** An annotated bibliography of woodwind instruction books, 1600–1830. Detroit, Information Coordinators, Inc., 1967. 138 p. (Detroit studies in music bibliography, 11.)

A bibliography of 450 items arranged chronologically; includes a number of "unlocated" titles. Contains a list of modern works cited; indexed by author and anonymous titles and by type of instrument.

785 / **Williams, David Russell.** A bibliography of the history of music theory. 2nd ed. Fairport, New York, Rochester Music Publishers, 1971. 58 p.
First printed in 1970.
A bibliography of selected theory works and writings devoted to them. Organized chronologically in study units, as in a syllabus. Indexes of treatises and names.

Sacred Music

Bibliographies of writings on sacred music are surprisingly few. Additional references will be found in the various handbooks to hymnology (nos. 326 ff.). See also current listings in the *Jahrbuch für Liturgik und Hymnologie* (no. 586) and Gregório Suñol's bibliography of works related to Gregorian chant (no. 717).

786 / **Buszin, Walter** [*et al.*]. A bibliography on music and the church. Prepared for the Commission on Music, Department of Worship and the Arts, National Council of Churches of Christ in the U.S.A. New York, National Council of Churches of Christ, 1958. 16 p.

Individual Composers

In this section are a few representative examples of bibliographies devoted to writings about specific composers. These are to be distinguished from bibliographies made up of entries for the composer's own works, which will be found in "Bibliographies of Music" under the heading "Individual composers" (see no. 981 ff.).

BEETHOVEN, LUDWIG VAN

787 / **Ludwig van Beethoven.** A magyar könyvtárakban és gyüjteményekben. Bibliográfia I-III. Ed. by Ferenc Gyimes and Veronika Vavrinecz. Budapest, Allami Gorkij Könyvtár, 1970–1972. 3 v

A union catalog of Beethoven documentation in Hungarian libraries.
Vol. 1: a bibliography of literature on Beethoven.

Vol. 2: a discography of 738 items, with index of performing artists and organizations.

Vol. 3: a bibliography of Beethoven compositions, 1,378 items, with indexes of titles, editors, and publishers.

CHOPIN, FRÉDÉRIC

788 / **Michałowski, Kornel.** Bibliografia chopinowska. Chopin bibliography 1849–1969. Kraków, Polskie Wydawnictwo muzyczne, 1970. 268 p.

A well-organized bibliography of literature about Chopin, covering documentary evidence, life, works, interpretation, studies of Chopin's reception, and bibliographical publications.

3,970 items. Text in Polish and English. Indexes of subjects, Chopin's works, and authors.

HANDEL, GEORGE FRIEDRICH

789 / **Sasse, Konrad.** Händel Bibliographie. Zusammengestellt von Konrad Sasse unter Verwendung des im Händel-Jahrbuch 1933 von Kurt Taut veröffentlichten Verzeichnisses des Schrifttums über Georg Friedrich Händel. Abgeschlossen im Jahre 1961. Leipzig, Deutscher Verlag für Musik, 1963. 352 p.

The expansion of a bibliography compiled by Kurt Taut for the 1933 Händel-Jahrbuch, with a supplement by Sasse published in the 1955 Jahrbuch. A highly organized work citing literature on every aspect of the composer's life and work. Author index.

Review by Willi Reich in *Literature, music, fine arts*, 1 (1968), p. 87–89.

REGER, MAX

790 / **Rösner, Helmut.** Max-Reger-Bibliographie. Das internationale Schrifttum über Max Reger 1893–1966. Bonn. Hannover, München, Dümmler (1968). 138 p. (Veröffentlichungen des Max-Reger-Institutes, 5.)

SCHUMANN, ROBERT

791 / **Munte, Frank.** Verzeichnis des deutschsprachigen Schrifttums über Robert Schumann 1856–1970. Hamburg, Wagner, 1972. 151 p. (Schriftenreihe zur Musik, 1.)

Anhang: "Schrifttums über Clara Schumann."

SIBELIUS, JEAN

792 / **Blum, Fred.** Jean Sibelius, an international bibliography on the occasion of the centennial celebrations, 1965. Detroit, Information Coordinators, 1965. 114 p. (Detroit studies in music bibliography, 8.)

P. 1–11: books and dissertations devoted to Sibelius; p. 13–45: books partially devoted to Sibelius; p. 47–71; music journals; p. 73–94: nonmusic journals. Index of names.

Review by Gerhard Hahne in *Die Musikforschung*, 22 (1969), p. 100. By Ruth Watanabe in *Notes*, 23 (1966), p. 279.

STRAUSS, RICHARD

793 / **Ortner, Oswald, and Franz Grasberger.** Richard-Strauss-Bibliographie. Teil 1: 1882–1944. Wien, Georg Prachner, 1964. 124 p. (Museion. Veröffentlichungen der Österreichischen Nationalbibliothek. Neue Folge. Dritte Reihe, 2.)

A bibliography of 1,763 items, organized in terms of various aspects of Strauss's career. The largest section is devoted to writings related to individual works, operas, etc.

WAGNER, RICHARD

794 / **Internationale Wagner-Bibliographie.** International Wagner bibliography. Bibliographie internationale de la littérature sur Wagner 1945–1955. Herausgegeben von Herbert Barth. Bayreuth, Edition Musica, 1956. 56 p.

Contains selective listings of German, English, and French writings on Wagner. The appendix offers an international Wagner discography, statistics of performances by major opera companies, and a survey of important Wagner collections.

795 / **Internationale Wagner-Bibliographie.** International Wagner bibliography. Bibliographie internationale de la littérature sur

Wagner 1956–1960. Herausgegeben von Henrik Barth. Bayreuth, Edition Musica, 1961. 142 p.

This volume follows the same pattern of organization as the preceding but also includes a tabulation of the casts of all the Bayreuth Festivals from 1876 to 1960.

796 / **Kastner, Emerich.** Wagner-Catalog. Chronologisches Verzeichniss der von und über Richard Wagner erschienenen Schriften, Musikwerke etc., etc., nebst biographischen Notizen. Offenbach z.M., André, 1878. 140 p.

Reprint, 1966, by Fritz A. M. Knuf, Hilversum.

Chronological listing of Wagner's works and the literature about them from 1813 to 1877.

797 / **Oesterlein, Nikolaus.** Katalog einer Richard Wagner-Bibliothek; nach den vorliegenden Originalien systematisch-chronologisch geordnetes und mit Citaten und Anmerkungen versehenes authentisches Nachschlagebuch durch die gesammte Wagner-Literatur. Leipzig, Breitkopf & Härtel, 1882–1895. 4 v.

Vols. 1 and 2 of this work consist of a bibliography of late 19th-century writings on Wagner. The remaining volumes consist of a catalog of the holdings of the Richard Wagner-Museum in Eisenach. (See also item no. 1232.)

Bibliographies of Music

In this category are listed bibliographies of *musical scores* as distinct from *writings about music*. This section lends itself to fewer subdivisions than the preceding assemblage of "Bibliographies of Music Literature," the major approaches being that of the performer in search of music appropriate to his particular instrument or ensemble, on the one hand, and that of the student of early music on the other.

Not included here, except for a token listing of recent titles, are the numerous listings of the works of individual composers. One of the best approaches to information of this kind is through the biographical dictionaries such as *Baker* (no. 65) and *Riemann* (no. 46), or such comprehensive encyclopedias as *MGG* (no. 38). For thematic catalogs, a useful guide is found in Barry Brook's *Checklist of thematic catalogues* (no. 1839).

This section excludes the catalogs of individual music publishing firms except where their coverage extends beyond the output of a single business house, as in the case of *Hofmeister* or *Pazdirek* (no. 818). Bibliographies of the work of early music publishers are found in the section "Histories and Bibliographies of Music Printing and Publishing."

GENERAL

798 / **Aronowsky, Salomon.** Performing times of orchestral works. Foreword by Percival R. Kirby. London, E. Benn, 1959. 802 p.

Covers both standard and minor composers of all countries and periods, with some emphasis on British names. Arrangements listed under both composer and arranger. Operas, orchestral versions of single songs, and opera excerpts appear frequently. No precise indication of edition or publisher, but lists of publishers and publishers' organizations are given. The work is a more lavish and expensive publication than seems warranted by its contents.

Review by Howard Mitchell in *Notes*, 17 (1960), p. 237–39.

799 / **Berkowitz, Freda P.** Popular titles and subtitles of musical compositions. New York, Scarecrow Press, Inc., 1962. 182 p.

Alphabetical listing of 502 works by title, with brief accounts of the origins of their popular titles. Bibliography. Composer index.

800 / **Boustead, Alan.** Music to Shakespeare, a practical catalogue of current incidental music, song settings and other related music. . . . London, printed by Novello and Co., sole distributor. Oxford Univ. Press, 1964. 40 p.

Shakespearean works entered alphabetically, with music given under three headings: (1) incidental music, (2) songs, (3) other music. Minimum bibliographical information. Indexes of song titles and of composers. No key to publishers.

For other listings of Shakespeare music, see no. 803.

801 / **British Broadcasting Corporation. Central Music Library.** [Catalogues] London, British Broadcasting Corp., 1965–67. 9 v.

[1] Chamber music catalogue: chamber music, violin and keyboard, cello and keyboard, various (1965), 1 v., various pagings.

[2] Piano and organ catalogue (1965). 2 v., various pagings.

[3] Song catalogue (1966). 4 v. Vols. 1–2, composers; vols. 3–4, titles.

[4] Choral and opera catalogue (1967). 2 v.

These volumes record the holdings of one of the world's great radio libraries. Each volume is devoted to a special category of materials. Entries include composer's full name, dates if known, title of the work, score or parts, duration, publisher. A bibliography of relevant reference works and a listing of the principal music publishers are given in each volume. The chief value of this set lies in the information it offers as a reference tool. The BBC Music Library is not a lending library.

Published under the supervision of John H. Davies, BBC Music Librarian; with an introduction by William Glock.

Review of vol. 1 (Chamber music catalogue) by Donald W. Krummel in *Notes*, 23 (1966), p. 46–48.

802 / **Bryant, Eric T.** Music librarianship; a practical guide. London, James Clarke; New York, Hafner [1959], 503 p.

Part II, p. 287–487, is a series of lists of recommended musical scores for libraries, classified under instrumental music, vocal music, miniature scores. Detailed annotations.

The Bryant work is also entered as no. 1841.

803 / **"Catalogue of Musical Works Based on the Plays and Poetry of Shakespeare."** Compiled by Winton Dean, Dorothy Moore, and Phyllis Hartnoll. In *Shakespeare in music*. London, Macmillan, 1964. P. 243–321.

Works listed under the titles of the plays, in three categories: opera, incidental music, song settings. Checklist of composers. The bibliography of operatic settings, by Winton Dean, is also published in *Shakespeare survey*, no. 18 (1965), p. 75–93.

804 / **Cudworth, Charles.** "Ye olde spuriosity shoppe or, put it in the *Anhang*." In *Notes*, 12 (1954–55), p. 25–40, 533–53.

A lively discussion of the problems of plagiarism, hoaxes, misattribution, and the use of pseudonyms in the music field. The article contains three useful supplements: (1) spuriosities proper, listed under their supposed composers; (2) nicknames and falsely titled compositions; (3) pseudonyms, altered forms of names, and nicknames.

For works covering similar material, see nos. 799, 814.

805 / **Cushing, Helen G.** Children's song index, an index to more than 22,000 songs in 189 collections comprising 222 volumes. New York, H. W. Wilson, 1936. 798 p.

A dictionary catalog of children's song literature. Main entry is by song title, with subordinate entries under composer, author of the words, and subject. References from first line to title. Foreign titles given in the original language. There is a preliminary "catalog of collections indexed," and a "directory of publishers" at the end of the volume.

806 / **Davies, Hugh.** Répertoire international des musiques electroacoustiques. International electronic music catalog. A cooperative publication of le Groupe de recherches musicales de l'O.R.T.F., Paris, and the Independent Electronic Music Center, New York. Cambridge, Mass., Distributed by M.I.T. Press, 1968. 330 p. (*Electronic music review*, nos. 2/3, April/July 1967.)
Text in French and English.

The aim of this new catalog is to document all the electronic music ever composed in the almost 20 years since composers first began to work in this media.

Main alphabet is by country, subdivided by city and state (if in U.S.A.). Gives data as to composer, title of work, function, date of composition, duration, and number of tape tracks involved.
Some 5,000 compositions listed. Appendixes include a discography, a directory of permanent studies, and an index of composers.
Review by Jon Appleton in *Notes*, 25 (1968), p. 34–35.

807 / **De Charms, Desiree, and Paul F. Breed.** Songs in collections, an index. [Detroit] Information Service, Inc., 1966. 588 p.
Indexes 411 collections of solo songs published between 1940 and 1957. Entries for more than 9,400 songs. Composed songs entered under composer, with anonymous and folk songs entered alphabetically by title under nationality. Separate sections for carols and for sea chanties. Complete title and first line index.
This work articulates with the Sears *Song Index*, no 816.
Review by Donald Ivey in *Journal of research in music education*, 15 (1967), p. 169–70; by Imogen Fellinger in *Die Musikforschung*, 23 (1970), p. 96–97; by Ellen Kenny in *Notes*, 23 (1966), p. 269–70.

808 / **"Documents du Demi-Siècle.** Tableau chronologique des principales oeuvres musicales de 1900 à 1950 établi par genre et par année. Numéro spécial." *La revue musicale*, no. 216 (1952), 146 p.

A listing, year by year, of the important musical works of the first half of the 20th century, together with miscellaneous information relating to music for each year. Catalogs of six publishers, with significant work issued by them between 1900 and 1950: Heugel, Costallat, Amphion, Ricordi, Choudens, Ouvrières. Minimal bibliographical information.

809 / **Foster, Myles B.** Anthems and anthem composers, an essay upon the development of the anthem from the time of the Reformation to the end of the 19th century; with a complete list of anthems (in alphabetical order) belonging to each of the four centuries. . . . London, Novello, 1901. 225 p.

Reprint by Da Capo Press, New York, 1970.

810 / **Hofmeister, Friedrich.** Verzeichnis der in Deutschland seit 1868 erschienenen Werke russischer Komponisten. Leipzig, Druck der Buchdruckerei Frankenstein, 1949. 253 p.

Alphabetical listing of composers, with their works in order of opus number. Detailed bibliographical information including price but lacking date of publication.

811 / **Leigh, Robert.** Index to song books, a title index to over 11,000 copies of almost 6,800 songs in 111 song books published between 1933 and 1962. Stockton, Calif. Robert Leigh, 1964. 273 p.

Intended to supplement the Sears *Song index,* no. 816.

Reprint published by Da Capo Press, New York, 1972.

812 / **McCarty, Clifford.** Film composers in America: a checklist of their work. Foreword by Lawrence Morton. Glendale, Calif., John Valentine [1953], 193 p.

163 names, with film scores listed by date. Index of film titles; index of orchestrators. Reprint by Da Capo Press, New York, 1972.

Review by F. W. Sternfeld in *Notes,* 11 (1953), p. 105.

Also entered as no. 180.

813 / **McColvin, Lionel R., and Harold Reeves.** "Music: a comprehensive classified list." In their *Music libraries.* London, Grafton, 1937–38. V. 2, p. 1–209.

A guide to selection for music librarians. A classified list containing, for the most part, music in print at the time of compilation. Emphasis on British publishers, though some foreign material is included. This list has been superseded, to a large extent, by the one given in Bryant, see no. 802.

814 / **Mies, Paul.** Volkstümliche Namen musikalischer Werke. Bonn, Musikhandel-Verlags [1960], 32 p.

Nicknames and popular titles for musical compositions listed under composers, with an alphabetical index of titles. Similar compilations are cited as no 799, 804.

815 / **Reddick, William.** The standard musical repertoire, with accurate timings. Garden City, N.Y., Doubleday & Co., 1947. 192 p.

Reprint by the Greenwood Press, New York, 1969.

A classified list of overtures, orchestral works, works for piano and for violin, songs, and choral numbers, with timings to the nearest 5 seconds. Designed primarily for program directors of radio stations.

816 / **Sears, Minnie E.** Song index: an index to more than 12,000 songs in 177 song collections . . . New York, H. W. Wilson Co., 1926. 650 p.

Supplement: an index to more than 7,000 songs in 104 collections . . . 1934. 366 p. Reprint by the Shoe String Press.

Contains titles, first lines, authors' names, and composers' names in one alphabet. Each song is cited under title, with added entry under composer and author, and cross references for first line and variant or translated titles. Classified and alphabetical listings of the song collections indexed.

The work of Sears has been continued in *Songs in collections* by De Charms and Breed (1966). See no 807.

817 / **Taylor, Jed H.** Vocal and instrumental music in print. New York and London, The Scarecrow Press, 1965. 166 p.

A highly selective list, containing much material of purely pedagogical interest. Classified under instrumental and vocal headings. Entries give title of work, with English translation, medium, publisher, and price. Of limited value, although there is a useful list of publishers and dealers, with their current addresses.

Review by Donald W. Krummel in *Notes*, 23 (1966), p. 58.

818 / **Universal-Handbuch der Musikliteratur Aller Zeiten und Völker.** Als Nachschlagewerk und Studienquelle der Welt-Musikliteratur. Wien, Pazdirek & Co. [1904–10?] 14 v.

Reprint 34 v. in 12 by Knuf, Hilversum [1966?]

The nearest thing to a comprehensive listing of "music in print" ever published. Primarily useful for 19th-century material in establishing the existence of and dates of editions. Arrangement under composer by opus number, if known; otherwise by title.

819 / **Upton, Raymond.** Index of miniature scores: British availability. London, C. Jackson, 1956. 120 p.

Review by Betty Buyck in *Notes*, 14 (1957), p. 367.

CURRENT

The current music bibliographies listed below restrict their entries to music only. For a full coverage, one should be acquainted with the various national bibliographies in which music appears in company with listings from other fields. An excellent introduction to the use of these major bibliographical tools is an article by Donald W. Krummel and James B. Coover, "Current national bibliographies, their music coverage," in *Notes*, 17 (1960), p. 375–88.

See also the current listings and reviews in such periodicals as *Notes*, *Fontes artis musicae*, *Acta Musicologica*, and the *Music review*.

820 / **Le Bibliograph Musical.** Paraissant tour les deux mois avec le concours d'une Réunion d'artistes et d'érudits. Première Année (1872)—Cinquième Année (1876) Numéro 1–29. Paris, 1872–76. Continuous pagination 499 p.

Reprint of the complete set by Schnase, 1968.

A bibliographical journal issued bimonthly by a group of scholars, librarians, and musicians (the number varies). Contains short articles of bibliographical interest, reports of auction sales, reviews, descriptions of music institutions, etc. The most frequent contributor is Arthur Pougin.

821 / **Bibliographia Hungarica 1945–1960.** Catalogus systematicus notarum musicarum in hungaria editarum. Edidit Bibliotheca

Nationalis Hungariae a Francisco Széchényi fundata. Budapest, Országos Széchényi Könyvtár, 1969. 361 p.

A classified listing of all Hungarian music publications between 1945 and 1960. Indexed by composers and by first line of texts. P. 353–361: a schematic outline of the classification system. A publication of the national Széchényi Library, the principal editors are Iván Pethes, Veronika Vavrineca, and Jenö Vécsey (deceased).

822 / **Bibliographie Musicale Française,** publiée par la Chambre Syndicale des Éditeurs de Musique. Année 1–26, Numéro 1–192. Paris, La Chambre Syndicale des Éditeurs de Musique, 1875–1920. 47 v. in 23.

Reprint of the original edition by Annemarie Schnase, Scarsdale, New York, 1968.

A monthly trade list of music issued by the major French publishers over a period of 45 years. The lists are classified by performing media. Some of the publishers represented are: Colombier, Choudens, Lemoine, Brandus, Durand, Gauthier, Grus, Heugel, Le Bailly, Leduc, and E. Mathieu.

823 / **The British Catalogue of Music.** 1– . London, The Council of the British National Bibliography, 1957– .

Published quarterly; the list issue of each year is a cumulated annual volume. Organized in two parts: a classified and an alphabetical section. There is also a section devoted to musical literature. Lists of music publishers with their British agents specified.

The classification scheme used in this catalog has been published separately; see no. 1838.

824 / **Brünn. Universita. Knihovna.** Prírustky hudebnin v cesko. Slovenských knihovnäch. Spracoval Zdeněk Zouhar. Praha, Statní Pedagogicke Nakladatelstvi, 1953– .

Joint accession list of 10 principal music libraries in Czechoslovakia, listing 2,000–3,000 items per year. Classified by medium, without index.

825 / **Composium Directory of New Music.** Vol. 1– . Los Angeles, Crystal Record Company, 1971– .

Composium, a quarterly index of contemporary compositions, is a list of recent works by living composers, and includes both published and currently unpublished compositions. The *Directory of new music,* published annually, includes all the works that have been listed in the Quarterly during the preceding year. These are indexed here by instrumentation as well as by composer. Also included are brief biographical sketches of each of the composers listed. [From the *Preface* by Peter Christ, Editor, *Composium,* President, Crystal Record Co.]

The 1971 ed. of the *Directory* has 59 pages. The 1972 issue has 64 p.; the 1973 issue, 48 p.

826 / **Dansk Musikfortegnelse.** Udgivet af Dansk Musikhandlerforening. Vol. 1– . Kobenhavn, 1931– .
An index to music issued by Danish music publishers. Arranged alphabetically with composers and titles interfiled. Each volume ordinarily covers three years of publication. Since 1962 the entries have been classified.

827 / **Deutsche Musikbibliographie.** Jahrgang 1– . Leipzig, F. Hofmeister, 1829– .
See no 578 for full annotation.

828 / **Deutscher Büchereiverband. Arbeitsstelle für das Büchereiwesen.** Musikbibliographischer Dienst (MD). 1. Jahrgang,—Berlin, Deutscher Büchereiverband, 1970– .
A periodical publication issued six times yearly, the sixth issue being a cumulation listing all of the current publications of serious music. International in scope, but German in practice since information is reported by 12 German public libraries. The editors are Burchard Bulling and Helmut Fösner. Entries are printed in catalog card format on one side of the page so that they can be cut and filed in a card tray. The publication can also be purchased in loose sheets for this purpose.

829 / **Fontes Artis Musicae.** Review of the International Association of Music Libraries, 1954– .
Each issue contains a "Liste internationale sélective" largely devoted to listings of current music publications by country, compiled by a series of national editors.
This entry is also found under "Bibliographies of Music Literature: Current or annual," no. 565 ff.

830 / **Hofmeisters Handbuch der Musikliteratur.** Bd. 1– . Leipzig, F. Hofmeister, 1844– .
See no. 583 for full annotation.

831 / **Jahresverzeichnis der Deutschen Musikalien und Musikschriften.** Jahrgang 1– . Leipzig, F. Hofmeister, 1852– .
See no. 588 for full annotation.

832 / **Letopis' Muzykal'noĭ Literatury;** organ gosudarstzennoĭ bibliografiĭ SSSR. Izdaetsia s 1931 goda; vykhodit 4 raza v god. Moskva, Izdatel'stvo vsesoĭuznoĭ knizhnoi palaty, 1931– .
Quarterly. Organization and content vary slightly. In 1960 a classified list of publications in musical notation. Includes literary works with musical supplements or extensive musical illustrations, and music issued in periodicals. Index by composer for each issue, and separate lists of books, magazines, newspapers containing music. Annual index of vocal works by title and first line, and by language of text. Entries give full bibliographical information, including complete contents, price, size of edition.

833 / **Přirůstky Hudebnin v Československých Knihovnách.** [Vol. 1–] Praha, Státni Pedagogické Nakladatelstvi, 1955– .
A classified union list of music accessions for seven major Czech libraries. The principal editor is Vladimír Telec.

834 / **U.S. Copyright Office.** Catalog of copyright entries. Music. Third series, v. 1– , 1947– . Washington, D.C., Copyright Office, The Library of Congress, 1947– .
From 1891 to 1906, the quarterly copyright index was issued by the Treasury Department and musical compositions were included as part of the general series. In a series, from 1906 to 1946, a music catalog was published separately. In 1946 it was subdivided into separate sections: published music, unpublished music, and renewal registrations, with main entries by composer and a classified index. This arrangement was maintained until vol. 11 of the third series (1958), when the listings were grouped under "current registrations" and "renewal registrations," with the main entry under title and a name index for composers.

835 / **U.S. Library of Congress.** Library of Congress catalog, music and phonorecords, a cumulative list of works represented by

Library of Congress printed cards. Washington, D.C., The Library of Congress, 1954– .

Current music accessions, printed or sound recordings, of the Library of Congress and of libraries participating in its cooperative cataloging program. Includes purchased current or retrospective materials and a selection of recent copyright deposits. Entries are reproduced from the library's printed cards. Name and subject index. Semiannual, with annual cumulation.

NATIONAL MUSIC

In this section are to be found bibliographies of music (scores) concerned with the music of particular nations. Many of these bibliographies originate in various national music centers that exist for the purpose of promoting the works of native composers. For a survey of such organizations, their history, services, publications, see "Directory of national music centers," compiled by Keith MacMillan, with and introduction by André Jurres, in *Notes*, 27 (1971), p. 680–693. This article describes 19 different national music centers.

Several of the works cited in the section "Bibliographies of music literature: National Music" also include listings of composers' works.

AUSTRALIA

836 / **Australasian Performing Right Association.** Catalogue of major musical compositions by Australian and New Zealand composers. Sydney, 1967? 53 p.

Supplementary catalogue of New Zealand composers. 9 p.

BELGIUM

837 / **Centre Belge de Documentation Musicale.** Catalogus van werken van Belgische componisten. Bruxelles, Centre Belge de Documentation Musicale, 1953–57. 20 numbers.

An irregularly published series of catalogs averaging 20 pages each, devoted to contemporary Belgian composers and their works. 11 in French, 9 in Flemish.

CANADA

838 / **Canadian Music Centre.** Catalogue of Canadian choral music available for perusal from the library of the Canadian Music Centre. Toronto, Canadian Music Centre, 1970. 207 p.

First issued in 1966, with an *Addendum* bringing the coverage up to 1970.

Classified listing with colored paper identifying sections devoted to mixed voices, female voices, and male voices. Composer listing and list of publishers.

Other Canadian Music Centre publications:

1. Canadian music for orchestra (1963)
2. Canadian chamber music (1967), 288 p.
3. Canadian keyboard music (1971), 91 p.
4. Canadian vocal music. 2nd ed. (1971), 81 p.

DENMARK

839 / **Samfundet Til Udgivelse af Dansk Musik 1871–1971.** The Society for Publishing Danish Music. Catalogue. København, Dan Fog Musikforlag, 1972. 115 p.

A similar listing was published in 1956 by Knud Larsen Musikforlag, with a *Supplement* in 1968.

The catalog is preceded by a history of the society, and "An outline of Danish music history."

P. 20–38: brief biographies of the composers; p. 39–85: the catalog, arranged alphabetically by composer. Chronological and systematic lists of publications; recordings issued by the society, a general index, and a 1972 price list.

FINLAND

840 / **Säveltäjain Tekijänoikeustoimisto Teosto.** Catalogue of Finnish orchestral and vocal compositions. Helsinki, Teosto (Composers' copyright bureau) 1961. 88 p.

Lists works by 57 Finnish composers giving titles, instrumentation, timings, publishers. Brief biographical sketches. English translations of Finnish titles.

FRANCE

841 / **Boll, André.** Répertoire analytique de la musique française des origines à nos jours. Paris, Horizons de France, 1948. 299 p.

Not as comprehensive as the title suggests. Part I: a list of composers of the French school, with dates, arranged alphabetically within historical periods. Part II: classified list of published French secular music, alphabetical by composer, followed by a similar listing of sacred music. Publishers given; indexed by works and by composers.

GERMANY (BUNDESREPUBLIK)

842 / **Deutscher Musikverleger-Verband.** Bonner Katalog. Verzeichnis der urheberrechtlich geschützten musikalischen Werke mit reversgebundenem Aufführungsmateriel. Bonn. Musikhandel-Verlagsgesellschaft M.B.H., 1959. 326 p.

Not a catalog of German music, strictly speaking, but a listing by composer of musical works protected by international copyright under the Bern Convention. Copyright editions of works by early composers included. Types of works indicated by symbols; duration and publishers given. Excellent source of information on published contemporary music.

GERMANY (DEUTSCHE DEMOKRATISCHE REPUBLIK)

843 / **Simbriger, Heinrich.** Werkkatalog zeitgenössischer Komponisten aus den deutschen Ostgebieten. Esslingen-Necker, Künstlergilde, 1955. 203 p.

Ergänzungsband, 1961. 151 p.

A classified bibliography of works by East German composers. Entries give title of work, instrumentation, publisher if any, and timing. A preliminary section is devoted to biographical sketches of the composers.

844 / **Was Wir Singen. Katalog des in der Deutschen Demokratischen Republik erschienenen weltlichen Lied- und Chormaterials.** Band I: 1945–58 Auswahl. Herausgegeben vom Zentralhaus für Volkskunst. Leipzig, Friedrich Hofmeister, 1959. 255 p.

Title listing of 6,582 entries, supplemented by lists of collections and of cantatas and oratorios. Indexed by subtitles or working titles, by voice combination and by affective theme, and by national character. Further indices by writer of text and composer.

GREAT BRITAIN

The British Catalogue of Music . . . see no. 811.

845 / **The Composers' Guild of Great Britain.** Chamber music by living British composers. London, British Music Information Centre, 1969. 42 p.

Alphabetical listing of composers and their works for three or more instruments. Information tabulated includes instrumentation, duration, publisher or agent, and availability of the material. Unpublished works also included.

846 / **The Composers' Guild of Great Britain.** British orchestral music. Vol. I of the catalogue of works by members of The Composers' Guild of Great Britain. London, Composers' Guild, 1958. 55 p.

Part 1: works for full, small or chamber orchestra.
Part 2: works for string orchestra.
The listings give composer, title of work, orchestration, publisher or agent, and availability of the material.

847 / **The Composers' Guild of Great Britain.** Orchestral music. Vol. II. By living British composers. London, British Information Centre, 1970. 82 p.

A sequel to the preceding catalog. Adds a listing of works for brass or military bands.

848 / **The Music Trader's Guide to Works by Twentieth-Century British Composers,** together with the names of their publishers; comprising instrumental works, songs, text books and manuals up to and including June, 1955. Compiled by L. D. Gibbin. London, Boosey and Hawkes, 1956. 132 p.

Brief entries for works by 76 composers; a listing alphabetical by title under the composers' names. Supplementary listing for "other British composers and their principal publishers."

HUNGARY

849 / **Bibliographia Hungarica 1945–1960.** Catalogus systematicus notarum musicarum in Hungaria editarum . . . edit. Bibliotheca Nationalis Hungariae. Budapest, 1969. 360 p.

850 / **Dedinsky, Izabella K.** Zeneművek, 1936—40. Budapest, Kiadja az országos széchényi könyvtár, 1944. 286 p.
Classified bibliography of music published in Hungary, 1936–1940. Includes both popular and serious music.

ISRAEL

851 / **Goldberg, Ira S.** Bibliography of instrumental music of Jewish interest. Part 2: Ensemble and solo. Compiled by Ira S. Goldberg. Rev. and enl. ed. New York, National Jewish Music Council, 1970. 181 p.

852 / **National Jewish Welfare Board. Bibliography Committee.** Bibliography of Jewish instrumental music. New York, National Jewish Music Council, 1948. 16 p.
Addenda, 1950. 7 leaves.
A selective list of the "best and most interesting works that are easily available . . . either in published form or through rental." Classified according to various combinations of instruments. Publishers indicated.

853 / **National Jewish Welfare Board. Bibliography Committee.** Bibliography of Jewish vocal music. New York, National Jewish Music Council. *c.* 1948. 36 p.
Addenda, 1950. 15 leaves.
A selective list of available Jewish vocal music "in good taste, and suited for programming." Classified by genre. Language or languages of text; publishers indicated.

854 / **Sendrey, Alfred.** Bibliography of Jewish music. New York, Columbia Univ. Press, 1951. 404 p.
Part I of this work is concerned with writings on Jewish music (entered as no. 765). Part II, p. 209–339, is a classified list of about 4,000 pieces of Jewish music, alphabetical by composer within class-

ifications, giving scoring, author, and language of text. Publisher and date indicated for published works; some manuscripts also listed.

LATIN AMERICA

855 / **Pan American Union, Music Section.** Latin American orchestral music available in the United States. Washington, Pan American Union, 1956. 79 p.

Supersedes a shorter list issued in 1955.

Part I: classified list of Latin American music available through publishing houses and other agencies. Part II: Latin American music in the Edwin A. Fleisher Collection in the Free Library of Philadelphia.

856 / **Thompson, Leila Fern.** Partial list of Latin American music obtainable in the U.S., and Supplement. 3rd ed., revised and enlarged. Washington, D.C., Pan American Union. 1948. 56 leaves.

Supplement, 17 leaves.

The first and second editions were prepared by Gilbert Chase, 1941 and 1942.

Concerned with concert music to the exclusion of popular and folk music. Classified by genre and country. Scoring, language of text, and publisher indicated. Indexed by country and by composer.

NORWAY

857 / **Society of Norwegian Composers.** Contemporary Norwegian orchestral and chamber music. Johan Grundt Tanam Forlag, 1970. 385 p.

Lists, with portraits, timings of the works, instrumentation.

SCOTLAND

858 / **Scottish Music Archive.** Catalogue of printed and manuscript music, May 1970. Glasgow, Scottish Music Archive, 74 p.

A classified list of music by contemporary Scottish composers giving instrumentation, duration, publisher, and availability of the material. The archive is centered at the University of Glasgow, but its policies are dictated by a committee made up of a number of Scottish musical institutions.

Supplement, 1972.

SWEDEN

859 / **Föreningen Svenska Tonsättare.** Nyare svenska orkester-verk samt instrumental—och vokalverk med orkester. Katalog of Swedish orchestral works (20th century) including instrumental soli and vocal works with orchestra. Stockholm, Society of Swedish Composers, 1956. 109 p. *Supplement*, 1959. 15 p.

Earlier lists were issued in 1937 and 1944 under a slightly varied title.

Classified listings of works under composers' names. Information includes publisher, instrumentation, timings.

860 / **Nordiska Musikförlaget.** Swedish orchestral works. Annotated catalogue. Commentary by Edvin Kallstenius. Stockholm, Nordiska Musikförlaget, 1948. 85 p.

This catalogue is intended to guide conductors, members of programme committees and other music lovers who wish to learn something about Swedish composition. [*Foreword*]

Selected works by 25 Swedish composers. Portraits and brief biographical sketches.

SWITZERLAND

861 / **Archives Musicales Suisses (Schweizerisches Musikarchiv).** Liste des oeuvres. Werkverzeichnis. Vol. 1– . Zürich, Archives musicales suisses, 1968– .

A series of pamphlets reproduced from typescript, each devoted to the work of a contemporary Swiss composer. Information includes instrumentation, timings, and availability of the works whether printed or in manuscript. Following is a list of publications through August 1971:

Jean Daetwyler (Janvier 1968), 15 leaves.
Paul Müller–Zürich (Juni 1968), 16 leaves.
Fernande Peyrot (Juin 1968), 5 leaves.
Edward Staempfli (Juni 1968), 10 leaves.
Frank Martin (Mars 1969), 10 leaves.
Jean Binet (Avril 1970), 17 leaves.
Luc Balmer (Mai 1970), 6 leaves.

Richard Sturzenegger (Mai 1970), 10 leaves.
Hans Haug (Juni 1970), 17 leaves.
Robert Oboussier (Juni 1970), 6 leaves.
Aloys Fornerod (Juin 1970), 6 leaves.
Raffaele d'Alessandro (Juillet 1970), 6 leaves.
Robert Blum (September 1970), 21 leaves.
Roger Vuataz (Octobre 1970), 30 leaves.
Bernard Reichel (Janvier 1971), 19 leaves.
Othmar Schoeck (August 1971), 27 leaves.

UNITED STATES

862 / **American Society of Composers, Authors and Publishers.**
ASCAP symphonic catalog. Second edition, including 1966 supplement. New York, American Society of Composers, Authors and Publishers, 1966. 369 p. (bound with *1966 Supplement*, 376 p.)

Alphabetical listing, by composers and arrangers, of symphonic literature controlled by ASCAP. Entries give instrumentation, duration, publisher. Supplementary list of publishers' addresses.

863 / **Broadcast Music Inc.** Symphonic catalogue. New York, Broadcast Music Inc., 1963. 132 p.

An alphabetical listing, by composer, of symphonic works the performing rights of which are controlled by Broadcast Music Inc. Entries give instrumentation, duration, and publishers of the works.

864 / **Catalog of Published Concert Music by American Composers.** Second edition. By Angelo Eagon. Metuchen, N.J., Scarecrow Press, 1969. 348 p.

Supplement to the second edition, 1971. 150 p.

This work first appeared as a publication of the U.S. Office of Information (1964), with a *Supplement* in 1965. The Scarecrow Press publication is an unacknowledged descendant.

Classified bibliography, including vocal and instrumental music; much relevant information as to performing groups required, instrumentation, publisher, etc.

865 / **Hixon, Donald L.** Music in early America: a bibliography of music in Evans. Metuchen, N.J., The Scarecrow Press, Inc., 1970. 607 p.

"An index to the music published in 17th and 18th-century America as represented by Charles Evans' *American Bibliography* and the Readex Corporation's microprint edition of *Early American Imprints, 1639-1800*." The major part of the work is devoted to entries for the music under composer, editor, or compiler. There is also a valuable section of biographical sketches; followed by indices of names, titles, and Evans serial numbers.

This work is also entered under no 1076.

YUGOSLAVIA

866 / **Kompozitori i Muzicki Pisci Jugoslavije.** (Yugoslav composers and music writers. Members of the Union of Yugoslav Composers, 1945–1967.) Catalogue. Beograd, SAKOJ, 1968. 663 p.

Edited by Milena Milosavljević-Pesić.

"An introduction to contemporary Yugoslav musical creation," by Kresimir Kovacevic.

Portraits, brief biographical accounts and lists of works. Text in Serbo-Croatian and English.

MUSIC FOR PERFORMANCE

The reference tools listed here are designed for the musician who has a specific objective in view; namely, the selection of material for performance purposes, whether for solo or ensemble use. The need for such tools, incorporating the latest publications, is a perpetual one that has given rise to a generous number of resources. Following is a summary classification of the items within this section.

Bagpipes—no. 878
Band—no. 879
Chamber Ensemble—nos. 869, 870, 871, 872, 873, 913, 933
Harpsichord—no. 868
Orchestra—nos. 875, 881, 884, 888, 908, 919, 924, 938, 942
Organ—nos. 868, 890, 917, 920, 939, 950
Piano—nos. 876, 895, 898, 904, 908, 918, 925, 936, 937, 944, 953
Voice (Choral)—nos. 883, 910, 915, 935, 940, 948
Voice (Solo)—nos. 886, 887, 909
String Ensemble—nos. 872, 874, 880, 893, 901
Violin—nos. 880, 891, 892, 914, 945
Viola—nos. 877, 914, 954

Cello—nos. 922, 951
String Bass—nos. 900, 928
Viols—no. 941
Wind Ensemble—nos. 885, 896,
    902, 903, 907, 927, 931, 932

Flute—nos. 897, 926, 949
Oboe—nos. 905, 906
Clarinet—nos. 894, 911, 923,
    946, 947
Bassoon—no. 934
Horn—nos. 882, 899
Recorder—nos. 867, 952
Saxophone—no. 916

867 / **Alker, Hugo.** Blockflöten-Bibliographie. Aufführungspraxis-Literatur-Spielgut. Wien, Universitätsbibliothek, 1960–61. 2 v. (Biblios-Schriften, 27–28.)

A source book of bibliographical information for performers on the recorder. Each volume contains a bibliography of writings on the instrument and its performance, including early accounts; a bibliography of instruction manuals; and a classified listing of modern editions of recorder music. Supplementary essays on history and performance practice. Facsimile plates from early methods.

868 / **Alker, Hugo.** Literatur für alte Tasteninstrumente; Versuch einer Bibliographie für die Praxis. 2nd verm. und verg. Aufl. Wien, Wissenschaftliches Antiquariat H. Geyer, 1967. 79 p. (Wiener Abhandlungen zur Musikwissenschaft und Instrumentenkunde, 2.)

First published in 1962.

The main division is between music for harpsichord and music for organ (without pedals). Brief entries, with publishers and editors given. Collections are entered by title and filed in the same alphabet with composers. The emphasis is on music currently available in practical editions.

869 / **Altmann, Wilhelm.** Handbuch für Klavierquartettspieler . . . Mit 237 Notenbeispielen. . . . Wolfenbüttel, Verlag für musikalische Kultur und Wissenschaft, 1937. 147 p.

Notenbeispiele in pocket at end of *Handbuch.*

A companion to a selective list of piano quartets, arranged chronologically by birthdates of the composers. German works curtailed in an effort toward international coverage. Brief descriptive and critical commentaries. Index of composers.

870 / **Altmann, Wilhelm.** Handbuch für Klavierquintettspieler . . . Mit 343 Notenbeispielen. Wolfenbüttel, Verlag für musikalische Kultur und Wissenschaft, 1936. 178 p.

Notenbeispiele in pocket at end of *Handbuch.*
Similar to the above, with emphasis on piano quintets.

871 / **Altmann, Wilhelm.** Handbuch für Klaviertriospieler; Wegweiser durch die Trios für Klavier, Violine und Violoncell. Mit fast 400 Notenbeispielen. Wolfenbüttel, Verlag für musikalische Kultur und Wissenschaft, 1934. 237 p.

872 / **Altmann, Wilhelm.** Handbuch für Streichquartettspieler. . . . Berlin, M. Hesse, 1928–31. 4 v. (Hesses Handbücher, 86, 87, 92, 94.)

A reprint of the 4 volumes has been announced on a subscription basis by Heinrichshofen's Verlag, Wilhelmshaven, together with a volume 5: *Ergänzungsband von 1935 bis zur Gegenwart.*

Vols. 1–2: string quartets; vol. 3: string trios, quintets, sextets, octets, addenda to quartets; vol. 4: works for strings and winds.

A companion to quartet literature giving brief descriptions and analyses of works in the standard repertory as well as lesser known works. Arrangement within each category is chronological.

873 / **Altman, Wilhelm.** Kammermusik-Katalog; ein Verzeichnis von seit 1841 veröffentlichten Kammermusikwerken. 6. bis August 1944 ergänzte Auflage. Leipzig, F. Hofmeister, 1945. 400 p.

Succeeded by Richter's *Kammermusik-Katalog.* . . . See no. 933.

Chamber music published since 1841, separate works or works in collections. Classified by medium, with composer indexes. International coverage.

Altmann, Wilhelm. Katalog der seit 1861 in den Handel gekommenen theatralischen Musik. . . .
See no. 337.

874 / **Altmann, Wilhelm.** Kleiner Führer durch die Streichquartette für Haus und Schule. . . . Berlin/Halensee, Deutscher Musikliteratur-Verlag [1950], 166 p.

An abridgement of the author's *Handbuch für Streichquartettspieler* (no. 872) concentrating on the classical literature for the ensemble, curtailing all post-Brahms works.

875 / **Altmann, Wilhelm.** Orchester-Literatur-Katalog; Verzeichnis von seit 1850 erschienenen Orchester-Werken. . . . Leipzig, F. E. C. Leuckart, 1926–36. 2 v.

Orchestral music published since 1850, listing scores, miniature scores, parts, and arrangements. Vol. 2 gives, in addition, instrumentation and timing and contains a composer index to both volumes. Thematic quotations given for works whose serial numbers are often confused, e.g. Haydn's symphonies, Händel's concertos, etc.

876 / **Altmann, Wilhelm.** Verzeichnis von Werken für Klavier vier- und sechshändig, sowie für zwei und mehr Klaviere. Liepzig, F. Hofmeister, 1943. 133 p.

Classified catalog of works for piano, 4 and 6 hands, and for 2 or more pianos with and without other instruments. Original works and arrangements included. Alphabetical by composer within classifications. Index.

877 / **Altmann, Wilhelm und W. Borissowsky.** Literaturverzeichnis für Bratsche und Viola d'amore. Wolfenbüttel, Verlag für musikalische Kultur und Wissenschaft, 1937. 148 p.

Classified catalog, including solo works, duos, and other combinations in which the viola has the leading role. Lists some works in manuscript and all known editions of published works, with dates. Includes transcriptions as well as original works.

878 / **Bagpipe Music Index.** Current alphabetical tune listing. Glen Ridge, New Jersey, Bagpipe Music Index, 1966. [unpaged]

Reproduced from typescript. Contains 2,430 listings from 35 tune books. Tunes identified by title, location in tune book, tune type, meter and number of parts.

879 / **Band Music Guide;** alphabetical listing of titles of all band music and composers of band music. 5th ed. Evanston, Ill., Instrumentalist Co., 1970.

The 2nd edition of this work appeared in 1960.

880 / **Baudet-Maget, A.** Guide du violoniste; œuvres choisies pour violon, ainsi que pour alto et musique de chambre, classées

d'après leur dégré de difficulté. Lausanne, Paris [etc.] Foetisch Frères [n.d.] 295 p.

Selective list of violin, viola, and string ensemble music from mid-17th century to the present. Classified according to genre and degree of difficulty.

881 / **Beck, Georges H.** Compositeurs contemporains: œuvres d'orchestre. Paris, Heugel & Cie [1960], 35 p.

A descriptive listing of recent orchestral works by 27 composers, chiefly French. Brief biographies of the composers. Entries give instrumentation, timings. Scores and performance materials available on rental from Heugel.

882 / **Brüchle, Bernhard.** Horn Bibliographie. Wilhelmshaven, Heinrichshofen, 1970. 272 p.

With a 14-page supplement of plates.

Entries classified according to ensembles: horn solo, horn and keyboard, various duo combinations, trios, quartets, etc. The work contains a bibliography of literature on the instrument, list of publishers, and index of names.

883 / **Burnsworth, Charles C.** Choral music for women's voices: an annotated bibliography of recommended works. Metuchen, N.J., Scarecrow Press, 1968. 180 p.

Detailed critical and descriptive annotations given for some 135 choral works for women's voices and a like number of arrangements. Indexed by title, number of voice parts, grade of difficulty, extended compositions, and collections. The work is overloaded with apparatus and verbosity which serve to diminish its value.

884 / **Buschkötter, Wilhelm.** Handbuch der internationalen Konzertliteratur. Berlin, Walter de Gruyter & Co., 1961. 374 p.

Compiled as a successor to Theodor Müller-Reuter's *Lexikon der deutschen Konzertliteratur* (no. 919). Works listed chronologically under composer. Information includes performance time, instrumentation, date of composition, performance, publisher.

Review by Richard Schaal in *Die Musikforschung*, 17 (1961), p. 84–85.

885 / **Chapman, James, Sheldon Fine and Mary Rasmussen.** "Music for wind instruments in historical editions, collected works

and numbered series: a bibliography," in *Brass Quarterly*, v. 1, nos. 3 & 4 (Spring–Winter, 1968), p. 115–149.

Part I: Music, without voices, for specified instrumentation, and for unspecified instrumentation with basso continuo, in historical editions and numbered series.

Indexes 42 historical editions and series.

Classified by instruments, ensembles, and forms.

886 / **Coffin, Berton.** Singer's repertoire. 2nd ed. New York, Scarecrow Press, 1960. 4 v.

First published in one volume, 1956.

Classified catalog of solo songs, each volume devoted to a particular voice range; information on subject, accompaniment, publisher.

Review by Arnold Caswell in *Journal of research in music education*, 9 (1961), p. 76.

887 / **Coffin, Berton, and Werner Singer.** Program notes for the singer's repertoire. Metuchen, N.J., Scarecrow Press, 1962. 230 p.

888 / **Daniels, David.** Orchestral music: a source book. Metuchen, N.J., The Scarecrow Press, Inc., 1972. 301 p.

The purpose of this work is to gather together into one volume the diverse information about orchestral works needed to plan programs and organize rehearsals: instrumentation, duration, and source of performance materials. [Editor's *Foreword*]

Particularly useful are the listings of materials for orchestra and various solo instruments or voices.

889 / **Eagon, Angelo.** Catalog of published concert music by American composers. Second edition. Metuchen, N.J., Scarecrow Press, 1969. 348 p.

This work was issued originally in 1964 as a publication of the Music Branch of the U.S. Information Agency. 175 p.

Also entered as no. 864.

Works are entered alphabetically by composer under a classified arrangement: vocal solo, instrumental solo, instrumental ensembles, concert jazz, percussion, orchestra, etc. There is a key to publishers and an author index. Information includes duration of orchestral works, author of text for vocal compositions. A useful, well-organized publication.

Review by Karl Kroeger, of the 1964 edition, in *Notes*, 22 (1966), p. 1032–33; by Richard Hunter, of the 1969 edition, in *Notes*, 26 (1970), p. 759–60.

890 / **Edson, Jean Slater.** Organ preludes, an index to composition on hymn tunes, chorales, plainsong melodies, Gregorian tunes and carols. Metuchen, N.J., Scarecrow Press, 1970. 2 v.

Vol. I: composer index, with settings listed alphabetically under composer's name. Publishers are identified.

Vol. II: index of tune names, identified by thematic incipits. Each tune name is followed by a list of the composers who have set it.

891 / **Emery, Frederic B.** The violin concerto through a period of nearly 300 years, covering about 3,300 concertos with brief biographies of 1,000 composers. Chicago, The Violin Literature Publishing Co., 1928. 615 p., with index p. i–xl.

Brief discussions of concerto composers grouped chronologically and by nationality. A mass of somewhat indiscriminate fact and information. Illustrated with portraits of musicians.

892 / **Farish, Margaret K.** String music in print. New York, R. R. Bowker, 1965. 420 p.

Supplement to string music in print. N.Y., Bowker, 1968. 204 p.

The work was first issued in a "preliminary edition" in 1963.

The work is

> . . . a guide to published music for the violin, viola, violoncello and double-bass. It contains information on solo music, accompanied and unaccompanied; chamber music, including combinations of stringed instruments with wind instruments, keyboard instruments, harp, guitar, percussion and voice; methods and studies. [Author's *Preface*]

Arrangement is alphabetical by composer within each category; composers' dates given. Brief titles, with instrumentation. Publishers indicated by symbols, with a comprehensive list of publishers, p. 411–20.

Review of the preliminary edition by Joal H. Berman in *Notes*, 20 (1963), p. 229; of the 1965 edition by Katherine Holum in *Journal of*

212

research in music education, 13 (1965), p. 190–91; of the *Supplement* by Dena J. Epstein in *Notes,* 25 (1969), p. 746.

893 / **Feinland, Alexander.** The combination violin and violencello without accompaniment. [Paramaribo, Surinam, Printed by J. H. Oliviera, 1944.] 121 p.

Classified catalog, including manuscripts, of music from the baroque to the present. Original publisher or location given. Biographical sketches of the composers represented.

894 / **Foster, Levin W.** A directory of clarinet music. Pittsfield, Mass., printed by A. E. Johnson & Son [1940], 128 p.

The work claims to list practically all the music known to be published for the clarinet. Classified arrangement, alphabetical by composer within each classification; publishers indicated. Some transcriptions and arrangements included, as well as more than 50 methods and studies.

895 / **Friskin, James, and Irwin Freundlich.** Music for the piano. A handbook of concert and teaching material from 1580 to 1952. New York, Rinehart [1954], 432 p. (The field of music, 5.)

Selective listing of standard works in the piano repertory. Classified arrangement. Remarks are concerned largely with the technical demands of the material and with its interpretation.

896 / **Gillespie, James E., Jr.** The reed trio: an annotated bibliography of original published works. Detroit, Information Coordinators, 1971. 84 p. (Detroit studies in music bibliography, 20.)

897 / **Girard, Adrien.** Histoire et richesse de la flûte. Paris, Libraire Gründ, 1953. 143 p.

A handsome, illustrated volume printed in an edition of 1,500 copies. Chapter IV, "Les flûtistes," lists the principal performers from the 15th to the 20th centuries, with brief comments on each. Chapter V, "Littérature," is a chronological listing of the important composers of flute music with their works, from Louis Couperin to the present, followed by an alphabetical listing, by composer, of works for solo flute accompanied by keyboard, harp, or orchestra. Manuscript works included.

898 / **Gratia, L. E.** Répertoire pratique du pianiste. . . . Préface de I. Philipp. Paris, Delagrave, 1931. 117 p.

A list of 2,500 piano pieces by 271 composers arranged alphabetically by composer, with categories of varying degree of difficulty. Four-hand pieces, p. 112–17.

899 / **Gregory, Robin.** The horn, a comprehensive guide to the modern instrument and its music. New York, Praeger, 1969. 410 p.

First printed in 1961 in London.

P. 181–393: Appendix C. A list of music for the horn. A classified list of music for horn solo or in combination with various ensembles, instrumental or vocal. Entries give composer, title, ensemble, and publisher.

900 / **Grodner, Murray.** Comprehensive catalogue of available literature for the double bass. 2nd ed. Bloomington, Indiana, Lemur Musical Research [1964], 84 p. (typescript)

First published in 1958.

Lists works in print, 1964. Solos and ensembles for from 2 to 14 instruments, using string bass. Each entry gives composer, title, instrumentation, grade of difficulty, publisher, price, with occasional annotations as to availability. A short bibliography of works about the bass and bass playing. Index of names.

Review of the first edition by Darius Thieme in *Notes*, 16 (1969), p. 258.

901 / **Grünberg, Max.** Führer durch die Literatur der Streichinstrumente . . . Kritisches, progressiv geordnetes Repertorium von instruktiven Solo- und Ensemble-Werken. . . . Leipzig, Breitkopf & Härtel, 1913. 218 p. (Handbücher der Musiklehre . . . hrsg. von X. Scharwenka, 10.)

A listing of music for violin, viola, cello, and ensemble from the baroque through the 19th century classified according to genre and degree of difficulty. Publishers and prices indicated. Bibliography, p. 207–09. Index.

902 / **Heller, George N.** Ensemble music for wind and percussion instruments: a catalog. Washington, D.C., Music Educators' National Conference, 1970. 142 p.

903 / **Helm, Sanford Marion.** Catalog of chamber music for wind instruments. Revised reprint. New York, Da Capo Press, 1969. 85 p.
First printed in 1952 at Ann Arbor, Michigan.
Chamber music for from 3 to 12 instruments employing at least one wind instrument. Classified according to the size of the ensemble and instrumentation. Gives publisher, date, American agent for currently available editions. Composer index.

904 / **Hodges, Mabelle L.** A catalogue of representative teaching materials for piano since 1900. Chicago, De Paul University Press, 1970. 108 p.

905 / **Hošek, Miroslav.** Katalog der Oboeliteratur tschechischer und slowakischer Autoren. Herausgegeben vom Tschechoslowakischen Musikinformationszentrum. Praha, 1969. 89 p.
Alphabetical listing by composer of chamber works for oboe and as many as 13 other instruments. Concertos and other orchestral works featuring the oboe are also included. Indexes of libraries, publishers, and instrumental combinations.

906 / **Hošek, Miroslav.** Oboen-Bibliographie. Bd. 1. 1972.
Lists more than 5,000 compositions for and with oboe.
Cited in Katzbichler, Kat. 25, Addenda, n. 1240.

907 / **Houser, Roy.** Catalogue of chamber music for woodwind instruments. 2nd ed. [Bloomington, Indiana], Indiana University, 1960. 158 leaves (typescript).
Supplement: Woodwind ensembles bibliography.
Material for from 3 to 10 instruments, classified according to ensemble. P. 147–48: A list of woodwind music found in the Moravian archives at Winston-Salem, North Carolina, and at Bethlehem, Pennsylvania. P. 152–55: Selected publications from the catalog of the Donemus Foundation, Amsterdam.

908 / **International Music Council.** Répertoires internationaux de musique contemporaine à l'usage des amateurs et des jeunes. I. Musique symphonique de 1880 à 1954. Frankfurt, New York, C. F. Peters, 1937– (v. 1, 63 p.).
A catalog of recently composed symphonic works suitable for young

215

people's and amateur orchestras. Material listed alphabetically by country; publisher, date, and instrumentation given. Indexes of composers, types of ensemble. List of publishers.

909 / **Kagen, Sergius.** Music for the voice, a descriptive list of concert and teaching material. Revised edition. Bloomington, Indiana University Press, 1968. 780 p.

First published in 1949 by Rinehart, New York, as no. 3 in the "Field of music" series.

Songs are listed alphabetically by composer and nationality within four large categories: (1) Songs and airs before the 19th century; (2) songs of the 19th and 20th centuries; (3) folk songs; (4) operatic excerpts. Each section has its own bibliography, and there are numerous biographical sketches of song writers. Data includes title, compass, tessitura, type, with descriptive remarks.

910 / **Knapp, J. Merrill.** Selected list of music for men's voices. Princeton, N.J., Princeton Univ. Press, 1952. 165 p.

Original works and arrangements, published and unpublished. Alphabetical by composer within main classification scheme. Each entry gives dates of composer, scoring, language, publisher, and editor. Index of composers.

Review by Archibald Davison in *Notes*, 10 (1952), p. 104–05.

911 / **Kroll, Oskar.** The clarinet. Revised, and with a repertory by Diethard Riehm. Translated by Hilda Morris. New York, Taplinger Pub. Co., 1968. 183 p.

Translation of *Die Klarinette; ihre Geschichte, ihre Literatur, ihre grossen Meister.*

Bibliography: p. 133–35. "Repertory of the clarinet": p. 136–175.

912 / **Leigh, Robert.** Index to song books, a title index to over 11,000 copies of almost 6,800 songs in 111 song books published between 1933 and 1962. Stockton, Calif., Robert Leigh, 1964. 273 p.

913 / **Lemacher, Heinrich.** Handbuch der Hausmusik. Graz, A. Pustet, 1948. 454 p.

The second part of the volume, p. 219 to end, lists works for solo instruments and various chamber ensembles. Many lesser known works included. Arranged alphabetically by composer within various categories. Publisher and brief description of works given. Bibliography, p. 435–39. Index.

914 / **Letz, Hans.** Music for violin and viola. New York, Rinehart [1948], 107 p. (The field of music, 2.)

Selective, graded list of music for unaccompanied violin, or violin and piano (p. 1–94); followed by a similar list of music for the viola (p. 96–107).

915 / **Locke, Arthur W., and Charles K. Fassett.** Selected list of choruses for women's voices. 3rd ed., revised and enlarged. Northampton, Mass., Smith College, 1964. 253 p.

First published in 1927; 2nd edition, 1946, edited by A. W. Locke.

Principal section is an alphabetical catalog by composers, with titles of choruses, voice combination, publisher, or source in a collection. Foreign titles usually translated. Collections listed separately and their contents given. Indexes include a chronological list of composers, compositions by categories, authors and sources of texts, first lines and titles.

Review by Karl Kroeger in *Notes*, 23 (1966), p. 63–64.

916 / **Londeix, Jean-Marie.** 125 ans de musique pour saxophone. Répertoire général des œuvres et des ouvrages d'enseignement pour le saxophone. Paris, Alphonse Leduc, 1971. 398 p.

A general listing of works involving saxophone by composer, followed by indexes under individual instruments (soprano, alto, tenor, baritone) and by ensembles. Composers are identified, and rather full biographical information, with critical quotations, is given for major composers. Supplementary lists of addresses for composers and publishers of saxophone music.

917 / **Lukas, Viktor.** Orgelmusikführer. Stuttgart, Philipp Reclam Jun. [1963], 271 p.

A listener's guide to concert organ literature, quite selective and confined to European repertory. Brief biographies of the composers; numerous thematic quotations. Contains a section on the organ with other instruments, a glossary of organ terms, and a description of the mechanics of the instrument. Index of composers and works.

918 / **Moldenhauer, Hans.** Duo-pianism; a dissertation. [Chicago, Chicago Musical College Press, 1951.] 400 p.

Contains a list of original two-piano music arranged alphabetically by composer. Publishers indicated. The main part of the dissertation concerns itself with practical rather than historical aspects of the subject. Also contains a list of recorded two-piano music.

919 / **Müller-Reuter, Theodor.** Lexikon der deutschen Konzertliteratur; ein Ratgeber für Dirigenten, Konzertveranstalter, Musikschriftsteller und Musikfreunde. Leipzig, G. F. Kahnt nachf., 1909. V. 1. 626 p.

Nachtrag zu Band I. Leipzig, Kahnt, 1921. 238 p.

The standard guide to orchestral and chamber music by the major composers of the romantic period, with detailed information as to date of composition, first performance, duration, instrumentation, relation to the composer's other works. Band I covers the following composers: Schubert, Mendelssohn, Schumann, Berlioz, Liszt, Raff, Wagner, Draeseke, Reinecke, Bruch, Gernsheim, and Richard Strauss. The *Nachtrag* is devoted to Beethoven, Brahms, and Haydn (symphonies only).

Buschkötter's *Handbuch* . . . (no. 884) is intended to supplement Müller-Reuter and bring it up to date.

920 / **Münger, Fritz.** Choralbearbeitungen für Orgel. Verzeichnis zu den Chorälen des Deutschen Evangelischen Kirchengesangbuches und des Gesangbuches der evang.–reform. Kirchen der deutschsprachigen Schweiz. Kassel, Bärenreiter [1952], 148 p.

Alphabetical listing by chorale text incipit, locating each in the German or Swiss chorale books and indicating the organ settings available in some 56 collections of chorale preludes.

921 / **National Association of Schools of Music.** Solo literature for the wind instruments. 32 p. (The Bulletin of the National Association of Schools of Music, no. 31. January, 1951.)

Lists of solos, including concertos, for flute, oboe, clarinet, bassoon, French horn, cornet and trumpet, trombone. Graded as to difficulty; brief critical or descriptive annotations. Publishers indicated.

922 / **Nogué, Edouard.** La littérature du violoncelle . . . Préface de M. Paul Bazelaire. . . . Paris, Delagrave, 1925. 151 p.

Lists nearly 2,000 works for violoncello, solo or with other instruments. Classified and graded, with short descriptions of most of the works. Publishers indicated.

923 / **Opperman, Kalmen.** Repertory of the clarinet. New York, Ricordi [1960], 140 p.

Classified index of music for the clarinet, including methods, etudes, and music for the instrument as solo and in combination with other instruments. List of publishers given, and a short bibliography of books on the clarinet.

Review by Roger P. Phelps in *Notes*, 18 (1960), p. 63–64.

924 / **Orchestra Music Guide. . . .** Evanston, Ill., Instrumentalist Co., n.d., 98 p.

Lists over 5,000 titles including full and string orchestra music, also vocal and instrumental solos, ensembles with orchestral accompaniment.

925 / **Parent, Charlotte F. H.** Répertoire encyclopédique du pianiste; analyse rainsonnée d'œuvres choisies pour le piano, du XVIe siècle, au XXe siècle, avec renseignements pratiques degré de difficulté, nombre de pages, éditeur et prix. . . . Paris, Hachette et Cie. (1900–1907), 2 v.

926 / **Pellerite, James J.** A handbook of literature for the flute (a list of graded method materials, solos, and ensemble music for the flute). Bloomington, Indiana, Zalo Publications [1963], 96 p.

This listing of flute literature is specifically designed to familiarize the music teachers, music educators, and students of the flute with a portion of available materials presently appearing in publishers' catalogs. [*Foreword*]

Graded and annotated.

927 / **Peters, Harry B.** The literature of the woodwind quintet. Metuchen, N.J., Scarecrow Press, 1971. 174 p.

A basic listing of woodwind quintet music, followed by a section devoted to the quintet with one, two, three, four, or five additional performers.

928 / **Planyavsky, Alfred.** Geschichte des Kontrabasses. Tutzing, Hans Schneider, 1970. 537 p.

Primarily a historical study of the string bass from the 16th century to the present—its construction, technique, and repertoire.

P. 433–506: classified catalog of string bass music, treating the instrument as solo and in a variety of ensembles. The work also contains a bibliography of relevant literature, a discography of string bass music, and an index of names and subjects.

929 / **Rapée, Erno.** Encyclopedia of music for pictures. New York, Arno Press, 1970. 510 p. (The literature of cinema.)
Reprint of the 1925 edition.

930 / **Rapée, Erno.** Motion picture moods for pianists and organists. New York, Arno Press, 1970. 678 p.
Reprint of the 1925 edition.
This and the preceding volume are reference works that were designed to assist musicians of the 1920s and early 1930s select the appropriate musical themes, or moods, to accompany motion pictures.

931 / **Rasmussen, Mary.** A teacher's guide to the literature of brass instruments. Durham, New Hampshire, Brass Quarterly, 1964. 84 p.
General discussion of music available for brass ensembles and solos, followed by extensive listings giving publisher, price, instrumentation, and grade level of the works cited.

932 / **Rasmussen, Mary.** A teacher's guide to the literature of woodwind instruments, by Mary Rasmussen and Donald Mattran. Durham, New Hampshire, Brass and Woodwind Quarterly, 1966, 226 p.
Bibliographies of woodwind music for solos or ensembles.

933 / **Richter, Johannes F.** Kammermusik-Katalog. Verzeichnis der von 1944 bis 1958 veröffentlichten Werke für Kammermusik und für Klavier vier- und sechshändig sowie für zwei und mehr Klaviere. Leipzig, F. Hofmeister, 1960. 318 p.
Successor to Wilhelm Altmann's work of the same title (no. 873.) Covers chamber music from 1945 through 1958. A classified bibliography, including chamber works with voice, piano four-hands, etc. Alphabetical index of composers and titles of collections. List of publishers.

934 / **Risdon, Howard.** Musical literature for the bassoon; a compilation of music for the basoon as an instrument in ensemble. Seattle, Berdon [1963], 24 p.

935 / **Roberts, Kenneth C.** A checklist of 20th-century choral music for male voices. Detroit, Information Coordinators, 1970. 32 p. (Detroit studies in music bibliography, 17.)

936 / **Rowley, Alec.** Four hands—one piano. A list of works for duet players. London/New York, Oxford Univ. Press, 1940. 38 p.

Classified list, with composer index, of original works for the medium, 1750 to date. Alphabetical arrangement with each class (the classics, the French school, etc.). Entries give composer's name and dates, title—usually in the original language, opus number, publisher.

937 / **Ruthardt, Adolf.** Wegweiser durch die Klavier-Literatur. 10. Aufl. Leipzig, Zürich, Hug & Co., 1925. 398 p.

First published in 1888.

Selective list of keyboard music including works for four or more hands from the Renaissance to the early 20th century. Classified according to genre and degree of difficulty. Brief descriptions of lesser-known works. Bibliography of writings on keyboard music, p. 359–76. Index.

938 / **Saltonstall, Cecilia D., and Hannah C. Smith.** Catalogue of music for small orchestra. Washington, D.C., Music Library Association, 1947. 267 p.

Selective list of works for orchestras with basic strings plus from two to eight winds. Arranged by composer. Entries give movements, scoring, timing, and publisher. Many American compositions included. Indexed by title and by number of winds employed.

939 / **Sartorius, Richard H.** Bibliography of concertos for organ and orchestra. Evanston, Ill., Instrumentalist Co. [1961], 68 p.

Includes primary sources as well as modern publications. Extensive annotations, biographical and descriptive of the music. Locations of original materials given. The list includes much material not exclusively for organ, i.e. concertos for "harpsichord or organ."

940 / **Schünemann, Georg.** Führer durch die deutsche Chor-literatur. Wolfenbüttell, Verlag für musikalische Kultur und Wissenschaft, 1935–36. 2 v.

Vol. 1: Männerchor. Vol. 2: Gemischter Chor.

Classified according to type of composition. Entries give composer, title, publisher, grade of difficulty, number of parts, duration. Indexed by first line of text, title, composer and arranger, author of text. Includes both secular and sacred works.

941 / **Smet, Robin de.** Published music for the viola da gamba and other viols. Detroit, Information Coordinators, 1971. 105 p. (Detroit studies in music bibliography, 18.)

942 / **Stein, Franz A.** Verzeichnis der Orchestermusik von 1700 bis zur Gegenwart. Bern und München, Francke Verlag [1963], 126 p.

A pocket guide to orchestral literature. Selective list of composers and their principal orchestral works. Entries give title, instrumentation, date of composition, movements if a composite work. No publishers given.

943 / **Swan, Alfred J.** The music director's guide to musical literature (for voices and instruments). New York, Prentice-Hall, 1941. 164 p.

P. 117–64: A selected list of works from the early Middle Ages through the 20th century. Arranged chronologically, with subdivisions by genre and country. Occasional annotations. The earlier part of the book contains brief comments on the composers represented in the bibliography.

944 / **Teichmüller, Robert und Kurt Herrmann.** Internationale moderne Klaviermusik, ein Wegweiser und Berater. Leipzig und Zürich, Hug & Co., 1927. 300 p.

Supplement, 1934.

Critical and selective bibliography of piano music from about 1890 to date of publication, arranged alphabetically by composer, with an index by country. Gives date of composition, opus number, title, publisher, price, grade, and critical comment.

945 / **Tottmann, Albert.** Führer durch die Violin-literatur. . . . 4. wesentlich vervollständigte, bis auf die Gegenwart seit 1901 forgeführte und neu bearbeitete Auflage von Wilhelm Altmann. Leipzig, J. Schuberth, 1935. 472 p.

Title varies: first published as *Führer durch den Violin-Unterricht*, 1873; 2nd ed., 1886; 3rd ed., 1902.

Classified bibliography including etudes, solo or accompanied violin works, duos, trios, quartets, etc., for violins. Gives full bibliographical information and brief critical comments. Supplements Altmann's *Kammermusik-Katalog* (no. 861) for solo works.

946 / **Tuthill, Burnet C.** "The concertos for clarinet," in *Journal of research in music education*, 10 (1962), p. 47–58.

Brief introduction to the history of the clarinet concerto and its literature, followed by annotated listing of such concertos from the 18th century to the present.

This list has been supplemented by Robert A. Titus in an article in the *Journal of research in music education*, 13 (1965), p. 169–76.

947 / **Tuthill, Burnet C.** "The sonatas for clarinet and piano," in *Journal of research in music education*, 14 (1966), p. 197–212.

An annotated listing similar to no. 946 above. A few transcriptions and works in manuscript are included.

948 / **Valentin, Erich.** Handbuch der Chormusik. Hrsg. im Auftrag der Arbeitsgemeinschaft deutscher Chorverbände. Regensburg, G. Bosse [1953–58], 2 v.

These volumes serve as general source books of information useful to choral directors. Special sections include a discography of choral music, listings of the contents of *Denkmäler,* writings on choral conducting. Major sections devoted to classified bibliographies of choral music, with full performance details. Each volume has a composer index.

949 / **Vester, Frans.** Flute repertoire catalogue. 10,000 titles. London, Musica Rara, 1967. 363 p.

Lists music for flute alphabetically under composer, with indexes directing the user to music for flute in combination with other instruments and with orchestra and voice. There is a short bibliography of literature on the flute and a listing of publishers of flute music.

950 / **Weigl, Bruno.** Handbuch der Orgelliteratur. . . . Leipzig, F. E. C. Leuckart, 1931. 318 p.

Classified listing of compositions for organ solo or organ with orchestra, instruments, or voices. Original works and transcriptions listed separately. International coverage.

951 / **Weigl, Bruno.** Handbuch der Violoncell-Literatur; systematisch geordnetes Verzeichnis der solo- und instruktiven Werke . . . 3. Auflage. Wien, Universal, 1929. 357 p.

Classified listing of compositions of cello and orchestra, cello and piano, cello solo, or accompanied by other instruments. Comparable in arrangement and content to his *Handbuch der Orgelliteratur* (above).

952 / **Winterfeld, Linde H. Von, und Harald Kunz.** Handbuch der Blockflöten-Literatur. Berlin/Wiesbaden, Bote & Bock, 1959. 139 p.

Listings of music for recorder, solo, ensemble, and in combination with other instruments. Publisher and price given. Composer and title index, and a short list of books on the recorder.

953 / **Wolters, Klaus, and Franzpeter Goebels.** Handbuch der Klavierliteratur. I. Klaviermusik zu zwei Händen, von Klaus Wolters. Zürich, Atlantis Verlag, 1967. 650 p.

954 / **Zeyringer, Franz.** Literatur für Viola: Verzeichnis der Werke für Viola-Solo, Duos mit Voila, Trios mit Viola, Viola-Solo mit Begleitung, Blockflöte mit Viola, Gesang mit Viola und der Schul- und Studienwerke für Viola. Hartberg, Oesterreich, Julius Schönwetter, 1963. 151 p.

With indexes of publishers and composers.
Ergänzungsband, 1965. 82 p.

JAZZ AND POPULAR MUSIC

Within recent years the field of jazz and popular music has developed its own bibliographical resources. Some of the principal items in this area are listed below. Others will be found in the section on "Dictionaries and Encyclopedias," e.g., Leonard Feather's *The encyclopedia of jazz* (no. 199) or the Lewine and Simon *Encyclopedia of theater music* (no. 352). Still others are cited under *Collectors' guides to jazz recordings* (nos. 1767 ff.) or belong in the category of early American popular song: see *Dichter* (no. 1059), *Sonneck* (no. 1107), or *Wolfe* (no. 1114).

955 / **Burton, Jack.** The blue book of Tin Pan Alley, a human interest encyclopedia of American popular music. Vol. 1: 1776–1860–1910. Watkins Glen, N.Y., Century House [1962], 304 p.

First published in 1951.

The 1962 publication is the first volume of an expanded new edition which, when completed, will carry the survey through the 1960s. The approach is chronological, with detailed listings of songs by the principal popular composers.

956 / **Burton, Jack.** The index of American popular music; thousands of titles cross-referenced to our basic anthologies of popular songs. Watkins Glen, N.Y., Century House, 1957. 1 v.

957 / **Chipman, John H.** Index to top-hit tunes (1900–1950) . . . with a foreword by Arthur Fiedler. Boston, Bruce Humphries [1962], 249 p.

An alphabetical index, by title, of the most popular American songs of the first half of the 20th century. Gives key, composer and author, publisher and original publication date, source in film or musical comedy. Chronological index, short bibliography.

958 / **Ewen, David.** American popular songs: from the Revolutionary War to the present. New York, Random House, 1966. 507 p.

Provides information on more than 3,600 songs popular in America from 1775 to 1966. Cites composer, lyricist, place, medium, and date, including the performer who made the song popular.

Review by Ruth Hilton in *Notes*, 24 (1968), p. 501–01.

959 / **Fuld, James J.** American popular music (reference book) 1875–1950. Philadelphia, Pa., Musical Americana, 1955. 94 p.

Supplement . . . 1956. 9 p.

A bibliography of some 250 selected American popular songs. Detailed information as to first printing, copyright date, description of cover. 20 plates of song covers. An interesting attempt to approach American popular song with the methods of descriptive bibliography.

960 / **Fuld, James J.** The book of world-famous music: classical popular and folk. Foreword by William Lichtenwanger. Rev. and enl. ed. New York, Crown Publishers, 1971. 688 p.

The work was first published in 1966.

225

A reference book that traces the linage, in printing or in manuscript, of the most familiar ("world-famous") compositions of the Western world. A thematic index with detailed commentary on sources, composers, history. An admirable exercise in applied bibliography.

Review of the 1966 edition by Ruth Hilton in *Notes*, 23 (1966), p. 56–57. Review of the 1971 edition by Nyal Williams in *Notes* 29 (1973), p. 448–49.

961 / **Huerta, Jorge A.** A bibliography of Chicano and Mexican dance, drama and music. Oxnard, Calif., Colegio Quetzalcoatl, 1972. 59 p.

The three major divisions of the bibliography cover dance, drama, and music subdivided by Pre-Columbia, Mexican, and Aztlan.

962 / **Mattfeld, Julius.** Variety music cavalcade, 1620–1961; a chronology of vocal and instrumental music popular in the United States. With an introduction by Abel Green. 3rd ed. Englewood Cliffs, N.J., Prentice-Hall, 1971. 766 p.

First issued in 1952 as *Variety music cavalcade, 1620–1950.* Originally appeared in a modified form as *Variety radio directory 1938–39,* supplemented in weekly issues of the periodical *Variety.* A revised edition appeared in 1962.

A chronological bibliography of American popular music, with parallel social and historical events listed for each year. Index of musical works by title, with dates of first publication.

Review by Irving Lowens in *Notes*, 20 (1963), p. 233–34.

Also entered as no. 503.

963 / **Shapiro, Nat.** Popular music: an annotated index of American popular songs. [NewYork] Adrian Press, 1964–69. 5 v.

Vol. 1: 1950–59. Vol. 2: 1940–49. Vol. 3: 1960–64. Vol. 4: 1930–39. Vol. 5: 1920–29.

A series which aims "to set down in permanent and practical form a selective annotated list of the significant popular songs of the 20th century." (author's preface)

Songs are listed alphabetically by title under each year of the decade. Each volume has its own index of titles and list of publishers.

Review by Ruth Hilton in *Notes*, 25 (1968), p. 247–48, and 27 (1970), p. 60–61.

LOCAL OPERA REPERTOIRES

A useful type of reference work is that which traces the chronology of opera as it has been performed in a particular place or theater: New York, Milan, Rome, Paris, Bologna, etc. Many of the leading opera companies of the world have been provided with such chronicles, which often include valuable data about first productions, the original cast of singers and dancers, information about the frequency of performance, etc.

These works are, strictly speaking, bibliographies of music, and they can be distinguished from other reference tools devoted to the musical theater; namely, dictionaries of opera and theater music and bibliographies of music literature devoted to the same subject.

964 / **Allacci, Leone.** Drammaturgia di Lione Allacci, accresciuta e continuata fino all'anno MDCCLV. Venezia, Presso G. Pasquali, 1755.

First edition, Rome, 1666. Revised and continued by Giovanni Cendoni, Apostolo Zeno, and others. Reprint of the 1755 edition by Bottega d'Erasmo, Torino, 1966.

A listing, alphabetical by title, of dramatic works produced in the Italian theater from the late 15th century to 1755. Not restricted to music but includes many operas and oratorios. See introduction to the facsimile reprint by Francesco Bernardelli.

965 / **Bauer, Anton.** Opern und Operetten in Wien; Verzeichnis ihrer Erstaufführungen in der Zeit von 1629 bis zur Gegenwart. Graz-Köln, Hermann Böhlaus Nachf., 1955. 156 p. (Wiener musikwissenschaftliche Beiträge, 2.)

4,856 stage works, listed by title, with indexes by composer, author, and chronology.

966 / **Bignami, Luigi.** Cronologia di tuttie gli spettacoli rappresentati al Teatro Comunale di Bologna della sua apertura 14 Maggio 1763 a tutto l'autunno 1881. Bologna, Mattiuzzi, 1882. 248 p.

The entries consist of transcriptions of theater bills for the period under consideration. All types of dramatic works are included, but by

227

far the largest part of the repertory is opera. Numerous indexes of performers, composers, authors, and other categories of theater personnel.

967 / **Bolongaro-Crevenna, Hubertus.** L'Arpa festante; die Münchner Oper 1651–1825, von den Anfängen bis zum "Freyschützen". München, Callwey, 1963. 272 p.

A cultural history of the Munich opera from its beginnings to 1825.

P. 209–272: a chronological listing of the repertory, with factual information drawn from the Munich theater archives.

968 / **Filippis, Felice de, et R. Arnese.** Cronache del Teatro di S. Carlo (1737–1960). Napoli, Edizioni Politica Popolare, 1961. 466 p.

P. 25–112: chronological listing, by year, of first performances of operas given at the San Carlo Opera in Naples from 1737 to 1960.

P. 113–304: a biographical dictionary of opera composers, with lists of their major works.

Indexes of librettists and singers; a summary of the seasons in which each work was performed. 76 full-page illustrations.

969 / **Fog, Dan.** The Royal Danish Ballet, 1760–1958, and August Bournonville. A chronological catalogue of the ballets and ballet-divertissements performed at the Royal Theatres of Copenhagen, and a catalogue of August Bournonville's works. Copenhagen, Dan Fog, 1961. 79 p.

Lists 516 ballet works performed by the Royal Danish Ballet, citing the choreographer, composer, and publisher of the music if available. Index of titles and of persons. Facsimile plates of music title pages.

970 / **Galvani, Livio Niso.** I teatri musicali di Venezia nel secolo XVII (1637–1700). Memorie storiche e bibliografiche. Milano, Ricordi, 1878. 193 p.

Operas performed in Venice during the 17th century, listed chronologically under 16 different theaters or opera houses. Entries listed by title, with composer, librettist, publication data of libretti, dedicatee, and much useful information. Indexes of names, titles, librettists, and composers.

971 / **Gatti, Carlo.** Il teatro alla Scala, nella storia e nell'arte (1778–1963). Milano, Ricordi, 1964. 2 v.

A handsome set, the second volume of which contains the chronicles of La Scala—complete inventories of the opera, ballet, and concert performances from 1778 to the present, with an analytical index. The chronologies were compiled by Giampiero Tintori.

972 / **Groppo, Antonio.** "Catalogo di tutti i drammi per musica recitati ne'Teatri di Venezia dell'anno 1637, in cui ebbere principio le pubbliche rappresentazioni de'medesmi fin all'anno presente 1745." In *Bollettino bibliografico musicale*. Nuova serie. Milano, 1952.
Published serially in four installments.
Lists 811 operas performed in Venice between 1637 and 1745, in chronological order, with title, librettist, composer, theater, and date of performance. Index of titles.

973 / **Lajarte, Théodore de.** Bibliothèque musicale du Theâtre de l'Opéra. Paris, Libr. des Bibliophiles, 1878. 2 v.
Reprint by Olms, Hildesheim, 1969.
Descriptive list of 594 stage works arranged in order of first production at the Paris Opéra, 1671–1876. Classified by period. Each period concludes with a biographical section listing composers and librettists alphabetically. Composer and title index to works in the repertoire.

974 / **Mooser, Robert-Aloys.** Opéras, intermezzos, ballets, cantates, oratorios joués en Russie durant le XVIIIe siècle. . . . Essai d'un répertoire alphabétique et chronologique. 3e édition revue et complétée. Bâle, Bärenreiter, 1964. 177 p.
First published in 1945; 2nd edition, 1955.
Gives librettist, translators of work, date and place of first performance, language of performance, date of publication of the libretto, etc. Sources of information are well documented. Indexes.
Review of the 2nd ed. by Anna A. Abert in *Die Musikforschung*, 9 (1956), p. 106.

975 / **Radiciotti, Giuseppe.** "Teatro e musica in Roma nel secondo quarto del secolo XIX (1825–50)." In *Storia dell'arte musicale e drammatica. Sezione 4*. Roma Tip. della R. Academia dei Lincei, 1906. P. 157–318.
Parte seconda: A chronical of the musical-dramatic productions given in the three major theaters in Rome during the early 19th century, Teatro Valle, Teatro Argentina, and Teatro Apollo.

976 / **Seltsam, William H.** Metropolitan opera annals. New York, H. W. Wilson Co., 1947. 751 p.

Chronological listing of Metropolitan Opera performances, with casts, from the initial season (1883–84) through 1946–47. Coverage for each season includes roster, excerpts from press reviews of noteworthy performances. Indexed by artist, opera.

Supplements issued annually in the final issue of each volume of the periodical *Opera news. First supplement*, 1957, cumulates information for 1945–57. *Second supplement: 1957–1966—a chronicle of artists and performers.* Foreword by Francis Robinson. N.Y., H. W. Wilson, 1968. 126 p.

977 / **Trezzini, Lamberto.** Due secoli di vita musicale. Storia del Teatro Comunale di Bologna. Bologna, Edizioni ALFA, 1966. 2 v.

Vol. 1 contains a series of essays on the history of various aspects of musical life in Bologna, chiefly related to the theater.

Vol. 2 consists of a "Repertorio critico degli spettacoli e delle esecuzioni musicali dal 1763 al 1966," by Sergio Paganelli. This is a chronological listing of opera, oratorio, and symphony productions, giving the names of members of the casts, soloists, and symphony conductors represented.

978 / **Wiel, Taddeo.** I teatri musicali veneziani del settecento. Catalogo delle opere in musica rappresentate nel secolo XVIII in Venezia (1701–1800). Venezia, Fratelli Visentini, 1897. 600 p.

Chronological listing of operas performed in Venice during the 18th century. 1,274 items. Entries give librettist, composer, place of performance, cast if known, ballet if included. Indexes of titles, librettists, composers, singers, dancers, etc. Introductory essay of 80 pages on the Venetian musical theater.

979 / **Wolff, Stéphane.** Un demi-siècle d'opéra-comique (1900–50): les œuvres, les interprètes. Paris, Éditions André Bonne, 1953. 339 p.

I. p. 15–231: the works arranged alphabetically by title, with much detailed information as to cast, production, etc. II. p. 233–339: the interpreters and their roles, a series of biographical sections treating the singers, dancers, conductors and other personnel involved in *opéra-comique* productions.

980 / **Wolff, Stéphane.** L'Opéra au Palais Garnier, 1875–1962: les oeuvres, les interprètes. Paris, "L'Entr'acte" [1963], 565 p.

A book of facts related to the Paris opéra and its productions from 1875 to the present.

I, p. 23–378: productions listed in several alphabets according to type ("oeuvres lyriques et oratories," "oeuvres chorégraphiques, oeuvres dramatiques," etc.). II, p. 379–552: persons affiliated with the opéra (singers, conductors, dancers, composers, administrative personnel).

MUSIC OF INDIVIDUAL COMPOSERS

A large number of bibliographical tools have been created to serve as guides to the music of individual composers; work lists and thematic catalogs exist in abundance. To cite them all would extend the present work beyond reasonable limits. For an exhaustive listing of thematic catalogs the reader can be referred to Barry Brook's compilation (see no. 1839). Important nonthematic inventories are to be found in the major encyclopedias, such as *Grove*, *MGG*, and *La Musica*.

The entries in the following section have been selected as representative of recent compilations of composers' work lists.

ABEL, KARL FRIEDRICH

981 / **Knape, Walter.** Bibliographisch-thematisches Verzeichnis der Kompositionen von Karl Friedrich Abel (1723–1787). Cuxhaven, W. Knape (1972?), 299 p.

ARNE, THOMAS AUGUSTINE

982 / **Parkinson, John A.** An index to the vocal works of Thomas Augustine Arne and Michael Arne. Detroit, Information Coordinators, 1972. 82 p. (Detroit studies in music bibliography, 21.)

BACH, JOHANN SEBASTIAN

983 **Whaples, Miriam K.** Bach aria index. Ann Arbor, Michigan, Music Library Association, 1971 (MLA index series, 11).

The main index classifies the arias by performing forces. Works are identified by text incipit, location in the Bach *Thematisch-syste-*

matiches Verzeichnis, and in the principal editions. Alphabetical index of first lines and of instruments.

BANCHIERI, ADRIANO

984 / **Mischiati, Oscar.** "Adriano Banchieri (1568–1634): Profilo biografico e bibliografia delle opere." In *Annuario* (1965–1970) Conservatorio di Musica "G. B. Martini," Bologna. Bologna, 1971, p. 39–201.

Also printed as separate by Casa Editrice Pàtron, Bologna, 1971.

A model bibliographical study of one of the most versatile composers and theorists of the Bolognese school of the early 17th century. Preliminary biographical essay followed by a systematic bibliography of Banchieri's sacred music, instrumental music, secular music, music theory, and literary writings. Copies of the works are located in major European libraries and the Library of Congress. Facsimile plates.

BEETHOVEN, LUDWIG VAN

985 / **Hess, Willy.** Verzeichnis der nicht in der Gesamtausgabe veröffentlichten Werke Ludwig van Beethovens. Wiesbaden, Breitkopf & Härtel, 1957. 116 p.

Cites 335 works not included in the complete edition, plus 66 doubtful works.

BERLIOZ, HECTOR

986 / **Bibliography Committee, New York Chapter, MLA.** An alphabetical index to Hector Berlioz: *Werke.* Ann Arbor, Michigan, Music Library Association, 1963. (MLA Index series, 2.)

BOCCHERINI, LUIGI

987 / **Gérard, Yves.** Thematic, bibliographical, and critical catalogue of the works of Luigi Boccherini. Trans. by Andreas Mayor. London, Oxford Univ. Press, 1969. 716 p.

Review by Ellen Amsterdam in *JAMS,* 24 (1971), p. 131–33.

CLEMENTI, MUZIO

988 / **Tyson, Alan.** Thematic catalogue of the works of Muzio Clementi. Tutzing, Hans Schneider, 1967. 136 p.

Review by Donald W. Krummel in *Notes,* 25 (1969), p. 725–26.

EISLER, HANNS

989 / **Notowicz, Nathan, and Jürgen Elsner.** Hanns Eisler Quellennachweise. Hrsg. im Auftrag des Hanns-Eisler Archives bei der Deutschen Akademie der Künste zu Berlin. Leipzig, Deutscher Verlag für Musik, 1966. 174 p.

A bibliographical source book of the work of Hans Eisler (1898–1962) based on the holdings of an archive in East Berlin. Coverage includes a listing of his compositions, an annotated bibliography of his literary work, and a discography of his music.

FRANZ, ROBERT

990 / **Boonin, Joseph M.** An index to the solo songs of Robert Franz. Hackensack, New Jersey, Joseph Boonin, Inc., 1970. 19 p. (Music indexes and bibliographies 4.)

A listing of Franz's songs by opus numbers; a brief survey of their publishing history, including the various collections issued in the late 19th century; title and first-line index and a listing of the poets set by the composer.

GOTTSCHALK, LOUIS MOREAU

991 / **Offergeld, Robert.** The centennial catalogue of the published and unpublished compositions of Louis Morau Gottschalk. Prepared for *Stereo Review*. New York, Ziff-Davis Publishing Co., 1970. 34 p.

The introduction discusses Gottschalk's output and the state of research based on the source materials. This is followed by an annotated listing of 298 compositions. The annotations are entertaining and informative; a model of bibliographical technique.

Review by Alan Mandel in *Notes*, 28 (1971), p. 42–43.

HANDEL, GEORGE FRIEDRICH

992 / **Bell, A. Craig.** Chronological catalogue of Handel's works. Greenock, The Grain-Aig Press, 1969. 68 p.

The chronological listing includes 157 works covering the period between 1695–1757, followed by a section of works of unknown or uncertain dates, and a group of spurious or doubtful works. Notes on the circumstances or composition and on availability in modern editions.

993 / **Bell, A. Craig.** Handel: a chronological thematic catalogue. Greenock, The Grain-Aig Press, 1972. 452 p.

Contains some 3,000 thematic incipits. Appendices list spurious and doubtful works, unpublished and lost works, and works with opus numbers. Indexed by librettists, instrumental and vocal titles, instrumental interludes. Classified index and first-line index.

994 / **Smith, William Charles.** Handel: a descriptive catalogue of the early editions. 2nd ed. with suppl. Oxford, B. Blackwell, 1970. 378 p.

First published in 1960 by Cassell, London.

The *Supplement*, p. 331–340, serves to bring the 1960 work up to date.

HASSE, JOHANN ADOLF

995 / **Hansell, Sven Hostrup.** Works for solo voice of Johann Adolf Hasse (1699–1783). Detroit, Information Coordinators, 1968. 110 p. (Detroit studies in music bibliography, 12.)

Review by Robert L. Marshall in *Die Musikforschung*, 24 (1971), p. 463–64; by Owen Jander in *Notes*, 25 (1969), p. 722–23.

HAYDN, JOSEPH

996 / **Haydn, Joseph.** Thematisches Verzeichnis sämtlichen Kompositionen . . . zusammengestellt von Aloys Fuchs 1839. Facsimile-Ausgabe. Hrsg. von Richard Schaal. Wilhelmshaven, Heinrichshofen's Verlag, 1968. 204 p. (Quellen-Kataloge zur Musikgeschichte, 2.)

Thematic catalog of Haydn's works compiled by the Viennese collector Aloys Fuchs in 1839. Reproduced in facsimile.

Review by H. C. Robbins Landon in *Haydn yearbook*, 6 (1969), p. 217-18.

IVES, CHARLES

997 / **De Lerma, Dominique-René.** Charles Edward Ives, 1874–1954: a bibliography of his music. Kent State University Press, 1970. 212 p.

Works listed alphabetically by title, with indexes of publishers, medium, chronology, arrangers, poets and librettists, phonorecords, and performers.

LOCKE, MATTHEW

998 / **Harding, Rosamund.** A thematic catalogue of the works of Matthew Locke; with a calendar of the main events of his life. Oxford, R. E. M. Harding; Distributed by Blackwell, 1971. 177 p.

Review by J. A. Westrup in *Music and Letters*, 53 (1972), p. 442–44; and *Anon* in *Times Literary Supplement*, no. 3,658 (April 1972), p. 387. Review by Michael Tilmouth in *The Musical Times*, 113 (1972), p. 561–62; by Gloria Rose in *Notes*, 29 (1973), p. 457.

MARCELLO, BENEDETTO

999 / **Fruchtman, Caroline S.** Checklist of vocal chamber works by Benedetto Marcello. Detroit, Information Coordinators, Inc., 1967. 37 p. (Detroit studies in music bibliography, 10.)

Review by Owen Jander in *Notes*, 24 (1968), p. 491–92.

MONTEVERDI, CLAUDIO

1000 / **Bibliography Committee, New York Chapter, MLA.** An alphabetical index to Claudio Monteverdi: *Tutti le opere*. Ann Arbor, Michigan, Music Library Association, 1963. (MLA Index series, 1.)

MOSCHELES, IGNAZ

1001 / **[Kistner, Friedrich, firm, Leipzig]** Thematisches Verzeichniss im Druck erschienener Compositionen von Ignaz Moscheles. London, H. Baron, 1966. 66 p.

MOZART, WOLFGANG AMADEUS

1002 / **Hill, George R., Murray Gould** [*et al.*]. A thematic locator for Mozart's works as listed in Köchel's *Chronologisch-Thematisches Verzeichnis*, 6th edition. Hackensack, N.J., Joseph Boonin, 1970. 76 p. (Music indexes and bibliographies, 1.)

The thematic locator contained in this volume presents the incipits of Mozart's musical works systematically, enabling the user to determine quickly the Köchel number and movement of any piece by Mozart. [*Preface*]

In two sections, one arranging the themes by interval size, the other arranging them by pitch name.

NICHELMANN, CHRISTOPH

1003 / **Lee, Douglas A.** The works of Christoph Nichelmann: a thematic index. Detroit, Information Coordinators, 1971. 100 p. (Detroit studies in music bibliography, 19.)

REGER, MAX

1004 / **Rösner, Helmut.** Max-Reger-Bibliographies. Das internationale Schrifttum über Max Reger 1893–1966. Bonn, Ferd. Dümmlers Verlag, 1968. 138 p.

Review by Gerd Sievers in *Die Musikforschung*, 24 (1971), p. 93–95.

REGNART, JACOB

1005 / **Pass, Walter.** Thematischer Katalog sämtlicher Werke Jacob Regnarts [c. 1540–1599]. Wien, Köln, Graz, Böhlau in Komm., 1969. 244 p. (Tabulae musicae Austriacae, 5.)

Review by John Graziano in *Notes*, 27 (1971), p. 493–94; by Wilhelm Schepping in *Jahrbuch für Volksliedforschung*, 16 (1971), p. 186; by Jürgen Kindermann in *Die Musikforschung*, 25 (1972), p. 371–72.

ROSETTI, ANTON

1006 / **Kaul, Oskar.** Thematisches Verzeichnis der Instrumentalwerke von Anton Rosetti. Wiesbaden, Breitkopf & Härtel (1968). 27 p.

ROSSI, SALAMON

1007 / **Newman, Joel, and Fritz Rikko.** A thematic index to the works of Salamon Rossi. Hackensack, N.J., Joseph Boonin, Inc., 1972. 140 p.

SCHUMANN, ROBERT

1008 / **Ochs, Michael.** Schumann index, part 1: an alphabetical index to Robert Schumann: *Werke*. Ann Arbor, Michigan, Music Library Association, 1967. (MLA Index series, 6.)

1009 / **Weichlein, William.** Schumann index, part 2: an alphabetical index to the solo songs of Robert Schumann. Ann Arbor, Michigan, Music Library Association, 1967. (Music index series, 7.)

STRADELLA, ALESSANDRO

1010 / **Jander, Owen H.** A catalogue of the manuscripts of compositions by Alessandro Stradella found in European and American libraries. Wellesley, Mass., Wellesley College, 1962. 72 leaves (typescript).
First issued in 1960.
A classified catalog of Stradella's works with locations of the manuscript sources. The principal divisions are instrumental music, vocal music with sacred texts, vocal music with secular texts.

STRAVINSKY, IGOR

1011 / **White, Eric Walter.** Stravinsky, the composer and his works. London, Faber and Faber, 1966. 608 p.

SULLIVAN, ARTHUR

1012 / **Poladian, Sirvart.** Sir Arthur Sullivan: an index to the texts of his vocal works. Detroit, Information Coordinators, Inc., 1961. 91 p. (Detroit studies in music bibliography, 2.)
A comprehensive index of first lines, titles, and refrains to the composer's vocal works, sacred and secular.
Review by William Lichtenwanger in *Notes*, 19 (1962), p. 428–30.

VERDI, GIUSEPPE

1013 / **Chusid, Martin.** A catalog of Verdi's operas. Hackensack, N.J., Joseph Boonin, Inc., 1973? 125 p. (Music indexes and bibliographies, 5.)

VICTORIA, TOMÁS LUIS DE

1014 / **Bibliography Committee, New York Chapter, MLA.** An alphabetical index to Tomás Luis de Victoria: *Opera omnia*. Ann Arbor, Michigan, Music Library Association, 1966. (MLA Index series, 5.)

VIVALDI, ANTONIO

1015 / **Coral, Lenore.** A concordance of the thematic indexes to the instrumental works of Antonio Vivaldi. Ann Arbor, Michigan, Music Library Association, 1965. (MLA Index series, 4.) 2nd edition, Ann Arbor, 1972.

WAGENSEIL, GEORG

1016 / **Scholz-Michelitsch, Helga.** Das Orchester- und Kammermusikwerk von Georg Christoph Wagenseil. Thematischer Katalog. Wien, Hermann Böhlaus Nachf., 1972. 228 p.

The incipits reflect all parts and movements in the works. Sources are located in libraries throughout the world. Bibliographical references.

EARLY MUSIC IN MODERN EDITIONS
(Including Collections and Monuments)

The purpose of the bibliographies listed in this category is to direct the user to new editions of old music—one of the most pressing needs of the performer, the teacher, and the music historian. Some of the items listed below are focused on the contents of the major critical editions (*Denkmäler, Gesamtausgaben*); others emphasize the more practical, performing editions of early music. In either case, listings of this kind are soon out of date. To keep abreast of new publications in this area, one should consult the music review sections of a variety of current periodicals: *Notes, Music and letters, Die Musikforschung, and JAMS,* as well as such regular listings as may be found in *Fontes artis musicae.* See also the entries in this volume under "Guides to Systematic and Historical Musicology." Many of the works listed there have bibliographical supplements which cite and evaluate historical editions and monuments.

By far the most useful guide to the contents of the historical sets and critical editions is *Heyer,* no. 1028 below.

1017 / **Apel, Willi.** "Editions, historical." In his *Harvard dictionary of music.* Cambridge, Mass., Harvard Univ. Press, 1947. P. 226–34.

Lists 31 important serial publications of early music, from plainsong through the 18th century. Contents of such large collections as the German and Austrian *Denkmäler* arranged alphabetically by composer.

1018 / **Bukofzer, Manfred F.** "A check-list of instrumental ensemble music before Haydn." In *Music Teachers' National Association Proceedings*, 1946. P. 470–79.
Includes only practical editions available through American publishers at the time of compilation.

1019 / **Bukofzer, Manfred F.** "List of editions [of Baroque music]." In his *Music in the Baroque era*. New York, Norton, 1947. P. 461–69.
A selective list organized under 4 main headings: (1) general anthologies; (2) historical collections; (3) smaller collections and performing editions; and (4) complete or collected editions of individual composers. Minimum bibliographical information.

1020 / **Charles, Sydney Robinson.** A handbook of music and music literature in sets and series. New York, The Free Press, 1972. 497 p.
Useful guide to the contents of critical editions, both collective and devoted to the works of individual composers. Two further sections treat (1) monographs and facsimile series and (2) music periodicals and yearbooks.

1021 / **Coover, James B.** Gesamtausgaben: a checklist. n.p. Distant Press, 1970. 27 leaves.
A practical listing, alphabetical by composer, of 376 *Gesamtausgaben*. The list was designed to help with acquisitions in a college or university music library. Includes all works "for which completeness was the professed goal, disregarding failure to accomplish it."

1022 / **"Denkmäler der Tonkunst"** [by Wolfgang Schmieder]. In *MGG*, v. 3, col. 164–92.
Lists 213 major editions, practical and scholarly, with contents given in considerable detail. Classified as to national or international coverage.

1023 / **"Denkmäler und Gesamtausgaben."** In *Repertorium der Musikwissenschaft* . . . bearb. von Willi Kahl und Wilhelm-Martin Luther. Kassel & Basel, Bärenreiter, 1953. P. 232–43.

140 entries for major historical sets. Full bibliographical information, but no listing of contents.

1024 / **"Editions et Rééditions de Musique Ancienne** (avant 1800)." In *Fontes artis musicae*, no. 1– . Paris, Assoc. Internationale des Bibliothèques Musicales, 1954– .

One of the few current listings of new editions of early music. International coverage. Full bibliographical information, including price.

1025 / **"Editions, Historical."** In *Reference works in music and music literature in five libraries of Los Angeles County*. Ed. by Helen W. Azhderian. Los Angeles, Univ. of Southern California, 1953. P. 116–37.

360 editions listed, both critical and practical. No detailed content analysis, but good coverage of the important sets.

1026 / **Eitner, Robert.** Verzeichnis neuer Ausgaben alter Musikwerke aus der frühesten Zeit bis zum Jahre 1800. Berlin, Trautwein, 1871. 208 p. (Monatshefte für Musikgeschichte. Beilage. 1871.)

Nachträge, published in *Monatshefte*, 9 (1877); "Register zu den Nachträgen" as its Beilage, 1877; and 10 (1878).

Still useful as a guide to the contents of early historical collections, including music in histories. *Abtheilung I*: annotated list of collections and literary works containing music; *Abtheilung II*: index of composers and their works, with separate listings of anonymous works and of German secular song through the 16th century.

1027 / **"Gesamtausgaben"** [by Wolfgang Schmieder]. In *MGG*, v. 4, col. 1850–76.

A valuable discussion of the historical development of critical editions of the work of individual composers followed by entries for 84 such editions, with detailed listings of contents.

1028 / **Heyer, Anna Harriet.** Historical sets, collected editions, and monuments of music; a guide to their contents. 2d ed. Chicago, American Library Association, 1969. 573 p.

First published in 1957.

An indispensible guide to editorial work in the field of early music. Detailed listings of the contents of sets, including important publishers' series (e.g. Bärenreiter's *Hortus musicus*, Nagel's *Musik*

Archiv, Kistner und Siegel's *Organum*, etc.) Numerous cross references. Comprehensive index of composers, editors, titles.

Review of the first edition by Irene Millen in *Notes*, 15 (1958), p. 390–91; by Harriet Nicewonger in *The Library Journal* (Sept. 1958), p. 2380. Of the second edition by Lenore Coral in *JAMS*, 24 (1971), p. 308–09; by Richard H. Hunter in *Notes*, 26 (1969), p. 275–77.

1029 / **Hirsch, Paul, and Kathi Meyer.** "Sammelwerke und Gesamtausgaben." In their *Katalog der Musikbibliothek Paul Hirsch*. Bd. IV, Cambridge, England, Cambridge Univ. Press, 1947. P. 331–409.

Lists 90 complete editions and collections, with a detailed survey of their contents.

1030 / **"Novae Editiones Musicae Classicae."** In *Acta M*, v. 3– . Leipzig & Copenhagen, Internationale Gesellschaft für Musikwissenschaft, Jan., 1931– .

Regular listing of the new editions of early music arranged alphabetically by composer, giving title, scoring, editor, place, publisher, date, and price. Discontinued after 1952.

1031 / **Ochs, Michael.** An index to *Das Chorwerk*, volumes 1–110. Ann Arbor, Michigan, Music Library Association, 1970. 38 p. (MLA Index series, 10.)

Composer index and title index. Information includes volume, page, type of composition and vocal ensemble.

1032 / **Schering, Arnold.** "Übersicht über die musikgeschichtlichen Sammelwerke und kritische Gesamtausgaben der Werke der grossen Meister der Musik aus dem Verlage von Breitkopf & Härtel." In his *Tabellen zur Musikgeschichte*. Leipzig, Breitkopf & Härtel, 1934. *Anhang*, 30 p.

A useful breakdown of the contents of the critical editions published by Breitkopf & Härtel. This supplement is omitted from the 1962 edition of the *Tabellen*.

1033 / **Schiedermair, Ludwig.** "Gesamtausgaben und Publikationsreihen in Ubersichten." In his *Einführung in das Studium der Musikgeschichte*. Bonn, F. Bümmlers Verlag, 1947. *Anhang*, p. 104–61. Surveys the contents of the major sets and publishers' series.

241

1034 / **Verzeichnis der Neudrucke alter Musik.** Herausgegeben im Auftrage des Staatlichen Instituts für deutsche Musikforschung von Walter Lott. Leipzig, F. Holmeister, 1937–43. 7 v.

An annual bibliography of new editions of music composed before 1800, covering the years of publication 1936–42. Includes separate works and contents of collections. German publications emphasized. Works listed by composer; medium and title index.

PRIMARY SOURCES OF EARLY MUSIC: MANUSCRIPTS AND PRINTED BOOKS

This section will direct users to bibliographies of original source materials, chiefly those prior to 1800. The list is highly selective. Nearly every dissertation or research study devoted to early music contains its bibliography of primary sources. Some of these bibliographies are of great value, but any attempt to cite them all would extend far beyond the scope of the present work. The user should be reminded that the major reference works such as *MGG* or Riemann's *Lexikon* contain abundant listings of primary sources. See, for example, the *MGG* entries under "Ars antiqua," "Ars nova," or "Chanson." Since the second edition of the present work was published, several important volumes in the *International Inventory of Musical Sources* have made their appearance (see nos. 1079 ff).

It should be obvious that one of the most direct approaches to primary sources will be found in the section entitled "Catalogs of Music Libraries and Collections." Another useful approach, although not employed here apart from one or two exceptions, is through the catalogs of antiquarian music and book dealers such as Leo Liepmannssohn, Otto Haas, Maggs Bros., etc.

See also the section "Histories and Bibliographies of Music Printing and Publishing for bibliographies of the output of some of the major music publishing houses from the 16th through the 18th centuries.

1035 / **Anderson, Gordon A.** "Notre Dame and related conductus: a catalogue raisonné." In *Miscellanea musicologica. Adelaide studies in musicology*, 6 (1972), p. 153–229.

A "work in progress" designed to give systematic coverage to all pieces which may be designated conductus and which issue from ca. 1170 to the close of the 13th century." Sources are identified and bibliographical references cited.

1036 / **Apel, Willi.** "Sources, musical (pre–1450)." In his *Harvard dictionary of music*, 2nd edition. Cambridge, Mass., Harvard Univ. Press, 1969. p. 797–99.

A brief but useful listing of some of the major sources of Gregorian chant, secular monophonic and polyphonic music to 1450. Locations of the sources are given with references to modern editions, if any.

1037 / **Becker, Carl Ferdinand.** Die Tonwerke des XVI. und XVII. Jahrhunderts, oder systematisch-chronologische Zusammenstellung der in diesen zwei Jahrhunderten gedruckten Musikalien. Zweite Ausgabe. Leipzig, E. Fleischer, 1855.

First published in 1847. Reprint of the second edition by Olms, Hildesheim, 1969.

An early classified bibliography of musical source materials, chronologically arranged under categories, with an index of composers and a general index to the whole. Attempts to list all musical compositions published in the 16th and 17th centuries to which actual or approximate dates could be assigned. An abridgement of Rimbault's *Bibliotheca madrigaliana* (no. 1100) is included as a supplement.

1038 / **Besseler, Heinrich.** "Studien zur Musik des Mittelalters: 1. Neue Quellen des 14. und beginnenden 15. Jahrhunderts. 2. Die Motette von Franko von Köln bis Philipp von Vitry." In *Archiv für Musikwissenschaft*, 7 (1925), p. 167–252, and 9 (1927), p. 137–258.

Two articles that are basic source studies for the music of the late medieval period, containing numerous inventories and descriptions of *ars nova* manuscripts. They supplement the work of Friedrich Ludwig covering the *ars antiqua* sources (see no. 1086).

1039 / **Bibliotheca Musico-Liturgica.** A descriptive handlist of the musical and Latin-Liturgical mss. of the Middle Ages preserved in the libraries of Great Britain and Ireland. Drawn up by W. H. Frere . . . and printed for the members of The Plainsong and Mediaeval Music Society. . . . London, Quaritch, 1901–1932. 2 v.

A union list of manuscript sources of early music in Great Britain. Vol. 1 (nos. 1–545): manuscripts at Lambeth and Oxford. Vol. 2 (nos.

546–1,031): manuscripts in cathedral chapter libraries and at Manchester, Dublin, Cambridge, etc. Full descriptions of the manuscripts; 17 plates. Indexes of service books, places, persons, and of Oxford Bodleian and Cambridge University Library manuscripts.

1040 / **Bohn, Emil.** "Bibliothek des gedruckten mehrstimmigen weltlichen deutschen Liedes vom Anfange des 16. Jahrhunderts bis ca. 1640." In the author's *Fünfzig historische Concerte in Breslau, 1881– 1892.* Breslau, Hainauer, 1893. p. 77–188.

A bibliography of German printed secular polyphonic song. The collections are listed chronologically to 1625; the volumes containing works by individual composers are listed alphabetically. Detailed bibliographical information, but contents not given. A useful guide to the printed sources of early German song.

1041 / **Bolle, W.** Die gedruckten englischen Liederbücher in der Zeit Shakespeares. Mit Abdruck aller Texte aus den bisher noch nicht neugedruckten Liederbüchern und den zeitgenössischen deutschen Übertragungen. Berlin, 1903.

Reprint by Johnson Reprint Company, 1969.

1042 / **Borren, Charles van den.** "Inventaire des manuscrits de musique polyphonique qui se trouvent en Belgique." In *Acta musicologica,* 5 (1933), p. 66–71, 120–27, 177–83; 6 (1934), p. 23–29, 65–73, 116–21.

An inventory of the manuscript sources of early polyphony in Belgian libraries. Detailed descriptions, with listings of contents, of manuscripts in the libraries in Brussels, Ghent, Liège, Louvain, Malines, and Tournai.

1043 / **The Breitkopf Thematic Catalogue.** The six parts and sixteen supplements, 1762–1787. Edited and with an introduction and indexes by Barry S. Brook. New York, Dover, 1966. 888 p.

Facsimile reproduction of the major 18th-century thematic catalog, giving almost 15,000 musical incipits and 1,300 first lines of texts representing over 1,000 composers. Preceded by an informative essay and an outline of the contents. Index of first lines of texts and a general index of names and topics.

Review by Bernard E. Wilson in *JAMS,* 21 (1968), p. 400–404; by Donald W. Krummel in *Notes,* 24 (1968), p. 697–700; by H. C. Robbins Landon in the *Haydn yearbook,* 6 (1969), p. 218.

1044 / **Breslauer, Martin** (Firm, Booksellers, Berlin). Das deutsche Lied, geistlich und weltlich bis zum 18. Jahrhundert. Berlin, M. Breslauer, 1908. 304 p. (Documente frühen deutschen Lebens, Reihe 1.)
Reprint by Olms, Hildesheim, 1966.
An important music dealer's catalog listing 556 items in the field of early German song. Full bibliographical entries with descriptive annotations. Numerous facsimiles of title pages. Prices given. Index of first lines of song texts, melodies, persons.

1045 / **Bridgman, Nanie.** "Musique profane italienne des 16e et 17e siècles dans les bibliothèques françaises," in *Fontes artis musicae,* 2 (1955), p. 40–59.
Full bibliographical descriptions of thirty-two 16th and 17th century prints of Italian secular music in branch libraries.

1046 / **British Museum (London) Department of Printed Books.** Hand-list of music published in some British and foreign periodicals between 1787 and 1848, now in the British Museum, London, The Trustees of the British Museum, 1962. 80 p.
Indexes to music, chiefly songs, in 12 periodicals. 1,855 entries arranged by composer.
Review by Richard Schaal in *Die Musikforschung,* 17 (1964), p. 423.

1047 / **The British Union-Catalogue of Early Music Printed before the Year 1801.** A record of the holdings of over 100 libraries throughout the British Isles. Editor: Edith B. Schnapper. London, Butterworths Scientific Publications, 1957. 2 v.
A major reference tool for work with early printed sources of music. These volumes provide the key to sources in British libraries. Brief bibliographical entries; locations established in more than 100 libraries in England, Scotland, and Ireland.
Review by A. Hyatt King in *Music and letters,* 39 (1958), p. 77–79; by Richard S. Hill in *Notes,* 15 (1958), p. 565–58; by Richard Schaal in *Die Musikforschung,* 12 (1959), p. 367–69.

1048 / **Brook, Barry S.** La symphonie française dans la seconde moitié du XVIIIe siècle. Paris, Publications de l'Institut de Musicologie de l'Université de Paris, 1962. 3 v.
Vol. 1 is a study of the French symphony of the latter half of the 18th century, with important bibliographical supplements: *Annexe IV*: "Index thematique arrangé par tonalites et temps" (p. 511–73); *An-*

245

nexe V: "Index alphabetique des incipits transposés en do majeur ou do mineur et indiqués par les lettres" (p. 574–84); *Annexe XI*: "Inventaire sommaire de la symphonie et de la symphonie concertante françaises" (p. 585–633); *Annexe VII*: "Reeditions et enregistrements" (p. 634–39). Bibliography (p. 643–65); general index.

Vol. 2: "Catalogue thématique et bibliographique." Full descriptions of the works, location of sources, short biographies of each composer.

Vol. 3: Scores of 6 previously unedited symphonies.

The work treats some 1,200 symphonies by 150 composers.

Review by Marc Pincherle in *Revue de musicologie*, 49 (1963), p. 131–33; by H. C. Robbins Landon in *Die Musikforschung*, 17 (1964), p. 435–39; by Jan LaRue in *MO* (1963), p. 384–88.

1049 / **Brown, Howard M.** Instrumental music printed before 1600; a bibliography. Cambridge, Mass., Harvard Univ. Press, 1965. 559 p.

A bibliography of the greatest importance for students of early instrumental music. Chronologically arranged beginning with Michel de Toulouze's *L'Art et instruction de bien dancer* (148?) and ending with works printed in 1599. Full bibliographical descriptions incorporating much valuable commentary. Includes references to works now lost.

P. 441–69: list of works cited. Indexes: (1) list of libraries and their holdings; (2) volumes described, arranged by types of notation; (3) volumes described, arranged by performing medium; (4) names; (5) first lines and titles.

Review by Claudio Sartori in *Notes*, 22 (1966), p. 1,209–212; by Jack Westrup in *Music and letters*, 47 (1966), p. 354–55; by Jeremy Noble in *JAMS*, 19 (1966), p. 415–17; by Ingrid Brainard in *Die Musikforschung*, 20 (1967), p. 465–70; by Martin Picker in *MO*, 28 (1967), p. 136–39; by A. Hyatt King in *The Library*, ser. 5, 22 (June 1969), p. 154–58.

1050 / **Bryden, John R., and David G. Hughes.** An index of Gregorian Chant. Cambridge, Mass., Harvard University Press, 1969. 2 v.

An index of chants found chiefly in modern service books. Vol. 1 gives text incipits; vol. 2, melodic incipits in number notation. A useful tool for identifying the chants used in polyphonic composition.

Review by Don M. Randel in *Notes*, 27 (1971), p. 477–78. By Andrew Hughes in *Music & letters*, 51 (1970), p. 317–19.

1051 / **Chaillon, Paule.** "Les fonds musicaux de quelques bibliothèques de province," in *Fontes artis musicae*, 2 (1955), p. 151–63.

A listing of libraries in 24 French provinces with descriptions of their catalogs, if any, followed by a list of *unica* or of rare or unusual works in their collections.

1052 / **Corbin, Solange,** ed. Répertoire de manuscrits médiévaux contenant des notations musicales. Paris, Éditions du Centre National de la Recherche Scientifique, 1965– .

Vol. 1: Bibliothèque Sainte-Geneviève (1965)

Vol. 2: Bibliothèque Mazarine, par Madeleine Bernard (1966)

This series promises to provide descriptions and inventories of all the manuscripts containing medieval chant notation.

Review by John Emerson in *JAMS*, 22 (1969), p. 119–22; by Ewald Jammers in *Die Musikforschung*, 21 (1968), p. 103–04.

1053 / **Crane, Frederick.** Materials for the study of the 15th-century *Basse danse*. New York, Institute of Medieval Music, 1968. 131 p. (Wissenschaftliche Abhandlungen, 16.)

Review by Peter Gülke in *Die Musikforschung*, 24 (1971), p. 339–40.

1054 / **Daniel, Ralph T., and Peter Le Hurray.** The sources of English church music 1549–1660. London, Published for the British Academy by Stainer and Bell, 1972. 2 v.

This is the first attempt to compile a complete inventory of sacred music in English covering the period from the early years of the Reformation to the mid-17th century. [*Preface*]

Part I is a listing of the sources, printed or in manuscript, a thematic catalog of all anonymous works, and a first-line index of anthems. Part II: services and anthems arranged in alphabetical order by composer, with all the data as to sources and locations of sources.

1055 / **Danner, Peter.** "Bibliography of guitar tablatures, 1546–1764." In *Journal of the lute society of America*, 5 (1972), p. 40–51.

A bibliography of 165 printed and 50 manuscript sources. Brief descriptive annotations.

1056 / **Daschner, Hubert.** Die gedruckten mehrstimmigen Chansons von 1500–1600. Bonn, Rheinische Friedrich-Wilhelms-Universität, 1962. 195 p.

A dissertation the greater part of which consists of a first-line index of polyphonic chansons from the printed collections of the 16th century. 4,273 chansons entered.

P. 175–82: "Verzeichnis der Musikdrucke," p. 184–86: "Verzeichnis der anonymen Gedichtsammlungen." P. 187–95; "Literaturverzeichnis."

1057 / **Davidsson, Åke.** Catalogue critique et descriptif des imprimés de musique des XVIe et XVIIe siècles conservés dans les bibliothèques suédoises. (Excepté la Bibliothèque de L'Université Royale d'Upsala). Upsala, Almquist et Wiksells, 1952. 471 p. (Studia musicologica upsaliensia, 1.)

A union catalog of early music in 18 Swedish libraries, excluding the University of Uppsala, which is treated elsewhere (see no. 1497). Full descriptions, contents, references; p. 455–71: bibliography of works cited.

1058 / **Deakin, Andrew.** Outlines of musical bibliography: a catalogue of early music and musical works printed or otherwise produced in the British Isles; the whole chronologically arranged with descriptive and critical notes on the principal works. Birmingham, A. Deakin, 1899. 112 p.

Reprint of the 1899 edition by Olms, Hildesheim, c. 1971.

A work projected on a much larger scale, but not completed. P. 5–18: a listing of manuscript sources. P. 19–96: chiefly printed music of the 16th and 17th centuries, but with a few manuscripts included. The entries are not precise, and the locations given are indefinite. Indexed by composer and title.

1059 / **Dichter, Harry, and Elliott Shapiro.** Early American sheet music, its lure and its lore, 1768–1889. . . . including a directory of early American music publishers. . . . New York, R. R. Bowker, 1941. 287 p.

A cross-section of early American sheet music, classified as to subject content. Composer, main title, publisher, and date included. The directory of publishers is an alphabetical listing of firms active from 1768 to 1899 and carries their histories to 1940. Additional lists of lithographers and artists active before 1870. Plates of illustrated title pages. Index.

1060 / **Dichter, Harry.** Handbook of American sheet music . . . first annual issue, 1947. Philadelphia, H. Dichter, 1947. 100 p.
Second series, with Bernice Larrabee. Philadelphia, 1953.
Catalogs of early American sheet music for sale by the author. Full of useful bibliographical data. Classified under selected headings: topic, author, title. Prices given. No index. The 1947 volume lists over 2,000 items.

1061 / **Draudius, Georg.** Verzeichnisse deutscher musikalischer Bücher, 1611–1625. In originalgetreuem Nachdruck herausgegeben von Konrad Ameln. Bonn, Deutschen Musikverleger-Verband, 1957.
Facsimile reprint of the music sections from the 1611 and 1625 editions of Draudius's *Bibliotheca librorum germanicorum classica*, an early document in the history of music bibliography. ("Musikalischer Bücher" here means "scores.") Classified according to type of composition. Primarily of historical interest.

1062 / **Duckles, Vincent.** "The music for the lyrics in early seventeenth-century English drama: a bibliography of the primary sources." In *Music in English renaissance drama*. Ed. by John H. Long. Lexington, University of Kentucky Press, 1968. p. 117–160.
Directs the reader to manuscript and early printed sources for the songs introduced into English drama from 1603–1642. Modern editions of these songs are cited when available.

1063 / **Duyse, Florimond Van.** Het oude Nederlandsche lied; wereldlijke en geestelijke liederen uit vroegeren tijd, teksten en melodieën, verzameld en toegelicht door Fl. van Duyse. . . . 's-Gravenhage, M. Nijhoff, 1903–1908. 4 v.
First issued in parts, 1900–1908; unaltered reprint by Frits A. M. Knuf, Hilversum, 1965.
The standard reference book for the study of early Dutch song. Actually an edition of 714 melodies given with their variants and with an abundance of related information on texts and music. Sacred song

is treated in vol. 3; vol. 4 contains indexes of names, of song titles, and of first lines of text.

1064 / **Eitner, Robert.** Bibliographie der Musik-Sammelwerke des XVI. und XVII. Jahrhunderts. Im Vereine mit Frz. Xav. Haberl, A. Lagerberg und C. F. Pohl. Berlin, L. Liepmannssohn, 1877. 964 p.

Supplemented by additions and corrections published in Eitner's *Monatshefte für Musikgeschichte*, 14 (1882), p. 152–55; 161–64.

Reprint of the original edition by Olms, Hildesheim, 1963.

Chronological bibliography of some 795 collections of music published between 1501 and 1700, with full descriptions, summary of contents, lists of composers represented, and library locations of individual copies. The second part of the work, p. 297–938, is a first-line index of the vocal texts, arranged alphabetically by composer.

Eitner's *Sammelwerke* is one of the major bibliographical tools for historical research in music, although it has been superseded, in part, by the first volume of the *International inventory of musical sources*. (See no. 1079).

1065 / **Eitner, Robert.** Biographisch-bibliographische Quellen-Lexikon der Musiker und Musikgelehrten der christlichen Zeitrechnung bis zur Mitte des 19. Jahrhunderts. . . . Leipzig, Breitkopf & Härtel, 1898–1904. 10 v.

Supplemented by the *Miscellanea musicae bio-bibliographica* (no. 1089), and by G. Radiciotti's "Aggiunte e correzioni ai dizionari biografici dei musicisti" (no. 1094).

Reprinted with the supplements by Musurgia, New York, 1947. *Neuauflage* published by Breitkopf & Härtel, Wiesbaden, 1959–60. "2. verbesserte Auflage," Graz, Akademische Druck- und Verlagsanstalt, 1959–60.

Eitner's *Quellen-Lexikon* remains the basic reference tool for locating primary sources of music before 1800. Both printed music and manuscripts are included, with their locations in European libraries. The work is badly out of date; much of the information, particularly as regards locations, is no longer correct. Work is proceeding on the *International inventory*, which will ultimately replace Eitner as a key to the sources of early music. See nos. 1079 ff.

1066 / **Fischer, Kurt von.** Studien zur italienischen Musik des Trecento und frühen Quattrocento. Bern, P. Haupt, 1956. 132 p. (Publikationen der Schweizerischen Musikforschenden Gesellschaft, ser. 2, v. 5.)

A bibliography of Italian secular music of the 14th and early 15th centuries. Text incipits, arranged alphabetically, for 177 madrigals, 25 caccie, and 423 ballate, with information as to sources and modern editions.

Review by Hans Tischler in *Notes*, 15 (1958), p. 405–406.

1067 / **Fortune, Nigel.** "A handlist of printed Italian secular monody books, 1602–1635." In *R.M.A. Research Chronicle*, No. 3. Published for the Royal Musical Association, 1963, p. 27–50.

A list of all publications containing at least one Italian secular monody from the first in 1602 to 1635. Location symbols given for the scarcer volumes. The notes indicate contemporary reprints and modern editions where they exist. By far the most comprehensive listing of Italian monody books available.

1068 / **Friedlaender, Max.** Das deutsche Lied im 18. Jahrhundert, Quellen und Studien. . . . Stuttgart und Berlin, Cotta, 1902. 2 v. in 3.

Vol. 1:1, p. 1–62: a chronological listing of 798 German songbooks of the 18th century (1689–1799), followed by a detailed commentary on the most important examples. Vol. 1:2, a collection of musical examples. Vol. 2: discussion of the poets, with indexes of names, text incipits.

1069 / **Geck, Martin.** Deutsche Oratorien, 1800 bis 1840. Verzeichnis der Quellen und Aufführungen. Wilhelmshaven, Heinrichshofen's Verlag, 1971. 105 p. (Quellen-Kataloge zur Musikgeschichte, 4.)

The bibliography has three major parts: (1) an alphabetical listing of the oratorios under composer; (2) a listing of performances by place; and (3) a listing by chronology. Some reviews and notices in contemporary periodicals are indicated. Oratorios by some 100 composers are cited.

1070 / **Geering, Arnold.** Die Organa und mehrstimmigen Conductus in den Handschriften des deutschen Sprachgebietes vom 13. bis 16. Jahrhundert. Bern, P. Haupt, 1952. 99 p. (Publikationen der Schweizerischen Musikforschenden Gesellschaft, ser. 2:1.)

A study concerned with the sources of early polyphony in the German-speaking countries, with a listing of the relevant manuscripts and an inventory of the organum and conductus settings they contain.

1071 / **Gennrich, Friedrich.** Bibliographie der ältesten französischen und lateinischen Motetten. Darmstadt, Selbstverlag, 1957. 124 p. (Summa musicae medii aevi, 2.)

A bibliography of the 13th-century motet, serving also as a guide to the manuscript sources and a record of scholarly work done in this field. Gennrich expands the work begun by Friedrich Ludwig in his *Repertorium* (see no. 1087). Motets are grouped under their respective tenors, with references to all known concordances and modern editions. Supplementary bibliographies of literature and of scripts, indexes of Latin and French tenors, and incipits to motettus and triplum parts.

Review by Hans Tischler in *Notes*, 16 (1959), p. 561–62.

1072 / **Gennrich, Friedrich.** Der musikalische Nachlass der Troubadours. Kommentar. Darmstadt, Selbstverlag, 1960. 176 p. (Summa musicae medii aevi, 4)

A complete bibliography of the surviving musical settings of Troubadour song, 302 entries in all, with information as to source, editions of text and music, verse forms, use of the melody as a contrafactum. Songs are numbered consecutively but grouped under composer, with bibliographical references to work done on the individual musicians. 25 manuscript sources are described and discussed.

Vol. 3 of the series, *Summa musicae medii aevi* (1958), is a musical edition of the surviving Troubadour melodies.

1073 / **Göhler, Albert.** Verzeichnis der in den Frankfurter und Leipziger Messkatalogen der Jahre 1564 bis 1759 angezeigten Musikalien. . . . Leipzig, C. F. Kahnt Nachf., 1902. (4 parts in 1 vol.)

Unaltered reprint by Frits A. M. Knuf, Hilversum, 1965.

A bibliograph of the music listed in the Frankfurt and Leipzig trade catalogs from 1564 to 1759. Works listed separately by century, under composer. Works identified by type.

1074 / **Gröninger, Eduard.** Repertoire-Untersuchungen zum mehrstimmigen Notre Dame-Conductus. Regensburg, Bosse, 1939. 163 p. (Kölner Beiträge zur Musikforschung, 2.)

An introductory essay of 59 pages, followed by tabulations, with concordances, of the polyphonic conductus compositions found in the four major Notre Dame sources.

1075 / **Hagopian, Viola L.** Italian *ars nova* music, a bibliographic guide to modern editions and related literature. Second edition, revised and expanded. Berkeley and Los Angeles, Univ. of Calif. Press, 1973. 175 p.

First printed in 1964.

An organized, annotated bibliography treating the work done by scholars in the field of 14th-century Italian music.

Review of the first edition by Ursula Günther in *Die Musikforschung*, 20 (1967), p. 83–84.

1076 / **Hixon, Donald L.** Music in early America: a bibliography of music in Evans. Metuchen, N.J., Scarecrow Press, 1970. 607 p.

This bibliography is an index to the music published in seventeenth- and eighteenth-century America as represented by Charles Evans' *American Bibliography* and the Readex Corporation's microprint edition of *Early American Imprints, 1639–1800.* . . .

The first two parts consist of an alphabetical composer-editor-compiler arrangement. Part III is devoted to biographical sketches. Parts III–VI are indexes: composer-compiler, title, and numerical index.

1077 / **Index to Early American Periodicals to 1850.** E. SONGS. (Cards E1 to E11). New York, Readex Microfilm Corp. [1965]. (Bibliographic aids in microprint.)

Microprint edition of the entries under "Songs" from an index of some 650,000 cards compiled by members of the English department of Washington Square College, New York University, with the aid of the WPA. Indexes some 340 early American magazines by authors, composers, analymous titles, first lines.

1078 / **International Association of Music Libraries. Radio Commission.** Catalogue of rare materials, and first supplement. Editor: Folke Lindberg. Stockholm, 1959. 185 leaves.

Supplement I: leaves 175–185.

A list designed for the use of radio librarians in locating copies of rare material that can be used for performance purposes.

1079 / **International Inventory of Musical Sources.** Handschriften mit mehrstimmiger Musik des 14. 15. und 16. Jahrhunderts. Mehrstimmige Musik in italienischen, polnischen, und tschechischen Quellen des 14. Jahrhunderts. Mehrstimmige Stücke in Handschriften aller Länder aus der Zeit um 1400–1425/30. Organale Sätze im älteren Stil und mehrstimmige Stücke in Choralhandschriften des 15. und 16. Jahrhunderts. Beschreiben und inventarisiert von Kurt von Fischer und herausgegeben in Zusammenarbeit mit Max Lütolf. München-Duisburg, G. Henle, 1972. 2 v. (RISM ser. B, vol. 4: 3–4.)

1080 / **International Inventory of Musical Sources.** Manuscripts of polyphonic music, 11th–early 14th century. Edited by Gilbert Reaney. München-Duisburg, G. Henle, 1966. 876 p. (RISM ser. B, vol. 4:1.)

The manuscripts are grouped by nationality of location; described individually with detailed bibliographical references. Thematic incipits in square notation.

1081 / **International Inventory of Musical Sources.** Manuscripts of polyphonic music (c. 1320–1400). By Gilbert Reaney. München-Duisburg, G. Henle, 1969. 427 p. (RISM ser. B, vol. 4:2.)

Organized as in the preceding volume.

Review by Ernest Sanders in *Music and letters*, 51 (1970), p. 458–59.

1082 / **International Inventory of Musical Sources.** Recueils imprimés XVIe–XVIIe siècles. Ouvrage publié sous la direction de François Lesure. I. Liste chronologique. München-Duisburg, G. Henle Verlag [1960–   ]. 639 p. (RISM ser. B, vol. 1.)

This volume is Part I of the systematic-chronological section of a comprehensive bibliography of musical sources currently being compiled under the joint auspices of the International Musicological Society and the International Association of Music Libraries. The present volume supersedes Eitner's *Bibliographie der Musik-Sammelwerke* (no. 1064) and, when completed, the project will replace his *Quellen-Lexikon* (no. 1065) as a modern, comprehensive reference tool for locating primary source materials for musical research.

This volume lists collections of music published between 1501 and 1700, with a summary of their contents and with the locations of copies in major European and American libraries. Index of editors and printers, and of titles and authors.

Review by Vincent Duckles in *Notes*, 18 (1961), p. 225–27; by Jack A. Westrup in *Music and letters*, 42 (1961), p. 76; by Daniel Heartz in *JAMS*, 14 (1961), p. 268–73; by Gustave Reese in *Fontes Artis Musicae*, 8 (1961), p. 4–7.

For documentation on U.S. response to the International Inventory, see "RISM: a report on U.S. activities," by Wayne D. Shirley in *Notes*, 23 (1967), p. 477–97.

1083 / **International Inventory of Musical Sources.** Recueils imprimés XVIIIe siècle. Ouvrage publié sous la direction de François Lesure. München-Duisburg, G. Henle Verlag [1964] 461 p. (RISM ser. B, vol. 2.)

Cites about 1,800 collections printed between 1701 and 1801, giving basic bibliographic descriptions, composers represented, and locations of copies throughout the world. This volume is organized alphabetically by title rather than chronologically as in the preceding entry.

1084 / **International Inventory of Musical Sources.** Tropen- und Sequenzenhandschriften. Von Heinrich Husmann. München-Duisburg, G. Henle Verlag [1964] 236 p. (RISM ser. B, vol. 5:1)

A volume of the *Inventory* set devoted to the manuscript sources of tropes and sequences. Sources grouped by country. Each entry gives information as to the signature, provenance, type of liturgical book, notation, structure of the source, contents, and related literature. Indexes of manuscripts arranged by libraries and by places of origin. Further indexes of places and subjects, names of saints, names of persons. Bibliography.

Review by Edward H. Roesner in *JAMS*, 21 (1968), p. 212–15.

1085 / **Linker, Robert W.** Music of the Minnesinger and early Meistersinger, a bibliography. Chapel Hill, University of North Carolina Press [1961], 79 p.

A bibliography of German medieval song arranged alphabetically under the composers' names. A preliminary list gives 40 manuscript sources and 41 modern publications of literary history, music, and text editions.

Review by Walter Salmen in *Die Musikforschung*, 17 (1964), p. 432.

Loewenberg, Alfred. Annals of opera, 1597–1940. . . .
See no. 353.

1086 / **Ludwig, Friedrich.** "Die Quellen der Motetten ältesten Stils." In *Archiv für Musikwissenschaft,* 5 (1923), p. 185–222, 273–315.

A basic source study of medieval polyphony, in which the author gives complete or partial inventories for some 50 manuscripts containing motets of the *ars antique* period.

This study has been reprinted as a supplement to Gennrich's edition of Ludwig's *Repertorium, Abteilung 2* (see below).

1087 / **Ludwig, Friedrich.** Repertorium organorum recentioris et motetorum vetustissimi stili. Band 1: Catalogue raisonné der Quellen. Abteilung 1: Handschriften in Quadrat-Notation. Halle, Niemeyer, 1910. 344 p.

Ludwig's *Repertorium,* although incomplete, is the starting point for all studies in the music of the *ars antiqua* period. It is essentially an inventory, with concordances, of the contents of the major manuscripts of the Notre Dame repertory.

Band 1, Abteilung 2: Handschriften in Mensuralnotation. Besorgt von Friedrich Gennrich. Langen bei Frankfurt, 1961. (Summa musicae medii aevi, 7.)

This portion of the *Repertorium* appeared in proof copy but was never published in Ludwig's lifetime. It consists chiefly of inventories of two major sources of the 13th-century motet, the *Montpellier Codex* and the *Clayette MS.* Included as a supplement to this volume is a reprint of Ludwig's study, "Die Quellen der Motetten ältesten Stils," which appeared in the *Archiv für Musikwissenschaft,* 5 (1925). See no. 1086 above.

A "2. erweiterte Auflage" of *Band 1,* edited by Luther A Ditmer, appeared in 1964 as a joint publication of the Institute of Mediaeval Music, New York, and Georg Olms, Hildeshiem.

Band 2: Musikalisches Anfangs-Verzeichnis des nach Tenores geordneten Repertorium. Besorgt von Friedrich Gennrich. Langen bei Frankfurt, 1962. 71 p. (Summa musicae medii aevi, 8.)

A thematic catalog of 515 motets based on 50 tenors taken from the liturgy of the Mass. Reprinted, incomplete, from Ludwig's unpublished proof copy.

1088 / **Meyer, Ernst H.** "Quellennachweise." In his *Die mehrstimmige Spielmusik des 17. Jahrhunderts in Nord- und Mittel-Europa.* . . . Kassel, Bärenreiter, 1934. P. 128–258.

A bibliography of the sources of 17th-century chamber music of the North-European school. Partially thematic for the English sources.

1089 / **Miscellanea Musicae Bio-Bibliographica.** . . . Hrsg. von H. Springer, M. Schneider und W. Wolffheim. 2., um einen Anhang verhehrte Auflage. New York, Musurgia, 1947. 435 p.

Originally published by Breitkopf & Härtel in quarterly issues, 1912–16, with annual index for each of the years covered. Provides corrections and additions to all the kinds of information in Eitner's *Quellen-Lexikon*, no. 1065.

Reprinted in vol. 11 of the Akademische Druck- und Verlagsanstalt *2. verbesserte Auflage* of the *Quellen-Lexikon*, which also contains marginal numerical references to the *Miscellanea*.

1090 / **Musiker Handschriften** . . . Composers' autographs; translated from the German with a new preface by Ernst Roth. London, Cassell, 1968. 2 v.

Translation of *Musikerhandschriften von Palestrina bis Beethoven*, edited by W. Gerstenberg, and *Musikhandschriften von Schubert bis Strawinsky*, edited by M. Hürlimann, both of which are based on *Musikerhandschriften von Bach bis Schumann*, by G. Schünemann, (1936).

Two handsome volumes of facsimiles made chiefly from composers' autographs in the Berlin State Library. Vol. 1 contains 159 plates; vol. 2, 140, with brief descriptive commentaries and identification of the sources.

Published in the U.S.A. under the imprint of Fairleigh Dickinson University Press.

Review by Werner Neumann in *Die Musikforschung*, 17 (1964), p. 454–55.

1091 / **Newman, Joel.** An index to capoversi and titles cited in Einstein's *The Italian madrigal*. New York, Publications of the Renaissance Society of America. 1967. 39 p. (Indexes and bibliographies, 3.)

Indexes more than 2,000 madrigal titles cited in Einstein's work. Composer and poet are cited where known. Those with musical settings in the Einstein book are identified.

1092 / **Nisser, Carl M.** Svensk instrumentalkomposition, 1770–1830. Nominalkatalog. Stockholm, Bokförlaget Gothia [1943]. 467 p.

Swedish instrumental music, native composers or composers living in Sweden. Alphabetical listing by composer, with detailed bibliographical and analytical descriptions, including key, movements, time signature, measure count. Bibliographical references. Index of names and places.

1093 / **Pillet, Alfred.** Bibliographie der Troubadours. Erg., weitergeführt und herausgegeben von Dr. Henry Carstens. Halle, Niemeyer [1933]. 518 p. (Schriften der Königsberger Gelehrten Gesellschaft. Sonderreihe, 2.)

Based on a bibliography of troubadour songs compiled by Karl Bartsch in 1872. Songs arranged alphabetically by first word of text, with inclusive numeration and subseries of numbers for works by individual authors. The emphasis is directed toward literary rather than musical scholarship.

1094 / **Radiciotti, Giuseppe.** "Aggiunte e correzioni ai dizionari biografici dei musicisti." In *Sammelbände der Internationalen Musikgesellschaft*, 14 (1914), p. 551–67; 15 (1915), p. 566–86.

Corrections and additions to Eitner's *Quellen-Lexikon* (no. 1065) with special attention to Italian composers.

Reprinted in the Musurgia edition of the *Quellen-Lexikon*, and as vol. 11 of the Akademische Druck- und Verlagsanstalt, 2. *verbesserte Auflage*, 1960.

1095 / **Randel, Don M.** An index to the chants of the Mozarabic rite. Princeton, New Jersey, Princeton Univ. Press, 1973. 670 p.

A comprehensive bibliography of the manuscript sources of Mozarabic chant, indicating the parts of the Office for which each chant would have been used.

1096 / **Raynaud, Gaston.** Bibliographie des altfranzösischen Liedes. Neu bearbeitet und ergänzt von Hans Spanke. Erster Teil. Leiden, E. J. Brill, 1955. 386 p.

The first part of a projected revision of Raynaud's *Bibliographie des chansonniers français des XIIIe et XIVe siècles*. Paris, 1884. 2 v. This work serves as a guide to trouvère songs, similar to that offered by the *Pillet* (no. 1093) or the *Gennrich* (no. 1072) for the troubadour repertory. Lists more than 2,130 songs, arranged according to the rhyme word of the first stanza, with references to the manuscript source and to literary and musical studies concerned with the item. P. 1–32: a bibliography of the manuscript sources and of modern editions and studies.

1097 / **Reich, Wolfgang.** Threnodiae sacrae. Katalog der gedruckten Kompositionen des 16.–18. Jahrhunderts in Leichenpredigtsammlungen innerhalb der Deutschen Demokratischen Republik. Dresden, 1966. 75 p. (Veröffentlichungen der Sächsischen Landesbibliothek, 7.)

A catalog of 434 funereal compositions of the 16th through the 18th centuries found in East German collections, chiefly Goth, Dresden, East Berlin, and Zwickau.

Review by Martin Geck in *Die Musikforschung*, 22 (1969), p. 389–90.

1098 / **Riaño, Juan F.** Critical and bibliographical notes on early Spanish music. . . . London, B. Quartich, 1887. 154 p.

Reprint by the Da Capo Press, New York, 1971.

Manuscripts and printed music to 1600, classified, giving descriptions and library locations of manuscripts. Numerous facsimile plates.

1099 / **Riedel, Friedrich W.** Quellenkundliche Beiträge zur Geschichte der Musik für Tasteninstrumente in der zweiten Hälfte des 17. Jahrhunderts (vornehmlich in Deutschland). Kassel und Basel, Bärenreiter, 1960. 224 p. (Schriften des Landesinstituts für Musikforschung Kiel, 10.)

A "source study" concerned with late-17th-century prints and manuscripts of keyboard music, with emphasis on the German school. Numerous useful lists and inventories incorporated into the work, e.g., "Verzeichnis der von 1648–1700 im Druck veröffentlichen Musik für Tasteninstrumente" (p. 57–72); "Quellenregister" [Handschriften], p. 219–24.

1100 / **Rimbault, Edward F.** Bibliotheca madrigaliana; a bibliographical account of the musical and poetical works published in England during the 16th and 17th centuries under the titles of madrigals, ballets, ayres, canzonets, etc. London, J. Smith, 1847. 88 p.

Reprint by B. Franklin, New York (196–?).

An early, and rather faulty, chronological list of vocal music published in England, 1588–1638, giving bibliographical descriptions and contents, source references. First-line index of madrigals and songs. Composer index.

1101 / **Sartori, Claudio.** Bibliografia della musica strumentale italiana stampata in Italia fino al 1700. Firenze, L. Olschki, 1952. 652 p. (Biblioteca di bibliografia italiana, 23.)

Chronological list of instrumental music, collections of vocal music containing one or more instrumental pieces or vocal music with one or more instrumental parts, published in Italy to 1700. Includes a few works by Italian composers published outside Italy. Excludes lute music and dramatic music. Complete bibliographical data, including dedications, prefaces, tables of contents. Composer index.

Review by Dragan Placmenac in *Notes*, 10 (1953), p. 616–19; by Harvey Olnick in *MQ*, 40 (1954), p. 98–102; by Willi Apel in *JAMS*, 7 (1954), p. 84–86; by Richard Schaal in *Die Musikforschung*, 7 (1954), p. 342.

Vol. II. (Volume secondo di aggiunte e correzioni con indici). Firenze, Leo S. Olschki, 1968. 216 p. (Biblioteca di bibliografia italiana, 56.)

Review by Owen Jander in *Notes*, 26 (1970), p. 738–39, and by Howard M. Brown in *JAMS*, 23 (1970), p. 531–33.

1102 / **Sartori, Claudio.** "Finalmente svelati i misteri delle biblioteche italiane" in *Fontes artis musicae*, 2 (1955), p. 15–37; 3 (1956), p. 192–202.

A product of the work on the International Inventory in Italy, this article contains a summary report of the holdings of 40 Italian libraries and an alphabetical listing of early printed music newly discovered in these collections.

1103 / **Schanzlin, Hans Peter.** "Musik-Sammeldrucke des 16. und 17. Jahrhunderts in schweizerischen Bibliotheken." In *Fontes artis musicae*, 4 (1957), p. 38–42.

1104 / **Schanzlin, Hans Peter.** "Musik-Sammeldrucke des 18. Jahrhunderts in schweizerischen Bibliotheken (I)." In *Fontes artis musicae*, 6 (1959), p. 20–26; II. *ibid.* (1961), p. 26–29.

Preliminary reports prepared by the Swiss office of the International Inventory of Musical Sources.

1105 / **Scheurleer, Daniel F.** Nederlandsche liedboeken; lijst der in Nederland tot het jaar 1800 uitgegevan liedboeken. . . . 's-Gravenhage, M. Nijhoff, 1912. 321 p.
Erste supplement, 1923.
A bibliography of song books published in the Netherlands from 1487 to 1800, with or without music, arranged chronologically under main headings of sacred and secular music, with index by author, editor, publisher, main word of title. 3,887 titles in the main work, 660 in the supplement.

1106 / **Smith, Carleton Sprague.** "Music manuscripts lost during World War II," in the *Book Collector*, 17 (1968), p. 26–36.
Deals with holographs by Bach, Beethoven, Haydn, Mozart *et al.* stored in Silesia and now presumably in Wroclaw (formerly Breslau), Poland.

1107 / **Sonneck, Oscar G. T.** A bibliography of early secular American music (18th century) . . . rev. and enl. by W. T. Upton. [Washington, D.C.] Library of Congress, Music Division, 1945. 617 p.
First published in 1905. Reprinted, with a new preface by Irving Lowens, by Da Capo Press, New York, 1964.
A title list, with full bibliographical descriptions, including first lines of texts. Completely indexed, with lists of composers, first lines, publishers, etc.
Review of the 1964 reprint by Harry Eskew in *Anuario, Inter-American Institute for Musical Research*, 1 (1965), p. 134.

1108 / **Stevenson, Robert.** "Sixteenth and seventeenth century resources in Mexico." In *Fontes artis musicae*, 1 (1954), p. 69–78; 2 (1955), p. 10–15.
The first installment is concerned with the manuscript resources of the Puebla Cathedral music archive, comprising some 365 sacred works by 36 composers. Arranged alphabetically by composer. The second part is a description of a 16th-century manuscript of sacred music in the library of Canon Octaviano Valdés of Mexico City.

1109 / **Thibault, Geneviève, et Louis Perceau.** Bibliographie des poésies de P. de Ronsard mises en musique au XVIe siècle. Paris, E.

Droz, 1941. 121 p. (Publications de la Société Française de Musicologie, 2 sér., t. 8.)

Chronological bibliography, 1552–1629, of some 148 collections containing musical settings of lyrics by Ronsard. Full bibliographical citations of the collections, with Ronsard settings listed for each. Index of text incipts and of collections and names.

1110 / **Vogel, Emil.** Bibliothek der gedruckten weltlichen Vocalmusik Italiens. Aus den Jahren 1500–1700. . . . Berlin, A. Haack, 1892. 2 v.

Partially revised and enlarged by Alfred Einstein under running title "Italian secular vocal music" in *Notes*, 2 (1945)–5 (1948), 232 p. in all. Einstein's revision treats only the second part of Vogel's original work, namely, the collections containing works by two or more composers.

Unaltered reissue. Hildesheim, Olms, 1962. 2 v. This issue incorporates Einstein's revision as published in *Notes*.

Vogel's *Bibliothek* is the basic source of information concerning early printed secular vocal music in Italy. In two parts: the first gives publications of the work of individual composers, arranged alphabetically by composer; the second gives collections, listed chronologically from 1501 to 1697. Full bibliographical citations, lists of contents, locations in European libraries. Index of collections, of places and publishers, of authors of texts, and of persons to whom works are dedicated.

A complete revision of Vogel is badly needed. It is reported that such a revision is being undertaken by Claudio Sartori and François Lesure and that the results of their work will be published in the near future. Meanwhile, there is a useful series of articles printed in *Analecta musicologica*, a publication of the Musikabteilung des Deutschen Historischen Instituts in Rom, bringing to light some recently noted additions to *Vogel* found in libraries in Europe and America. See Ernest Hilmar, "Ergänzungen zu Emil Vogel's Bibliothek . . ." in *Analecta musicologica*, 4 (1967), p. 154–206; *ibid*, 5 (1968), p. 295–98; Lorenzo Bianconi, 9 (1970), p. 142–202.

1111 / **Walther, Hans.** Initia carminum ac versuum medii aevi posterioris latinorum. Alphabetisches Verzeichnis der Versanfänge mittellateinischer Dichtungen. . . . Göttingen, Venderhoeck & Ruprecht, 1959. 1,186 p. (Carmina medii aevi posterioris latina, 1.)

Not a music bibliography but a most valuable reference tool for musicologist working in the field of medieval studies. An alphabetical index of text incipits for more than 20,000 medieval Latin lyrics, with references to manuscript sources and modern editions. Bibliography of literature; index of names and subjects.

1112 / **Winternitz, Emanuel.** Musical autographs from Monteverdi to Hindemith. Princeton, N.J., Princeton Univ. Press, 1955. 2 v.

Reissued by Dover Publications, New York, paperbound edition, 1965. 2 v.

Vol. 1 is devoted to commentary on the plates, with two introductory chapters: "The written sign" and "The writing act." Vol. 2 contains 196 full-page plates of autographs.

1113 / **Wolf, Johannes.** Handbuch der Notationskunde. 1. Teil: Tonschriften des Altertums und des Mittelalters. II. Teil: Tonschriften der Neuzeit, Tabulaturen, Paritur, Generalbass und Reformversuche. Leipzig, Breitkopf & Härtel, 1913–19. 2 v. (Kleine Handbücher der Musikgeschichte, 7.)

The Wolf *Handbuch* is cited here on the strength of its useful listings of early manuscript sources connected with the author's discussion of notational practices. For example: "Quellen der *ars antiqua*" (vol. 1, p. 258–63); "Die *ars nova*" (vol. 1, p. 351–54); "Handschriftliche Quellen des 15. und 16. Jahrhunderts" (vol. 1, p. 444–65); "Verzeichnis einiger wichtiger deutscher Lautentabulaturen" (vol. 2, p. 47–59); "Italienische Lautentabulaturen" (vol. 2, p. 66–71); "Quellen französischer Lautentabulatur" (vol. 2, p. 95–106); "Guitarretabulaturen" (vol. 2, p. 209–18).

1114 / **Wolfe, Richard J.** Secular music in America, 1801–1825. A bibliography. Introduction by Carleton Sprague Smith. New York, New York Public Library, Astor, Lenox and Tilden Foundations, 1964. 3 v.

A major work of bibliography in the field of early American music. Prepared as a continuation of the Sonneck-Upton *Bibliography* (no. 1107). The arrangement is alphabetical by composer. Brief biographies. Full bibliographical descriptions and locations of copies in American libraries and private collections.

Appendixes: (1) "Unrecorded 18th-century imprints located during the course of this work." (2) "A list of works in the Sonneck-Upton

Bibliography which have been redated into 19th century." (3) "Locations of newly discovered copies of works in the Sonneck-Upton *Bibliography*." Index of titles; of first lines; of publishers, engravers, and printers; of numbering systems. General index.

Review of James C. Downey in *Anuario of the Inter-American Institute for Musical Research*, 1 (1965), p. 122–24.

1115 / **Wotquenne, Alfred.** Table alphabétique des morceaux mesurés contenus dans les œuvres dramatiques de Zeno, Metastasio et Goldoni. Leipzig, Breitkopf & Härtel, 1905. 77 p.

An alphabetical first-line index of aria and ensemble texts by Zeno, Metastasio, and Goldoni, citing volume and page numbers in the standard editions of their works and title of the work from which the incipit is derived. Table of librettos by the three authors.

FOLK SONG AND BALLAD

This section should be used in conjunction with the section "Bibliographies of Music Literature: Ethnomusicology," which lists studies and monographs pertaining to folk song and ballad. Here, the emphasis is on the music itself. The user should bear in mind, however, that a work such as Haywood's *Bibliography of North American folklore and folksong* (no. 678) contains numerous entries for music, both printed and on sound recordings. Also relevant in certain respects are such bibliographies as Sears' *Song index* (no. 816), Fuld's *American popular music* (no. 959) and the bibliographies by Sonneck-Upton (no. 1107) and by Wolfe (no. 1114) which serve to bridge the uncertain gap between folk and popular song.

1116 / **Bronson, Bertrand H.** The traditional tunes of the Child ballads, with their texts, according to the extant records of Great Britain and America. Princeton, N.J., Princeton Univ. Press, 1959–1972. 4 v.

Vol. 1: ballads 1–53; vol. 2: ballads 54–113; vol. 3: ballads 114–243; vol. 4: with addenda to vols. 1–4.

A monumental work of scholarship in the field of English-Scottish ballads. Based on the work of Francis J. Child but far exceeding it in scope and authority. The literary and musical traditions of each ballad is discussed, together with a printing of all the known variants both literary and musical.

Review by Klaus Roth in *Jahrbuch für Volksliedforschung*, 13 (1968), p. 228–29.

1117 / **California. University. Department of Music.** Check list of California songs. Archive of California folk music. Part I: texts in print. Berkeley, California, University of Calif., 1940. 160 leaves (typescript).

Published in connection with a WPA project supervised by Sidney H. Robertson.

A list, alphabetical by title, of more than 2,500 songs from texts either published or known to have circulated in California, with an index of first lines. P. 157–60: bibliography of songsters and broadsides.

1118 / **Chappell, William.** Popular music of the olden time. A history of the ancient songs, ballads, and of the dance tunes of England. . . . Reprint by Dover Publications, Inc., of the original London publication of 1855–59. New York, Dover, 1965. 2 v.

A revision of this work, by H. Ellis Wooldridge, appeared in 1893. This edition was, in turn, reprinted by Jack Brussel, New York, 1961.

Chappell is the classic work on English popular song. It is the basis for the expanded work by Claude Simpson on *The British broadside ballad*. (See no. 1122.)

1119 / **Dean-Smith, Margaret.** A guide to English folksong collections. . . . Liverpool, University Press of Liverpool, in association with the English Folk Dance and Song Society, 1954. 120 p.

Foreword by Gerald Abraham.

Indexes approximately 62 collections of English folk song, 1822–1952. Main entry is by song title, with cross references from text incipit. Chronological list of collections. Detailed annotations.

Review by Bertrand H. Bronson in *JAMS*, 8 (1955), p. 57–58.

1120 / **Merwe, F. Z. van der.** . . **Suid-Afrikaanse** musiekbibliografie 1787–1952. Pretoria, J. L. Van Schaik, 1958. 410 p.

A comprehensive bibliography of music related to South Africa (by South African composers wherever published, writings on South African themes or subject matter). The largest part of the citations refer to songs, marches, dance music of a popular nature, although a few studies and monograms are interfiled. Entries are unclassified, arranged alphabetically by composer or author. Index of South African composers and musicians. The language is Afrikaans.

1121 / **Sidel'nikov, Viktor M.** . . Russkaĭa narodnaĭa pesnĭa: bibliograficheskiĭ ukazatel' 1735–1945. Moskva, Izd. Akademiĭ Nauk SSSR, 1962.

At head of title: Akademĭa Nauk SSSR, Institut mirovoi literatury im. A. M. Gor'kogo.

Part I: texts of folk poetry and folk songs, published in journals, newspapers, etc., with or without music. Part II: books, articles, etc., about Russian folksong. Index of names.

1122 / **Simpson, Claude M.** The British broadside ballad and its music. New Brunswick, N.J., Rutgers Univ. Press, 1966. 919 p.

An indispensable reference tool for students of English popular song from the 16th through the 18th centuries. Gives music for 540 broadside ballads and traces each melody from its earliest printed and manuscript sources. No ballad texts printed. The work takes its point of departure from William Chappell's *Popular music of the olden time* (1855–59, 2 v.) but far exceeds Chappell in coverage.

Review by Berti and Bronson in *MQ*, 52 (1966), p. 384–87; by John Ward in *JAMS*, 20 (1967), p. 131–34. See also Ward's extended commentary "*Apropos the British broadside ballad and its music*" in the same issue of *JAMS*, p. 28–86; by Walter Woodfill in *Journal of research in music education*, 14 (1955), p. 238–39; by Walter Suppan in *Jahrbuch für Volksliedforschung*, 13 (1968), p. 229–31; by Charles Heywood in *Ethnomusicology*, 11 (1967), p. 133–34.

SACRED MUSIC

Many of the items entered in this section are actually editions of Protestant or Catholic liturgical music. At the same time, they qualify as reference books because of the scope and authority of their documentation.

1123 / **Bäumker, Wilhelm.** Das katholische deutsche Kirchenlied in seinen Singweisen, von den frühesten Zeiten bis gegen Ende des 17.

Jahrhunderts. Freiburg, Herder'sche Verlagshandlung, 1883–1911. 4 v.
  Reprinted from the original by Georg Olms, Hildesheim, 1962.
  Bäumker's work is the basic study of the German Catholic church
song. The main body of the work consists of quotations and discussion of the individual melodies, classified according to the church year
or liturgical use. Each volume contains an extensive bibliography, arranged chronologically, of early printed song collections. Entries cover
the period from 1470 to 1800. Transcriptions from the prefaces of early
song collections are given.

1124 / **Chevalier, Ulysse.** Repertorium hymnologicum. Catalogue
des chants, hymnes, proses, séquences, tropes en usage dans l'église
latine depuis les origines jusqu'à nos jours. Louvain, 1892–1920. 6 v.
  The standard bibliography of Latin rhymed poetic texts for liturgical
use. A volume of additions and emendations was prepared by Clemens
Blume under the title *Repertorium repertorii*, Leipzig, 1901.
  The *Repertorium* has been reprinted by Bollandistes, 1959; the
Blume supplement by Olms, Hildesheim.

1125 / **Diehl, Katharine S.** Hymns and tunes—an index. Metuchen, N.J., Scarecrow Press, 1966. 1,242 p.
  A comprehensive finding tool for anyone interested in locating or
identifying a Protestant hymn or hymn tune. Approach offered through
first lines of text, authors, tune names, composers, and by melodies
given in alphabetical notation. The texts are almost exclusively English.
Appendices include a glossary and a chronological list of hymnals
indexed.

1126 / **Frost, Maurice.** English and Scottish psalm and hymn
tunes, *c.* 1543–1677. London, Oxford Univ. Press, 1953. 531 p.
  P. 3–50: a bibliography of English-Scottish "Old Version" psalters
from 1556 to 1677, with full descriptions and lists of contents. The
main body of the work is an edition of 457 psalm tunes or harmonized
versions thereof.
  For an index to this work compiled by Kirby Rogers, see no. 1908.

1127 / **Kirsch, Winifred.** Die Quellen der mehrstimmigen Mag-
nificat- und Te Deum-Vertonungen bis zur Mitte des 16. Jahrhunderts.
Tutzing, Hans Schneider, 1966. 588 p.
  Review by James Erb in *JAMS*, 22 (1969), p. 122–25; by Martin Just
in *Die Musikforschung*, 21 (1968), p. 523–24.

1128 / **Metcalf, Frank Johnson.** American psalmody; or titles of books containing tunes printed in America from 1721 to 1820. New introduction by Harry Eskew. New York, Da Capo Press, 1968.

An unabridged republication of the first edition published in New York in 1917.

Review by Richard A. Crawford in *Notes*, 26 (1969), p. 42–43.

1129 / **Monumenta Monodica Medii Aevi.** Herausgegeben im Auftrag des Musikwissenschaftlichen Seminars der Universität Erlangen-Nürnberg von Bruno Stäblein. Band I– . Kassel, Bärenreiter, 1956– .

Band I: Hymnen (1956), 724 p.

Band II: Die Gesänge des altrömischen Graduale. Vat. lat. 5319. (1970), 724 p.

Band III: Introitus-Tropen 1. Das Repertoire der südfranzösischen Tropare des 10. und 11. Jahrhunderts (1970), 470 p.

Band VII: Alleluia-Melodian I, bis 1100. (1968), 682 p.

A series devoted to the publication of medieval monody, chiefly sacred. The music is organized liturgically and given in neume notation, with copious documentation. A basic tool for research in medieval music.

1130 / **Parks, Edna D.** Early English hymns: an index. Metuchen, N.J., The Scarecrow Press, 1972. 168 p.

Lists 1,157 hymns from some 51 hymnals and psalters and other sources. No music is given, but the tune names are identified and metrical structure is given.

1131 / **Protestant Episcopal Church in the U.S.A. Joint Commission on Church Music.** Service music and anthems for the nonprofessional choir. Greenwich, Conn., Seabury Press, 1955. 56 p.

Service music classified by liturgical use; anthems by the church year. Information includes degree of difficulty, number of parts, presence of solos, type of accompaniment, publisher, and number in series.

1132 / **Radó Polycarpe.** Répertoire hymnologique des manuscrits liturgiques dans les bibliothèques publiques de Hongrie. Budapest, Stephaneum Nyomda, 1945. 59 p. (Az orságos széchenyi könyvtár kiadványai, 20.)

Alphabetical listing of 727 hymns found in 146 liturgical manuscripts in libraries in Hungary.

1133 / **Schreiber, Max.** Kirchenmusik von 1500–1600, Original-drucke und Manuskripte chronologisch zusammengestellt . . . [Regens-burg]. Druckerei St. Georgsheim Birkeneck, 1932. 88 p.

Chronological list of 16th-century sacred music, printed and manu-script sources. Entered alphabetically by composer under year of issue. Brief titles, and locations in British and continental libraries. Index of composers and classified index of forms.

1134 / **Schreiber, Max.** Kirchenmusik von 1600–1700, Original-drucke und Manuskripte chronologisch zusammengestellt . . . [Regens-burg]. Druckerei St. Georgsheim Birkeneck, 1934. 184 p.

Treats 17th-century sacred music as in the entry above.

1135 / **Stellhorn, Martin H.** Index to hymn preludes . . . and other organ compositions, based on hymns, chorales, and carols. A listing of 2,200 selections of various publishers according to key, difficulty, and length. St. Louis, Concordia Publishing House [1948], 151 p.

1136 / **Thuner, O. E.** Dansk Salme-Leksikon: Haandbog i dansk Salmesang. En hymnologisk Sammenstilling af Ord og Toner med his-toriske og bibliografiske Oplysninger. København, O. Lohse, 1930. 592 p.

Lists 1,108 Danish psalm settings, with detailed information as to sources of texts and music. Index of melody groups, personal names, first lines of texts.

1137 / **Wackernagel, Philipp.** Bibliographie zur Geschichte des deutschen Kirchenliedes im XVI. Jahrhundert. Frankfurt am Main, 1855. 718 p.

Unaltered reprint of the original edition by Georg Olms, Hildesheim, 1961.

A chronological listing of 1,050 editions of German sacred song pub-lished during the 16th century. Detailed bibliographical descriptions, with annotations. Transcriptions given of the introductions to 110 of the collections.

1138 / **Zahn, Johannes.** Die Melodien der deutschen evangeli-schen Kirchenlieder aus den Quellen geschöpft und mitgeteilt. . . . Gütersloh, Bertelsmann, 1889–93. 6 v.

Reprint of the original edition by Olms, Hildesheim, 1963.

Zahn is primarily an edition, giving 8,806 melodies, derived from the earliest sources, for the German Protestant liturgy. Classified according to metrical form.

Vol. 5, p. 307–494: biographical notices of 463 chorale composers or editors of chorale collections. Index of composers; first-line index of texts.

Vol. 6: a bibliography of 1,408 items listing the sources of the melodies and arranged chronologically from 1507 to 1892, with locations of copies in the principal European libraries. Further supplements give non-German sources and manuscript sources.

Catalogs of Music Libraries
and Collections

A KNOWLEDGE OF the published catalogs of the major music libraries and collections is essential for locating source materials for study or research. Access to this information has been made immeasurably easier in recent years by the appearance of Rita Benton's *Directory of music research libraries*, published under the auspices of the International Association of Music Libraries (see no. 1139 below). This work supplies international coverage for music libraries in Europe and North America. Substantial lists of libraries are found in *MGG* (by Alfons Ott) and in *Grove 5* (by Charles Cudworth), although these are both somewhat out of date. The German music libraries are separately described and their catalogs cited in Richard Schaal's *Führer durch deutsche Musikbibliotheken*, 1971 (see no. 1252), and Claudio Sartori has done likewise for the Italian institutions in a 1971 issue of *Fontes artis musicae* (see no. 1297).

The following section covers the catalogs of the principal music libraries of the world and also includes a number of important exhibition catalogs, although we have made no effort to be comprehensive in the latter category. Excluded are the auction or sale catalogs of music collections that have been dispersed—with a few exceptions such as the famous Wolffheim catalog (no. 1563), which is itself a bibliographical tool of first importance.

It goes without saying that a great many musical source materials have never been cited in special music catalogs. Information must be sought in general library catalogs of early printed books and manuscripts. The music manuscripts in the Bodleian Library at Oxford, for example, must be extracted from the seven volumes of Madan's *Summary catalogue of Western manuscripts in the Bodleian library . . .* (1895–1953). Likewise, Cambridge University music manuscripts are to be found in the series of college library catalogs compiled by Montague Rhodes James. No attempt has been made here to cite general catalogs of this kind, but the reader's attention may be called to the invaluable guide to *Latin manuscript books before 1600, a list of the printed catalogues and unpublished inventories of extant collections* by Paul Kristeller (revised edition, Fordham Univ. Press, 1960). The search for sources has, of course, been greatly facilitated by the continuing appearance of volumes in the series promoted by The International Inventory of Musical Sources.

In the present list the catalogs have been grouped, as far as is possible, by place. Place is ordinarily designated as a city followed by the appropriate country (or state in the case of the United States). Certain national union catalogs or descriptions of the holdings of several libraries within a country are entered under the name of the country in small capital letters (GERMANY, GREAT BRITAIN, SWEDEN, etc.).

There are a few catalogs of important collections that remain in private hands or that have been dispersed or changed their locations in recent years: the Hirsch, Cortot, and Wolffheim collections are examples. These catalogs are grouped in a special category at the end of this section. See nos. 1554–63.

Our first entry is for an international directory of music research libraries issued under the auspices of the International Association of Music Libraries.

1139 / **International Association of Music Libraries. Commission of Research Libraries.** Directory of music research libraries, including contributors to the International Inventory of Musical Sources (RISM). Edited by Rita Benton. Iowa City, University of Iowa, 1967–1972. 3 v.

Part I: Canada and the United States. Covers 36 entries for Canada and 297 for the United States.

Part II: Thirteen European countries. 784 entries for libraries in Austria, Belgium, Switzerland, Federal Republic of Germany, German Democratic Republic, Denmark, Ireland, Great Britain, Luxemburg, Norway, The Netherlands, Sweden, and Finland.

Part III: Spain, France, Italy, Portugal.

The information includes a brief description of each library, with addresses and phones, types of service, and a bibliography of relevant literature. Particularly valuable are the bibliographies covering not only the individual institutions but the countries as a whole, as well as general literature on music libraries and their holdings. These directories are to be reissued eventually as part of the International Inventory of Music Sources.

Review of Part I by A. Hyatt King in *Notes*, 24 (1963), p. 490; of Part II by Vincent Duckles in *Journal of research in music education*, 20 (1972), p. 293–94, and by Susan T. Sommer in *Notes*, 29 (1972), p. 259–60.

AARHUS, DENMARK

1140 / **Statsbiblioteket.** Fagkataloger (redigeret af Erling Winkel og Ingeborg Heilmann) 2. forogede udg. Aarhus, Aarhus Stiftsbogtrykkerie, 1946–57. 4 v.

Three volumes cover scores; one, music literature. Entries for scores include collections and separate publications, with contents given for collections.

Aldrich, Richard. A catalogue of books. . . .
See no. 1202.

AMSTERDAM, HOLLAND

1141 / **Toonkunst-Bibliotheek.** Catalogus van de uitleen-afdeling. Amsterdam-Zuid, Toonkunst-Bibliotheek, 1968. 43 p.

Catalog of a loan collection of music for performance in the Amsterdam municipal library. Classified by performance forces. Index of names.

1142 / **Vereniging Voor Nederlandse Muziekgeschiedenis. Bibliotheek.** Catalogus van de bibliotheek der Vereniging voor Nederlandse Muziekgeschiedenis. Amsterdam, G. Alsbach, 1919. 274 p.

Classified catalog, including both early and recent works. Contains a special section of manuscripts. Index of names and titles.

ANN ARBOR, MICHIGAN

1143 / **University of Michigan.** "The University of Michigan's purchase of the Stellfeld music library." By Louise E. Cuyler, Gordon A. Sutherland, and Hans T. David. In *Notes*, 12 (1954), p. 41–57.

Describes Michigan's acquisition of the collection of the jurist, musicologist, and collector Dr. J. A. Stellfeld of Antwerp. Hans David gives a brief summary of some of the important holdings of the library. Eight facsimile plates.

ASSISI, ITALY

Biblioteca Comunale. See no. 1292.

1144 / **La Cappella della Basilica di S. Francesco. Biblioteca.** Catalogo del fondo musicale nella Biblioteca Comunale di Assisi, a cura di Claudio Sartori. Milano, Istituto Editoriale Italiano, 1962. 449 p. (Bibliotheca musicae, 1.)

Expands the work of Francesco Pennacchi published in the series *Associazione dei musicologi italiani* (see no. 1292). Lists early printed music, books, and manuscripts separately. Most of the material is pre-1800, but a few 19th-century manuscripts are included. Entries give contents of early items, locations for rarities. Descriptive annotations.

Review by Walther Dürr in *Die Musikforschung*, 18 (1965), p. 83–84.

AUGSBURG, GERMANY

1145 / **Schaal, Richard.** Das Inventar der Kantorei St. Anna in Augsburg. Ein Beitrag zur protestantischen Musikpflege im 16. und beginnenden 17. Jahrhundert. Kassel, Bärenreiter, 1965. 107 p. (Catalogus musicus, 3.)

Transcription of an inventory compiled in the early 17th century of the music collection of the Lutheran church and school of St. Anna in Ausburg. The collection itself is no longer intact.

1146 / **Schletterer, Hans M.** Katalog der in der Kreis- und Stadtbibliothek dem Städtischen Archive und der Bibliothek des Historischen Vereins zu Augsburg befindlichen Musikwerke. Augsburg, Fidelis Butsch Sohn, 1879. 138 p. (Beilage. Monatsheft für Musikgeschichte, Jahrgang 10–11, 1878–79.)

BADAJOZ, SPAIN

1147 / **Monasterio de Guadalupe.** Catálogo del archivo musical del Monasterio de Guadalupe, por El. P. Dr. Arcángel Barrado, O.F.M., Bibliotecario y maestro de capilla. Badajoz, 1945. 181 p.

Catalog of a collection of accompanied sacred vocal music, chiefly late 18th century. 947 items, preceded by an historical study of the archive. Index of composers, and of musical forms.

BARCELONA, SPAIN

1148 / **Diputación Provincial. Biblioteca Central.** Catàlech de la Biblioteca Musical . . . per en Filipe Pedrell. Barcelona, Palau de la Diputació, 1908–1909. 2 v.

Classified catalog of 1,271 entries, including theory, history, practical music. Full bibliographical entries, collations, extensive notes, facsimiles, and musical quotations. Items listed by signature number, with an alphabetical index in volume 2.

1149 / **Diputación Provincial. Biblioteca Central.** La música española desde la edad media hasta nuestros días; catálogo de la exposición histórica . . . por Higinio Anglés. Barcelona, Diputación Provincial de Barcelona, Biblioteca Central, 1941. 82 p.

Exhibition catalog commemorating the centennial of the birth of Filipe Pedrell. 171 items, manuscripts and printed books, associated with the history of Spanish music, assembled from a number of collections. Chronological arrangement, full entries, 52 facsimiles.

BASEL, SWITZERLAND

1150 / **Universität. Bibliothek.** Catalog der Schweizerischen Musikbibliothek. Hrsg. von der Öffentlichen Bibliothek der Universität Basel. I. Musikgeschichtliche und theoretische Werke. Basel, E. Birkhäuser, 1906. 39 p.

A collection of music literature. The catalog of music which was to form vol. 2 was issued as vol. 1 of the library's *Katalog der Musikabteilung der Offentlichen Bibliothek* . . . (see next item).

1151 / **Universität. Bibliothek.** Katalog der Musikabteilung der Öffentlichen Bibliothek der Universität Basel und in ihr enthaltenen Schweizerischen Musikbibliothek. Band I: Musikalische Kompositionen. Hrsg. von Edgar Refardt. Basel, Universitäts-Bibliothek, 1925. 141 p.

Works listed in alphabetical order by composer; important collections analyzed. Separate listing of collections, followed by a summary of the contents of several manuscript collections of music by Swiss composers. Index of editors, arrangers, librettists.

1152 / **Universität. Bibliothek.** Katalog der Musik-Sammlung auf der Universitäts-Bibliothek in Basel (Schweiz) . . . von Julius Richter. Leipzig, Breitkopf & Härtel. 1892. 104 p. (Beilage. Monatschefte für Musikgeschichte. Jahrgang 23–24.)

Full descriptions, contents, musical quotations for manuscripts and early printed music in the university library.

1153 / **Universität. Bibliothek.** Thematischer Katalog der Instrumentalmusik des 18. Jahrhunderts in den Handschriften der Universitätsbibliothek Basel. Von Edgar Refardt. Bern, P. Haupt, 1957. 59 p. (Publikationen der Schweizerischen Musikforschenden Gesellschaft, ser. 2, v. 6.)

The major part of this collection was assembled by the Basel silk manufacturer Lucas Sarasin (1730–1802). Some 473 of the works cited were once part of his library. With these are incorporated the collection of the Basel *Collegium musicum* and that of the de Pury family. References are made to 18th-century printings of the works here found in manuscript.

BAVARIA

1154 / **Kataloge Bayerischer Musiksammlungen.** Hrsg. von der Generaldirektion der Bayerischen Staatlichen Bibliotheken. Thematischer Katalog der Musikhandschriften der ehemaligen Klosterkirchen Weyarn, Tegernsee, und Benediktburn. Hrsg. von Robert Münster und Robert Machold. München, Henle, 1971. 196 p.

Records the holdings of Bavarian cloisters and abbeys, catalogs of which are maintained in the Bavarian State Library in Munich.

1155 / **Musik in Bayern.** I. Bayerische Musikgeschichte, Überblick und Einzeldarstellungen. Hrsg. von Robert Münster und Hans Schmid. II. Ausstellungskatalog Augsburg, Juli bis Oktober 1972. Hrsg. von Folker Göthel. Tutzing, Hans Schneider, 1972. 2 v.

Vol. I is a collection of essays on various aspects of Bavarian music history; vol. II is an exhibition catalog of 850 items illustrative of Bavarian musical history and culture. Numerous facsimile plates.

BELGIUM

Borren, Charles van den. "Inventaire des manuscrits de musique polyphonique qui se trouvent en Belgique."
See no 1042.

BEREA, OHIO

1156 / **Baldwin-Wallace College. Riemenschneider Memorial Bach Library.** Catalog of the Emilie and Karl Riemenschneider Memorial Bach Library. Ed. by Sylvia W. Kenney. New York, Columbia Univ. Press, 1960. 295 p.

A numbered catalog of 2,537 items, of which the first 520 are writings on Bach and his time. No. 521–31: music of Bach's sons and contemporaries. No. 532 to end: music of J. S. Bach. The principal grouping is by musical forms; manuscripts listed separately. Index of cantatas, and general index.

Two *Supplemental catalogs*, compiled by J. B. Winzenburger, have been issued to members of the Riemanschneider Bach Institute (Dec. 1970 and Jan. 1972). Current acquisitions reported in the periodical *Bach*, 1970–   .

Review by Walter Emery in *Music and letters*, 42 (1961), p. 376–77.

BERGAMO, ITALY

1157 / **Biblioteca Civica.** Il fondo musicale Mayr della Biblioteca Civica di Bergamo, nel secondo centenario della nascita di Giovanni Simone Mayr (1763–1963). Ed. Arrigo Gazzaniga. Bergamo, Edizioni "Monumenta Bergomensia," 1963. 149 p. (Monument bergomensia, 11.)

A classified catalog of works by Simone Mayr and his contemporaries in the Biblioteca Civica in Bergamo. Chiefly manuscripts, including many autographs. 24 pages of facsimiles.

1158 / **Il Museo Donizettiano.** Catalogo. Bergamo, Centro di Studi Donizettiani, 1970. 273 p.

First published in 1936.

The present edition gives a brief historical introduction, followed by a tabulation of important Donizetti performances between 1946 and 1969.

The *Catalogo* (p. 53–273) is subdivided into six sections: (1) autographs and manuscripts, (2) musical publications, (3) theatrical publications, (4) letters and documents, (5) iconography, and (6) artifacts.

BERKELEY, CALIFORNIA

1159 / **University of California. Music Library.** Autograph manuscripts of Ernest Bloch at the University of California. Berkeley, Univ. of Calif., 1962. 20 p.

Describes 35 autograph manuscripts bequeathed to the University of California Music Library from the estate of Ernest Bloch. The catalog was compiled by Minnie Elmer.

1160 / **University of California. Music Library.** "Musique classique française à Berkeley: pièces inédites de Louis Couperin, Lebègue, La Barre, etc." By Alan Curtis. In *Revue de musicologie*, 55 (1969), p. 123–164.

Describes and inventories 14 manuscripts of French music, chiefly keyboard, of the late 17th and early 18th centuries in the Music Library of the University of California at Berkeley.

1161 / **University of California. Music Library.** Thematic catalog of a manuscript collection of 18th-century Italian instrumental music in the University of California, Berkeley, Music Library. By Vincent Duckles and Minnie Elmer. Berkeley and Los Angeles, University of Calif. Press, 1963. 403 p.

A collection comprising some 990 manuscripts containing works by 82 composers of the Tartini school at Padua. The central figures are Giuseppe Tartini and Michele Stratico. Preliminary chapters discuss the historical background of the collection, and tabulate the handwritings and the watermarks represented.

Review by Charles Cudworth in *Galpin society journal*, 18 (March 1965), p. 140–41; by Denis Stevens in *Musical times*, 105 (July 1964), p. 513–14; by Donald Krummel in *Notes*, 22 (1966), p. 1025–26.

BERLIN, GERMANY

1162 / Die Amalien-Bibliothek. Musikbibliothek der Prinzessin Anna Amalia von Preussen (1732–1787). Historische Einordnung und Katalog mit Hinweisen auf die Schreiber der Handschriften. Von Eva Renate Blechschmidt. Berlin, Merseburger, 1965. 346 p. (Berliner Studien zur Musikwissenschaft, 8.)

Reconstruction of the catalog of an important 18th century music collection formed by the youngest sister of Friedrich the Great. The bulk of the collection was acquired by the Joachimsthalsche Gymnasium in the late 18th century. The collection was dispersed for safekeeping in World War II, and since then parts of it have found their way to libraries in Tübingen, Marburg, and the Deutsche Staatsbibliothek in Berlin. Blechschmidt's study treats the history of the collection and describes each item in detail, including both printed music and manuscripts. Special attention is given to the identification of the scribes responsible for the manuscript copies.

1163 / Deutsche Staatsbibliothek. Die Bach-Handschriften der Berliner Staatsbibliothek, von Paul Kast. Trossingen, Hohner-Verlag, 1958. 150 p. (Tübinger Bach-Studien, 2/3.)

A catalog of manuscripts of music by members of the Bach family, once a part of the collection of the Prussian State Library, now distributed between the two Deutsche Staatsbibliotheken (West and East) and the University Library at Tübingen. Essentially a finding list for one of the world's great collections of Bach sources now dispersed. Brief entries; indices of composers, scribes, and former owners of the manuscripts.

1164 / Deutsche Staatsbibliothek. Die Beethoven-Sammlung in der Musikabteilung der Deutschen Staatsbibliothek. Verzeichnis: Autographe, Abschriften, Dokumente, Briefe. Aufgenommen und zusammengestellt von Eveline Bartlitz. Berlin, Deutsche Staatsbibliothek, 1970. 229 p.

A well-organized bibliography of all types of materials in the extensive Beethoven collections of the German State Library (East). Includes manuscripts, sketches, first editions, letters, items from Beethoven's library, etc. Numerous bibliographical references.

Review by William Drabkin in *Notes*, 28 (1972), p. 692–94.

1165 / Deutsche Staatsbibliothek. "Die Musikabteilung," von Karl-Heinz Köhler. In *Deutsche Staatsbibliothek*, 1661–1961. Band I: Geschichte und Gegenwart, p. 241–74.

A narrative account of the founding of the music division of the Berlin State Library, the work of its successive directors, and the growth of its collections up to the restoration of the music room after its destruction in World War II. The riches of the collection are summarized, particularly the Bach, Mozart, and Beethoven holdings. The author is director of the Music Division.

1166 / Internationale Musikleihbibliothek. Katalog. Berlin, 1952. 276 p.

Classified catalog of an international lending library of instrumental, vocal, and choral works. Includes parts for orchestral music. Strong in works by Soviet composers, but other countries are also well represented. Composer index.

1167 / Joachimsthalsches Gymnasium. Bibliothek. Katalog der Musikaliensammlung des Joachimsthalschen Gymnasium zu Berlin. Verfasst von Robert Eitner. Berlin, T. Trautwein, 1884. 106 p. (Beilage, Monatshefte für Musikgeschichte. Jahrgang 16.)

This collection incorporates the library of Princess Anna Amalie, sister of Friedrich the Great (see also no. 1162.) Strong in 18th-century music of the North-German school. 627 numbered items. Author-composer index. The collection was partially dispersed and destroyed in World War II.

1168 / Joachimsthalsches Gymnasium. Bibliothek. Thematischer Katalog der von Thulemeir'schen Musikalien-Sammlung in der Bibliothek des Joachimsthal'schen Gymnasiums zu Berlin. Hrsg. von Robert Eitner. Leipzig, Breitkopf & Härtel, 1899. 110 p. (Beilage, Monatshefte für Musikgeschichte. Jahrgang 30–31.)

The collection covers the period 1700–1800.

1169 / **Königliche Hausbibliothek.** Katalog der Musiksammlung aus der Königlichen Hausbibliothek im Schlosse zu Berlin, Verfasst und erläutert von Georg Thouret. . . . Leipzig, Breitkopf & Härtel, 1895. 356 p.

Supplemented by *Neue Erwerbungen der Königliche Hausbibliothek zu Berlin* (Beilage. Monatshefte . . . Jahrgang 35, 1903).

Brief entries, alphabetical by composer. 6,836 items, printed and manuscript, with a special section of works dedicated to members of the royal family and a supplementary section for military music.

1170 / **Staatsbibliothek der Stiftung Preussischer Kultur-besitz.** Katalog der Sammlung Bokemeyer. By Harald Kümmerling. Kassel, Bärenreiter, 1970. 423 p. (Kieler Schriften zur Musikwissenschaft, 18.)

Reconstruction of an 18th-century private music library of more than 3,000 manuscripts, printed music, and theoretical works. Partially dispersed. Parts of the collection surviving in the West Berlin State Library have been identified by Kümmerling.

Review by Richard H. Hunter in *Notes*, 28 (1971), p. 57–58.

BERN, SWITZERLAND

1171 / **Schweizerische Landesbibliothek.** Katalog der Schweizerischen Landesbibliothek. Musik Werke der Mitgleider des Schweizerischen Tonkünstlervereins veröffentlicht von 1848–1925. . . . Ed. by K. Joss. Bern-Bümpliz, Buchdruckerei Benteli, 1927. 152 p.

About 5,000 titles, abridged to essential information, in a classified arrangement.

BETHLEHEM, PENNSYLVANIA

1172 / **Archives of the Moravian Church.** A catalogue of music by American Moravians, 1724–1842, from the Archives of the Moravian Church at Bethlehem, Pa. Bethlehem, Pennsylvania, The Moravian Seminary and College for Women, 1938. 118 p. Reprint by AMS press, New York, 1970.

Short biographies and lists of compositions by 17 Moravian-American composers. Appendix of 24 plates of selected compositions and sample pages from the original manuscripts.

BLOOMINGTON, INDIANA

1173 / **Indiana University. School of Music. Latin-American Music Center.** Latin American music available at Indiana University: score library, tape archive (art music), folk and primitive music. Bloomington, Indiana, Indiana University, 1964. 101 leaves (typescript).

BOLOGNA, ITALY

Accademia Filarmonica. Archivio. See no. 1280.

1174 / **Accademia Filarmonica.** Catalogo descrittivo degli autografi e ritratti du musicisti lasciati alla Reale Accademia Filarmonica di Bologna dall'Abb. Dott. Masseangelo Masseangeli. Compilato a cura degli Accademici Prof. Cav. Federico Parisini e Maestro Ernesto Colombani. Bologna, Regia Tipografia, 1896. 435 p.

This catalog first appeared, under a slightly different title, in 1881. Reprint of the 1881 edition by Forni, Bologna, 1969.

1175 / **Accademia Filarmonica.** Mostra internazionale di musica in Bologna 1888. Catalogo con brevi cenni biografici e succinte discrizioni degli autografi e documenti de celebri o distinti musicisti posseduti da Emilla Succi. Accademia Filarmonica di Bologna. Bologna, Società Tipografica già Compositori, 1888. 179 p.

A collection of 886 items, chiefly letters of musicians of the 18th and 19th centuries, mostly autograph. Arranged alphabetically, with brief biographical notices and descriptions of the items.

Archivio di S. Petronio. See no. 1280.

Biblioteca Ambrosini. See no. 1280.

1176 / **Biblioteca Universitaria.** "Codidi musicali della R. Biblioteca Universitaria di Bologna," by Lodovico Frati, in *Rivista musicale italiana*, 23 (1916), p. 219–42.

A general description of the resources of the music collection in the library of the University of Bologna, drawing attention to major holdings in plainchant, early theory, and polyphony.

1177 / **Civico Museo Bibliografico Musicale.** (Formerly Conservatorio di Musica "G. B. Martini.") Catalogo della biblioteca del Liceo Musicale di Bologna, compilato da Gaetano Gaspari, compiuto e pubblicato da Federico Parisini per cura del municipio. . . . Bologna, Libreria Romagnoli dall'Acqua, 1890–1943. 5 v.

Vols. 1–4 are reissued in photo-offset by Arnaldo Forni (Bologna, 1961) with corrections by Napoleone Fanti, Oscar Mischiati, and Luigi Ferdinando Tagliavini.

Vol 1: music theory. Vol. 2: sacred vocal music (ed. Luigi Torchi). Vol. 3: secular vocal music and opera (ed. Luigi Torchi). Vol. 4: instrumental music and pedagogy (ed. Raffaele Caldolini). Vol. 5: Libretti (ed. Ugo Sesini).

This catalog provides access to one of the richest collections of early music in the world, incorporating the library of the 18th-century scholar Padre Giambattista Martini. Full bibliographical descriptions; contents given for collections, transcriptions of numerous prefaces and dedications. Entries are alphabetical within each category. General index of names.

1178 / **Il Convento di S. Francesco.** Catalogo del fondo musicale. By Gino Zanotti. Bologna, Forni, 1970. 2 v. (Bibliotheca musica bononiensis, sezione VI, n. 3.)

Vol. I: "Le edizioni." 324 p. Vol. II: "I manoscritti." 393 p.

Catalogs the music collection of the Franciscan church where Padre Martini lived and worked during the 18th century. The collection includes a considerable amount of his music.

BONN, GERMANY

1179 / **Beethoven-Haus.** "Die Beethovenhandschriften des Beethovenhauses in Bonn." By Hans Schmidt. In *Beethoven-Jahrbuch.* Jahrgang 1969/70. Bonn, Beethovenhaus, 1971. p. 1–443.

A catalog of 776 items. Major sections are letters (489 items), documents partially or wholly in Beethoven's hand (29 items), works (76 items), copies by Beethoven of other composers' works (9 items), sketches (106 items), copyists' work (31 items), and early printed music with annotations by the composer (11 items). Detailed indexes.

1180 / **Beethoven-Haus.** Eine Schweizer Beethovensammlung. Von Max Unger. Zürich, Verlag der Corona, 1939. 235 p. (Schriften der Corona, 24.)

Catalog of the Bodmer collection, perhaps the world's greatest accumulation of Beethoven documents, once in private hands but now part of the archive of the Beethoven House in Bonn. The catalog is organized in 12 categories, the most important of which are 389 letters, including those of the composer's contemporaries, 108 manuscripts of music; 43 early or first editions; 17 pictures. 16 facsimile plates; index of names.

1181 / **Friedrich-Wilhelms-Universität. Bibliothek.** "Die musikalischen Autographen der Universitäts-Bibliothek Bonn." Von Theo Clasen. In *Festschrift Joseph Schmidt-Görg zum 60. Geburtstag.* Bonn, Beethoven-Haus, 1957. p. 26–65.

567 autographs by 245 musicians, extracted from bequests or autograph books. Wide representation of musicians and musical scholars of the early 19th century.

1182 / **Friedrich-Wilhelms-Universität. Musikwissenschaftliche Seminar.** Katalog der Musikhandschriften im Besitz des Musikwissenschaftlichen Seminars der Rheinischen Friedrich-Wilhelms-Universität zu Bonn. By Magda Marx-Weber. Köln, Arno Volk-Verlag, 1971. 138 p. (Beiträge zur Rheinischen Musikgeschichte, 89.)

A collection of 595 manuscripts, some 550 of which were assembled by the organist-cantor Christian Benjamin Klein (1754–1825). Prominent among the composers represented are Benda, Bernabei, Homilius, Reichardt, Weinlig, Wirbach, and Zumsteeg.

BORDEAUX, FRANCE

1183 / **Galerie des Beaux-Arts.** L'art et la musique dix-neuvième. Exposition du Mai organisée à l'initiative de Monsieur Jacques Chaban-Delmas, Maire de Bordeaux. . . . Bordeaux, Galerie des Beaux-Arts, 1969. 119 p.

Catalog for an exhibition held in Bordeaux from 30 May to 30 September, 1969.

206 items, including 30 instruments. 81 plates. Brief descriptions including bibliographies and some information as to provenance.

BOSTON, MASSACHUSETTS

1184 / **Boston Public Library.** Catalogue of the Allen A. Brown collection of music. Boston, Mass., 1910–16. 4 v.

A dictionary catalog of composers, titles, subjects, with explicit contents and analytics given for all collections. One of the first, and one of the few printed catalogs for a major American music collection. Rich in opera and in orchestral scores, primarily 19th-century editions.

1185 / **Boston Public Library.** Dictionary catalog of the music collection of the Boston Public Library. Boston, Mass., G. K. Hall and Co., 1972. 20 v.

Photo-offset publication of the card file for a collection of some 80,000 volumes covering music, biography, history and criticism, theory and composition, music education, collected editions and monuments, bibliographical works, libretti, and periodicals. This catalog incorporates the Allen A. Brown music collection, but excludes sheet music, clippings and programs, and recordings.

BRANDENBURG, GERMANY

1186 / **St. Katharinenkirche. Bibliothek.** Die musikalischen Schätze der St. Katherinenkirche zu Brandenburg a.d. Havel. Ein Beitrag zur musikalischen Literatur des 16. und 17. Jahrhunderts. Von Johann F. Täglichsbeck. Brandenburg, A. Müller, 1857. 50 p.

Manuscripts and printed works, 1564–1671, chronologically arranged, with full bibliographical information and descriptive notes.

BRASOV, RUMANIA

1187 / **Honterusgymnasium. Bibliothek.** Dis Musiksammlung der Bibliothek zu Kronstadt, von Erich H. Müller. Kronstadt, J. Gött's Sohn, 1930. 176 p.

Manuscripts, printed music and books. Brief biographical sketches of authors or composers. Publication dates, plate numbers.

BRESLAU, GERMANY and BRIEG, GERMANY

See WROCLAW, POLAND.

BRÜNN, CZECHOSLOVAKIA

1188 / **Moravské Muzeum.** Průvodce po archívních fondech Ústavu dějin hudby Moravského musea v Brně. Zprac. Theodora Straková, *et al.* 1. vyd. Brno, Ustav dějin hudby. Mor. musea, rozmn., 1971. 256 p. 22 plates.

Summary in Russian, German, and English.
Catalog of the music holdings of the Moravian Museum in Brünn.

1189 / **Universitätsbibliothek.** Alte Drucke der Werke von tschechischen Komponisten des 18. Jahrhunderts in der Universitäts- bibliothek in Brno. Von Vladimír Telec. Praha, Státní Pedagogické Nakladatelství, 1969. 163 p.

Cites 1,278 works by 42 Czech composers; a total of 522 biblio- graphical units. 278 of the items are on microfilm. Full bibliographical descriptions, including tempo and metrical indications for the move- ments of composite works. Introduction in German and Czech. Eight plates.

BRUSSELS, BELGIUM

1190 / **Bibliothèque Royale de Belgique.** Catalogue de la bib- liothèque de F. J. Fétis, acquise par l'État belge. Bruxelles, C. Muquardt, 1877. 946 p.

The Fétis library was acquired by the Bibliothèque Royale in 1872 and contains many rarities. 7,325 items classified under two main headings: (1) "Bibliothèque générale" and (2) "Bibliothèque musicale."

1191 / **Bibliothèque Royale de Belgique.** Catalogue des imprimés musicaux des XVe, XVIe et XVIIe siècles. Fonds général. Par Bernard Huys. Bruxelles, Bibliothèque Royale de Belgique, 1965. 422 p.

446 numbered items. The catalog lists those works not part of the Fétis collection (above), although if another copy or a more complete copy is found in *Fétis*, this information is given. Contents listed for each item. Of particular interest is the listing of music excerpted from theoretical works such as Kircher, Glareanus, Zarlino, etc.

Review by François Lesure in *Revue de musicologie*, 51 (1965), p. 102; by Ute Schwab in *Die Musikforschung*, 21 (1968), p. 104–105.

1192 / **Bibliothèque Royale de Belgique.** François-Joseph Fétis et la vie musicale de son temps, 1784–1871. Bruxelles, Bibliothèque Royale, 1972. 254 p. 64 plates.

"Exposition organisée à l'occasion du centième anniversaire de l'achat de la collection Fétis." May 27 to August 26, 1972.

An admirably documented exhibition catalog treating the multiple interests and activities of Fétis as a musicologist, historian, composer, and collector.

1193 / **Bibliothèque Royale de Belgique.** De Grégoire le Grand à Stockhausen. Douze siècles de notation musicale. Catalogue de l'exposition rédigé par Bernard Huys. Bruxelles, Bibliothèque Royale, 1966. 169 p.

Catalog of a well-organized exposition of 100 items tracing the history of musical notation. 16 facsimile plates and 48 illustrations in the text. Each entry is fully described, with bibliographical references.

1194 / **Conservatoire Royal de Musique. Bibliothèque.** Catalogue de la bibliothèque . . . par A. Wotquenne. Bruxelles, Coosemans, 1898–1912. 4 v.

Annexe I: "Libretti d'opéras et d'oratorios italiens du XVIIe siècle." Bruxelles, O. Schepens, 1901. 189 p.

A classified catalog to one of the richest European music collections. Printed scores and manuscripts interfiled.

BUDAPEST, HUNGARY

1195 / **Orzágos Széchényi Könyvtár.** "Catalogue raisonné der Esterházy Opernsammlung, in chronologischer Ordnung der Premièren." In *Haydn als Opernkapellmeister; die Haydn-Dokumente der Esterházy Opernsammlung.* Bearbeitet von Dénes Bartha und László Somfai. Budapest, Verlag der Ungarischen Akademie der Wissenschaften, 1960. p. 179–403.

Chronological listing of the operatic works preserved in the Esterházy archive in the National Széchényi Library. Each work is fully described, with special attention given to Haydn's annotations on works performed under his direction. An important new approach to Haydn research.

1196 / **Országos Széchényi Könyvtár.** Haydn compositions in the music collection of the National Széchényi Library, Budapest. Published on the occasion of the 150th anniversary of Haydn's death (1809–1959). Edited by Jenö Vécsey. Budapest, Publishing House of the Hungarian Academy of Sciences, 1960. 167 p.

Also published in Hungarian and German.

A classified listing of 372 items, 72 of which are Haydn autographs. 42 facsimiles of manuscripts, prints, and other documents related to the composer's career.

1197 / **Országos Széchényi Könyvtár.** "Die Musikalien der Pfarrkirche zu St. Aegidi in Bárfa." By Otto Gombosi. In *Festschrift für Johannes Wolf*. Berlin 1929. p. 38–47.

The collection described here is now in the National Széchényi Library at Budapest. Gombosi discusses some 20 music prints of the 16th century and a number of important 16th- and 17th-century manuscripts.

1198 / **Országos Széchényi Könyvtár.** Zenei kéziratok jegyzéke. Budapest, Kiádja a Magyar Nemzeti Múzeum Orzágos Széchényi Könyvtár, 1921–40. 2 v. (Catalogus bibliothecae musaei nat. hungarici. Musica, I, II.)

Vol. 1 (391 p.): editor, Isoz Kálmán. Catalog of 1,449 autograph letters of musicians, including some of Haydn and Liszt. Vol. 2 (237 p.): editor, Lavotta Rezsö. Catalog of music manuscripts.

CAMBRAI, FRANCE

1199 / **Coussemaker, Edmond de.** Notice sur les collections musicales de la Bibliothèque de Cambrai et des autres villes du Départment du Nord. . . . Paris, Techener, 1843. 180, 40 p.

Concerned chiefly with 16 manuscripts and 4 printed collections in the Cambrai library. The descriptions are brief, faulty, and outdated.

CAMBRIDGE, ENGLAND

1200 / **University. Fitzwilliam Museum.** Catalogue of the music in the Fitzwilliam Museum, Cambridge, by J. A. Fuller-Maitland and A. H. Mann. London, C. J. Clay and Sons, 1893. 298 p.

209 manuscripts, 196 printed books, and an important collection of Handel materials.

1201 / **University. Peterhouse College.** Catalogue of the musical manuscripts at Peterhouse, Cambridge, compiled by Anselm Hughes. Cambridge, Cambridge Univ. Press, 1953. 75 p.

Important source materials for the study of English church music of the 16th and 17th centuries comprising four Latin partbooks of *c.* 1540 and two sets of English partbooks *c.* 1630–40.

CAMBRIDGE, MASSACHUSETTS

1202 / **Harvard University. Music Library.** A catalogue of books relating to music in the library of Richard Aldrich. New York (printed at the Plimpton Press, Norwood, Mass.), 1931. 435 p.

A classified catalog of music literature, primarily of the 19th and 20th centuries, with a small collection of books printed before 1800 (p. 35–55). This library has been incorporated into the Harvard University music collection.

CARPENTRAS, FRANCE

1203 / **Bibliothèque d'Inguimbert.** Catalogue de la collection musicale J. B. Laurens donnée a la ville de Carpentras pour la Bibliothèque d'Inguimbert. Carpentras, J. Seguin, 1901. 151 p.

Classified catalog of music books and scores; a 19th-century scholar's library. Preceded by a biography of the donor, J. B. Laurens, archeologist, painter, writer, organist, composer, and musicologist.

CESENA, ITALY

1204 / **Biblioteca Comunale.** "Catalogo delle opere musicali a stampa dal'500 al'700 conservate presso la Biblioteca Comunale di Cesena." By Sergio Paganelli. In *Collectanea historiae musicae,* 2 (1957), p. 311–38.

95 early prints of vocal and instrumental music; 6 theory works.

CHICAGO, ILLINOIS

1205 / **The Newberry Library.** "The Newberry Library, Chicago." By Donald W. Krummel. In *Fontes artis musicae* (July-December, 1969), p. 119–24.

A narrative account of the music resources of the Newberry Library in the areas of medieval music, Renaissance and baroque music, music of the 18th and 19th centuries, music of master composers, and Americana.

COIMBRA, PORTUGAL

1206 / **Universidade. Biblioteca.** Inventário dos inéditos e impressos musicais (subsídios para um catálogo). Fasc. I. Prefaciado por Santiago Kastner. Coimbra, Impresso nas oficinas da "Atlântida." 1937. 47 & 55 p.

Separate alphabets and pagination for manuscripts and early printed works. Full descriptions.

1207 / **Universidade. Biblioteca.** Os manuscritos musicais nos. 6 e 12 da Biblioteca Geral da Universidade de Coimbra (Contribuïção para um catálogo definitivo). Por Mário de Sampayo Ribeiro. Coimbra, 1941. 112 p.

A detailed study of two manuscripts of polyphonic music in the university library at Coimbra.

COLLEGEVILLE, MINNESOTA

1208 / **St. John's University. Alcuin Library.** "The monastic manuscript microfilm library," by Julian G. Plante, in *Notes*, 25 (1968), p. 12–14.

The article describes a microfilm library of nearly 11,000 codices filmed from the monastic libraries in Europe (Göttweig, Heiligenkreuz, Herzogenburg, Klosterneuburg, Kremsmünster, Lambach, Lilienfeld, Melk, etc.). The author cites 27 manuscripts of early music theory available for study in the collection at Collegeville.

COLOGNE, GERMANY

1209 / **Domcapelle.** Die Leiblsche Sammlung. Katalog der Musikalien der Kölner Domcapelle. Von Gottfried Göller. Köln, Arno Volk-Verlag, 1964. 133 p. (Beiträge zur rheinischen Musikgeschichte, 57.)

Thematic catalog of 291 sacred choral works, chiefly early 19th century, formerly in the chapel of Cologne Cathedral. The collection is now in the Diözesanbibliothek of the Archbishopric of Cologne. Former owner—Carl Leibl, Kapellmeister.

Review by Winfried Kirsch in *Die Musikforschung*, 20 (1967), p. 95.

1210 / **Universitäts- und Stadtbibliothek.** Katalog der in der Universitäts- und Stadtbibliothek Köln vorhandenen Musikdrucke des 16., 17., und 18. Jahrhunderts. By Willi Kahl. Köln, 1958. 20 p.

118 items. Bibliographical references.

COPENHAGEN, DENMARK

1211 / **Kommunebiblioteker.** Katalog over dansk og udenlandsk musik og musiklitteratur. 2. udgave. København, B. Lunos Bogtrykkeri, 1932. 157 p.

First published in 1921.

Tilvaext (supplement), 1932–39. København, B. Lunos, 1939.

1212 / **Kommunebiblioteker.** Katalog over musik og musiklitteratur. København, Nordlunde, 1954–58. 4 v.

Vol. 1: orkestermusik, kammermusik, enkelte instrumenter, 1956, 72 p. Vol. 2: klaver, orgel, harmonium, 1954. 65 p. Vol. 3: vokalmusik, 1958, 118 p. Vol. 4: operaer, operetter, balletter, 1955, 46 p.

A fifth volume devoted to books on music was never published.

CREMONA, ITALY

1213 / **Biblioteca Governativa e Libreria Civica.** Mostra bibliografica dei musicisti cremonesi: catalogo storico-critico degli autori e catalogo bibliografico. Cremona, Biblioteca Governativa e Libreria Civica, 1951. 149 p.

Catalog of an exhibition held in 1949. P. 1–106: biographical notices of Cremonese musicians; p. 107–45: exhibition catalog, arranged chronologically; about 140 items related to the history of music in Cremona.

CRESPANO VENETO, ITALY

1214 / **Biblioteca Musicale del Prof. Pietro Canal** in Crespano Veneto. Bassano, Prem. Stabilimento Tipogr. Sante Pezzato, 1885. 104 p.

A scholar's library of 1,152 items, of which the first 1,034 are books on music. Contains many rarities. The owner was a professor at the University of Padua and wrote studies of music in Mantua and Venice.

1215 / **Cathedral. Archivo.** Catálogo musical del Archivo de la Santa Iglesia Catedral Basilica de Cuenca. Recogido por Restituto Navarro Gonzalo. Revisado por Jesús López Cobos. Dirigido por Antonio Iglesias. Cuenca, Ediciones del Instituto de Música Religiosa, 1965. 372 p.

CZECHOSLOVAKIA

1216 / **Fischer, Kurt von.** "Repertorium der Quellen tschechischer Mehrstimmigkeit des 14. bis 16. Jahrhunderts." In *Essays in musicology in honor of Dragan Plamenac on his 70th birthday*. Pittsburgh, Univ. of Pittsburgh Press, 1969. p. 49–60.

Identifies 73 manuscript sources of early Czech polyphony in 23 institutions, chiefly in Czechoslovakia but including the Austrian National Library at Vienna.

1217 / **Plamenac, Dragan.** "Music libraries in Eastern Europe, a visit in the summer of 1961." In *Notes*, 19 (1962), p. 217–34; 411–20; 584–98.

An illuminating account of present conditions in some of the major East-European music libraries, including those in Czechoslovakia. Locations of important bodies of source materials are indicated.

1218 / **Pruvodce po pramenech k dějinám Hudby.** Fondy a sbirky uložené v. Čechách. (Music collections and archives in the CSSR.) Zpracovali; Jaroslav Bužga, Jan Kouba, Eva Mikanová a Tomislav Volek. Redigoval: Jan Kouba. Praha, Ceskoslovenská Akademie Ved, 1969. 323 p.

General descriptions of the music resources of Czech museums, libraries, and archives. Name index.

1219 / **Svobodová, Maria.** "Musikbücherein, Archive und Museen in der CSSR." in AIBM, Ländergruppe Deutsche Demokratische Republik. Internationaler Sommerkurs für Musikbibliothekare, 1964. Berlin, 1965. p. 48–69.

A descriptive account of the major music archives, libraries, and museums in Czechoslovakia.

1220 / **Terrayová, Maria J.** "Súpis archívnych hudobných fondov na Slovensku." In *Hudobnovedné stúdie*. VI. Bratislava, Vydavetel'stvo Slovenskej Akadémie, Vied, 1960. p. 197–328.

Thematic catalog of the music manuscripts in two hitherto undescribed Czech archives: the archive of the Pfarrkirche of Púchov (on deposit in the Musicological Institute of the Slovakian Academy of Sciences) and the archive of the Príleský Ostrolúcky family (on deposit in the Slovakian National Museum in Martin). The manuscripts are chiefly of late-18th-century instrumental and vocal music by Italianate Czech composers of the period.

DAGENHAM, ENGLAND

1221 / **Public Libraries.** Catalogue of music; a complete catalogue of the scores, miniature scores, recorded music and books . . . in the Dagenham Public Libraries. Compiled by W. C. Pugsley and G. Atkinson. Dagenham (Essex) 1958. 299 p.

DANZIG

See GDAŃSK, POLAND.

DARMSTADT, GERMANY

1222 / **Hofbibliothek.** "Musik-Handschriften der Darmstädter Hofbibliothek." Beschrieben von F. W. E. Roth, in *Monatshefte für Musikgeschichte*, 20 (1888), p. 64–73; 82–92.

117 items, 10th to 19th centuries. Brief descriptions.

1223 / **Hofbibliothek.** "Zur Bibliographie der Musikdrucke des XV. bis XVII. Jahrhunderts in der Darmstädter Hofbibliothek." Von F. W. E. Roth, in *Monatshefte für Musikgeschichte* 20 (1888), p. 118–25; 134–41; 154–61.

75 items, fully described.

1224 / **Internationales Musikinstitut Darmstadt.** Informationszentrum für zeitgenössische Musik. Katalog der Abteilung Noten. Darmstadt, Internationales Musikinstitut, 1966. 293 p.

Title varies, began as *Kranichsteiner Musikinstitut*.

An international lending library established in 1948 to further the study and performance of contemporary music. Classified catalog, chiefly scores, but a small collection of books.
Review by Karl Kroeger in *Notes*, 23 (1967), p. 531–32.

DENTON, TEXAS

1225 / **North Texas State College. Music Library.** A bibliography of contemporary music in the Music Library of North Texas State College, March 1955. Compiled by Anna Harriet Heyer. . . . Denton, Texas, 1955. 128 leaves (typescript).
Alphabetical listing by composer, and by title under composer. Chiefly scores and chamber music with parts. No index.
Review by Dorothy A. Linder in *Notes*, 13 (1956), p. 656–57.

DRESDEN, GERMANY

1226 / **Sächsische Landesbibliothek.** Katalog der Musiksammlung der Kgl. öffentlichen Bibliothek zu Dresden (im Japanischen Palais). Bearb. von Robert Eitner und Otto Kade. . . . Leipzig, Breitkopf & Härtel. 1890. 150 p. (Monatshefte für Musikgeschichte. Beilage. Jahrgang 21–22.)
Music manuscripts to the date of compilation; printed music and books on music to 1700.

1227 / **Sächsische Landesbibliothek.** Klaviermusik der sozialistischen Länder aus der Sächsischen Landesbibliothek. Bestandsverzeichnis zusammengestellt von Wolfgang Reich. Dresden, Sächsische Landesbibliothek, 1962. 79 p.
A list, grouped alphabetically by country, of keyboard music by East-European composers. Date, publisher, and pagination given for each entry.

DUBLIN, IRELAND

1228 / **Trinity College Library.** "The lute books of Trinity College, Dublin." by John Ward. In *The Lute Society journal*, 9 (1967), p. 17–40; 10 (1968), p. 15–32.

1229 / **Durham Cathedral. Library.** A catalogue of the printed music and books on music in Durham Cathedral Library. By Alec Harman. London–New York–Toronto, Oxford Univ. Press, 1968. 136 p.

Review by Imogen Fellinger in *Die Musikforschung*, 25 (1972), p. 99–100; by Henry Leland Clarke in *Notes*, 25 (1969), p. 501–502.

1230 / **L'Institut Français d'Ecosse.** Hector Berlioz (1803–1869), an exhibition at L'Institut Français d'Ecosse on the occasion of the 1963 Edinburgh International Festival. Edinburgh, Institut Français d'Ecosse, 1963. 40 p.

An exhibition catalog compiled by Richard Macnutt. 127 items, arranged chronologically with respect to the composer's career. Fully annotated with connecting commentary.

1231 / **University. Reid Library.** Catalogue of manuscripts, printed music, and books on music up to 1850 in the library of the Music Department of the University of Edinburgh . . . Edited by Hans Gál. Edinburgh, Oliver and Boyd, 1941. 78 p.

Important for its holdings in 18th-century music, printed and in manuscript, from the private collection of John Reid, 1721–1807. Brief entries.

1232 / **Richard Wagner-Museum.** Katalog einer Richard Wagner Bibliothek; nach den vorliegenden Originalien systematisch-chronologisch geordnetes und mit Citaten und Anmerkungen versehenes authentisches Nachschlagebuch durch die gesammte Wagner-Literatur. By Nikolaus Oesterlein. Leipzig, Breitkopf & Härtel, 1882–95. 4 v.

Apart from the bibliography of Wagner literature (vols. 1–2), this work provides a catalog of a collection of Wagner documents, formerly in Vienna but purchased by the city of Eisenach in 1895 (vols. 3–4).

FERRARA, ITALY

Biblioteca Communale. See no. 1289.

ENGLAND

See under GREAT BRITAIN

FLORENCE, ITALY

1233 / **Biblioteca Nazionale Centrale.** Catalogo dei manoscritti musicali della Biblioteca Nazionale di Firenze. By Bianca Becherini. Kassel, Bärenreiter, 1959. 178 p.

144 numbered items; detailed descriptions, contents of collections. Indexes of text incipits, musicians, poets, and names mentioned in the descriptive notes.

Review by Frank L. Harrison in *Music and letters*, 42 (1961), p. 281; by Nanie Bridgman in *Fontes artis musicae*, 8 (1961), p. 31–33; by Walther Dürr in *Die Musikforschung*, 14 (1961), p. 234–35.

1234 / **Biblioteca Nazionale Centrale.** Mostre bibliografica di musica italiana dalle origini alla fine del secolo XVIII. Firenze, L. S. Olschki, 1937. 102 p.

An exhibition catalog. Preface signed: Anita Mondolfo.

Conservatorio di Musica "Luigi Cherubini" (formerly cited as R. Istituto Musicale). See also no. 1282.

1235 / **Conservatorio di Musica "Luigi Cherubini."** Esposizione nazionale dei Conservatori Musicali e delle Biblioteche. Palazzo Devanzati, 27 Ottobre 1949–8 Gennaio 1950. Firenze, G. Barbèra, 1950. 121 p.

Exposition catalog celebrating the 100th anniversary of the founding of the conservatory. Includes manuscripts, printed music, and some musical instruments.

1236 / **Conservatorio di Musica "Luigi Cherubini."** "I manoscritti e le stampe rare della Biblioteca del Conservatorio 'L. Cherubini' di Ferenze." In *La Bibliofilia*, 66 (1964), p. 255–99.

20 manuscripts and 21 early printed books "nuova catalogazione e reintegrazione."

A catalog compiled by Bianca Becherini for the purpose of giving full descriptions of those items in the collection that are most rare and most interesting to foreign scholars.

1237 / **Conservatorio di Musica "Luigi Cherubini."** Indice di alcuni cimeli esposti appartenenti alla Biblioteca del R. Istituto. By Riccardo Gandolfi. Firenze, Tipografia Galletti e Cocci, 1911. 32 p.

At head of title: "Nella commemorazione cinquantenaria dalla fondazione del R. Istituo Musicale 'Luigi Cherubini' di Firenze."

Brief descriptive entries for 30 manuscripts and 37 early printed books, 32 theory works, and 4 "Curisità diversi."

1238 / **Galleria degli Uffizi.** I disegni musicali del Gabinetto degli "Uffizi" e delle minori collezioni pubbliche a Firenze. By Luigi Parigi. Firenze, L. S. Olschki, 1951. 233 p.

A catalog of prints and drawings with musical content or subject matter: musicians, musical instruments, performance practice, etc. Indexed by instruments and by subjects.

1239 / **Galleria degli Uffizi.** Mostra di strummenti musicali in disegni degli "Uffizi." Catalogo a cura di Luisa Marcucci con prefazione di Luigi Parigi. Firenze, L. S. Olschki, 1952. 47 p.

An exhibition of 65 items from the Uffizi print collection; 25 plates.

1240 / **Galleria degli Uffizi.** Gli strumenti musicali nei dipinti della Galleria degli Uffizi. By Marziano Bernardi e Andrea Della Corte. Torino, Edizioni Radio Italiana, 1952. 177 p. 51 plates.

A handsome volume devoted to representations of musical activity in paintings in the Uffizi gallery. Index of artists and of instruments depicted.

1241 / **Illustrazioni di Alcuni Cimeli Concernenti l'Arte Musicale in Firenze.** . . . Di Riccardo Gandolfi. In Firenze, a cura della Commissione per la Esposizione di Vienna, 1892.

A lavish, illustrated catalog prepared for the Vienna exposition of 1892. Limited edition, elephant folio, 39 facsimile plates of Italian

297

musical documents from the 11th to the 19th centuries. Historical introduction and notes on the plates.

FRANCE

1242 / **Bridgman, Nanie.** "Musique profane italienne des 16e et 17e siècles dans les bibliothèques françaises." In *Fontes artis musicae* (1955:1), p. 40–59.

Precise description of 32 rarities of the 16th and 17th centuries found in 5 public or private libraries in France.

1243 / **Chaillon, Paule.** "Les fonds musicaux de quelques bibliothèques de province." In *Fontes artis musicae* (1955:2), p. 151–63.

Describes a group of source materials found in 24 French provincial libraries, sources that came to light in connection with work done in preparation for the RISM volumes.

FRANKFURT AM MAIN, GERMANY

1244 / **International Exhibition "Music in the Life of the People."** Katalog der Internationalen Austellung "Musik im Leben der Völker," von Kathi Meyer. Frankfurt am Main, Hauserpresse Werner U. Winter, 1927. 340 p.

Catalog of the large international music exhibition held June 11 to August 28, 1927. Organized according to the systematic arrangement of the exhibition halls. Includes printed books, manuscripts, instruments, pictures and other artifacts. 49 plates.

A separate catalog of the Italian section was printed in Rome, 1927. 161 p.

1245 / **Lessing-Gymnasium. Bibliothek.** Die musikalischen Schätze der Gymnasialbibliothek und der Peterskirche zu Frankfurt a.M., von Carl Isräel. Frankfurt a.M., Mahlau und Waldschmidt, 1872. 118 p.

Covers the period to about 1800; full bibliographical data.

1246 / **Stadtbibliothek.** Kirchliche Musikhandschriften des XVII. und XVIII. Jahrhunderts; Katalog von Carl Süss, im Auftrage der Gesellschaft der Freunde der Stadtbibliothek, bearb. und hrsg. von Peter Epstein. Berlin, Frankfurter Verlags-Anstalt, 1926. 224 p.

Chiefly cantatas arranged alphabetically under composer, with a separate section of 834 works by G. P. Telemann. Entries give date if known, title, instrumentation.

1247 / **Gamber, Klaus.** Codices liturgici latini antiquiores. Freiburg, Universitätsverlag, 1963. (Spicilegii friburgensis subsidia, 1.)
Liturgical music manuscripts in the library of the University at Freiburg.

1248 / **Kade, Otto.** Die älteren Musikalien der Stadt Frieburg in Sachsen. Leipzig, Breitkopf & Härtel, 188, 32 p. (Beilage. Monatshefte für Musikgeschichte. Jahrgang 20.)

GDAŃSK, POLAND (formerly DANZIG)

1249 / **Stadtbibliothek.** Die musikalischen Handschriften der Stadtbibliothek und in ihrer Verwaltung befindlichen Kirchenbibliotheken von St. Katharinen und St. Johann in Danzig. Von Otto Günther. Danzig, 1911. (Katalog der Handschriften der Danziger Stadtbibliothek, Bd. 4: Handschriften, Teil 4.)
The surviving music manuscripts and early printed books of the Danzig Stadbibliothek have been filmed and are listed in the catalog of music sources published by the Polish National Library in Warsaw (see no 1528). Professor Plamenac in his articles on East European music libraries (no. 1217), has given a summary listing of the major holdings of this collection.

GENOA, ITALY

1250 / **Biblioteca dell'Istituto Musicale "Nicolo Paganini."** Catalogo del fondo antico a cura di Salvatore Pintacuda. Milano, Istituto Editoriale Italiano, 1966. 489 p. (Bibliotheca musicae, 4.)
Review by Frank A. D'Accone in *Notes*, 23 (1967), p. 530–31.

Biblioteca Universitaria. See no. 1287.

GERMANY

1251 / **Kahl, Willi, and Wilhelm-Martin Luther.** Repertorium der Musikwissenschaft. . . .
For complete citation and annotation, see no 551.

1252 / **Schaal, Richard.** Führer durch deutsche Musikbibliotheken. Wilhelmshaven, Heinrichshoven's Verlag, 1971, 163 p. (Taschenbücher zur Musikwissenschaft, 7.)

German libraries are listed alphabetically by place, covering both West and East Germany. For the major libraries there are descriptions given of the collection, with some historical information. Bibliographies include catalogs and other publications related to the libraries under consideration.

GERMANY (DEUTSCHE DEMOKRATISCHE REPUBLIK)

1253 / **Deutscher Bibliotheksverband. Sektion Musikbibliotheken.** Musikbibliotheken und Musikaliensammlungen in der Deutschen Demokratischen Republik. Red. Peter Thüringer. Mitarb. Jutta Theurich und Rose Hebenstreit. Halle, Internat. Vereinigung d. Musikbibliotheken, Ländergruppe DDR. 1969. 62 p.

A publication sponsored by the East German section of the International Association of Music Libraries.

91 institutions are described, with pertinent data concerning their resources and services. Catalogs and other publications cited.

GLASGOW, SCOTLAND

1254 / **Anderson's College. Library. Euing Collection.** The Euing musical library. Catalogue of the musical library of the late Wm. Euing, Esq., bequeathed to Anderson's University, Glasgow. . . . Glasgow, Printed by W. M. Ferguson, 1878. 256 p.

Classified catalog. The collection is strong in theoretical works from 1487 and liturgical music of the Church of England, 16th to 19th centuries.

GOTTINGEN, GERMANY

1255 / **Niedersächsische Staats- und Universitäts-Bibliothek.** Johann Sebastian Bach Documenta. Hrsg. von Wilhelm Martin Luther zum Bachfest 1950 in Göttingen. Kassel, Bärenreiter, 1950. 148 p.

545 numbered items from an exhibition illustrating J. S. Bach's influence from his own time to the present day. Covers a wide area of documentation. 54 plates.

1256 / **Niedersächsische Staats- und Universitäts-Bibliothek.** Die Musikwerke der Kgl. Universitäts-Bibliothek in Göttingen. Verzeichnet von Albert Quantz. Berlin, T. Trautwein, 1883. 45 p. (Monatshefte für Musikgeschichte. Beilage, Jahrgang 15.)

45 theoretical works and some 100 music prints of the 16th and 17th centuries. Good representation of German composers of the period.

GOTTWEIG. (BENEDICTINE ABBEY) AUSTRIA

1257 / **Göttweig. Graphisches Kabinett.** Musik, Theater, Tanz vom 16. Jahrhundert bis zum 19. Jahrhundert in ihrem Beziehungen zur Gesellschaft, Ausstellung Stift Göttweig, Niederösterreich, 28. Mai–23. Okt. 1966. 86 p.

This library has been enriched by materials from the collection of the Viennese collector Aloys Fuchs.

GRANADA, SPAIN

1258 / **Capilla Real. Archivo.** "El Archivo de música de la Capilla Real de Grenada." By José López Calo. In *Anuario musical*, 13 (1958), p. 103–28.

A small collection of manuscripts, early printed books, and documents. Lists full contents for polyphonic sources.

GRAZ, AUSTRIA

1259 / **Neue Galerie.** Bilder aus Beethovens Leben, aus der Beethoven Sammlung G. L. de Baranyai. Ausstellung des Landes Steiermark und der Stadt Graz. Graz, 1962. 77 p.

GREAT BRITAIN

1260 / **Bibliotheca Musico-Liturgica.** A descriptive handlist of the musical and Latin-liturgical mss. of the Middle Ages preserved in the libraries of Great Britain and Ireland. Drawn up by W. H. Frere . . . and printed for the members of the Plainsong and Mediaeval Music Society. London, B. Quaritch, 1901–1932. 2 v.

Reprint by Georg Olms, Hildesheim, 1967.

See no. 1039 for complete annotation.

1261 / **The British Union-Catalogue of Early Music Printed Before the Year 1801.** A record of the holdings of over 100 libraries throughout the British Isles. Editor: Edith B. Schnapper. London, Butterworths Scientific Publications, 1957. 2 v.

See no. 1047 for complete annotation.

1262 / **Long, Maureen W.** Music in British libraries—a directory of resources. London, The Library Association and The Polytechnic of North London, 1971. 183 p. (Library Association research publication, 7.)

GRIMMA, GERMANY

1263 / **Königl. Landesschule. Bibliothek.** Verzeichniss der in der Bibliothek der Königl. Landdesschule zu Grimma vorhandenen Musikalien aus dem 16. und 17. Jahrhundert, von N. M. Petersen. . . . Grimma, G. Gensel, 1861. 24 p.

The greater part of this collection is now in the Sächsischen Landesbibliothek in Dresden.

GROTTAFERRATA, ITALY

1264 / **Biblioteca della Badia di Grottaferrata.** "La musica bizantina e i codici di melurgia della biblioteca di Grottaferrata." In *Accademie e biblioteche d'Italia*, 1930–31.

Library of the principal center of Byzantine musical studies in Italy.

THE HAGUE, HOLLAND

1265 / **Gemeentemuseum.** Catalogue of the music library. Vol. 1: Historical and theoretical works to 1800, by Marie H. Charbon. New York, Da Capo Press, 1969– .

Also published in Dutch by Frits Knuf. Introduction in Dutch and English.

First of a series of catalogs projected to cover the resources, printed and in manuscript, of the Music Library of the Gemeentemuseum at The Hague. This series will incorporate the holdings of the Scheurleer collection (see no. 1267). A parallel series is devoted to the musical instruments in the Gemeentemuseum. (See no 1587.)

1266 / **Gemeentemuseum.** Nederlandsche muziekleven 1600–1800. 's-Gravenhage, Gemeentemuseum, 6 Juni–6 September, 1936. 124 p.

Catalog of an exhibition on Dutch musical life of the 17th and 18th centuries. Includes printed books, manuscripts, musical instruments, and paintings with musical subjects. Illustrated. Introduction by D. J. Balfoort.

1267 / **Muziekhistorisch Museum van Dr. D. F. Scheurleer.** Catlogus van de muziek-werken en de boeken oven muziek. 's-Gravenhage, M. Nijhoff, 1923–25. 3 v.

The catalog was preceded by two earlier compilations, one in two volumes in 1885–87 and one in three volumes, 1893–1910.

A classified catalog; volume 3 is a general index. Numerous facsimiles of early title pages. The Scheurleer collection is an outstanding working library of musicology as well as containing many rarities. It is now the property of the city of The Hague.

HALLE, GERMANY

1268 / **Händel-Haus.** Katalog zu den Sammlungen des Händel-Hauses in Halle. v. 1– . Halle an der Saale, Händel-Haus, 1961– .

Teil 1: Handschriftensammlung (1961); Teil 2: Bildsammlung, Porträts (1962). Teil 3: Bildsammlung, Städte- und Gebäudedarstellung (1964). Teil 5: Musikinstrumentensammlung. Besaitete Tasteninstrumente (1966). See no. 1590.

A growing series of catalogs concerned not only with Handel documents but with material on early-19th-century German song, iconography. Numerous plates.

HAMBURG, GERMANY

1269 / **Hamburger Musikbücherei.** Oper, Operette, Singspiel. Ein Katalog der Hamburger Musikbücherei, 1965. Hamburg, Herausgegeben von den Hamburger Öffentlichen Bücherhallen, 1965. 207 p.

A catalog of the theatre holdings of the Hamburg Musikbücherei comprising some 3,198 volumes, 1,590 titles. Full scores and vocal scores are indicated, with publishers and plate numbers. Chiefly 19th and 20th century works, but with some early items. Arranged alphabetically by composer, with indexes of Singspiele, of full scores, of titles. Editor: Annemarie Eckhoff.

Review by Klaus Hortschansky in *Die Musikforschung*, 22 (1969), p. 521–22.

HEILBRONN, GERMANY

1270 / **Gymnasium. Bibliothek.** Alter Musikschatz, geordnet und beschreiben von Edwin Mayers. Heilbronn, C. F. Schmidt, 1893. 82 p. (Mitteilungen aus der Bibliothek des Heilbronner Gymnasiums, 2.)

1271 / **Stadtarchiv.** Die Musiksammlung der Stadtarchiv Heilbronn. Katalog mit Beiträgen zur Geschichte der Sammlung und zur Quellenkunde des XVI. Jahrhunderts. By Ulrich Siegele. Heilbronn, Stadtarchiv, 1967. 323 p. (Veröff. des Archivs der Stadt Heilbronn, 13.)

Gives full bibliographical descriptions with contents of collections. RISM items are identified. 16 plates of early manuscripts, bindings, and editions. First line index; index of names and subjects.

HRADEC KRÁLOVÉ (KÖNIGGRÄTZ), CZECHOSLOVAKIA

1272 / **Černý, Jaromir.** Soupis hudeních rukopisů muzea v. Hradci Králové (Catalog of musical manuscripts in the Museum at Hradec Králové). Praha, Universita Karlova, 1966. 240 p. (Miscellanea musicologica, 19.)

Catalog of 56 items, chiefly manuscripts of liturgical music. Copiously indexed by form, texts by language, with a bibliography of relevant literature; 16 facsimile plates.

HUNGARY

1273 / **Pethas, Iván.** "Musikbibliotheken in Ungarn." In *Fontes artis musicae* (Mai-Dezember, 1968), p. 114–18.

Describes 15 current Hungarian music libraries, with a table giving comparative statistics on their holdings and services.

Rado, Polycarpe. Répertoire hymnologique . . .
See no. 1132.

IOWA CITY, IOWA

1274 / **University Library.** An exhibit of music and materials on music, early and rare. Preface by Albert T. Luper. Iowa City, The Graduate College and The University Libraries, State University of Iowa, April 1953. 39 p.

An annotated exhibition catalog of materials on loan from the Library of Congress, The Newberry Library, The University of Illinois, The Sibley Musical Library, and private sources. Part I: autograph scores (13 items). Part II: early music editions and manuscripts. Part III: books on music (45 items).

1275 / **University Library.** An annotated catalog of rare musical items in the libraries of the University of Iowa. Additions: 1963–1972. Compiled by Gordon S. Rowley, with a preface by Rita Benton. Iowa City, 1973. 121 p.

A catalog of 278 items, articulating with the volume entered below. Extended annotations, descriptive and biograical. RISM items identified. Bibliography (p. 107–116). Index of names.

1276 / **University Library.** Rare musical items in the libraries of Iowa. By Frederick K. Gable. Foreword by Albert T. Luper. Iowa City, 1963. 130 p.

A carefully annotated catalog of 275 items. Part I: books on music. Part II: music scores. Index of names and of selected subjects. Selected bibliography.

For an account of the history, resources, and services of this rapidly growing music library, see Rita Benton, The music library of the University of Iowa." In *Fontes artis musicae* (Juli-Dezember 1969), p. 124–29.

ITALY

1277 / **Associazione dei Musicologi Italiani.** Catalogo generale delle opere musicali, teoriche o pratiche, manoscritti o stampate, di autori vissuti fino ai primi decenni del XIX secolo, esistenti nelle biblioteche e negli archivi d'Italia. . . . Parma, Freschig. 1911–38. 14 v.

The *Associazione* catalogs are of mixed quality and completeness, but in many cases they represent the best available listings of the holdings of important Italian libraries. Their coverage is confined to music and theoretical works written or published before 1810.

1278 / (i) 1. Città di Parma. (Compilatori: Guido Gasperini, Nestore Pellicelli.) 1909–11. 295 p.
Reprint by Forni, Bologna, 1970.

1279 / (i) 2. Città di Reggio-Emilia. (Compilatore: Guido Gasperini, Nestore Pellicelli.) 1911. 24 p.
Reprint by Forni, Bologna, 1970.

1280 / (ii) Città di Bologna. (Compilatori: Alfredo Bonora, Emilio Giani.) 1910–11–38. 159 p.
Archivio della R. Accademia Filarmonica (p. 1–43).
Biblioteca dell'Avv. Raimondo Ambrosini (p. 47–66).
Archivio di S. Petronio (p. 71–159).

1281 / (iii) Città di Milano. Biblioteca Ambrosiana. (Compilatore: Gaetano Cesari.) 1910–11. 20 p. (incomplete)

1282 / (iv) 1. Città di Firenze. Biblioteca del R. Istituto Musicale. (Compilatori: Riccardo Gandolfi, Carlo Cordara.) 1910–11. 321 p.

1283 / (iv) 2. Città di Pistoia. Archivio capitolare della cattedrale. (Compilatore: Umberto de Laugier.) 1936–37. 106 p.

1284 / (v) Città di Roma. Biblioteca della R. Accademia di S. Cecilia. (Compilatore: Otello Andolfi.) 1912–13 (incomplete)

1285 / (vi) 1. Città di Venezia. (Compilatore: Giovanni Concina.) 1913–13. 382 p.
Biblioteca Querini Stampalia (p. 1–25).
Museo Correr (p. 29–113).
Pia Casa di Ricovero (p. 117–161).
R. Biblioteca di S. Marco. (Compilatori: Taddeo Wiel, A. d'Este, R. Faustini.) p. 169–382.

1286 / (vi) 2. Città di Vicenza. Biblioteca bertoliana . . . de Sebastiano Rumor; Archivio della cattedrale . . . da Primo Zanini. 1923. 48 p.

1287 / (vii) Città di Genova. R. Biblioteca Universitaria (Schedatore: Raffaele Bresciano.) n.d., 21 p.

1288 / (viii) Città di Modena. R. Biblioteca Estense. (Compilatore: Pio Lodi.) 1916–24. 561 p.
Reprint by Forni, Bologna, 1967.

1289 / (ix) Città di Ferrara. Biblioteca Comunale. (Compilatori: Emmanuele Davia, Alessandro Lombardi.) 1917. 40 p.

1290 / (x) 1. Città di Napoli. Archivio dell'Oratorio dei Filippini. (Compilatore: Salvatore di Giacomo.) 1918. 108 p.

1291 / (x) 2. Città di Napoli. Biblioteca del R. Conservatorio di S. Pietro a Majella. (Compilatori: Guido Gasperini, Franca Gallo.) 1918–34. 696 p.

1292 / (xi) Città di Assisi. Biblioteca comunale. (Compilatore: Francesco Pennacchi.) 1921. 45 p.

1293 / (xii) Città di Torino. R. Biblioteca Nazionale. (Compilatori: Attilio Cimbro, Alberto Gentili.) 1928. 38 p.

1294 / (xiii) Biblioteche e archivi dell città di Pisa. (Compilatore: Pietro Pecchiai.) 1932–35. 90 p.

1295 / (xiv) Città di Verona. Biblioteca della Soc. Accademica Filarmonica di Verona. Fondo musicale antico. (Compilatore: Giuseppe Turrini.) 1935–36. 54 p.

1296 / **Rubsamen, Walter H.** "Music research in Italian libraries." In Notes, · 6 (1948–49), p. 220–33; 543–69; 8 (1950–51), p. 70–89, 513.
A narrative account of the author's experiences working in Italian libraries shortly after World War II. Contains useful inventories, partially thematic, of manuscripts of early music in Italian libraries.

1297 / **Sartori, Claudio.** "Italian music libraries." In Fontes artis musicae, 18 (1971), p. 93–157.
An issue of Fontes devoted primarily to the description of Italian

music libraries and their resources; preceded by an illuminating discussion, in Italian, English, and German, of the general situation.

1298 / **Smijers, Albert.** "Vijftiende en zestiende eeuwsche muziek handschriften in Italie met werken van Nederlandsche componisten." In *Tijdschrift der Vereeniging voor Nederl. Muziekgeschiedenis,* 14 (1935), p. 165–81.

Describes a card file of compositions by Netherland composers of the 15th and 16th centuries in 50 manuscripts in Italian libraries. By means of collation, the author has been able to clarify numerous misattributions and identify anonymous works in these sources.

JENA, GERMANY

1299 / **Universitätsbibliothek.** Die geistlichen Musikhandschriften der Universitätsbibliothek Jena, von Karl Erich Roediger. Jena, Frommannsche Buchhandlung Walter Biedermann, 1935. 2 v.
Vol. 1: *Textband.* Vol. 2: *Notenverzeichnis.*

Primarily a source study with inventories of 18 choirbooks containing music of the Burgundian-Netherland repertory in the University Library at Jena. Vol. 1 treats the sources and their contents, with indexes of liturgical settings, of cantus fermi, of composers. Vol. 2 is a thematic catalog of the choirbooks. Vol. 1, p. 111–14: a listing of sixty-three 16th-century prints in the Jena library.

JONKÖPING, SWEDEN

1300 / **Ruuth, Gustaf.** Katalog over aldere musikalier i Per Brahegymnasiet i Jonköping. (Catalog of the music collection in Per Brahegymnasiet, Jonköping.) Stockholm, Svenskt Musikhistoriskt Arkov, 1971. 131 p. (Musik i Sverige, 2.)

A collection of 18th- and 19th-century music reflecting the repertoires of local musicians.

KALININGRAD, U.S.S.R. (formerly KÖNIGSBERG, GERMANY.)

1301 / **Staats- und Universitäts-Bibliothek. Bibliotheca Gottholdiana.** Die musikalischen Schätze der Königlichen- und Universitäts-Bibliothek zu Königsberg in Preussen. Aus dem Nachlasse Friedrich August Gottholds. Ein Beitrag zur Geschichte und Theorie der Tonkunst, von Joseph Müller. Im Anhang: Joseph Müller-Blattau, Die musikalischen Schätze der Staats- und Universitäts-Bibliothek zu Königsberg in Preussen." Hildesheim and New York, Georg Olms, 1971. 731 p.

Reprint of the edition originally published by Adolph Marcus, Bonn, 1870. The article by Müller-Blattau was published in the *Zeitschrift für Musikwissenschaft*, 6 (1924), p. 215–39.

An important collection of 55,000 volumes, strong in 17th-century church music, in print and in manuscript; also vocal music from the 16th to the 19th centuries. Works by various Königsberger Kapellmeister such as Eccard, Stobaeus, Sebastini. Also numerous first editions of Beethoven, Haydn, Mozart.

KASSEL, GERMANY

1302 / **Deutsches Musikgeschichtliches Archiv.** Katalog der Filmsammlung. Zusammengestellt und bearbeitet von Harald Heckmann. Band I, Nr. 1– . Kassel, Bärenreiter, 1955– .

Title varies: Nr. 1, *Mitteilungen und Katalog.* . . .

A series of lists documenting the holdings of a microfilm archive of primary source materials for the study of German music history. Includes manuscripts and early printed books. For a description of this project and its catalogs, see Harald Heckmann, "Archive of German music history," in *Notes*, 16 (1958), p. 35–39.

1303 / **Landesbibliothek.** Übersichtlicher Katalog der ständischen Landesbibliothek zu Cassel. Bearbeitet von Carl Israël. Cassel, A. Freyschmidt, 1881. 78 p.

Works from the 16th and 17th centuries, both manuscripts and printed books. Rich in German and Italian church and chamber music. An unpublished catalog by Wilhelm Lange, available in Kassel, supplements the coverage supplied by Israël's work.

KIEL, GERMANY

1304 / **Hortschansky, Klaus.** Katalog der Kieler Musiksammlungen: die Notendrucke, Handschriften, Libretti und Bücher über Musik aus der Zeit bis 1830. Kassel, Bärenreiter, 1963. 270 p. (Kieler Schriften zur Musikwissenschaft, 14.)

A catalog of the music in three libraries in Kiel: the Schleswig-

Holsteinische Landesbibliothek; Bibliothek des Musikwissenschaftlichen Instituts des Universität; Universitätsbibliothek.
Review by Donald W. Krummel in *Notes*, 21 (1963–64), p. 129–31.

KÖNIGSBERG, GERMANY. See KALININGRAD, U.S.S.R.

KRAKOW, POLAND

1305 / **Uniwersytet Jagielloński. Bibljoteka.** Ksiazki o muzyce w Bibljotece Jagielloński. Kraków, 1924–38. 3 v.
At head of title: Józef Reiss.

KREMSMÜNSTER, AUSTRIA

1306 / **Benediktiner-Stift Kremsmünster. Bibliothek.** Die Lautentabulaturen des Stiftes Kremsmünster. Thematischer Katalog. By Rudolf Flotzinger. Wien, Hermann Böhlaus, 1965. 274 p. (Tabulae musicae austriacae, 2.)
Describes and inventories a group of 9 manuscripts and two early prints of lute music in the library of the Benedictine Abbey at Kremsmünster.
Review by Hans Radke in *Die Musikforschung*, 21 (1968), p. 242-44.

ŁAŃCUT, POLAND

1307 / **Biblioteka Muzyczna Zamku w łańcucie.** Katalog. By Krzysztof Bieganski. Kraków, Polskie Wydawnictwo Muzyczne, 1968. 430 p.
A library of some 2,637 items, strong in late-18th- and early-19th-century music. Broadly classified as to vocal and instrumental music, theory and didactic works, with very specific subdivisions. Index of composers, of arrangers, of publishers (listed by place), ballets, operas, first-line index of texts.

LAUSANNE, SWITZERLAND

1308 / **Vaud. Bibliothèque Cantonale et Universitaire.** Inventaire du fonds musical François Olivier, par Jean Louis Matthey. Lausanne, 1971. 69 p. (Its Inventaire des fonds manuscrits, 2.)

LEGNICA, POLAND (formerly LIEGNITZ, GERMANY)

1309 / **Ritter-Akademie.** "Katalog der in der Kgl. Ritter-Akademie zu Liegnitz gedruckten und handschriftlichen Musikalien nebst den hymnologischen und musikalisch-theoretischen Werken." By Robert Eitner. In *Monatshefte für Musikgeschichte*, 1 (1869), p. 25–39, 50–56, 70–76 (incomplete).

1310 / **Ritter-Akademie.** Die Musik-handschriften der Königl. Ritter-Akademie zu Liegnitz. Verzeichnet von Ernst Pfudel. Leipzig, Breitkopf & Härtel, 1886–89. 74 p. (Monatshefte für Musikgeschichte. Beilage. Jahrgang 18 u. 21.)

LEIPZIG, GERMANY

1311 / **Musikbibliothek der Stadt Leipzig.** Erst und Frühdrucke von Robert Schumann in der Musikbibliothek Leipzig. Leipzig, 1960. 64 p. (Bibliographische Veröffenlichungen der Musikbibliothek der Stadt Leipzig.)

The exhibition also included pictures, autographs, and literature on Robert Schumann.

1312 / **Musikbibliothek der Stadt Leipzig.** Handschriften der Werke Johann Sebastian Bachs in der Musikbibliothek der Stadt Leipzig. Bearb. von Peter Krause. Leipzig, 1964. 62 p.

1313 / **Musikbibliothek der Stadt Leipzig.** Quellenwerke zur Händelforschung: Katalog. Hrsg. anlässlich der wissenschaftlichen Konferenz zur Händel-Ehrung der D.D.R., 11–19 April, 1959, in Halle. Leipzig, 1959. 29 p.

1314 / **Musikbibliothek Peters.** Katalog der Musikbibliothek Peters, neu bearb. von Rudolf Schwartz. Band I: Bücher und Schriften. Leipzig, C. F. Peters, 1910. 227 p.

An earlier edition by Emil Vogel (1894) included both books and music.

Classified catalog of a large reference library of music literature maintained by C. F. Peters before the war. All publishers represented. Many early works, although the chief strength is in 19th-century literature. Entries give place and date of publication but not publisher.

Major classes: dictionaries, periodicals, music history, biographies and monographs, instruction, instruments, aesthetics, etc.

1315 / **Breitkopf & Härtel.** Catalogo delle sinfonie, partite, overture, soli, trii, quattri e concerti per il viollino, flauto traverso, cembalo ad altri stromenti, che si trovano in manuscritto nella officina musica di Giovanni Gottlob Breitkopf in Lipsia. Leipzig, 1762–65 (six parts). *Supplemento* I–XVI (1766–87).

Reprint by Dover Publications, New York, with an introduction by Barry S. Brook (1966).

An 18th-century thematic catalog of great importance. Chiefly instrumental music, but some vocal, from the archives of Breitkopf & Härtel. Useful in tracing or identifying works of the period.

1316 / **Breitkopf & Härtel.** Katalog des Archive von Breitkopf & Härtel, Leipzig, im Auftrage der Firma. Hrsg. von Wilhelm Hitzig. Leipzig, Breitkopf & Härtel, 1925–26. 2 v. in 1.

1. Musik-Autographe; 2. Briefe.

348 autograph scores from Handel to Hindemith, fully described, with a composer index. Autograph letters are limited to persons born before 1780. Separate index to letters.

LENINGRAD, U.S.S.R.

1317 / **Golubovskiĭ, I. V.** Muzyakl'nyĭ Leningrad. Leningrad, Gosudarstvennoe Muzykalnoe Izdatel'stvo. 1958.

"Biblioteki i muzei," p. 351–411.

Describes in general terms the musical content of 14 libraries, 2 record libraries, and 12 museums. Lists manuscripts of Russian composers and mentions a few examples of Western manuscripts and early books in various collections. Details as to organization, cataloging, circulation, etc.

LIÈGE, BELGIUM

1318 / **Conservatoire Royal de Musique. Fonds Terry.** Catalogue de la Bibliothèque du Conservatoire Royal de Musique de Liège. Par Eugène Monseur. Fonds Terry: Musique dramatique. Liège, Conservatoire Royal, 1960. 75 p.

A second volume covers "Musique instrumentale." 51 p.

The Terry collection was acquired by the Liège Conservatory in 1882. The dramatic works stem chiefly from the period 1780 to 1880. Broadly classified as to full or vocal scores and by language of the libretto: French or foreign. The instrumental music is late-18th- or early-19th-century material, both printed and in manuscript.

LIEGNITZ, GERMANY

See LEGNICA, POLAND

LILLE, FRANCE

1319 / **Bibliothèque de Lille.** Catalogue des ouvrages sur la musique et des compositions musicales de la Bibliothèque de Lille. Lille, Imprimerie de Lefebvre-Ducrocq, 1879. 752 p.

2,721 items. The collection is particularly rich in late-18th- and early-19th-century French operas, which exist here in complete sets of performance materials. Also a large collection of symphonies, overtures, chamber music.

LISBON, PORTUGAL

1320 / **Biblioteca da Ajuda.** Catálogo de música manuscrita . . . Elaborado sob a direcçao de Mariana Amélia Machado Santos, directora da biblioteca. Lisboa, 1958–63. 6 v.

A collection of manuscripts, 3,617 items, entered alphabetically by composer and running consecutively through the six volumes. The collection is strong in 18th- and early-19th-century music, particularly opera.

1321 / **Library of João IV, King of Portugal.** Primeira parte do index de livraria de musica do muyto alto, e poderoso Rey Dom João o IV . . . Por ordem de sua Mag. por Paulo Crasbeck. Anno 1649. (Edited by J. de Vasconcellos. Porto, 1874–76.) 525 p.

Reprinting of a catalog, compiled in 1649 by Paul Crasbeck, for the royal library in Lisbon, which was destroyed in the earthquake of 1755. The catalog, although of a nonexistent collection, remains an important bibliographical tool for the study of early Spanish and Portuguese music.

LIVERPOOL, ENGLAND

1322 / **Public Library.** Catalogue of the music library. Liverpool, Central Public Libraries, 1954. 572 p.

Supersedes an earlier catalog of the same type, 1933.

About 45,000 entries for books and music published for the most part after 1800.

LONDON, ENGLAND

British Broadcasting Corporation. Central Music Library. See no. 801.

1323 / **British Museum.** Beethoven and England: an account of sources in the British Museum. By Pamela J. Willetts. London, The Trustees of the British Museum, 1970. 76 p. 16 plates.

Review by William Drabkin in *Notes*, 28 (1972), p. 692–94.

1324 / **British Museum.** "Early Dutch librettos and plays with music in the British Museum," By Alfred Loewenberg. In *The journal of documentation*, 2 (March 1947), 30 p.

Catalog of 97 Dutch librettos of the 17th and 18th centuries. The list was projected as the first installment of a complete bibliography of librettos in the Museum, a project never carried out.

1325 / **British Museum.** Four hundred years of music printing. By A. Hyatt King. London, Trustees of the British Museum, 1954. 48 p.

An exhibition catalog. Also entered as no. 1674.

1326 / **British Museum.** Henry Purcell, 1659—1695; George Fredric Handel, 1685–1759; catalogue of a commemorative exhibition, May-August 1959. London, Published by the Trustees, 1959. 47 p.

66 items related to Purcell, 180 to Handel. Introduction; annotations; eight full-page plates.

1327 / **British Museum.** Mozart in the British Museum. London, Published for the Trustees, 1956. 27 p. 12 plates.

Catalog of an exhibition of 196 prints, autographs, early editions, etc., drawn from various collections in the British Museum, including the Department of Prints and Drawings, the Burney collection, Maps, Hirsch, and Zweig collections.

1328 / **British Museum. Department of Manuscripts.** Catalogue of manuscript music in the British Museum, by A. Hughes-Hughes. London, 1906–1909. 3 v.

Reprint of the first edition, London, 1964.

Vol. 1: sacred vocal music. Vol. 2: secular vocal music. Vol. 3: instrumental music, treatises, etc.

Entries are classified by genre or form, which means that the contents of the manuscripts are often separated and distributed through the three volumes. Author indexes; title, first-line index of songs.

1329 / **British Museum. Department of Manuscripts.** Handlist of music manuscripts acquired 1908–67. By Pamela J. Willetts, Assistant Keeper, Department of Manuscripts. London, Published by the Trustees of the British Museum, 1970. 112 p.

This handlist supplements the Hughes-Hughes *Catalogue of manuscript music* (above).

Covers *Additional Mss, Egerton Mss*, music Mss on loan to the Department of Manuscripts, and music Mss preserved with printed collections in the Department of Printed Books. Index of names.

Review by Gordon Dodd in *Cheyls, journal of the Viola da Gamba Society*, 2 (1970), p. 41–42. By J. A. Westrup in *Music & letters*, 52 (1971), p. 184–85.

1330 / **British Museum. Department of Printed Books.** Catalogue of music. Accessions, Vol. 1–   . London, British Museum, 1884–   .

An annual publication compiled from the printing catalog slips. It is ordinarily reserved for departmental use in the British Museum, but there are copies in the New York Public Library and the Library Congress. Occasional volumes of special bibliographical interest, like the Paul Hirsch collection, have been given wider distribution. See nos. 1333, 1334.

1331 / **British Museum. Department of Printed Books.** Catalogue of printed music published between 1487 and 1800 now in the British Museum, by W. Barclay Squire. London, Printed by order of the Trustees, 1912. 2 v.

Reprint by Kraus, 1969.

First Supplement, 34 p., bound in. *Second supplement*, by W. C. Smith. Cambridge Univ. Press, 1940. 85 p.

Includes early music of all countries, but particularly rich in British sources. Early theory and some literary works on music included. Brief entries with dates, or estimated dates, of publication.

1332 / British Museum. Department of Printed Books. Hand-list of music published in some British and foreign periodicals between 1787 and 1848, now in the British Museum. London, Trustees of the British Museum, 1962. 80 p.

Indexes the music, chiefly songs, in 12 periodicals. 1,855 entries arranged by composer. Printed from slips prepared for entry in the British Museum catalog.

This item also appears as no. 1046.

Review by Richard Schaal in *Die Musikforschung*, 17 (1964), p. 423.

1333 / British Museum. Department of Printed Books. Hirsch Music Library. Books in the Hirsch Library, with supplementary list of music. London, Trustees of the British Museum, 1959. 542 p. (Catalogue of printed books in the British Museum. Accessions, 3rd ser., Pt. 291B.)

A catalog of over 11,500 books on music, acquired by the British Museum in 1946 as part of the Paul Hirsch library. Brief entries printed from slips prepared for the Museum catalog.

Review by Richard S. Hill in *Notes*, 17 (1960), p. 225–27.

See also no. 1559 under "Catalogs of Private Collections."

1334 / British Museum. Department of Printed Books. Hirsch Music Library. Music in the Hirsch Library. London, Trustees of the British Museum, 1951. 438 p. (Catalogue of printed music in the British Museum, Accessions, Pt. 53.)

About 9,000 entries listed in two sections: "Music printed before 1800," p. 1–112; "Music printed since 1800," p. 113 to end.

See also the "Supplementary list of music" printed in the catalog of *Books in the Hirsch Library*, above.

Review by Vincent Duckles in *Notes*, 10 (1952), p. 281–82.

See also no. 1559 under "Catalogs of Private Collections."

1335 / British Museum. King's Music Library. Catalogue of an exhibition of music held in the King's Library, October 1953. London, 1953. 52 p.

1336 / **British Museum. King's Music Library.** Catalogue of the King's Music Library, by William Barclay Squire and Hilda Andrews. London, Printed by order of the Trustees, 1927–29. 3 v.

Part I: the Handel manuscripts, by William Barclay Squire, 143 p., five facsimile plates. Part II: the miscellaneous manuscripts, by Hilda Andrews, 277 p. Part III: printed music and musical literature, by William Barclay Squire, 383 p.

The King's Music Library, once on loan, is now part of the permanent collection of the British Museum. It is now generally referred to as the Royal Music Library.

1337 / **British Museum. Royal Music Library.** A list of manuscript and printed music available on positive microfilm. London, British Museum Photographic Service, 1968. 17 p.

A useful listing of primary source material on positive microfilm. Costs come to 9 pence per foot, with a minimum charge of 10 shillings. Lengths of film strips are noted so that estimates can be made.

1338 / **Guildhall Library. Gresham Music Library.** A catalogue of the printed books and manuscripts deposited in Guildhall Library. London, The Corporation of London. Printed by authority of The Library Committee, 1965. 93 p.

A collection made up chiefly of late 18th-century materials reflecting the collecting activity of Edward Taylor, Gresham Professor from 1837 to 1883.

The section on manuscripts was prepared by Margery Anthea Baird. Index of names.

1339 / **Historical Music Loan Exhibition, 1885.** . . . A descriptive catalogue of rare manuscripts and printed books, chiefly liturgical . . . by W. H. James Weale. London, B. Quaritch, 1886. 191 p.

An exhibition held at Albert Hall, London, June–October 1885.

Full bibliographical citations, with descriptive annotations, for 23 liturgical manuscripts, 73 liturgical books, 46 theory works, and some 56 items of early music. 14 plates.

1340 / **Musicians' Company.** An illustrated catalogue of the music loan exhibition held . . . by the Worshipful Company of Musicians at Fishmongers' Hall, June and July 1904. London, Novello, 1909. 353 p.

Includes early printed music, manuscripts, instruments, portraits, concert and theater bills, etc. Descriptive annotations; numerous plates and facsimiles.

1341 / Plainsong and Mediaeval Music Society. Catalogue of the Society's library. Nashdom Abbey, Burnham, Bucks., 1928. 39 p.

A short title catalog. Four facsimile plates. The collection is now on deposit in the Music Library of the University of London.

1342 / Royal College of Music. Catalogue of the manuscripts in the Royal College of Music, by William Barclay Squire, with additions by Rupert Erlebach. . . . (London, 1931) 568, 216 leaves (typescript).

This catalog was never published. Typewritten copies are available in the major British libraries, and the catalog may be obtained on microfilm.

1343 / Royal College of Music. Catalogue of the printed music in the library of the Royal College of Music, by William Barclay Squire. . . . London, Printed by order of the Council . . . 1909. 368 p.

This collection, rich in sources of early English music, incorporates the holdings of the Sacred Harmonic Society, below, and the library of Sir George Grove.

1344 / Sacred Harmonic Society. Catalogue of the library . . . new edition, revised and augmented. London, Published by the Society, 1872. 399 p.

First printed in 1862, with a *Supplement* in 1882.

Classified catalog of printed music, manuscript music, and musical literature. 2,923 numbered items. General index.

1345 / Westminster Abbey. Musik-katalog der Bibliothek der Westminster-Abtei in London. Angefertigt von William Barclay Squire. Leipzig, Breitkopf und Härtel, 1903. 45 p. (Beilage. Monatshefte für Musikgeschichte, Jahrgang, 35.)

Broadly classified catalog, including both printed and manuscript music, sacred and secular.

LORETO, ITALY

1346 / Santa Casa di Loreto. L'Archivio Musicale. L'Archivio musicale della Cappella Laurentana. Catalogo storico-critico. By Giovanni Tebaldini. Loreto, A cura dell'Administrazione di S. Casa, 1921. 198 p.

Printed music, 16th–18th centuries; manuscripts of the same period; an archive of manuscript scores by the Maestri della Cappella, anonymous works, etc. Full descriptions. Detailed history of the chapel. Index of composers.

LUCCA, ITALY

1347 / **Biblioteca del Seminario.** Catalogo delle musiche stampate e manoscritto del fondo antico. Ed. by Emilio Maggini. Milano, Istituto Editoriale Italiano, 1965. 405 p. (Bibliotheca musicae, 3.)

Early printed music and manuscripts from the 16th to the early 19th centuries, with a small collection of writings on music. Contents of collections and locations of other copies listed. The collection is rich in early-17th-century prints of sacred music.

1348 / **Biblioteca del Seminario.** "Il fondo di musiche a stampa della Biblioteca del Seminario di Lucca." By Claudio Sartori. In *Fontes artis musicae* (1955:2), p. 134–47.

A listing, alphabetical by composer, of the early music prints in the Seminary library, including, at the end of the list, five anthologies and three manuscripts.

1349 / **Bonaccorsi, Alfredo.** "Catalogo con notizie biografiche delle musiche dei maestri lucchesi esistenti nelle biblioteche di Lucca." In *Collectanea historiae musicae*, 2 (1957), p. 73–95.

Sources listed from three libraries in Lucca: the Seminario Arcivescovile; the Istituto Musicale "L. Boccherini"; and the Biblioteca Governativa.

1350 / **Lucca All'esposizione della Musica e del Teatro in Vienna nel 1892.** Lucca, Dalla Tipografia Giusti, 1892.

50 p.

A rare exposition catalog of music from Lucca displayed at the exposition in Vienna in 1892. 37 facsimile plates, with detailed discussions, and a brief introduction on the history of music in Lucca.

LÜBECK, GERMANY

1351 / **Stadtbibliothek.** Katalog der Musik-Sammlung auf der Stadtbibliothek zu Lübeck. Verzeichnet von Carl Stiehl. Lübeck, Druck von Gebrüder Borchers [1893], 59 p.

1352 / Stadtbibliothek. Die Musikabteilung der Lübecker Stadt-bibliothek in ihren älteren Beständen: Noten und Bücher aus der Zeit von 12. bis zum Anfang des 19. Jahrhunderts, verzeichnet von Wilhelm Stahl. Lübeck, 1931. 61 p.

1353 / Stadtbibliothek. Musik-Bücher der Lübecker Stadtbibliothek, verzeichnet von Prof. Wilhelm Stahl. Lübeck, Verlag der Lübecker Stadtbibliothek, 1927. 42 p.

Classified catalog of 19th- and 20th-century music literature.

LÜNEBURG, GERMANY

1354 / Ratsbücherei. Katalog der Musikalien der Ratsbücherei Lüneburg, von Friedrich Welter. Lippstadt, Kistner & Siegel, 1950. 332 p.

Music prints and manuscripts, theory and practical music to 1850, holdings in 17th- and 18th-century instrumental music, particularly in the manuscript collections, which are listed separately. Numerous thematic incipits given.

LUZERN, SWITZERLAND

1355 / Theater- und Musik-Liebhabergesellschaft. Die Haydn-drucke aus dem Archiv der "Theater- und Musik- Liebhabergesellschaft zu Luzern," nebst Materialien zum Musikleben in Luzern um 1800. Von Wilhelm Jerger. Freiburg in der Schweiz, Universitätsverlag, 1959. 45 p. (Freiburger Studien zur Musikwissenschaft, 7.)

Entries for 64 early Haydn editions, with a table of concordances with the Hoboken *Thematisch-bibliographisches Werkverzeichnis* of Haydn's compositions.

MACERATA, ITALY

1356 / Biblioteca Communale. Studi sulla Biblioteca Comunale e sui tipografi di Macerata. Miscellanea a cura di Aldo Adversi. Casa di Risparmio della Provincia de Macerata, 1966.

P. 63–77: "La raccolta musicale ed in particulare gli spartiti autografi della Cappella del Duomo di Macerata nella Biblioteca Comunale Mozzi-Borgetti," by Lepanto de Angelis.

320

P. 79–122: "Catalogo del fondo musicale fino all'anno 1800 della Biblioteca Comunale di Macerata," by Antoni Garbelatto.

A small collection comprising 22 items of early printed music, 24 of music literature, and 23 of music manuscripts.

MADRID, SPAIN

1357 / **Ayuntamiento. Biblioteca Musical Circulante.** Catálogo. Ed. ilus. Madrid, Ayuntamiento, Sección de Cultura e información, 1946. 610 p.

Apéndice 1, 1954. 213 p.

Music arranged in 16 classes, by instrument and form. Class T, "Bibliografia," contains books on music almost exclusively in Spanish. No publishers or dates given for entries. Many light and popular works. No index.

1358 / **Biblioteca Medinaceli.** "Catalogue of the music in the Biblioteca Medinaceli, Madrid." By J. B. Trend. In *Revue hispanique*, 71 (1927), p. 485–554.

"The Medinaceli library is notable for possessing almost the entire corpus of Spanish (Castilian) madrigals." 34 items fully described, with inventories of contents and biographical sketches of the composers. Appendix: musical settings of famous poets.

1359 / **Biblioteca Municipal.** Catálogo de la sección de música de la Biblioteca Municipal de Madrid. By José Subirá. Tomo primero: Teatro Menor tonadillas y sainetes. Madrid, Sección de Cultura Artes Gráficas Municipales, 1965. 394 p.

A collection of Spanish popular drama. Works are identified by text incipits.

1360 / **Biblioteca Nacional.** Catálogo músical de la Biblioteca Nacional de Madrid, por Higinio Anglés y José Subirá. Barcelona, Consejo Superior de Investigaciones Científicas, Instituto Español de Musicología, 1946–51. 3 v.

Vol. 1: Manuscritos (490 p., 27 facsimile plates). Vol. 2: Impresos: Libros litúrgicos y teóricos musicales (292 p., 12 facsimile plates). Vol. 3: Impressos: Música práctica (410 p., 13 facsimile plates).

Entries for 234 manuscripts, 285 liturgical and theoretical prints,

337 music prints. Full descriptions with bibliographical references, lists of contents.

1361 / **Biblioteca Nacional.** Esposicion de música sagrada española. Catalog de los codices, manuscritos y libros musicales expuestos por Jaime Moll Roqueta. Madrid, 1954. 41 p.

120 items. 12 facsimile plates.

1362 / **La Casa de Alba.** La música en la Casa de Alba; estudios históricos y biográficos, por José Subirá. Madrid [Establecimiento tipográfico "Sucesores de Rivadeneyra"], 1927. 374 p.

Not a catalog, but a mine of bibliographical information concerning the early music and books on music in the library of the Casa de Alba. Numerous early prints and manuscripts cited and described; 60 plates, chiefly facsimiles of bibliographical interest.

1363 / **La Casa de Alba.** "La musique de chambre espagnole et française du XVIIIe siècle dans la bibliothèque du Duc d'Alba," par José Subira, in *Revue de musicologie*, 7 (1926), p. 78–82.

1364 / **Palacio Nacional. Capilla. Archivo de Música.** Catálogo del Archivo de Música de la Real Capilla del Palacio, por Jose Garcia Marcellan. Madrid, Editorial del Patrimonio Nacional [1938], 361 p.

P. 13–142: listing of works by composer. P. 151–247: brief biographies of the composers represented. P. 249–361: classified listing of works.

MAINZ, GERMANY

1365 / **Gutenberg-Museum.** Tausend Jahre Mainzer Musik; Katalog der Ausstellung, 1957 [Text: Adam Gottron], Mainz, 1957. 32 p. (Kleiner Druck der Gutenberg-Gesellschaft, 63.)

An illustrated exhibition catalog of 138 items related to the history of music in Mainz.

1366 / **Stadtbibliothek.** "Zur Bibliographie der Musikdrucke des XV.–XVIII. Jahrhunderts der Mainzer Stadtbibliothek." By F. W. E. Roth, in *Monatshefte für Musikgeschichte*, 21 (1889), p. 25–33.

A catalog of 45 early music prints, including both theory works and practical music. Full bibliographical citations for some items, otherwise reference to citations in the catalogs of other collections.

MANCHESTER, ENGLAND

1367 / **Henry Watson Music Library.** George Frideric Handel. The Newman Flower collection in the Henry Watson Music Library. A catalogue compiled by Arthur D. Walker, with a foreword by Winton Dean. Manchester, The Manchester Public Libraries, 1972. 134 p.

1368 / **Henry Watson Music Library.** List of glees, madrigals, part-songs, etc. in the Henry Watson Music Library. Compiled by J. A. Cartledge. New York, B. Franklin, 1970. 197 p.
Reprint of the original edition of 1913.

MANNHEIM, GERMANY

1369 / **Hof- und Nationaltheater.** Archiv und Bibliothek des Grossh. Hof- und Nationaltheaters in Mannheim, 1779–1839. . . . von Dr. Friedrich Walter. Leipzig, S. Hirzel, 1899. 2 v.
Band I: Das Theater-Archiv . . . Repertorium mit vielen Auszügen aus den Akten und Briefen, Inhalts-Ausgaben, usw.
Band II: Die Theater-Bibliothek . . . Katalog der gedruckten Bücher, Manuskripte und Musikalien der älteren Periode nebst einem Repertoire der Dalbergschen Zeit.
An important collection of theater history, in which music is well represented.

MEKLENBURG-SCHWERIN. See SCHWERIN, GERMANY

MEXICO, D.F.

1370 / **Spiess, Lincoln, and Thomas Stanford.** An introduction to certain Mexican musical archives. Detroit, Information Coordinators, 1969. 185 p. (Detroit studies in music bibliography, 15.)
Review by Henry Cobos in *Notes*, 27 (1971), p. 491–92.

MILAN, ITALY

Biblioteca Ambrosiana. See no. 1281.

1371 / **Biblioteca Nazionale Braidense.** La musica nelle biblioteche milanesi. Mostra di libri e documenti, Milano, 28 Maggio–8 Guigno 1963. . . . Milano, U. Allegretto di Campi, 1963. 55 p.

An exhibition catalog compiled by Mariangela Donà.

1372 / **Biblioteca Nazionale Braidense.** "Musiche a stampa nella Biblioteca Braidense di Milano." By Mariangela Donà. In *Fontes artis musicae*, 7 (1960), p. 66–69.

Although it does not have a music collection as such, the National Library at Milan has a number of important items cataloged under "musica." This article describes some 30 such items.

1373 / **Biblioteca Trivulziana. Civica Raccolta delle Stampe.** Ritratti di musicisti ed artisti di teatro conservati nella raccolta delle stampe e dei disegni. Catalogo descrittivo. By Paolo Arrigoni e Achille Bertarelli. Milano, Tipografia del "Popolo d'Italia," 1934. 454 p. 30 plates.

Catalog of the Bertarelli collection of portraits of musicians, singers, comedians, dancers, and persons connected with the theater. Separate sections for acrobats, extemporaneous poets, child prodigies, etc. Entries give full names of subjects, descriptions of pictures, biographical information. Numerous indexes: names, places, theatrical performances, etc.

1374 / **Cappella del Duomo. Archivo.** La Cappella del Duomo di Milano. Catalogo delle musiche dell'archivio. By Claudio Sàrtori. Milano, a cura dell Ven. Fabbrica del Duomo, 1957. 366 p.

The archive, established in 1394, contains important manuscript holdings of the 15th century and sacred vocal works to the 19th. Separate sections for manuscripts and printed music. Brief entries; contents for anthologies.

1375 / **Conservatorio di Musica "Giuseppe Verdi."** Catalogo della biblioteca. Letteratura musicale e opere teoriche. Parte prima: Manoscritti e stampe fino al 1899. Milan, 1969. 151 p. (Distributed by Casa Editrice Leo S. Olschki, Florence.)

This and the following entry are part of a series of catalogs devoted to the holdings of the library of the Milan conservatory, edited under the supervision of Guglielmo Barblan. This volume lists 2,458 writings on music published before 1900. Index of subjects, of editors, compilers, translators.

Review by Susan Summer in *Notes*, 27 (1971), p. 730–31.

1376 / **Conservatorio di Musica "Giuseppe Verdi."** Catalogo della biblioteca . . . Fondi speciali I: Musiche della Cappella di Santa Barbara in Mantova. Schede compilate da Gilda Grigolato. Prefazione di Guglielmo Barblan. Indici a cura di Agostina Zecca Laterza. Milan, 1972. 530 p.

The collection of the Cappella di Santa Barbara in Mantua has been incorporated into the collection of the Milan conservatory.

1377 / **Conservatorio di Musica "Giuseppe Verdi."** Indice generale dell'Archivio Musicale Noseda; compilato dal Prof. Eugenio de' Guarinoni . . . con una breve biografia del fondatore e con alcuni cenni intorno all'archivio stesso ed alla Biblioteca del R. Conservatorio di musica di Milano. Milano, E. Reggiani, 1898. 419 p.

First published in the *Anuario* of the Milan conservatory. 1889–96. 10,253 titles.

The strength of the collection is centered in late-18th- and early-19th-century music. Preceded by a brief historical introduction. Index of composers represented in autographs, and of operas in full score.

1378 / **Museo Teatrale alla Scala.** Catalogo del Museo teatrale alla Scala. Edito a cura del consiglio direttivo; compilato da Stefano Vittadini. . . . Milano, E. Bestetti, 1940. 401 p.

An illustrated catalog of the musical-theatrical collection at La Scala. Bibliography: p. 375–93.

1379 / **Parigi, Luigi.** La musica nelle gallerie di Milano. Con 21 illustrazioni in tavole fuori testo. Milano, Perrella, 1935. 71 p.

Paintings with musical subjects in the art galleries of Milan. Descriptions of each work and its subject matter. 21 plates.

MODENA, ITALY

1380 / **Archivio di Stato.** "Repertorio dei libri musicali di S.A.S. Francesco II d'Este nell'archivio di Stato di Modena." By E. J. Luin. In *La Bibliofilia*, 38 (1936), p. 419–45.

A catalog compiled in the late 17th century of the holdings of the music library of Francesco II d'Este. Much of the material has been incorporated into the collection of the Biblioteca Estense in Modena. Rich in late-17th-century opera, oratorios, cantatas, etc. Both manuscripts and prints.

Biblioteca Estense. See also no. 1288.

1381 / **Biblioteca Estense.** "Bibliografia delle stampe musicali della R. Biblioteca Estense." By Vittorio Finzi. In *Rivista delle biblioteche* (1892–95). v. 3, p. 77–89, 107–14, 162–76; v. 4, p. 16–28, 174–85; v. 5, p. 48–64, 89–142.

Full descriptions of 321 works. Index.

MONTECASSINO, ITALY

1382 / **Archivio Musicale.** "L'Archivio musicale di Montecassino." By Eduardo Dagnino. In *Casinensia*: miscellanea di studi Cassinesi publicati in occasione del XIV centenario della fondazione della Badia di Montecassino. V. 1 (1929), p. 273–96.

A summary account of the music holdings of the Montecassino archive, a collection of some 1,100 items, including more than 100 full scores of 18th-century operas, oratorios, etc. Four plates illustrating rarities from the collection.

1383 / **Archivio Musicale.** "I manoscritti musicali gregoriani dell'archivio di Montecassino." By Paolo M. Ferretti. In *Casinensia*: miscellanea di studi Cassinesi . . . v. 1 (1929), p. 187–203.

Detailed descriptions of 11 manuscripts of Gregorian chant in the Montecassino archive. The 11th consists of a group of fragments from various sources. Two facsimile plates.

MONTSERRAT, SPAIN

1384 / **Lenaerts, René B.** "Niederländische polyphone Musik in der Bibliothek von Montserrat." In *Festschrift Joseph Schmidt Gorg zum 60. Geburtstag.* Bonn, Beethovenhaus, 1957. P. 196–201.

Describes six manuscripts containing Netherlands polyphony: manuscript numbers 765, 766, 769, 771, 772, 778.

1385 / **Publichnaĭa Biblioteka. Otdel Rukopiseĭ.** Sobraniia D. V. Razumovskogo i V. F. Odoevskogo. Arkhiv D. V. Razumovskogo. Opisaniĭa pod radaktsiei I. M. Kudrĭavtseva. Moskva, 1960. 261 p.

Catalog of manuscripts, 15th–19th centuries, primarily of church music in various notations. The Razumovskii collection contains 135 manuscripts, the Odoevskii, 35. Description of biographical material, papers, letters, etc. in the Razumovskii archive. Chronological index; index of names and titles.

Biblioteca Antonnio Venturi. . . . See no. 1442.

1386 / **Bischöflichen Priesterseminars. Santini Bibliothek.** Kirchenmusikalische Schätze der Bibliothek des Abbate Fortunato Santini, ein Beitrag zur Geschichte des katholischen Kirchenmusik in Italien. By Joseph Killing. Düsseldorf, L. Schwann, 1910. 516 p.

A study based on the material in the Santini collection, a library of early music scored from the original partbooks by Fortunate Santini (1778–1862) and acquired about 1856 by the University Library at Münster.

P. 455–67: "Verzeichnis der in der Bibliothek Santini enthaltenen Druckwerke." P. 469–516: "Verzeichnis von Musikwerken die in der Santinischen Bibliothek als Handschriften enthalten sind."

1387 / **Bischöflichen Priesterseminars. Santini Bibliothek.** "Verzeichnis der kirchenmusikalische Werke der Santinischen Sammlung." in *Kirchenmusikalischen Jahrbuch*, 26–33 (1931–1938).

An incomplete inventory of the sacred music in the Santini collection.

1388 / **Universitätsbibliothek.** Die musikalischen Schätze der Santinischen Sammlung. Führer durch die Ausstellung der Universitäts-Bibliothek. . . . Münster, Westfälische Vereinsdruckerei, 1929. 32 p.

Exhibition catalog prepared by K. G. Fellerer.

MUNICH, GERMANY

1389 / **Bayerische Staatsbibliothek.** "Die Augsburger Bibliothek Herwart und ihre Lautentabulaturen. Ein Musikbestand der Bayerischen Staatsbibliothek aus dem 16. Jahrhundert," by Marie Louise Martinez-Göllner. *In Fontes artis musicae* (Januar–Juni, 1969) p. 29–48.

A study focused primarily on 15 manuscripts of lute tablature acquired in 1586 by the Bavarian State Library with the purchase of the private library of Johann Heinrich Herwart of Angsburg. The article includes publication of a 16th-century catalog of printed instrumental music in the Herwart collection.

1390 / **Bayerische Staatsbibliothek.** Die musikalischen Handschriften der K. Hof- und Staatsbibliothek in München, beschrieben von Jul. Jos. Maier. Erster Theil: Die Handschriften bis zum Ende des XVII. Jahrhunderts. München, in Commission der Palm'schen Hofbuchhandlung, 1879. 176 p.

278 items, chiefly anthologies, containing about 6,380 pieces of music. One of the richest collections of 16th-century music. A notable collection of 74 choirbooks belonging to the original Bavarian court chapel. "Inhalts Verzeichnis" of anonymous and attributed works.

1391 / **Städtische Musikbücherei.** Kataloge der städtischen Musikbücherei München . . . Erster Band: Klavier. Bearbeitet von Bibliotheksrat Dr. Willy Krienitz. München, 1931. 407 p.

Catalog of the holdings in keyboard music of one of the major public music libraries in Germany. Some 40,000 items, classified. Includes works for piano solo, duet, and two pianos. Index of names.

1392 / **Theatermuseum.** "Die vor 1801 gedruckten Libretti des Theatermuseums München." By Richard Schaal. In *Die Musikforschung,* 10 (1957), p. 388–96, 487–94; 11 (1958), p. 54–69, 168–77, 321–36, 462–77; 12 (1959), p. 60–75, 161–77, 299–306, 454–61; 13 (1960), p. 38–46, 164–72, 299–306, 441–48; 14 (1961), p. 36–43, 166–83.

Also published separately by Bärenreiter, Kassel, 1962.

983 librettos listed alphabetically by title, with date and place of first performance, name of composer, etc.

1393 / **Universitätsbibliothek.** Die Musikhandschriften der Universitätsbibliothek München. Beschrieben von Clytus Gottwald. Wiesbaden, Harrassowitz, 1968. 127 p. (Die Handschriften der Universitätsbibliothek München, 2.)

NAPLES, ITALY

1394 / **Biblioteca Nazionale.** I codici notate della Biblioteca Nazionale di Napoli. By Raffaele Arnese. Firenze, Leo S. Olschki, 1967. 257 p. (Biblioteca di bibliografia Italiano, 47.)

Concerned chiefly with liturgical manuscripts in which musical notation is present, but also including a few sources in mensural notation. Indexes of types of notation, types of script, chronological arrangement, titles, and names. Bibliography, p. 127–47.

Review by Ewald Jammers in *Die Musikforschung,* 21 (1968), p. 504–506.

1395 / **Biblioteca Nazionale.** "Il fondo musicale cinquecentesco della Biblioteca Nazionale di Napoli." By Anna Mondolfo. In *Collectanea historiae musicae,* 2 (1957), p. 277–90.

Describes fifty-one 16th-century works.

Conservatorio di Musica S. Pietro a Majella.
See no. 1291.

1396 / **Conservatorio di Musica S. Pietro a Majella.** "La biblioteca del Conservatorio di Napoli." In *Accademie e bibliotheche d'Italia,* 38 (1970), p. 286–92.

A brief narrative account stressing the important holdings of the library, particularly works related to the opera and cantata and documents of the Bellini-Donizetti period.

1397 / **Conservatorio di Musica S. Pietro a Majella.** Mostra autografi musicali della scuola napoletana . . . Settembre–Ottobre 1936. Napoli, Confederazione Fascista dei Professionisti e degli Artisti, 1936. 58 p.

An exhibition catalog of musical autographs and portraits of musicians of the Neapolitan school.

1398 / **Conservatorio di Musica S. Pietro a Majella.** "Mozart alla Biblioteca del Conservatorio di Napoli." By Francesco Bossarelli. In *Analecta musicologia,* 5 (1968), p. 248–66; 7 (1969), p. 190–212.

A bibliography of the Mozart holdings of the Naples conservatory.

1399 / **Conservatorio di Musica S. Pietro a Majella.** Il Museo storico musicale di S. Pietro a Majella. Napoli, R. Stabilimento Tipografico Francesco Giannini et Figli, 1930. 153 p.

A collection of musicians' portraits, busts, autographs, musical instruments, medals, and photographs. 734 items. Special archives of materials related to Vincenzo Bellini and Giuseppe Martucci.

Oratorio dei Filippini. Archivo. See no. 1290.

NEW HAVEN, CONNECTICUT

1400 / **Yale University School of Music. Library.** A temporary mimeographed catalog of the music manuscripts and related materials of Charles Edward Ives. . . . Compiled by John Kirkpatrick in 1954–60. New Haven, Conn., Yale School of Music, 1960. 279 p. (typescript)

NEW YORK CITY, NEW YORK

1401 / **Bartók Archives.** The Béla Bartók archives, history and catalogue. By Victor Bator. New York, Bartók Archives Publication, 1963. 39 p.

Description of the Archives and of their founding, with summary inventories of materials in such categories as letters, books, articles, clippings, concert programs, printed music, photographs, and recordings as well as autograph manuscripts.

This collection has been virtually inaccessible in recent years because of legal complications involving its ownership. Two reports by Fritz A. Kuttner, published in *Die Musikforschung,* will help to clarify its present status: (1) "Der Katalog des Bartók-Archives in New York City," 21 (1969), p. 61–63, and (2) "Das Bartók-Archiv in New York City, ein Nachtrag," 22 (1969), p. 75–76.

1402 / **New York Public Library. Music Division.** Catalogue of Jos. W. Drexel's musical library. Part I: Musical writings. Philadelphia, King and Baird, 1869. 48 p.

This catalog contains only 1,536 of the more than 6,000 items in the Drexel collection. Especially rich in English printed music and manuscripts in the 16th, 17th, and 18th centuries. The collection contains numerous items from the library of Edward F. Rimbault, English antiquarian and collector.

1403 / **New York Public Library. Music Division.** Dictionary catalog of the music collection, New York Public Library. Boston, G. K. Hall, 1965. 33 v.
Supplement 1, 1966.
Duplication by photo-offset of a catalog of some 522,000 cards, 21 cards per page, comprising the holdings of the Music Division of the New York Public Library. Books, pamphlets, and musical scores in one alphabet. The catalog includes numerous analytics for articles in Festschriften, periodicals, etc. A comprehensive reference tool based on the resources of one of the great music libraries of the United States.

1404 / **New York Public Library. Music Division.** "The Music Division of the New York Public Library," [by Frank C. Campbell] in *Fontes artis musicae* (Juli-Dezember 1969) p. 112–19.

General account of the history, holdings, special indexes, and collections of one of America's richest music libraries.

1405 / **New York Public Library. Music Division.** "Musicalia in der New York Public Library, mitgeteilt von Hugo Botstiber." In *Sammelbände der Internationalen Musikgesellschaft*, 4 (1902–1903), p. 738–50.

A summary account of some of the more interesting and important items in the Drexel collection. Gives a full inventory of the "Sambrook MS," with brief entries for other manuscripts and early printed books. Includes a listing of musicians' autographs.

1406 / **New York Public Library. Vincent Astor Gallery.** Musical treasures in American libraries. An exhibition in the Vincent Astor Gallery. Reprinted from the *Bulletin* of the New York Public Library, vol. 72 (Spring 1968), 16 p.

33 items fully described, illustrated in four full-page plates.

1407 / **The Pierpoint Morgan Library.** The Mary Flager Cary music collection: printed books and music, manuscripts, autograph letters, documents, portraits. New York, The Pierpoint Morgan Library, 1970. 108 p. 49 plates.

Introduction signed by Charles Ryskamp, Director.

Collection comprises 64 printed books and 216 manuscripts as well as a large list of autograph letters and 18 items under "portraits and miscellany."

Compiled by Otto E. Albrecht (manuscripts), Herbert Cahoon (autograph letters and documents), and Douglas C. Ewing (printed books, portraits, and memorabilia).

Review by Susan T. Sommer in *Notes*, 28 (1972), p. 681–82.

OBERLIN, OHIO

1408 / **Oberlin College. Conservatory of Music. Mary M. Vial Music Library.** Mr. and Mrs. C. W. Best collection of autographs in the Mary M. Vial Music Library of the Oberlin College Conservatory of Music. Oberlin, Ohio, Oberlin College Library, 1967. 55 p.

A collection of 110 autograph letters, signed photographs, etc., chiefly related to 19th- and early-20th-century musicians. Partial translations given for many of the documents. 10 facsimile plates.

OXFORD, ENGLAND

1409 / **University. Bodleian Library.** [Catalog, in manuscript, of the music manuscripts in the Bodleian Library, with a list of books given to the University by Dr. Heather.] 1 v., unpaged.

An unpublished, handwritten catalog made in the early 19th century, available for study in the Bodleian Library. Gives contents for some 303 "Music School" manuscripts dating from the early 17th century.

1410 / **University. Bodleian Library.** English music, guide to an exhibition held in 1955. Oxford, Bodleian Library, 1955. 40 p.

An exhibition catalog of 101 items, well annotated. 8 full page plates. Informative introduction, unsigned. The exhibition covers English music from the 11th to the 20th century, although early music is stressed.

1411 / **University. Bodleian Library.** Manuscripts of Byzantine chant in Oxford [by] N. G. Wilson and D. I. Stefanovic. Oxford, Bodleian Library, 1963. 56 p.

An exhibition catalog. Facsimiles. Bibliography, p. 5–6.

1412 / **University. Bodleian Library.** Medieval polyphony in the Bodleian Library, by Dom Anselm Hughes. Oxford, Bodleian Library, 1951. 63 p.

Descriptions and inventories of contents for 51 manuscripts and fragments in the Bodleian. Index of text incipits and of composers and places of origin.

Review by Manfred Bukofzer in *JAMS*, 5 (1952), p. 53–65.

1413 / **University. Bodleian Library.** "Seventeenth-century Italian instrumental music in the Bodleian Library," by Denis Stevens. In *Acta M*, 26 (1954), p. 67–74.

The author lists some 85 sets of parts of early Italian instrumental music in the Bodleian, by composer in alphabetical order, with essential bibliographical information. In an article in *Collectanea historiae musicae*, 2 (1957), p. 401–12, he discusses nine unica from the above collection.

1414 / **University. Christ Church College.** Catalogue of music [manuscripts] in the Library of Christ Church, Oxford, by G. E. P. Arkwright. London, Oxford Univ. Press, 1915–23.

Part I: Works of ascertained authorship, 1915. 128 p. Reprint of the 1915 volume by S. R. Publishers, East Ardsley, England, 1971, with a preface by T. B. Strong. Part II: 1: Manuscript works of unknown authorship. Vocal. 1923. 182 p. Part II: 2: [Manuscripts of instrumental music of unkown authorship.] An unpublished catalog, completed in 1935, available for examination in the Christ Church College library.

1415 / **University. Christ Church College.** Catalogue of printed music published prior to 1801, now in the Library of Christ Church, Oxford. Edited by Aloys Hiff. London, Oxford Univ. Press, 1919. 76 p.

A collection rich in Italian and English music of the 16th and 17th centuries. Alphabetical arrangement by composer, with analytics for collections.

PADUA, ITALY

1416 / **Basilica di San'Antonio. Archivo Musicale.** . . . L'Archivo musicale della Cappella Antoniana in Padova; illustrazione storico-critico, con cinque eliotipie. Padova, Tipografia e Libreria Antoniana, 1895. 175 p.

Compiled by Giovanni Tebaldini.

P. 1–92: Historical essay on the chapel of St. Anthony. P. 93–149: partial catalog of manuscripts and prints. Complete lists of works for Vallotti, Sabbatini; thematic incipits for Tartini concertos.

1417 / **Biblioteca Capitolare.** "Codici musici della Biblioteca Capitolare di Padova." [By Antonio Garbelotti.] In *Revista musicale italiana*, 53 (1951), p. 289–314; 54 (1952), p. 218–30.

A summary description of the manuscript holdings of the Biblioteca Capitolare in Padua. Sources discussed chronologically by centuries. Both plainchant and polyphonic manuscripts considered.

PARIS, FRANCE

1418 / **Archives Nationale. Minutier Central.** Documents du Minutier Central concernant l'histoire de la musique (1600–1650). Tome I. Comp. by Madeleine Jurgens. Préface de François Lesure. Paris, S.E.V.P.E.N., 1967. 1053 p. (Ministère des Affaires Culturelles. Direction des Archives de France. Archives Nationales.)

An organized presentation of documents related to musicians of the first half of the 17th century in the French national archives. Musicians are grouped according to their occupations: musicians of the court, of the city, instrument makers, music printers, etc. General index, p. 895–1038.

Review by Albert Cohen in *JAMS*, 22 (1969), p. 126–29; by James R. Anthony in *Notes*, 26 (1970), p. 511–13.

1419 / **Bibliothèque de L'Arsenal.** Catalogue des livres de musique (manuscrits et imprimés) de la Bibliothèque de l'Arsenal à Paris, par L. de La Laurencie . . . et A. Gastoué. Paris, E. Droz, 1936. 184 p. (Publications de la Société française de musicologie, 2. sér., t. 7.)

Manuscripts and printed music arranged alphabetically by composer, or catchword of title if anonymous, under main divisions of sacred and secular. Manuscripts from the 10th century; printed works of the 16th–18th centuries. Exceptionally rich in editions of little-known French composers of the 18th century.

1420 / **Bibliothèque Nationale.** Claude Debussy. Paris, Bibliothèque Nationale, 1962. 73 p.

An exposition catalog of 335 items celebrating the centennial of Debussy's birth. Arranged chronologically. Eight plates.

1421 / **Bibliothèque Nationale.** Frédéric Chopin. Exposition du centenaire. Paris [Bibliothèque Nationale], 1949. 82 p.

234 items, eight plates; documents arranged to parallel the chronology of the composer's life.

1422 / **Bibliothèque Nationale.** Gabriel Fauré. Paris [Bibliothèque Nationale], 1963. 16 p.

An exhibition catalog of 100 items, with a chronology of the composer's life and work.

1423 / **Bibliothèque Nationale.** Introduction a la paléographie musicale byzantine catalogue des manuscrits de musique byzantine de la Bibliothèque Nationale de Paris et des bibliothèques publiques de France. [Paris, Impressions artistiques L. M. Fortin, 1928.] 99 p. (Publications de la Société internationale de musique. Section de Paris.)

Compiled by Amédée Gastoué.

1424 / **Bibliothèque Nationale.** Jean-Philippe Rameau, 1683–1764. Paris [Bibliothèque Nationale], 1964. 100 p.

Illustrated exhibition catalog celebrating the 200th anniversary of the death of Rameau.

1425 / **Bibliothèque Nationale.** Mozart en France. Paris [Bibliothèque Nationale], 1956. 76 p.

Illustrated exhibition catalog of 234 items related to Mozart's life in France. P. 67–76: a bibliography of early French editions of Mozart's music.

1426 / **Bibliothèque Nationale.** La musique française du moyen âge à la révolution, catalogue rédigé par Amédée Gastoué [*et al.*], Paris, Édition des Bibliothèques Nationales de France, 1934. 196 p.

Illustrated catalog of 660 manuscripts, books, and works of art from major French public and private collections, displayed at the "Exposition de la musique française," 1933, in the Galérie Mazarine of the Bibliothèque Nationale.

1427 / **Bibliothèque Nationale. Department des Imprimés.** Catalogue du fonds de musique ancienne de la Bibliothèque Nationale. [By Jules Ecorcheville.] Paris, 1910–14. 8 v.
　Reprint by Da Capo Press, New York, 1972.
　Manuscripts, printed music, and theoretical and literary works on music not included in the general catalog of the library, to 1750. Partially thematic. Arranged alphabetically by composer, with collections analyzed. Brief bibliographical descriptions.

1428 / **Bibljoteka Polska.** Frédéric Chopin, George Sand et leurs amis. Exposition à la Bibliothèque Polonaise. Paris, 1937. 63 p.
　An exposition of 638 items related to Chopin, George Sand, and their circle. Includes manuscripts, letters, portraits. Illustrated.

1429 / **Bibliothèque Sainte-Geneviève.** Catalogue du fonds musical de la Bibliothèque Sainte-Geneviève de Paris. Manuscrits et imprimés. Par Madeleine Garros et Simone Wallon. Kassel, Internationale Vereinigung der Musikbibliotheken; Internationale Gesellschaft für Musikwissenschaft, 1967. 156 p. (Catalogus musicus, 4.)

1430 / **Conservatoire National de Musique et de Déclamation** . . . Catalogue bibliographique . . . par J. B. Weckerlin, bibliothécaire. Paris, Firmin-Didot et Cie., 1885. 512 p.
　Covers the period to about 1800. Includes only part of the early materials in the collection. Following a prefatory history of the library, three sections are given: early treatises, vocal music, early instrumental music of the French school.

1431 / **Conservatoire Nationale de Musique et de Déclamation. Fonds Blancheton.** . . . Inventaire critique du Fonds Blancheton. . . . Paris, E. Droz, 1930–31. 2 v. (Publications de la Société française de musicologie. 2. sér., 2: 1–2.)
　Compiled by Lionel de La Laurencie.
　The Blancheton collection consists of 27 volumes containing some 300 instrumental compositions by 104 composers. It was assembled

before 1750. Important source materials for the history of the symphony. Full descriptions, with critical and biographical notes on the composers.

1432 / **Opéra. Bibliothèque, Archives et Musée.** Bibliothèque musicale du Théâtre de l'Opéra. Catalogue historique, chronologique, anecdotique . . . rédigé par Théodore de Lajarte. Paris, Librairie des Bibliophiles, 1878. 2 v.

Reprint by Olms, Hildesheim, 1969.

A descriptive list of 594 stage works arranged in order of their first production at the Paris Opéra, 1671–1876. Classified by periods. Each period is included with a biographical section which lists composers and librettists alphabetically. Composer and title index to works in the repertoire.

PARMA, ITALY

Città di Parma. See no. 1278.

1433 / **Conservatorio di Musica "Arrigo Boito."** Biblioteche musicali in Italia: La Biblioteca del Conservatorio di Parma e un fondo di edizioni dei sec. XVI e XVII non comprese nel catalogo a stampa." [By Riccardo Allorto.] In *Fontes artis musicae*, (1955: 2), p. 147–51.

Describes a collection of 31 sets of 16th- and 17th-century partbooks acquired by the library in 1925.

1434 / **Conservatorio di Musica "Arrigo Boito."** "Osservazioni sulla Biblioteca Musicale di Parma." [By Mario Medici.] In *Avrea Parma*, 48 (May–August, 1964), p. 3–49.

Provides copius data on the library of the Conservatorio. Many of the rare manuscripts and printed books are cited in full, along with an account of the history of the institution and its administrative structure.

PHILADELPHIA, PENNSYLVANIA

1435 / **Curtis Institute of Music.** Catalogue of the Burrell Collection of Wagner documents, letters, and bibliographical material. London, The Nonpareil Press, 1929. 99 p.

1436 / **Free Library. Drinker Library of Choral Music.** Catalog. [By Henry S. Drinker.] Philadelphia, 1957. 116 p.

First published in 1947 by the Association of American Choruses, Princeton, New Jersey, with a *Supplement*, July, 1948.

Catalog of a lending library of choral materials, made available to members of the Association of American Choruses.

1437 / **Free Library. Edwin A. Fleisher Music Collection.** The Edwin A. Fleisher music collection in the Free Library of Philadelphia; a descriptive catalogue. Rev. ed. Philadelphia, 1965– .

First published in 1933–45, two volumes, with a *Supplementary List*, 1945–55. (1956), 33 p.

Catalog of a loan collection of orchestral music, much of the material unpublished. Classified; information includes dates of composer, title of each work in the original language, with English translation, publisher, instrumentation, timing, date of composition, and information relating to first performance.

1438 / **Library Company.** American song sheets, slip ballads and poetical broadsides, 1850–1970; a catalogue of the collection of the Library Company of Philadelphia, by Edwin Wolf 2nd. Philadelphia, 1963. 205 p.

A listing, alphabetical by title, of 2,722 American song sheets, ballads, and broadsides, with information as to author, composer, format, cover design, etc. Separate listing of 194 Confederate songs. Index of printers and publishers, of authors and composers, of singers. Reproduction of pictorial covers.

PIACENZA, ITALY

1439 / **Archivio del Duomo.** Catalogo del fondo musicale a cura di Francesco Bussi. Milano, Istituto editoriale italiano, 1967. 209 p.

A catalog in four parts: (1) printed music, chiefly of the 16th and 17th centuries; (2) music manuscripts, including anthologies; (3) manuscript and printed liturgical books; and (4) a small collection of books on music. Index of names.

1440 / **Archivio del Duomo.** "L'Archivio del Duomo di Piacenza e il Liber XIII di Constanzo Antegnati." [By Claudio Sartori.] in *Fontes artis musicae* (1957: 4), p. 28–37.

Description of the collection and catalog of its early printed music.

338

Special attention given to a unique copy of the *Liber XIII*, a collection of sacred and secular vocal music by C. Antegnati.

PIRNA, GERMANY

1441 / **Hoffmann-Erbrecht, Lothar.** "Die Chorbücher der Stadtkirche zu Pirna." In *Acta M*, 27 (1955), p. 121–37.

Detailed description of eight choirbooks of polyphonic music of the mid-16th century. Partially thematic; summary inventories; two facsimile plates. These manuscripts are now in the Sächsische Landesbibliothek in Dresden.

PISA, ITALY

Biblioteche e Archivi. . . . See no. 1294.

PISTOIA, ITALY

Archivio Capitolare della Cattedrale. See no. 1283.

1442 / **Biblioteca Antonio Venturi.** "La collection Antonio Venturi, Montecatini-Terme (Pistoia) Italie." [By Raymond Meylan.] In *Fontes artis musicae* (1958: 1), p. 21–44.

A private collection of late-18th-century vocal and instrumental music.

PITTSBURGH, PENNSYLVANIA

1443 / **Finney, Theodore M.** "A group of English manuscript volumes at the University of Pittsburgh," in *Essays in musicology in honor of Dragon Plamenac on his 70th birthday*. Pittsburgh, Univ. of Pittsburgh Press, 1969. p. 21–48.

Describes the contents of a collection of twelve 17th- and 18th-century manuscripts of English provenance, privately owned but currently on deposit in the music library of the University of Pittsburgh. The study incorporates two indexes, one of composers and the other of initial words and titles.

1444 / **Finney, Theodore M.** A union catalogue of music and books on music printed before 1801 in Pittsburgh libraries. 2nd ed. Pittsburgh, Pa., University of Pittsburgh, 1963. 106 leaves (typescript).

First published in 1959. *Second edition supplement,* 1964. 42 leaves.
Lists the holdings in early music in four Pittsburgh libraries: the
Carnegie Library, the University of Pittsburgh, St. Vincent's College,
and the private library of the compiler. There is a strong emphasis on
early English music.
Review by Donald Krummel in *Notes,* 21 (1963–64), p. 129–31.

PLASENCIA, SPAIN

1445 / **Catedral. Archivo.** "El Archivo de música en la catedral
de Plasencia." By Samuel Rubio. In *Anuario musical,* 5 (1950),
p. 147–68.
A small collection of early manuscripts and printed music, full de-
sribed and contents listed.

POLAND

See also WARSAW, POLAND. **Biblioteka Narodowa.** No. 1528.

See also Dragan Plamenac's article in *Notes,* 19
(1962). No. 1217.

1446 / **Thematic Catalogue of Early Musical Manuscripts in
Poland.** Vol. 1: collections of music copied for use at Wawel. Fasc. 1,
edited by Elżbieta Głuszcz-Zwolińska. Warsaw. Polskie Wydawnictwo
Muzyczne, 1969– . 61 leaves in portfolio.
The general editor is Zygmunt M. Szweykowski.

The edition will consist of a number of volumes constituting thematic
catalogues of individual early manuscripts or their groups. . . . The first
volumes will be devoted to the collections copied for use at Wawel, the
following to the collections from Sandomierz and Lowicz regions and
from the surroundings of Cracow. [Editor's description]

PRAGUE, CZECHOSLOVAKIA

1447 / **Cathedral.** Catalogue collectionis operum artis musicae
quae in bibliotheca capituli metropolitani pragensis asservantur. Com-
posuit Dr. Antonius Podlaha. Prague, Metropolitan Capitulary of
Prague. Prague, 1926. 87 p.

1448 / **National Museum.** Hudební sbírka Emiliána Troldy. (The music library of Emilián Trolda.) By Alexander Buchner. Prague, Národní Museum, 1954. 132 p.

Thematic catalog of the Trolda music collection deposited in the Music Department of the National Museum. The collection contains music from *c.* 1550–1820 scored by Trolda from numerous archives, native and foreign.

1449 / **University Library.** Catalogus codicum notis musicis instructorum qui in bibliotheca publica rdi publicae bohemiae socialisticae—in Bibliotheca Universitatis Pragensis servantur. (Catalog of Latin musical manuscripts in the State Library of the CSSR. Prague, University Library, 1971. 1,280 p.

Edited by V. Plocek.

REGGIO-EMILIA, ITALY

Città di Reggio-Emilia. See no. 1279.

RIO DE JANEIRO, BRAZIL

1450 / **Biblioteca Nacional.** "Estudio Brasilenos I. Manuscritos musicales en la Biblioteca Nacional de Rio de Janeiro." By Francisco Curt Lange. In *Revista de estudios musicales*, 1 (April 1950), p. 98–194.

Chiefly 19th-century composers. A: works by European composers. B: works by Brazilian composers or Europeans active in Brazil.

1451 / **Biblioteca Nacional.** Música no Rio de Janeiro imperial 1822–1870. Rio de Janeiro, Biblioteca Nacional, 1962. 100 p.

At head of title: "Exposiçio comemorativa do primeiro decênio da seçao de música e arquivo sonore."

391 items, chiefly Brazilian imprints of the period.

1452 / **Biblioteca Nacional.** Rio musical; crônica de uma cidade. Rio de Janeiro, Biblioteca Nacional, 1965. 51 p.

At head of title: "Exposiçao comemorativa do IV centenário da cidade do Rio de Janeiro."

ROME, ITALY (see also VATICAN CITY)

1453 / **Basilica of Santa Maria in Trastevere.** "Music in the archives of the Basilica of Santa Maria in Trastevere." By Beekman C. Cannon. In *Acta musicologica*, 41 (1969), p. 199–212.

Description and inventory of the music in one of the most renowned Roman churches. Most of the material comes from the latter half of the 17th century. The collection is rich in music by Angelo Berardi, who became *Maestro di Cappella* in 1693.

1454 / **Biblioteca Corsiniana.** Biblioteca corsiniana e dell'Accademia Nazionale dei Lincei; catalogo dei fondi musicali Chiti e Cor.-siniano Ed. Argia Bertini. Milano, Istituto editoriale italiano, 1964. 109 p. (Bibliotheca musicae, 2.)

Catalog covering printed music, theoretical works, and manuscripts. 17th- and early-18th-century vocal and instrumental music.

1455 / **Biblioteca Corsiniana.** "La collezione Corsini di antichi codici musicali e Girolamo Chiti." By Vito Raeli. In *Rivista musicale italiana*, 25 (1918–20).

Describes the founding of the Corsini library and the role played by the early-18th-century church musician, Girolamo Chiti, friend of Padre Martini.

Biblioteca della R. Accademia di S. Ceclia. See no. 1284.

1456 / **Biblioteca Doria-Pamphilj.** "Die Musiksammlung der Fürsten Doria-Pamphilj in Rom." By Andreas Holschneider. In *Archiv für Musikwissenschaft*, 18 (1961), p. 248–64.

Description of the collection and inventory of its contents, classified under five main headings: (1) collections, 16th and 17th centuries; (2) sacred music; (3) oratorios (early manuscripts); (4) operas, early manuscripts; (5) German instrumental music, chiefly 18th century.

1457 / **Biblioteca Doria-Pamphilj.** "Die Sinfonien-Manuskripte der Bibliothek Doria-Pamphilj in Rom." By Friedrich Lippmann. In *Analecta musicologica*, 5 (1968), p. 201–47.

Thematic catalog of some 119 symphonies by 36 composers. Many of the works are not known from other sources.

1458 / **Biblioteca Doria-Pamphilj.** "Die Streichquartettmanu-skripte der Bibliothek Doria-Pamphilj in Rom." By Friedrich Lipp-mann with Ludwig Finscher. In *Analecta musicologica*, 7 (1969), p. 120–44.
Thematic catalog of the string quartet repertory in the library.

1459 / **Biblioteca Doria-Pamphilj.** "Die Streichtriomanuskript der Bibliothek Doria-Pamphilj in Rom." By Friedrich Lippmann with Hubert Unverricht. In *Analecta musicologica*, 9 (1970), p. 299–335.
Thematic catalog of string trios in the Doria-Pamphilj collection.

1460 / **Congregazione dell'Oratorio di Roma.** Inventario del fondo musicale dell'Oratorio. A cura di Argia Bertini. Roma, 1968–70. 3 fascicles.
A fourth fascicle is to include anonymous works.

1461 / **Deutsches Historisches Instituts in Rom.** "Die Musik-geschichtliche Abteilung des Deutschen Historischen Instituts in Rom." By Karl Gustav Fellerer. In *Die Musikforschung* 20 (1967), p. 410–13.
Brief description of the leading musicological reference library in Italy, calling attention to its major areas of interest, special files, and indexes.

1462 / **Kast, Paul.** "Römische Handschriften." In *MGG*, 11 (1963), col. 750–61.
A narrative account citing and describing the principal manuscripts, chiefly polyphonic, in Rome. Much attention given to sources in the Vatican Library. Bibliography of writings on Roman libraries and their manuscript sources.

For the Vatican Library, see under VATICAN CITY, ROME.

SALT LAKE CITY, UTAH

1463 / **University of Utah. Library.** A catalogue of books and music acquired from the library of Hugo Leichtentritt. . . . Edited by Carol E. Selby. Salt Lake City, Univ. of Utah, 1954. 106 p. (Bulletin of the University of Utah, 45: 10).

A scholar's working library of music books and scores; a few early editions, but centered in the 19th and 20th centuries. The catalog is divided in two sections: books (p. 9–46) and music (p. 49–106).

1464 / **Mozart-Museum.** Katalog des Mozart-Museums im Geburts- und Wohnzimmer Mozarts zu Salzburg . . . 4. Aufl. Salzburg, Im Selbstverlage des obengenannten Stiftung. 1906, 62 p.

Describes a collection of Mozart memorabilia maintained in the composer's birthplace. The collection includes portraits, medals, letters, and music.

1465 / **Museum Carolino Augusteum.** Die Musikaliensammlung im Salzburger Museum Carolino Augusteum, von Josef Gassner. Salzburg, 1962. 247 p.

Originally published in the Museum's *Jahresschrift*, 1961. Salzburg, 1962, p. 119–325.

The collection, founded in 1834, is rich in 19th-century editions. Manuscripts and printed music interfiled. Full bibliographical citations, with publishers' plate numbers given. Facsimile plates.

1466 / **Die Musikaliensammlung der Erzabtei St. Peter in Salzburg.** Katalog. Erster Teil. Leopold und Wolfgang Amadeus Mozart, Joseph und Michael Haydn. Mit einer Einführung in die Geschichte der Sammlung vorgelegt von Manfred Hermann Schmid. Salzburg, 1970. 300 p. (Schriftenreihe der Internationalen Stiftung Mozarteum, Band 3/4. Zugleich Band I der Publikationen des Instituts für Musikwissenschaft der Universitäts Salzburg.)

Review by Susan T. Sommer in *Notes*, 29 (1972), p. 258.

1467 / **San Francisco State University. Frank V. De Bellis Collection.** Orchestra scores and parts in the Frank V. De Bellis collection of the California State Colleges. San Francisco State College, 1964. 24 unnumbered leaves (typescript).

A preliminary catalog of the orchestral portion of the De Bellis collection, a collection devoted exclusively to Italian music. Entries listed alphabetically by composer, with early and modern editions interfiled. Parts specified.

SAN MARINO, CALIFORNIA

1468 / **Henry E. Huntington Library and Art Gallery.** Catalogue of music in the Huntington Library printed before 1801. Compiled by E. N. Backus. San Marino, Calif., The Library, 1949. 773 p.

"Music publications and publications without music notation but of distinct interest to musicians and musicologists. . . ." Excluded are manuscripts, song texts, opera librettos. Includes music published in periodicals. Entry is under composer, with anonymous works under title. Index to composers and editors, chronological index, first-line index of songs. The collection is strong in 17th- and 18th-century English music.

Review by Cyrus L. Day in *Notes*, 6 (1949), p. 609–10; by Harold Spivacke in *MQ*, 35 (1949), p. 640–42.

SANTIAGO, CUBA

1469 / **Hernandez Balaguer, Pablo.** Catalogo de música de los archivos de la catedral de Santiago de Cuba y del Museo Bacardi. La Habana, Biblioteca Nacional "Jose Marti." 1961. 59 p.

Catalog of works by Cuban composers in the archives of the cathedral at Santiago and in the Bacardi Museum in the same city.

SCHLOSS LANCUT, POLAND

1470 / **Bieganski, Krzysztof.** Biblioteka muzyczna Zamku w Lancucie. Katalog. Kraków, 1969. 430 p.

Catalog of the music library of a castle (Schloss Lancut) in southern Poland.

SCHWERIN, GERMANY

1471 / **Grossherzogliche Regierungsbibliothek.** Die Musikalien-Sammlung des grossherzoglich Mecklenburg-Schweriner Fürsten-hauses aus den letzten zwei Jahrhunderten. Schwerin, Druck der Sandmeyerschen Hofbuchdruckerei, 1893. 2 v.

Compiled by Otto Kade.

Primarily 18th- and 19th-century manuscripts and printed music. Part I is a thematic catalog, alphabetical by composer, with a classified section under "Anonyma." Part II: librettos. Part III: index of dedications, autographs, etc.

1472 / Grossherzogliche Regierungsbibliothek. Der musikalische Nachlass der Frau Erbgrossherzogin Auguste von Mecklenburg-Schwerin . . . von Otto Kade. Schwerin, Druck der Sandmeyerschen Hofbuchdruckerei, 1899. 142 p.

SEVILLE, SPAIN

1473 / Biblioteca Colombina. "La música conservada en la Bibliotecta Colombina y en la Catedral de Sevilla." By Higinio Anglés. In *Anuario musical*, 2 (1947), p. 3–39.

88 manuscripts and prints from the Colombina library; 9 manuscripts and 22 prints from the cathedral archives. Bibliographical references and notes on all the items.

1474 / Biblioteca Colombina. "Printed collections of polyphonic music owned by Ferdinand Columbus." By Catherine Weeks Chapman. In *JAMS*, 21 (1968), p. 34–84.

Reconstruction of the 16th-century music library of the son of Christopher Columbus, based on a manuscript catalog preserved in that library. The catalog makes reference to a number of editions now lost.

SITTEN, SWITZERLAND (VALAIS)

1475 / Stenzl, Jurg. Repertorium der liturgischen Musikhandschriften der Diözesen Sitten, Lausanne und Genf. Band I: Diözese Sitten. Freiburg, Universitätsverlag. 1972– . Veröffentlichungen der Gregorianischen Akademie zu Freiburg in der Schweiz. Neue Folge, Band I.)

The first volume of a series devoted to the liturgical music manuscripts in the dioceses of Sitten, Lausanne, and Geneve. Band I has 383 pages, 100 illustrations, 60 facsimiles, and 72 pages of edition.

SORAU, GERMANY (NOW ZARY, POLAND)

SPAIN

1476 / Aubry, Pierre. "Iter Hispanicum: notices et extraits de manuscrits ancienne conservés dans les bibliothèques d'Espagne." In *Sammelbände der Internationalen Musikgesellschaft*, v. 8 and 9 (1907–08). Also issued as a separate.

A series of essays treating early Spanish sources of polyphony, Mozarabic chant, the "Cantigas de Santa Maria," and folk music.

1477 / **Riaño, Juan F.** Critical and bibliographical notes on early Spanish music. London, B. Quaritch, 1887. 154 p.

Reprint by the Da Capo Press, New York, 1971.

Manuscripts and printed music to 1600, classified, giving descriptions and library locations of manuscripts. Numerous facsimile plates. Also entered under no. 1098.

STANFORD, CALIFORNIA

1478 / **Stanford University. Library.** Catalogue of the Memorial Library of Music, Stanford University, by Nathan van Patten. Stanford, Calif., Stanford University Press, 1950. 310 p.

A collection of manuscripts, prints, inscribed copies of books and scores; the emphasis is on "association items." 1,226 entries.

Review by Otto Albrecht in *Notes*, 8 (1951), p. 706–709.

STOCKHOLM, SWEDEN

1479 / **Stiftelsen Musikkulturens Främjande** [Foundation for Furthering Musical Culture]. Förteckning över musikhandskrifter: musikalier, brev och biografica [Catalog of music manuscripts, letters and biographical documents. Compiled by Gunnar Holst]. Stockholm, Svenskt Musikhistoriskt Arkiv, 1972. 51 p. (Bulletin, 8.)

A preliminary catalog, or checklist, of the manuscript collection of Rudolf Nydahl, Stockholm, now owned by the Foundation for Furthering Musical Culture. About 4,500 items in all, including some 1,200 autographs, correspondence, and other documents. The catalog is in two parts: (1) music manuscripts, (2) letters and other documents. The collection is strong in the work of 19th-century musicians.

STUTTGART, GERMANY

1480 / **Landesbibliothek.** Die Handschriften der Württembergischen Landesbibliothek Stuttgart. Erste Reihe, erster Band: Codices musici (Cod. Mus. Fol. I 1–71). Beschrieben von Clytus Gottwald. Wiesbaden, Otto Harrassowitz, 1964. 184 p.

Describes 53 manuscripts in mensural notation and 18 plainchant sources, giving concordances for texts and music, index of text incipits, thematic catalog for anonymous works, with full bibliographical apparatus. An exemplary catalog.

Review by Franz Krautwurst in *Die Musikforschung*, 21 (1968), p. 233–37.

1481 / Landesbibliothek. Die Handschriften der Württembergischen Landesbibliothek Stuttgart. Zweite Reihe: Die Handschriften der ehemagligen königlichen Hofbibliothek. Sechster Band: Codices musici. Erster Teil . . . Beschrieben von Clytus Gottwald. Wiesbaden, Otto Harrassowitz, 1965. 66 p.

Continues the cataloging begun in the preceding volume, covering a different series of manuscripts.

Review by Ute Schwab in *Die Musikforschung*, 24 (1971), p. 210–12.

1482 / Landesbibliothek. Katalog über die Musik-Codices des 16. und 17. Jahrhunderts auf der K. Landesbibliothek in Stuttgart. Angefertigt von A. Halm. Langensalza, Beyer, 1902–1903. 58 p. (Beilage. Monatshefte für Musikgeschichte Jahrgang 34–35.)

Cites 70 manuscripts with listings of contents for each. Index to text incipits under individual composers.

SWEDEN

The Swedish bibliographer Åke Davidsson has prepared union catalogs of early printed music and of music theory works in Swedish libraries. See his *Catalogue critique et descriptif des ouvrages théoriques sur la musique imprimés au XVIe et au XVIIe siècles et conservés dans les bibliothèques suédoises*, (no. 776), and his *Catalogue critique et descriptif des imprimés de musique des XVIe et XVIIe siècles conservés dans les bibliothèques suédoises . . .* (no. 1057).

TENBURY WELLS, ENGLAND

1483 / St. Michael's College (Tenbury). Library. The catalog of manuscripts in the library of St. Michael's College, Tenbury. Compiled by E. H. Fellowes. Paris, Éditions de l'Oiseau Lyre, 1934. 319 p.

Manuscripts in the library bequeathed to the College by Sir Frederick Ouseley. 1,386 items; rich in early English music. The library also holds a large portion of the "Toulouse-Philidor collection," consisting of 290 volumes of manuscripts and 67 printed books devoted to the repertory of early 18th-century French opera. Composer index.

1484 / **St. Michael's College (Tenbury). Library.** A summary catalogue of the printed books and music in the library of St. Michael's College, Tenbury. Compiled by E. H. Fellowes, 1934. 143 leaves (unpublished manuscript).

An unpublished catalog of the printed books and music in the library of St. Michael's College. Intended as a companion volume to the manuscript catalog above, but never printed.

TOKYO, JAPAN

1485 / **Musashino Academia Musicae. Biblioteca.** List of acquisition. No. 1– . Tokyo, Musashino Academia Musicae, 1957– .

Text in Japanese and English.

An annual volume listing materials acquired from April of one year to March of the next. Classified listing of both books and scores. The first section of each issue is devoted to rare materials. No. 15 by March 1972.

1486 / **Musashino Academia Musicae. Biblioteca.** Litterae rarae. Liber primus– . Tokyo, Musashino Academia Musicae, 1962– .

A catalog of rare music materials added to the collection. Published irregularly, *Liber secundus* appeared in 1969. A library rich in first or early editions of music and music literature from the 16th through the 19th centuries. The librarian is Dr. Yoshio Ito.

Liber primus (1962), 141 p. *Liber secundus* (1969), 276 p.

1487 / **Nanki Music Library.** Catalogue of rare books and notes: the Ohki Collection, Nanki Music Library. Tokyo, 1970.

1488 / **Nanki Music Library.** Catalogue of the Nanki Music Library. Part I: Musicology. Tokyo, 1929. 372 p.

A reference library for the historical study of Western music. Much of the material came from the collection of W. H. Cummings, English collector whose library was sold at auction in 1918.

1489 / **Nanki Music Library.** Catalogue of the W. H. Cummings collection in the Nanki Music Library. Tokyo, 1925. 70 p.

A catalog focused on the rare materials acquired in the Cummings sale. About 450 items, including much important early English music.

TOLEDO, OHIO

1490 / **Museum of Art.** The printed note, 500 years of music printing and engraving, January 1957. Toledo, Museum of Art, 1957. 144 p.
Foreword by A. Beverly Barksdale.
Catalog of an exhibition devoted to the history of music printing and engraving. Splendidly illustrated, 188 items, on loan from major public and private collections throughout the country. Informative annotations; bibliography of 67 items.

TOLEDO, SPAIN

1491 / **Biblioteca Capitolar.** "Les manuscrits polyphoniques de la Bibliothèque Capitulaire de Tolede." By René Lenaerts. In *International Society for Musical Research, Fifth Congress, Utrecht, 1952.* p. 267–81.
Brief descriptions and discussion of about 30 sources of early polyphonic music in the Toledo library.

TREVISO, ITALY

1492 / **Archivio Musicale del Duomo.** La Cappella Musicale del Duomo di Treviso (1300–1633). By Giovanni d'Alessi. Vedelago, Tipografia "Ars et Religio," 1954. 272 p.
Historical study of the musical establishment of the cathedral at Treviso. Chapter 15, p. 169–218, deals with the musical archive and its resources. Manuscripts are listed briefly; printed works in greater detail.

TULLN, AUSTRIA

1493 / **Pfarrkirche St. Stephan.** Das alte Musikarchiv der Pfarrkirche St. Stephan in Tulln. By Karl Schnürl. Wien, Böhlaus, 1964. 88 p. (Tabulae musicae austriacae, 1.)
The catalog is chiefly concerned with manuscripts, although a short section of prints is included. Partially thematic. The principal composers represented are Albrechtsberger, Diabelli, Eybler, Joseph and

350

Michael Haydn, Krottendorfer, Mozart, Schneider, Schubert, Winter, etc.

Review by Imogene Horsley in *Notes*, 24 (1967), p. 52–53.

TURIN, ITALY

Biblioteca Nazionale. See also no. 1293.

1494 / **Biblioteca Nazionale.** "L'Intavolatura d'organo tedesca della Biblioteca Nazionale di Torino. Catalogo ragionato." By Oscar Mischiati. In *L'Organo, rivista di cultura organaria e organistica*, 4 (1963), p. 1–154.

An inventory of the contents of 16 volumes of German organ tablature in the National Library in Turin, the largest body of source material for German organ music known. The manuscripts contain 1,770 compositions on 2,703 written folios, compiled between 1637 and 1640. Appendices include paleographic descriptions of the volumes, author lists added by later hands, watermarks, concordant prints, manuscripts and modern editions, and an index of composers.

1495 / **Biblioteca Nazionale.** "La raccolta di rarità musicali "Mauro Foa" alla Biblioteca Nazionale di Torino." by Alberto Gentili. In *Accademie e biblioteche d'Italia*, 1 (1927), p. 36–50.

Descriptive account of a collection of 95 volumes, manuscripts, and prints founded by Count Giacomo Durazzo, Genoan Ambassador to Venice in 1765. Includes autographs of Vivaldi and Stradella, as well as the organ tablatures mentioned above.

1496 / **Biblioteca Nazionale.** Manoscritti e libri a stampa musicali esposti dalla Biblioteca Nazionale di Torino. Firenze, L. Franceschini, 1898. 24 p.

Exposition catalog of 20 manuscripts and 36 prints of the 16th–18th centuries.

UPPSALA, SWEDEN

1497 / **Universitetsbiblioteket.** Catalogue critique et descriptif des imprimés de musique des XVIe et XVIIe siècles, conservés à la Bibliothèque de l'Université Royale d'Upsala; par Rafael Mitjana, avec une introduction bibliographique par Isak Collijn. . . . Upsala, Impr. Almqvist et Wiksell, 1911–1951. 3 v.

Vol. 1: Musique religieuse, I, par Rafael Mitjana (1911). Vol. 2: Musique religieuse, II, musique profane; musique dramatique, musique instrumentale; additions au Tome I, par Åke Davidsson (1951). Vol. 3: Recueils de musique religieuse et profane, par Åke Davidsson (1951).

Entries in vols. 1 and 2 are arranged alphabetically within each category; vol. 3 is chronological, with an index of the contents of the collections under composer. Index of printers and publishers and a bibliography of works cited. Full bibliographical entries, with locations of copies in other libraries.

1498 / **Universitetsbiblioteket.** Catalogue of the Gimo collection of Italian manuscript music in the University Library of Uppsala. By Åke Davidsson. Uppsala, 1963. 101 p. (Acta bibliothecae R. Universitatis Upsaliensis, 14.)

A catalog of 360 items, comprising both vocal and instrumental music of the 18th century. An introduction relates the history of the collection. Useful bibliography of sources and related literature.

Review by Minnie Elmer in *Notes*, 22 (1965), p. 715–16; by R. Thurston Dart in *The Library*, 5th ser., 20 (June 1965), p. 166–67.

1499 / **Universitetsbiblioteket. Sammlung Düben.** "Die Dübensammlung. Ein Versuch ihrer chronologischen Ordnung." Von Bruno Grusnick. In *Svensk tidskrift för musikforskning*, 46 (1964), p. 27–82; 48 (1966), p. 63–186.

VALLADOLID, SPAIN

1500 / **Catedral. Archivo Musical.** "El Archivo Musical de la Catedral de Valladolid." By Higinio Angleś. In *Anuario musical*, 3 (1948), p. 59–108.

20 manuscripts and 97 early printed books. Inventories given for the contents of the manuscripts and full bibliographical citations for the prints, with references to Eitner and other bibliographies.

VATICAN CITY, ROME

1501 / **Biblioteca Vaticana.** Monumenti vaticani di paleografia musicale latina. By H. M. Bannister. Lipsia, O. Harrassowitz, 1913. 2 v. 130 plates. (Codices e vaticanis selecti, 12.) Reprint by the Gregg Press, 1969.

A volume of commentary and a volume of plates containing excerpts from Vatican manuscripts, assembled for the purposes of paleographical study. Contains a vast amount of information on the manuscript sources of plainchant in the Vatican Library.

1502 / **Biblioteca Vaticana.** "Die Sammlungen der Oratorienlibretti (1679–1725) und den restlichen Musikbestand der Fondo San Marcello der Biblioteca Vaticana in Rom." By Andreas Liess. In *Acta musicologica*, 31 (1959), p. 63–80.

Cites 106 oratorio libretti in the Fondo San Marcello of the Biblioteca Vaticana. References to whether or not the works are known to Eitner.

1503 / **Biblioteca Vaticana. Cappella Giulia.** Le opere musicali della Cappella Giulia. I. Manoscritti e edizioni fino al '700. By José M. Llorens. Città del Vaticano, Biblioteca Apostolica Vaticana, 1971. 412 p. (Studi e testi, 265.)

Review by Samuel F. Pogue in *Notes*, 29 (1973), p. 445–48.

1504 / **Biblioteca Vaticani. Cappella Sistina.** Bibliographischer und thematischer Musik-katalog des Päpstlichen Kapellarchives im Vatikan zu Rom . . . von Fr. X. Haberl. Leipzig, Breitkopf & Härtel, 1888. 183 p. (Beilage, Monatshefte für Musikgeschichte. Jahrgang 19/20.)

Descriptions of 269 items, manuscripts and early printed works, with a thematic catalog, by composer, of the early polyphonic sources. Considerable documentation on the Cappella Sistina and the musicians employed there. The Haberl catalog represents only a small part of the Cappella Sistina collection. See no. 1505 below.

1505 / **Biblioteca Vaticana. Cappella Sistina.** Capellae Sixtinae codices musicis notis instructi sive manuscripti sive praeli excussi. Rec. J. M. Llorens. Roma, Città del Vaticano, Biblioteca Apostolica Vaticana, 1960. 555 p. 10 facsimile plates.

A catalog of the collection treated by F. X. Haverl, above, but much more thoroughly, since Haberl covered only 269 of the 660 manuscripts and printed volumes present. Volumes listed by number, with detailed inventories of contents. Descriptive annotations in Latin. Thematic catalog of anonymous works.

Review by Dragan Plamenac in *Notes*, 19 (1961), p. 251–52; by

Peter Peacock in *Music and letters*, 42 (1961), p. 168–69; by Glen Haydon in MQ, 48 (1962), p. 127–29.

1506 / **Biblioteca del Palazzo Giustinian Lolin.** Stampe e manoscritti preziosi e rari della Biblioteca del Palazzo Giustinian Lolin a San Vidal. By Siro Cisilino. Venezia, A cura del fondatore Dott. Ugo Levi sotto gli auspici dell'Ateneo Veneto, 1966. 55 p.

At head of title: Fondazione Ugo e Olga Levi, Centro di Cultura Musicale Superiore.

Catalog of the library of a recently established musical foundation in Venice. 70 items listed, including printed books and manuscripts from the 16th to the early 19th centuries. Many of the manuscripts are composite in content. The collection contains important source materials for the study of 18th-century instrumental music.

Biblioteca Nazionale Marciana. See no. 1285.

1507 / **Biblioteca Nazionale Marciana.** I codici musicali contariniani del secolo XVII nella R. Biblioteca di San Marco in Venezia. Illustrati dal Dr. Taddeo Wiel. Venezia, F. Ongania, 1888. 121 p.

Reprinted by Forni, Bologna, 1969.

The Contarini collection is a special library of manuscript scores of 17th-century Venetian opera, by such composers as Cesti, Cavalli, Pallavicino, Ziani, etc. 120 numbered items. Entries give information as to date of first performance, librettist, cast, general description of the work. Composer index.

Biblioteca Querini Stampalia. See no. 1285.

Museo Correr. See no. 1285.

Pia Casa di Ricovero. See no. 1285.

1508 / **Archivio della Cattedrale.** "Il fondo musicale dell'archivio della Cattedrale di Vercelli." By Claudio Sartori. In *Fontes artis musicae*, 5 (1958), p. 24–31.

Accademia Filarmonica. See no. 1295.

1509 / **Accademia Filarmonica.** L'Accademia Filarmonica di Verona, dalla fondazione (Maggio 1543) al 1600 e il suo patrimonio musicale antico. By Giuseppe Turrini. Verona, "La Tipografica Veronese," 1941. 345 p.

A detailed history of the Accademia Filarmonica from its beginnings to 1600. Chapter 16 discusses the holdings of the library on the basis of early inventories. Chapter 17 continues the discussion to the first half of the 19th century. Chapter 18 includes a catalog of the existing materials in the "Fondo musicale antico," some 217 prints and 21 manuscripts.

1510 / **Biblioteca Capitolare.** Il patrimonio musicale della Biblioteca Capitolare di Verona dal sec. XV al XIX. By Giuseppe Turrini. Verona, "La Tipografica Veronese," 1953. 83 p. (Estratto dagli Atti dell'Academia di Agricoltura, Scienze e Lettere di Verona, ser. 6: 2, p. 95–176.)

Archivio della Cattedrale. See no. 1286.

Biblioteca Bertoliana. See no. 1286.

1511 / **Beethoven-Zentenarausstellung.** Führer durch die Beethoven Zentenarausstellung der Stadt Wien: "Beethoven und die wiener Kultur seiner Zeit." Wien, Selbstverlag der Gemeinde Wien, 1927. 248 p.

An exhibition catalog of 1,070 items, including letters, documents, pictures, musical instruments, scores, and prints related to Beethoven and his circle.

1512 / **Gesellschaft der Musikfreunde.** Geschichte der K. K. Gesellschaft der Musikfreunde in Wien. . . . In einem Zusatzbande: "Die Sammlungen und Statuten," von Dr. Eusebius Mandyczewski. Wien, Adolf Holzhausen, 1912. 2 v.

Vol. 1 is a history of the Gesellschaft from 1812–1870 and from 1870–1912. Vol. 2, "Zusatz-Band," is not a true catalog but a summary listing of the holdings of the archive, library, and museum. Of particular value is Mandyczewski's listing of "Bücher und Schriften über Musik. Druckwerke und Handschriften aus der Zeit bis zum Jahre 1800," p. 55–84. Also "Musik-Autographe," p. 85–123.

1513 / **Gesellschaft der Musikfreunde.** Geschichte der Gesellschaft der Musikfreunde in Wien, 1912–1927. (Fortsetzung der Festschrift zur Jahrhundertfeier vom Jahre 1912.) Wien, Gesellschaft der Musikfreunde, 1937.

Continues the documentation given in the preceding volume. Of particular interest is the account by Hedwig Kraus of "Die Sammlungen der Gesellschaft der Musikfreunde, 1912–1937." p. 1–42.

1514 / **Gesellschaft der Musikfreunde.** Die Volksmusiksammlung der Gesellschaft der Musikfreunde in Wien (Sonnleithner-Sammlung). 1. Teil, bearbeitet von Walther Deutsch und Gerlinde Hofer, mit einem Beitrag von Leopold Schmidt. Wien, A. Schendl, 1969. 186 p. (Schriften zur Volksmusik, 2.)

Catalog of a collection of folk music, chiefly Austrian, begun in 1818. Entries are grouped chiefly by region. First-line index of songs; indexes of places and names. 29 plates duplicating pages from the collection.

Review by Hartmut Braun in *Jahrbuch für Volksliedforschung*, 15 (1970), p. 159–60.

1515 / **Hoftheater.** Katalog der Portrait-Sammlung der K. V. K. Generalintendanz der K. K. Hoftheater. Zugleich ein biographisches Hilfsbuch auf dem Gebiet von Theater und Musik. Wien, Adolph W. Kunast, 1892–94. 3 v.

Catalogs a large collection of portraits and other graphic materials related to the theater; classified according to type of theater or kind of entertainment. *Gruppe III*, Vol. 1, p. 119–264, is concerned with pictorial documents on musicians: composers, librettists, concert singers, writers on music, etc.

1516 / **Internationale Ausstellung für Musik- und Theaterwesen.** Fach-Katalog der Musikhistorischen Abteilung von Deutschland und Österreich-Ungarn . . . Wien, 1892. 591 p.

Catalog for a large and varied music exhibition held in Vienna in

1892. Includes prints, manuscripts, instruments, portraits, letters, and other documents arranged roughly in chronological order from ancient times to the end of the 19th century.

1517 / **Künstlerhaus.** Katalog der Ausstellung anlässlich der Centenarfeier Domenico Cimarosas. Wien, Verlag des Comités, 1901. 163 p.

Exhibition catalog of 524 items related to Cimarosa and his contemporaries; includes scores, portraits, medals, etc.

1518 / **Minoritenkonvent.** Das Musikarchiv im Minoritenkonvent zu Wien (Katalog des älteren Bestandes vor 1784). By Friedrich Wilhelm Riedel. Kassel, Bärenreiter, 1963. 139 p. (Catalogus musicus, 1.)

Broadly classified catalog of manuscripts and printed music, chiefly 17th and 18th centuries. Strong in early keyboard music. Indexes of composers, copyists, and former owners.

Review by Othmar Wessely in *Die Musikforschung*, 18 (1965), p. 204–206.

1519 / **Museum des 20. Jahrhunderts.** Schönberg—Webern—Berg: Bilder—Partituren—Dokumente. (Catalog of an exhibition at the Museum des 20. Jahrhunderts, Vienna, 17 May–20 July, 1969.) Wien, Museum des 20. Jahrhunderts, 1969. 118 p.

Review by Dika Newlin in *Notes*, 27 (1971), p. 488–89.

1520 / **Österreichische Nationalbibliothek.** Die Estensischen Musikalien; thematisches Verzeichnis mit Einleitung von Robert Haas. Regensburg, G. Bosse, 1927. 232 p.

Reissued in 1957 as Bd. VII of *Forschungsbeiträge zur Musikwissenschaft*. Regensburg, G. Bosse.

Catalog, largely thematic, of an important collection of 18th century instrumental music originating in northern Italy. Includes a small group of cantatas and other vocal works. Classified within major sections of prints and manuscripts. Index of names, text incipits.

1521 / **Österreichische Nationalbibliothek.** "Die Musikbibliothek von Raimund Fugger d.J.: ein Beitrag zur Musiküberlieferung des 16. Jahrhunderts." By Richard Schaal. In *Acta musicologica* 29 (1957), p. 126–37.

Catalog of the Fugger library, from a 16th-century manuscript in the Staatsbibliothek, Munich. The bulk of the Fugger family music collection is now in the Vienna Library.

1522 / Österreichische Nationalbibliothek. "Die Musiksammlung der Nationalbibliothek." By Robert Haas. In *Jahrbuch der Musikbibliothek Peters*, 37 (1930), p. 48–62.

1523 / Österreichische Nationalbibliothek. "Die Musiksammlung." By Leopold Nowak. In *Die Österreichische Nationalbibliothek. Festschrift herausgegeben zum 25. Jährigen Dienstjubliäum des Generaldirektors Prof. Dr. Josef Bick.* Wien, H. Bauer-Verlag, 1948. p. 119–38.

1524 / Österreichische Nationalbiblothek. Die Musiksammlung der Österreichischen Nationalbibliothek. By Franz Grasberger. . . . Wien, Bundeskanzleramt, Bundespressedienst, 1970. 32 p.

1525 / Österreichische Nationalbibliothek. Richard Strauss Ausstellung zum 100. Geburtstag. Bearbeitet von Franz Grasberger und Franz Hadamowsky. Wien, Österreichische Nationalbibliothek, 1964. 360 p.

Exhibition catalog of a rich collection of documents related to Richard Strauss. Illustrated.

1526 / Österreichische Nationalbibliothek. Tabulae codicum manuscriptorum praeter graecos et orientales in Bibliotheca Palatina Vindobonensi asservatorum . . . x. IX–X: Codicum musicorum, Pars I–II. Vindobonae, venum dat. Geroldi filius, 1897–99. 2 v. in 1.

Catalog, compiled by Joseph Mantuani, of the manuscripts numbered 15,501–19,500 comprising the music holdings of the Austrian National Library. Introduction and descriptive notes in Latin. Each volume has an index of names, of subjects, and of text incipits.

1527 / Österreichische Nationalbibliothek. Photogrammarchiv. Katalog des Archiv für Photogramme musikalischer Meisterhandschriften, Widmung Anthony van Hoboken. Bearb. von Agnes Ziffer. Wien, Prachner, 1967– . 482 p.

An archive of photocopies of the autographs of a selected group of great composers, chiefly Viennese, founded in 1927 by Anthony van Hoboken and Heinrich Schenker. 2,684 entries, many references to related literature.

1528 / **Biblioteka Narodowa.** Katalog mikrofilmów muzycznych (Catalog of musical microfilms). Vol. 1– . Warszawa, Biblioteka Narodowa, 1956– .

A series of catalogs originating in the microfilm archive of the National Library at Warsaw. Three volumes—volumes 8, 9, and 10— of a larger series (Katalog mikrofilmow) are concerned with music. The holdings of numerous Polish libraries are represented.

Vol. 1 (1956): chiefly manuscripts and printed materials of the 19th century. Vol. 2 (1962): musical documents of the 17th and 18th centuries. Vol. 3 (1965): historical source materials related to Polish music.

1529 / **University Library.** Katalog druków muzycznych XVI, XVII e XVIII w. Biblioteki Uniwersytetu warszawskiego. Tom I: Wiek XVI. By Janina Mendysowa. Warszawa, Wydawn. Uniwers. warszawsk, 1970. 380 p. (Acta bibliothecae universitatis varsovensis, 7.)

Catalog of printed music of the 16th–18th centuries in the University Library at Warsaw.

This work is highly praised in a brief description in *Fontes artis musicae*, 19 (1972), p. 46.

UNITED STATES

1530 / **Albrecht, Otto E.** A census of autograph music manuscripts of European composers in American libraries. Philadelphia, Univ. of Pennsylvania Press, 1953. 331 p.

Lists 2,017 manuscripts now in America by 571 European composers, giving title, pagination, dimensions, and descriptive notes. Current and former owners indicated. Organized alphabetically by composer. Index of owners.

Review by Jack A. Westrup in *Music Review*, 16 (1955), p. 84–85.

WASHINGTON, DISTRICT OF COLUMBIA

1531 / **U.S. Copyright Office.** Dramatic compositions copyrighted in the United States, 1870–1916. Washington, D.C., Govt. Printing Office, 1918. 2 v.

Unaltered reprint by Johnson Reprint Corp., New York, 1968.

Review by Lenore Coral in *Notes*, 26 (1969), p. 52–53.

1532 / U.S. Library of Congress. Music Division. Catalogue of early books on music (before 1800) by Julia Gregory. . . . Washington, D.C., Govt. Printing Office, 1913. 312 p.

Supplement (Books acquired by the Library, 1913–42) by Hazel Bartlett . . . with a list of books on music in Chinese and Japanese. 1944. 143 p.

Republication in one volume of the original catalog and its supplement by the Da Capo Press, New York, 1969.

The Library of Congress has one of the richest collections of early music theory in the world. The entries conform to the Library's printed catalog cards.

Review by Ruth Watanabe in *Notes*, 26 (1970), p. 521–524.

1533 / U.S. Library of Congress. Music Division. Catalogue of first editions of Edward MacDowell (1861–1908) by O. G. Sonneck. Washington, D.C., Govt. Printing Office, 1917. 89 p.

Includes works with and without opus numbers, compositions written under pseudonyms, and works edited by the composer. Index of titles, first lines of texts, authors and translators, publishers.

1534 / U.S. Library of Congress. Music Division. Catalogue of first editions of Stephen C. Foster (1826–1864) by Walter R. Whittlesey and O. G. Sonneck. Washington, D.C., Govt. Printing Office, 1915. 79 p.

Works arranged by title; indexed by authors of text, publishers, first lines. Detailed annotations.

1535 / U.S. Library of Congress. Music Division. Catalogue of opera librettos printed before 1800, prepared by O. G. T. Sonneck. Washington, D.C., Govt. Printing Office, 1914. 2 v.

Reprint by Johnson Reprint Corp., New York, 1970; and by Burt Franklin, New York, 1967.

The Library's collection of librettos began in 1909 with the purchase of the Schatz collection. By 1914 it contained 17,000 items and was particularly strong in first editions of 17th- and 18th-century works. Vol. 1 is a title listing, with notes giving date of first performance, place, name of composer if known. Vol. 2 is an index by composers, by librettists, and of titles of specific arias mentioned.

1536 / U.S. Library of Congress. Music Division. Dramatic music. Catalogue of full scores, compiled by O. G. T. Sonneck. Washington, D.C., Govt. Printing Office, 1908. 170 p.

Reprint by Da Capo Press, New York, 1969.

Full scores of operas in original editions, some manuscript copies included, and some photocopies. Arranged alphabetically by composer.

Review by Ruth Watanabe in *Notes*, 26 (1970), p. 521–24.

1537 / **U.S. Library of Congress. Music Division.** The Music Division, a guide to its collections and services. Washington, D.C., Govt. Printing Office, 1972. 22 p.

Published in 1960 under the title: *The Music Division in the Library of Congress.*

A brief descriptive account of the work and resources of the Music Division, with illustrations.

1538 / **U.S. Library of Congress. Music Division.** Orchestral music . . . catalogue. Scores. Prepared under the direction of O. G. T. Sonneck. Washington, D.C., Govt. Printing Office, 1912. 663 p.

Reprint by Da Capo Press, New York, 1969.

Orchestra scores from about 1830 to 1912.

Review by Ruth Watanabe in *Notes*, 26 (1970), p. 521–24.

1539 / **U.S. Library of Congress. Music Division. Elizabeth Sprague Coolidge Foundation.** Coolidge Foundation program for contemporary chamber music; preliminary checklist of works available for loan (November 1961). Compiled by Frances G. Gewehr. Washington, D.C., Library of Congress, 1961. 38 p. (typescript)

Supplement, April 1963.

A classified list of contemporary chamber music scores and parts which may be borrowed by qualified ensembles for study purposes. Entries give publisher and price; recordings if available are also cited.

U.S. Library of Congress. Music Division. Dayton C. Miller Flute Collection. See nos. 701, 1634.

1540 / **Washington Cathedral. Library.** "The Douglas collection in the Washington Cathedral Library." In *The life and work of Charles Winfred Douglas*, by Leonard Ellinwood and Anne Woodward Douglas. New York, Hymn Society of America, 1958. p. 36–72. (Hymn Society of America, Papers, no. 23.)

A library of hymnology and liturgical music formed by one of the leading authorities in the field.

WINSTON-SALEM, NORTH CAROLINA

1541 / **Moravian Music Foundation.** Catalog of the Johannes Herbst collection. Ed. by Marilyn Gombosi. Chapel Hill, Univ. of North Carolina Press, 1970. 255 p.

A thematic catalog of some 500 manuscripts of sacred music for use in the Moravian service. There are about 1,000 anthems and arias in the collection. The catalog is preceded by an historical introduction describing the musical practices of the 18th-century Moravian church. Index of composers and titles.

Review by Susan T. Sommer in *Notes*, 29 (1972), p. 258–59.

WOLFENBÜTTEL, GERMANY

1542 / **Herzog-August-Bibliothek.** Die Handschriften nebst den älteren Druckwerken der Musikabteilung . . . Beschrieben von Emil Vogel. . . . Wolfenbüttel, J. Zwissler, 1890. 280 p. (Die Handschriften der Herzoglichen Bibliothek zu Wolfenbüttel . . . 8.)

1543 / **Herzog-August-Bibliothek.** . . . Musik: alte Drucke bis etwa 1750. Beschrieben von Wolfgang Schmieder. Mitarbeit von Gisela Hartwieg. Text- und Registerband. Frankfurt am Main, V. Klostermann, 1967. 2 v. (Kataloge der Herzog-August-Bibliothek Wolfenbüttel, 12 u. 13.)

Vol. I: Texaband. 764 p. Vol. II: Registerband. 310 p.

A splendid catalog of 1,334 entries, representing the resources of one of the great German libraries. Early printed music and theoretical treatises.

Review by Harald Heckmann in *Die Musikforschung*, 23 (1970), p. 207–209; by Donald W. Krummel in *Notes*, 26 (1969), p. 39–40.

1544 / **Herzog-August-Bibliothek.** Libretti: Verzeichnis der bis 1800 erschienenen Text bücher. Hrsg. von Eberhard Theil und Gisela Rohr. Frankfurt am Main, Klostermann, 1970. 395 p. (Katalog der Herzog-August-Bibliothek Wolfenbüttel, 14.)

The entire collection, 1742 listings, of pre-1800 libretti of operas, interludes, operettas, musical comedies, burlesques, and ballets is

available for purchase on microfiche from Kraus-Thomson, Nendeln, Lichtenstein.
Review by Susan T. Sommer in *Notes*, 29 (1972), p. 259.

WROCLAW, POLAND (formerly BRESLAU, GERMANY)

1545 / **Bohn, Emil.** Bibliographie der Musik-Druckwerke bis 1700 welche in der Stadbibliothek, der Bibliothek des Acad. Inst. für Kirchenmusik, und der K. und Universitäts-Bibliothek zu Breslau aufbewahrt werden. . . . Berlin, A. Cohn, 1883. 450 p.
Reprint by Georg Olms, Hildesheim, 1969.
The three collections cataloged here are outstanding for their 16th- and 17th-century manuscripts and prints, particularly of liturgical and vocal music. P. 1–31: theoretical works; p. 32–351: practical works (music); p. 371–74: collections of chronological order; p. 374–400: continuation of practical works. Full bibliographical descriptions.

1546 / **Stadtbibliothek.** Die musikalischen Handschriften des XVI. und XVII. Jahrhunderts in der Stadtbibliothek zu Breslau . . . von Emil Bohn. Breslau, Commissions-Verlag von J. Hainauer, 1890. 423 p.
Reprint by Georg Olms, Hildesheim, 1970.
356 items, with full inventories of contents. Numerous indexes and supplementary lists; first-line incipits of vocal texts, anonymous compositions, composer index, etc.

1547 / **Staats- und Universitäts-Bibliothek.** Beschreibendes Verzeichnis der alten Musikalien-Handschriften und Druckwerke des Königlichen Gymnasiums zu Brieg. Bearbeitet von Friedrich Kuhn. Leipzig, Breitkopf & Härtel, 1897. 98 p. (Monatshefte für Musikgeschichte. Beilage, Jahrgang 29.)
A collection placed in the library of Breslau University in 1890. 54 manuscripts and some 110 printed books, chiefly 16th century. Contents given for manuscript anthologies; full bibliographical description for prints. Index.

WUPPERTAL, GERMANY

1548 / **Stadtbibliothek.** Musikalien-Bestand der Stadtbibliothek. Wuppertal, 1960. 117 p.

YUGOSLAVIA

1549 / **Glasbeni Rokopisi in Tiski na Slovenskem do Leta 1800.** Music manuscripts and printed music in Slovenia before 1800. Catalogue. [Compiled by J. Höfler and I. Klemencic.] Ljubljani, Narodna in Univerzitetna knjiznica v Ljubljani, 1967. 105 p.

The present catalogue is an attempt to catalogue all surviving early musical material in libraries and archives throughout Slovenia. [From the introduction by the editors]

The material comprises 32 chant manuscripts, 343 general manuscripts, chiefly 18th and early 19th century, and an unnumbered section devoted to printed music. Items are located in 17 Slovenian libraries or collections.

SORAU, GERMANY (NOW ZARY, POLAND)

1550 / **Hauptkirche.** Musikalienkatalog der Hauptkirche zu Sorau N. L. Hergestellt von G. Tischer und K. Burchard. [Langensalza, H. Beyer & Söhne, 1902.] 24 p. (Monatshefte für Musikgeschichte. Beilage. Jahrgang 34.)
The collection contains 33 prints, chiefly 17th century, and a small group of manuscripts in which Telemann, Petri, and C. G. Tag are well represented.

ZURICH, SWITZERLAND

1551 / **Allgemeine Musikgesellschaft.** Katalog der gedruckten und handschriftlichen Musikalien des 17. bis 19. Jahrhunderts im Besitze der Allgemeinen Musikgesellschaft Zürich. Red. von Georg Walter. Zürich, Hug, 1960. 145 p.
A collection rich in 17th- and 18th-century instrumental music. Thematic incipits for works in manuscript.
Review by Donald Krummel in *Notes*, 19 (1961), p. 77; by Willi Kahl in *Die Musikforschung*, 16 (1963), p. 284.

1552 / **Zentralbibliothek.** "Die Österreichische Musiküberlieferung der Züricher Zentralbibliothek." [By Erich Schenk.] In *Die*

Osterreichische Nationalbibliothek. Festschrift hrsg. zum 25. jährigen Dienstjubiläum des Generaldirektors Prof. Dr. Josef Bick. Wien, H. Bauer-Verlag, 1948. p. 576–81.

Consists chiefly of a listing of works by Austrian composers in the Zurich library, giving place, publisher and library signature. Special attention given to works not mentioned in Eitner.

ZWICKAU, GERMANY

1553 / **Ratsschulbibliothek.** Bibliographie der Musikwerke in der Ratsschulbibliothek zu Zwickau, bearb. . . . von Reinhard Vollhardt. Leipzig, Breitkopf & Härtel, 1893–96. 299 p. (Monatshefte für Musikgeschichte. Beilage. Jahrgang 25–28.)

764 numbered items manuscripts and printed books, including liturgical works, theoretical works, instrumental and vocal music. Chiefly 16th- and 17-century materials.

CATALOGS OF PRIVATE COLLECTIONS

In this section some of the catalogs of major private music collections are cited. Few of these remain intact. Some, like the Cortot or the Wolffheim collections, have been dispersed; others have changed location in recent years. No attempt has been made here to list the numerous catalogs issued in connection with auction sales, although some of these are of great bibliographical interest. Some indication of the information to be gained from the study of early music auction catalogs, a field very little explored as yet, can be found in A. Hyatt King's recent book on *Some British collectors of music, c. 1600–1960,* Cambridge University Press, 1963.

Frits Knuf, Amsterdam, has announced the publication of a series of reprints of important auction catalogs of music. Those scheduled for publication in the *First Series* are catalogs of Selhof, Burney, Türk, Coussemaker, Novello, and Rimbault.

1554 / **Bokemeyer, Heinrich.** Collection. An important 18th-century music library assembled by the theorist Heinrich Bokemeyer

(1679–1751). Harald Kümmerling has reconstructed the collection and identified its surviving elements now in the Stiftung Preussischer Kulturbesitz in Berlin.

See under BERLIN, GERMANY. No. 1170.

1555 / **Cortot, Alfred.** Bibliothèque Alfred Cortot. . . . v.l. Catalogue établi par Alfred Cortot et rédigé par Frederik Goldbeck, avec la collaboration de A. Fehr. Préface de Henry Prunières. [Argentevil, Sur les presses de R. Coulouma, 1936] 221 p.

Première partie (all published): Traités et autres ouvrages théoriques des XVe, XVIe, XVIIe, & XVIIIe siècles.

The music theory holdings in the library of Alfred Cortot. Cortot's interests as a collector extended over a wide area of musical practice. The collection passed into the hands of a dealer at the owner's death in 1962.

Portions of the Cortot library have since been acquired by the British Museum, the Newberry Library in Chicago, the University of California Music Library at Berkeley, and the University of Kentucky at Lexington. For an account of this dispersal, and a complete list of Kentucky's acquisition of 290 treatises, see Frank Traficante, "The Alfred Cortot collection at the University of Kentucky Libraries," in *University of Kentucky Library Notes*, 1: 3 (Spring 1970), 19 p. A shorter version of the same paper is printed in *Notes*, 26 (1970), p. 713–17. The Cortot materials in the British Museum are described by A. Hyatt King and O. W. Neighbour in *The British Museum Quarterly*, 31 (1966), p. 8–16.

1556 / **Feininger, Laurence.** Repertorium cantus plani. Tridenti, Societas Universalis Sanctae Ceciliae, 1969. 2 v.

Catalog of a private collection of liturgical manuscripts. Vol. I: Antiphonaria. Vol. II: Gradualia.

Each volume treats 24 manuscripts. Descriptions are followed by complete inventories of the contents of each source. Indexes of liturgical incipits conclude each volume.

1557 / **Fuchs, Aloys.** "The autographs of the Viennese music collections of Aloys Fuchs, using the original catalogues". Edited by Richard Schaal, in *Haydn Yearbook*, Vol. VI (1969), p. 3–191.

The autographs are listed alphabetically by composer, with information as to provenance and destination if known. Introduction in German and English.

Fuchs (1799–1853) was the first great collector of musical autographs. His collection was dispersed, but portions of it can be found in the Berlin Staatsbibliothek, the Staatsbibliothek der Stiftung Preussischer Kulturbesitz, and the Benedictine Abbey at Göttweig.
See also no. 1257.

1558 / **Heyer, William.** Musikhistorisches Museum von Wilhelm Heyer in Köln, Katalog von Georg Kinsky. Band 4: Musik-Autographen. Leipzig, Breitkopf & Härtel, 1916. 870 p.

1,673 items, one of the finest collections of musical autographs ever assembled. Dispersed and sold at auction in 1926 by the firm of Henrici and Liepmannssohn. Kinsky's catalogs of the Heyer collection are models of music bibliography, full of biographical and descriptive detail. 64 facsimile plates.

For other volumes of the Heyer *Katalog*, see no. 1592.

1559 / **Hirsch, Paul.** Katalog der Musikbibliothek Paul Hirsch. . . . Frankfurt am Main, herausg. von K. Meyer und P. Hirsch. . . . Berlin, M. Breslauer, 1928–47. 4 v. (V.4 has imprint: Cambridge Univ. Press.)

Vol. 1: Theoretisch Drucke bis 1800. Vol. 2: Opera-Partituren. Vol. 3: Instrumental- und Vokalmusik bis etwa 1830. Vol. 4: Erstausgaben, Chorwerke in Partitur, Gesamtausgaben, Nachschlagewerke, etc. Ergänzungen zu Bd. I–III.

The Paul Hirsch Library, one of the great private music collections of the world, was removed from Frankfurt to Cambridge, England just prior to World War II and was acquired by the British Museum in 1946.

See also nos. 1333, 1334.

1560 / **Koch, Louis. Collection.** Katalog der Musikautographen Sammlung . . . Manuskripte, Briefe, Dokumente, von Scarlatti bis Stravinsky. Beschrieben und erläutert von Georg Kinsky. Stuttgart, Hoffmannsche Buchdruckerei F. Krais, 1953. 360 p.

An important collection of musical autographs. Strong in German music of the classic and romantic periods. 21 facsimile plates.

Review by Richard S. Hill in *Notes*, 11 (1953), p. 119–20.

1561 / **Meyer, André. Music Collection.** Collection musicale André Meyer: manuscrits, autographes, musique imprimée et manuscrite, ouvrages théoriques, historiques et pédagogiques, livrets, iconographie, instruments de musique. Abbeville, F. Paillart [1960], 118 p.

Catalog compiled by Francois Lesure and Nanie Bridgman.

A collection of manuscripts and early printed music, particularly noteworthy for its holdings in iconography. Beautifully illustrated by 292 plates.

Review by Hans Halm in *Die Musikforschung*, 17 (1964), p. 83–84.

1562 / Die Musikalien der Grafen von Schönborn-Wiesentheid.
Thematisch-bibliographischer Katalog. I. Theil: Das Repertoire des Grafen Rudolf Franz Erwein von Schönborn (1677–1754). Band I: Drucke aus den Jahren 1676 bis 1738. By Fritz Zobeley. Tutzing, Hans Schneider 1967. 143 p. (Veröffentlichungen der Gesellschaft für Bayerische Musikgeschichte e.V.)

Thematic catalog of a private collection of early vocal and instrumental music assembled by the Count von Schönborn-Wiesentheid in Schloss Weiler bei Aschaffenburg. 149 items, with full bibliographical descriptions and inventories of contents. Informative introductory chapters on the history of the collection and its composition. Further catalogs of the MSS and archive materials projected.

Review by W. Gordon Marigold in *Notes*, 24 (1968), p. 715–16.

1563 / Wolffheim, Werner J. Library. Versteigerung der Musikbibliothek des Herrn Dr. Werner Wolffheim . . . durch die Firmen: M. Breslauer & L. Liepmannssohn. . . . Berlin, 1928–29. 2 v. in 4.

One of the finest collections ever brought together by a private person . . . the 2-volume catalog compiled at the time of its sale will always rank as an indispensable work of reference. [*Grove's*]

Classified catalog of a library that included not only rarities but the standard reference books and editions as well. Full descriptions with copious notes. Numerous facsimile plates.

Catalogs of
Musical Instrument Collections

COLLECTIONS OF MUSICAL instruments are frequently annexed to music libraries. The reader will note that a number of the catalogs in the preceding section are concerned, in part, with Western or Oriental instruments. In the section that follows, the catalogs of some of the major specialized collections of musical instruments are listed along with a number of exhibition catalogs emphasizing this area of collecting activity.

For a comprehensive and historical view of instrument collections, see Alfred Berner's article, "Instrumentensammlungen," in *MGG*, 6, col. 1295–1310. There is also an illuminating paper by Georg Kinsky entitled "Musikinstrumentensammlungen in Vergangenheit und Gegenwart," in the *Jahrbuch Peters*, 27 (1920), p. 47–60. The article in *Grove's*, 5th edition, by Langwell (vol. 4, p. 509–15) provides the locations of the collections but no bibliographical information.

ANN ARBOR, MICHIGAN

1564 / **University of Michigan. Stearns Collection of Musical Instruments.** Catalog of the Stearns collection of musical instruments, by Albert A. Stanley. 2nd ed. Ann Arbor, Mich., University of Michigan, 1921. 276 p.

First published in 1918.

A catalog of 1,464 instruments, Western and Oriental. 13 plates, descriptive annotations. Bibliography and indexes of makers, geographical distribution, names of instruments.

A brief, informative survey of the history of the collection, its character and present condition. Three plates.

1565 / **University of Michigan. Stearns Collection of Musical Instruments.** Stearns collection of musical instruments—1965. By Robert Austin Warner. . . . Ann Arbor, School of Music, University of Michigan [1965], 10 p.

BASEL, SWITZERLAND

1566 / **Historisches Museum.** Katalog der Musikinstrumente im Historischen Museum zu Basel. Von Dr. Karl Nef. Basel, Universitäts-Buchdruckerei von Friedrich Reinhardt, 1906. 74 p.

Bound with *Festschrift zum zweiten Kongress der Internationalen Musikgesellschaft*, Basel, 1906. 294 instruments listed and described. 12 plates.

BERKELEY, CALIFORNIA

1567 / **University of California. Department of Music.** Catalogue of the collection of musical instruments in the Department of Music, University of California, Berkeley. Part I. Edited by David Boyden . . . Berkeley, California, 1972. 104 p.

A collection of 88 instruments, including early originals and modern replicas. Short essays on the principal instrument forms. Each instrument is introduced historically followed by its precise dimensions. A second part is projected.

BERLIN, GERMANY

1568 / **Institut für Musikforschung.** Die Berliner Musikinstrumentensammlung; Einführung mit historischen und technischen Erläuterungen von Alfred Berner. Berlin, 1952. 58 p.

Not strictly a catalog, but a guide to the principal types of instruments with reference to examples in the Berlin collection. 11 plates.

1569 / **Staatliche Akademische Hochschule für Musik.** Führer durch die Sammlung alter Musik-Instrumente, von Dr. Oskar Fleischer. Berlin, A. Haack, 1892. 145 p.
Classified catalog, chiefly early Western instruments, with a few Oriental.

1570 / **Staatliche Akademische Hochschule für Musik.** Sammlung alter Musikinstrumente bei der Staatlichen Hochschule für Musik zu Berlin; beschreibender Katalog von Curt Sachs. Berlin, J. Bard, 1922. 384 cols. 30 plates.
The collection contains some 3,200 items, of which about 250 are non-European instruments. Classified catalog. Entries give descriptions of instrument, maker, date and place of manufacture. Index of instruments, places, makers, etc.

1571 / **Staatliches Institut für Musikforschung.** Das Musikinstrumenten Museum Berlin. Eine Einführung in Wort und Bild. Berlin, 1968. 70 p.
Historical essay: "75 Jahre Musikinstrumenten-Sammlung" by Irmgard Otto; 56 photo plates of instruments.

1572 / **Staatliches Institut für Musikforschung.** Musikinstrumenten Museum Berlin. Ausstellungsverzeichnis mit Personen- und Sachregistern, bearbeitet von Irmgard Otto. Berlin, 1965. 144 p.
A guide to the Berlin musical instrument collection as currently displayed, with a diagram of the exposition halls, index of donors, a list of catalog numbers, and 12 pages of photo plates of instruments.

BOSTON, MASSACHUSETTS

1573 / **Museum of Fine Arts. Leslie Lindsey Mason Collection.** Ancient European musical instruments . . . by N. Bessaraboff . . . Pub. for the Museum . . . by the Harvard Univ. Press, 1941. 503 p.
An authoritative catalog, well illustrated, 213 items. Provides a wealth of background information for the historical study of instruments. Bibliography, p. 453–69. Indexes of names and subjects. 16 plates and 72 illustrations in text. The collection of Canon Francis W. Galpin forms the basis of the Mason collection.

Review by Curt Sachs in MQ (July, 1942), p. 380–83.

For a recent evaluation of the book, and a tribute to its author, see David Boyden's article "Nicholas Bessaraboff's Ancient European musical instruments," in Notes, 28 (1971), p. 21–27.

BRAUNSCHWEIG, GERMANY

1574 / **Städtisches Museum.** Verzeichnis der Sammlung alter Musikinstrumente im Städtischen Museum Braunschweig . . . Instrumente, Instrumentenmacher und Instrumentisten in Braunschweig. . . . Braunschweig, E. Appelhans, 1928. 124 p. (Werkstücke aus Museum, Archiv und Bibliothek der Stadt Braunschweig, 3.)

At head of title: Hans Schröder.

The catalog occupies p. 5–34; lists 113 items, all European. The remainder of the volume is devoted to studies of local instrument makers and performers.

BRUSSELS, BELGIUM

1575 / **Conservatoire Royal de Musique. Musée Instrumental.** Catalogue déscriptif et analytique du Musée . . . par Victor-Charles Mahillon, conservateur . . . 2nd ed. Gand, A. Hoste, 1893–1922. 5 v.

One of the great instrument collections of the world. More than 3,000 instruments of all cultures. Classified catalog. The descriptions include precise indications of each instrument's pitch, tuning, and range.

BUSSUM, HOLLAND

1576 / **Leewen Boomkamp, C. van, and J. H. van der Meer.** The Carel van Leeuwen Boomkamp collection of musical instruments. Amsterdam, Frits Knuf, 1971. 188 p. 80 plates.

A private collection of 112 items, expertly described and illustrated in photographs. The collection is strongest in its stringed instruments (57) and its bows (32).

Review by Anthony Baines in Galpin Society Journal, 25 (1972), p. 123–35.

CAIRO, EGYPT

1577 / **Museum of Egyptian Antiquities.** Catalogue général des antiquités égyptiennes du Musée du Caire. Nos. 69201–69852: Instruments de musique, par Hans Hickmann. Le Caire, Imprimerie de l'Institut français d'archéologie orientale, 1949. 216 p. 116 plates.

Classified catalog of 651 ancient Egyptian instruments, or fragments thereof, with detailed descriptions and photo reproductions.

CINCINNATI, OHIO

1578 / **Art Museum.** Musical instruments. [Collection of the Cincinnati Art Museum.] Cincinatti, 1949.

An illustrated brochure listing 110 instruments, 60 European, 50 non-European.

COPENHAGEN, DENMARK

1579 / **Carl Claudius Collection.** Carl Claudius' Samling af gamle musikinstrumenter. København, Levin og Munskgaard, 1931. 423 p.

A rich private collection of musical instruments, now administered by the University of Copenhagen. The catalog describes 757 items.

1580 / **Musikhistorisk Museum.** Das Musikhistorische Museum zu Kopenhagen: beschreibender Katalog von Angul Hammerich; deutsch von Erna Bobé. Mit 179 illustrationen. Kopenhagen, G. E. C. Gad; Leipzig, Kommissionsverlag von Breitkopf & Härtel, 1911. 172 p.

The Danish edition appeared in 1909.

Classified catalog of 631 items, 582 of which are instruments, Western and Oriental, followed by a short listing of liturgical manuscripts, prints, and miscellany.

EDINBURGH, SCOTLAND

1581 / **University. Dept. of Early Keyboard Instruments.** The Russell Collection and other early keyboard instruments in Saint Cecilia's Hall, Edinburgh. [Compiled by Sidney Newman and Peter Williams.] Edinburgh, Edinburgh Univ. Press, 1968. 79 p.

1582 / **University. Galpin Society Exhibition.** An exhibition of European musical instruments. Edinburgh International Festival, Aug. 18th–Sept. 7th, 1968, Reid School of Music, Edinburgh University. Edinburgh, 1968. 99 p. 40 plates.

The 21st anniversary exhibition of the Galpin Society.

An exhibition catalog of 716 items, including bibliography. Instruments described, dimensions given. The introductory paragraphs for each group of instruments are supplied by specialists. The editor of the catalog is Graham Melville-Mason.

See also the Galpin Society exhibition catalog, London 1951 (no. 1601).

EISENACH, GERMANY

1583 / **Bachmuseum.** Berzeichnis der Sammlung alter Musikinstrumente im Bachhaus zu Eisenach, hrsg. von der Neuen Bach Gesellschaft. 4., erweiterte Aufl. Leipzig, Breitkopf & Härtel, 1964. 97 p. (Veröffentlichungen der Neuen Bachgesellschaft. Vereinsjahr 50, 1962.)

First issued in 1913.

Classified catalog of more than 230 items. Illustrated with line drawings.

FLORENCE, ITALY

1584 / **Conservatorio di Musica "Luigi Cherubini."** Gli strumenti musicali raccolti nel Museo del R. Istituto L. Cherubini a Firenze. [By Leto Bargagna. Firenze, G. Ceccherini.] [1911] 70 p.

A catalog of 146 instruments; 12 plates.

1585 / **Museo del Conservatorio "Luigi Cherubini."** Gli strumenti musicali della corte medicea e il Museo del Conservatorio "Luigi Cherubini" di Firenze. Cenni storici e catalogo descrittivo. [By] Vincio Gai. Firenze, LICOSA, 1969. 286 p.

The instruments are illustrated by line drawings with precise measurements. P. 255–71: "Bibliografia." Preceded by an introduction relating the history of the collection.

374

GIJÓN, SPAIN

1586 / **Museo Internacional de la Gaita.** Catalogo. Gijón, Asturias (España), 1970. 152 p.

Catalog of a museum devoted to the bagpipe, its history and distribution. Organized by country, with numerous color plates and black-and-white illustrations.

THE HAGUE, HOLLAND

1587 / **Gemeentemuseum.** Catalogi van de muziekbibliotheek en de collectie muziekinstrumenten onder redactie van dr. C. C. J. von Gleich. Catalogus van de muziekinstrumenten. Deel I: Hoorn-en trompetachtige blaasinstrumenten door Leo J. Plenckers. Amsterdam, Frits Knuf, 1970. 85 p.

The first of a series of catalogs projected to cover the musical instrument collections at the Gemeentemuseum. Describes 136 instruments of the horn and trumpet type. Eight plates; a classified grouping of instrument types, and a glossary. Index of names.

This series is paralleled by another devoted to the holdings of the Museum's music library. (See no. 1265.)

1588 / **Gemeentemuseum.** Europese muziekinstrumenten in het Hagse Gemeentemuseum. [By A. W. Ligtvoet & W. Lievense.] 's-Gravenhage, Gemeentemuseum, 1965. 160 p.

With 64 full-page illustrations.

1589 / **Gemeentemuseum.** Exotische en oude Europese muziekinstrumenten, in de muziekafdeling van het Hagse Gemeentemuseum; 25 afbeeldingen toegelicht. [By A. W. Ligtvoet.] 's-Gravenhage, Nijgh & Van Ditmar [1955], 51 p.

A general, popular introduction to the collection. 25 plates. Text in Dutch and English.

HALLE, GERMANY

1590 / **Händel-Haus.** Katalog zu den Sammlungen des Händel-Hauses in Halle. 5. Teil: Musikinstrumentensammlung. Besaitete Tasteninstrumente. By Konrad Sasse. Halle, Händel-Haus, 1966. 292 p. 115 illustrations.

One of the largest collections of keyboard instruments in Europe, comprising some 115 items. Founded on the collection of J. C. Neupert of Nuremberg, acquired in the 1930s.

Review by Friedrich Ernst in *Die Musikforschung*, 21 (1968), p. 506–07.

For a catalog of the complete holdings of the Handel House in Halle, see no. 1268.

[HEYER COLLECTION]

1591 / **Heyer Collection.** Kleiner Katalog der Sammlung alter Musikinstrumente, verfasst von Georg Kinsky. Köln, 1913. 250 p.

An abridgement of the material in the following catalog; valuable because it contains entries for the wind instruments in the Heyer collection, not included in the larger catalog.

1592 / **Heyer Collection.** Musikhistorisches Museum von Wilhelm Heyer in Köln. Katalog von Georg Kinsky. Leipzig, Breitkopf & Härtel, 1910–16. 2 v.

The two volumes of this catalog are concerned with the instrument collection. Vol. 1: Besaitete Tasteninstruments. Orgel und orgelartige Instrumente. Friktionsinstrumente. Vol. 2: Zupf- und Streichinstrumente. Vol. 3 (not published) was intended to cover the wind instruments. The Heyer instrument collection, one of the finest in the world, was transferred to Leipzig in 1926, where it was destroyed in World War II.

Kinsky's catalog is a mine of information for the student of early instruments; copiously illustrated, rich in detail.

See also no. 1558, 1591.

HOLYOKE, MASSACHUSETTS

1593 / **Mount Holyoke College.** The Belle Skinner collection of old musical instruments. . . . A descriptive catalogue compiled under the direction of William Skinner. [Philadelphia, New York, etc. Printed by the Beck Engraving Co.] 1933. 210 p.

Illustrated catalog of 89 instruments, including some particularly fine examples of keyboard instruments. Colored plates.

Since 1959 this collection has been on loan to Yale University.

JOHANNESBURG, SOUTH AFRICA

1594 / **Kirby, Percival Robson.** Catalogue of the musical instruments in the collection of Percival R. Kirby, compiled by Margaret M. de Lange. Johannesburg, Africana Museum, 1967. 155 p.

[LACHMANN COLLECTION]

1595 / **Lachmann, Erich.** Erich Lachmann collection of historical stringed musical instruments. Los Angeles, Allan Hancock Foundation, Univ. of Southern California, 1950. 53 p.

A handsome catalog of 42 items; noteworthy for its photographic illustrations by Irvin Kershner.

LEIPZIG, GERMANY

1596 / **Karl-Marx-Universität.** Führer durch des Musikinstrumentenmuseum der Karl-Marx-Universität Leipzig. Von Paul Rubardt. Leipzig, Breitkopf & Härtel, 1955. 84 p. 16 plates.

1597 / **Universität. Musikwissenschaftlisches Instrumentenmuseum.** Führer durch das Musikwissenschaftliche Instrumentenmuseum der Universität Leipzig. Hrsg. von Helmut Schultz. Leipzig, Breitkopf & Härtel, 1929. 85 p. 19 plates.

A classified catalog organized according to the ground plan of the display.

LINZ, AUSTRIA

1598 / **Landesmuseum.** Die Musikinstrumentensammlung des Oberösterreichischen Landesmuseums. Bearbeitet von Othmar Wessely. Linz, Demokratische Druck- und Verlags-Gesellschaft [n.d.], 47 p. (Kataloge des Oberösterreichischen Landesmuseums, 9.)

A collection of 188 items, classified and described briefly.

LONDON, ENGLAND

1599 / **British Museum. Department of Western Asiatic Antiquities.** Ancient musical instruments of Western Asia in the Department of Western Asiatic Antiquities, the British Museum. By Joan Rimmer. London, British Museum, 1969. 51 p. 26 plates.

Actual instruments as well as depictions are described. Treats the use of string, wind, and percussion instruments in Sumerian, Babylonian, Anatolian, Assyrian, and Hellenistic Asiatic societies. Corrects several inaccurate reassemblies. Appendix gives a classified list of instruments and a table of musical references in the Old Testament.

1600 / **Fenton House. Benton Fletcher Collection.** Catalogue of the Benton Fletcher collection of early keyboard instruments at Fenton House, Hampstead. London, Country Life, Ltd., for the National Trust, 1957. 26 p.

A descriptive brochure by Raymond Russell for a collection of early keyboard instruments maintained in playing condition in a late-17th-century house in Hampstead, London.

1601 / **Galpin Society.** British musical instruments. August 7–30, 1951. [London, The Galpin Society, 1951.] 35 p.

A classified exhibition catalog of instruments, chiefly of British make or use. Includes 151 woodwind, 61 brass, 27 keyboard, 62 of the violin family, 16 of the viol family, and 16 miscellaneous. Brief descriptions, with short introductions for each class of instruments.

See also the Galpin Society exhibition catalog, Edinburgh, 1968.

1602 / **Horniman Museum.** The Adam Carse collection of old musical wind instruments [now in the Horniman Museum, London]. London, Staples Press for the London County Council, 1951. 88 p.

A collection of 320 instruments, briefly described, with historical notes for each family. Illustrated by drawings.

1603 / **Horniman Museum and Library.** Musical instruments: handbook to the Museum's collection, by Jean L. Jenkins. 2nd ed. London, Inner London Education Authority, 1970. 104 p.

First edition published in 1958.

A catalog which is at the same time a handbook for the study of musical instruments, chiefly non-Western. 32 plates; bibliography, discography, and index.

1604 / **Royal College of Music.** Catalog of historical musical instruments paintings, sculpture, and drawings. [London, Royal College, 1952.] 16 p.

Foreword by George Dyson.

Contains the Donaldson collection of musical instruments. Brief inventory with minimum description.

1605 / **Royal Military Exhibition, 1890.** A descriptive catalogue of the musical instruments recently exhibited at the Royal Military Exhibition, London, 1890. Compiled by Charles Russell Day. London, Eyre & Spottiswoode, 1891. 253 p.

An exhibition confined to wind and percussion instruments. 457 wind instruments (percussion not inventoried). Plates.

1606 / **South Kensington Museum.** A descriptive catalogue of the musical instruments of the South Kensington Museum . . . By Carl Engel. . . . London, Printed by G. E. Eyre and W. Spottiswoode for H.M. Stationery Office, 1874. 402 p.

Preceded by an essay on the history of musical instruments.

1607 / **Victoria and Albert Museum.** Catalogue of musical instruments. London, Her Majesty's Stationery Office, 1968. 2 v.

Vol. 1: Keyboard instruments, by Raymond Russell. 94 p. and 47 plates. Detailed descriptions of 52 keyboard instruments, including pianos and organs described by Austin Niland. Appendix B: The decoration of keyboard instruments by Peter Thornton; biographical notes on the makers, bibliography and index.

Vol. 2: Non-keyboard instruments, by Anthony Baines. 121 p. 138 plates. The instruments are grouped as stringed instruments and wind instruments, with 16 subgroups of the former, 8 of the latter. Full technical descriptions, clear plates of details; bibliography and index.

Review by Don L. Smithers in *Notes*, 26 (1969), p. 47–48.

1608 / **Victoria and Albert Museum.** Musical instruments as works of art. London, Victoria and Albert Museum, 1968. 50 unnumbered leaves.

Illustrated with more than 100 plates showing details of early musical instruments characterized by fine workmanship. All from the instrument collection of the Victoria and Albert.

LUCERNE, SWITZERLAND

1609. / **Richard Wagner Museum.** Katalog der städtischen Sammlung alter Musikinstrumente im Richard-Wagner-Museum, Tribschen, Luzern. Erstellt im Auftrag der Museum-Kommission von René Vannes. . . . Luzern, Otto Dreyer, 1956. 40 p.

A catalog of 95 stringed instruments, 46 wind, 11 idiophones, 37 exotic instruments. 16 plates.

1610 / **Museum and Art Gallery.** The Ridley collection of musical wind instruments in the Luton Museum. [Luton, the Corp. of Luton, Museum and Art Gallery, 1957.] 32 p.

65 wind instruments. Historical note, p. 1–21. Plates.

MILAN, ITALY

1611 / **Conservatorio di Musica "Giuseppe Verdi."** Gli strumenti musicali nel Museo del Conservatorio di Milano. Ed. E. Guarinoni. Milano, Hoepli, 1908. 109 p.

A collection of 278 instruments, 177 European and 91 non-European. Index of donors and of instruments.

1612 / **Museo degli Strumenti Musicali.** Catalogo, a cura di Natale e Franco Gallini. [Milano] Castello Sforzesco [1963] 448 p.

An earlier catalog of the same collection issued in 1958 under the title: *Civico Museo di antichi strumenti musicali.* The 1963 catalog, completely reorganized, lists 641 items, well described and illustrated in 141 plates.

1613 / **Museo degli Strumenti Musicali.** Mostra di antichi strumenti musicali della Collezione N. Gallini (Maggio, 1953). Milano, Villa Communale (Ex Reale) [1955], 43 p.

An exhibition catalog of 200 items dating from the time when the Gallini collection was in private hands. It has since become the property of the city of Milan, and its complete catalog appears above. Preface signed by Natale Gallini; 32 plates.

MUNICH, GERMANY

1614 / **Bayerisches Nationalmuseum.** Ausstellung alte Musik, Instrumente, Noten und Dokumente aus drei Jahrhunderten. Veranstaltet durch die Stadt München im Bayerischen Nationalmuseum, November–December, 1951. Katalog. München, Musikverlag Max Hieber, 1951, 71 p. 23 plates.

An exhibition devoted to music in cultural history. 636 items, of which the majority are early instruments.

1615 / **Yale University. Art Gallery.** Musical instruments at Yale, a selection of Western instruments from the 15th to 20th centuries. Catalog by Sibyl Marcuse. . . . [New Haven] Yale University Art Gallery [1960], 32 p.

An exhibition, Feb. 19–March 27, 1960, of 26 instruments as well as paintings, drawings, prints, and manuscripts. Illustrated.

1616 / **Yale University.** Checklist, Yale collection of musical instruments. New Haven, Conn., Yale University, 1968. 43 p.

Preface signed by Richard Rephann, Curator, 1968.

Checklist of 310 instruments comprising items from the Morris Steinert, the Belle Skinner, and the Emil Herrmann collections as well as gifts from private donors and Friends of Music at Yale. Brief descriptions, no bibliography, chiefly Western instruments.

1617 / **Yale University. Morris Steinert Collection.** The Morris Steinert collection of keyed and stringed instruments. New York, Tretbar [1893].

1618 / **Metropolitan Museum of Art.** . . . Catalog of keyboard instruments. New York, Metropolitan Museum of Art, 1903. 313 p.

1619 / **Metropolitan Museum of Art. Crosby Brown Collection.** Catalog of the Crosby Brown collection of musical instruments of all nations. . . . New York, Metropolitan Museum of Art, 1903–1907. 3 v. in 4.

Vol. 1: Europe (1904). Vol. 2: Asia (1903). Vol. 3: Instruments of savage tribes and semi-civilized people: Pt. 1, Africa (1907); Pt. 2, Oceanica (1907); Pt. 3, Historical groups (1905).

See the article by Emanuel Winternitz, "The Crosby Brown collection of musical instruments: its origin and development," in *Metropolitan Museum Journal*, 3 (1970). Also printed as a separate, 20 p.

1620 / **New York (City) Metropolitan Museum of Art.** Keyboard instruments in the Metropolitan Museum of Art, a picture book by

Emanuel Winternitz. New York, The Metropolitan Museum of Art, 1961. 48 p.

Not a catalog, but a book of photo reproductions of keyboard instruments from the Metropolitan's collection, including details, with commentary by the Curator.

OXFORD, ENGLAND

1621 / **Ashmolean Museum.** Catalogue of the Hill collection of musical instruments in the Ashmolean Museum, Oxford, by David D. Boyden. London, Oxford Univ. Press, 1969. 54 p. 57 plates.

Review by Joan Rimmer in *Notes*, 26 (1970), p. 741–44.

PARIS, FRANCE

1622 / **Conservatoire National.** . . . Le Musée du Conservatoire National de musique. Catalogue descriptif et raisonné, par Gustave Chouquet. Nouvelle ed. Paris, Firmin-Didot, 1884. 276 p.

First published in 1875. Supplement by Léon Pillaut, in 1894, 1899, and 1903.

A catalog of 1,006 instruments, subdivided into European and non-European sections. Index of instruments and of names. Catalogers of musical instruments owe much to the classification established by Chouquet in this catalog.

SALZBURG, AUSTRIA

1623 / **Museum Carolina Augusteum.** Alte Musik-Instrumente im Museum Carolino Augusteum Salzburg. Führer und beschreibendes Verzeichnis von Karl Geiringer. Leipzig, Breitkopf & Härtel, 1932. 46 p.

A catalog of 288 instruments, with an index of makers and four photographic plates showing 48 different instruments.

TOKYO, JAPAN

1624 / **Musashino Academiae Musicae.** Catalogue, museum of musical instruments. On the 40th anniversary of the Institute. Tokyo, Japan, 1969. 108 p. Four p. of illustrations.

Text in Japanese and English.

The collection was established in 1953. The catalog is classified by national origins of the instruments, with a taxonomy according to method of sound production. Part 2 is a catalog of accessories; part 3 a catalog of mechanical devices.

TORONTO, CANADA

1625 / **Royal Ontario Museum.** Musical instruments in the Royal Ontario Museum, by Ladislav Dselenyi. Toronto, Royal Ontario Museum, 1971. 96 p.

A well-illustrated catalog of more than 100 instruments. The instruments come from the bequest of R. S. Williams, beginning in 1913.

VIENNA, AUSTRIA

1626 / **Kunsthistorisches Museum.** Alte Musikinstrumente; die Sammlung des Kunsthistorischen Museums in der neuen Burg zu Wien. [By Victor Luithlen.] Wien, H. Bauer, 1954. 28 p.

A brief visitor's guide to the collection described below.

1627 / **Gesellschaft der Musikfreunde.** "Musikinstrumente," in *Zusatz-band zur Geschichte der K. K. Gesellschaft der Musicfreunde in Wien. Sammlung und Statuten* . . . von Dr. Eurebius Mandyczewski. Wien, 1912. p. 154–85.

Catalog of a collection of 355 instruments, of which 221 are of Western origin. The remaining are of ethnic interest: Turkey, Africa, Arabia, Persia, Siam, India, China, Japan, etc.

1628 / **Kunsthistorisches Museum.** Die Sammlung alter Musikinstrumente. Beschreibendes Verzeichnis von Julius Schlosser. Wien, Anton Schroll, 1920. 138 p.

The catalog describes 361 instruments, most of which are illustrated in 57 plates. 31 Oriental and folk instruments. Western instruments are entered in chronological order, grouped according to type, with full descriptions and an informative introduction to each major section: i.e., "Das Orchester des 16. und 17. Jahrhunderts;" "Die Entwicklung des Instrumentenbaus seit dem 18. Jahrhundert." Much useful historical information given, as, for example, a supplement quoting the descriptions of 20 early instruments from Mattheson's *Neu eröffnetes Orchester* (1713).

1629 / Kunsthistorisches Museum. Katalog der Sammlung alter Musikinstrumente. I. Teil. Saitenklaviere. Wien, Kunsthistorisches Museum, 1966. 95 p. 32 plates.

Classified catalog and description of 76 keyboard instruments. Full of detailed information respecting instrument makers, dimensions of the instruments, bibliographical references. The catalog is the work of the music instrument collection's director Victor Luithlen and his assistant Kurt Wegerer. This volume is the first of three that will eventually cover all of the museum's holdings.

Review by Friedrich Ernst in *Die Musikforschung*, 21 (1968), p. 506–07.

1630 / Museum für Völkerkunde. Aussereuropäische Musikinstrumente. Wien, Museum für Völkerkunde [1961]. 89 p.

Foreword by Alfred Janata.

Illustrated, classified catalog of 654 non-European instruments.

WASHINGTON, DISTRICT OF COLUMBIA

1631 / Smithsonian Institution. Division of Musical Instruments. A checklist of keyboard instruments at the Smithsonian Institution. Washington, D.C., Smithsonian Institution, 1967. 79 p.

Full description lacking, but remarkably rich in information: maker, place of origin, date, type, compass, etc. Five plates.

For another publication based on the Smithsonian's collection of keyboard instruments, see no. 1635.

1632 / Hoover, Cynthia A. Harpsichords and clavichords. Washington, Smithsonian Institution Press, 1969. 43 p.

1633 / U.S. Library of Congress. Gertrude Clarke Whittall Foundation. The Stradivari memorial at Washington, the national capital, by William Dana Orcutt. Library of Congress, Gertrude Clarke Whittall Foundation [1938], 49 p.

Description of the matched set of Stradivarius instruments donated to the Library of Congress.

1634 / U.S. Library of Congress. Music Division. Dayton C. Miller Flute Collection, a checklist of the instruments. Compiled by

Laura E. Gilliam and William Lichtenwanger. Washington, D.C., Library of Congress, 1961. 113 p.

Lists 1,593 instruments of the flute type. Indexes by maker, type of instrument, trade name, system of fingering, etc. 8 plates.

See also no. 701 for the Dayton C. Miller *Catalog of Books . . . relating to the flute.*

Review by Anthony Baines in *Galpin Society Journal*, No. 15 (March 1962), p. 100.

1635 / **U.S. National Museum [Smithsonian Institution].** Handbook of the collection of musical instruments in the United States National Museum. By Frances Densmore. Washington, D.C., Govt. Printing Office, 1927. 164 p. 49 plates. (Smithsonian Institution U.S. National Museum. Bulletin 136.)

Histories and Bibliographies of Music Printing and Publishing

Included here are bibliographies of the output of some of the major early music printers and publishers, such as Petrucci, Playford, Walsh, Ballard, etc.; studies of music publishing in particular regions or countries (England, Italy, Paris, Vienna, etc.); and a few works concerned with the technical processes of music printing or engraving. The most comprehensive bibliography on the history of music printing has been compiled by Åke Davidsson: see no. 1644, below.

1636 / **Bergmans, Paul.** "La typographie musicale en Belgique au XVIe siècle." In *Histoire du livre et de l'imprimerie en Belgique des origines à nos jours*, 5 (Bruxelles, 1929), p. 47–75.

An illustrated account of 16th-century Belgian music printers and printing.

1637 / **Berz, Ernst-Ludwig.** Die Notendrucker und ihre Verleger in Frankfurt am Main von den Anfängen bis etwa 1630. Eine bibliographische und drucktechnische Studie zur Musikpublikation. Kassel, International Association of Music Libraries and International Musicological Society, 1970. 336 p. (Catalogus musicus, 5.)

A thoroughly documented study of music printing in Frankfurt to 1630. With a bibliography of 258 printed works by some 43 printers.

1638 / **Bobillier, Marie.** "La librairie musicale en France de 1653 à 1790, d'après les Registres de privilèges." [Par Michel Brenet, *pseud.*] In *Sammelbände der Internationalen Musikgesellschaft*, 8 (1906– 1907), p. 401–66.

An examination with extensive transcriptions from the archives in the Bibliothèque Nationale pertaining to licenses granted for the publication of music and books on music in Paris from 1652 to 1790. Thorough discussion of the inception of the royal *privilège*, with transcriptions of sample 17th-century *privilèges*. Supplemented by Cucuel, no. 1641 below.

> **The Breitkopf Thematic Catalogue . . .**
> See no. 1043.

1639 / **Castelain, Raoul.** Histoire de l'édition musicale; ou, du droit d'èditeur au droit d'auteur, 1501–1793. Préf. de André Siegfried. Paris, H. Lemoine, 1957. 92 p.

Brief history of music publishing, with emphasis on legal aspects.

1640 / **Cohen, Paul.** Musikdruck und Drucker zu Nürnberg im 16. Jahrhundert erschienenen Noten und Musikbücher. . . . Nürnberg, H. Zierfuss, 1927. 63 p.

Also issued as a dissertation (Erlangen) under the title, *Die Nürnberger Musikdrucker im sechzehnten Jahrhundert*, 1927. Historical study, with brief accounts of the individual printers, followed by a chronological listing of 443 works published in Nürnberg from 1501 to 1600.

1641 / **Cucuel, Georges.** "Quelques documents sur la librairie musicale au XVIIIe siècle." In *Sammelbände der Internationalen Musikgesellschaft*, 13 (1911–1912). p. 385–92.

A further study of the archives related to the licensing of music publications in France supplementing the article by Bobillier, no. 1638 above.

1642 / **Davidsson, Åke.** Bibliographie zur Geschitchte des Musikdrucks. Uppsala, Almquist & Wiksell, 1965. 86 p. (Studia musicologica Upsaliensia, Nova Ser. 1.)

A bibliography of 598 items related to the history of music printing and publishing, with a brief introductory survey of the literature. The expansion of a bibliography first issued as a part of the author's *Musik-bibliographische Beiträge*. See no. 1644 below.

1643 / **Davidsson, Åke.** Danskt musiktryck intill 1700-talets mitt. Dänischer Musikdruck bis zur Mitte des 18. Jahrhunderts. Uppsala [Almquist & Wiksell], 1962. 100 p. (Studia musicologica upsaliensia, 7.)

An historical study of early Danish music printing, with a chronological listing of Danish prints issued during the period under consideration. Bibliography and index of names.

Review by Martin Geck in *Die Musikforschung*, 18 (1965), p. 346–47.

1644 / **Davidsson, Åke.** "Die Literatur zur Geschichte des Notendrucks." In his *Musikbibliographische Beiträge*. Uppsala, A.B. Lundequistska Bokhandeln, 1954. P. 91–115. (Uppsala Universitets Arsskrift, 1954: 9.)

A survey of writings on the history of music printing, with a bibliography of 268 items.

Superseded by the author's *Bibliographie zur Geschichte des Musikdrucks*, see no. 1642, above.

Review by Edward N. Waters in *Notes*, 12 (1955), p. 604; by Vincent Duckles in *The Library Quarterly*, 26 (1956), p. 73–74.

1645 / **Davidsson, Åke.** Studier rörande svenskt musiktryck före ar 1750. Studien über schwedischen Musikdruck vor 1750. Uppsala [Almquist & Wiksell], 1957. 167 p. (Studia musicologica upsaliensia, 5.)

Part I (Allmän del) is a general survey of early Swedish music printing. Part II (Speciell del) is a bibliography of 124 Swedish imprints issued between 1585 and 1750, in chronological order. Text in Swedish, summary in German. General bibliography and index of persons.

Review by Rudolph Gjelsness in *Notes*, 15 (1958), p. 569–70.

1646 / **Day, Cyrus L. & E. B. Murrie.** English song-books, 1651–1702; a bibliography with a first-line index of songs. London, Bibliographical Society, 1940 [for 1937], 439 p.

Lists and describes the contents of 252 secular song books published in England and Scotland. Arrangement is chronological, nonextant works included. First-line index of 4,150 songs by about 250 composers. Also indexed by composer, author of text, performer, tunes and airs, sources, titles of collections, printers, publishers, and booksellers. A model of descriptive bibliography, particularly valuable for its coverage of the publishing activity of John and Henry Playford and their contemporaries.

1647 / **Deutsch, Otto E.** Musikverlags Nummern. Eine Auswahl von 40 datierten Listen. Zweite, verbesserte und erste deutsche Ausgabe. Berlin, Merseburger, 1961. 32 p.

Revision and expansion of a list originally published in the *Journal of Documentation*, 1 (1946), under the title: "Music publishers' numbers, a selection of 40 dated lists, 1710–1900."

Treats 20 German, 14 Austrian, 3 Dutch, 1 English, 1 French, and 1 Swiss firm. Index of places and individual publishers. Supplemented by the author's "Musikverlags-Nummern, ein Nachtrag," in *Die Musikforschung*, 15 (1962), p. 155.

Review by Donald W. Krummel in *Notes*, 19 (1961), p. 76–77; by Richard Schaal in *Die Musikforschung*, 16 (1963), p. 389.

1648 / **Dona, Mariangela.** Le stampa musicale a Milano fino all'anno 1700. Firenze, Olschki, 1961. 167 p. (Biblioteca di bibliografia italiana, 39.)

Milanese music publishers given in alphabetical order, with chronological listings of their publications. Copies of rare works located in major European libraries. Index of composers and works, index of persons to whom works are dedicated.

Review by Richard Schaal in *Die Musikforschung*, 17 (1964), p. 183.

1649 / **Dunning, Albert.** De muziekuitgever Gerhard Fredrik Witvogel en zijn fonds. Ein bijrage tot de gescheidenis van de Nederlandse muziekuitgeverij in de achttiende eeuw. Utrecht, A. Oosthoek's Uitgeversmaatschappij N.V. 1966. 64 p. (Muziekhistorische Monografieën, 2.)

"Uitgegeven door de Vereniging voor Nederlandse Muziekgeschiedenis."

Discussion of the life and works of Witvogel, with an annotated bibliography of 95 music publications by the firm. Locations of copies given, list of composers whose works were published, bibliography and index of names.

1650 / **Eitner, Robert.** Buch- und Musikalienhändler, Buch- und Musikaliendrucker nebst Notenstecher, nur die Musik betreffend nach den Originaldrucken verzeichnet. . . . Leipzig, Breitkopf & Härtel, 1904. 248 p. (Monatshefte für Musikgeschichte. Beilage.)

Compiled as a by-product of the *Quellen-Lexikon*; limited to material before 1850. Alphabetical listing of publishers, printers, and dealers, their dates of location at various addresses, changes in name, branches if any. International coverage.

1651 / **Elvers, Rudolf.** "Musikdrucker, Musikalienhändler und Musikverleger in Berlin 1750–1850." In *Festschrift Walter Gerstenberg zum 60. Geburtstag*. Wolfenbüttel, Möseler Verlag, 1964. p. 37–44.

Lists 155 Berlin music printers, dealers, and publishers active during the century under consideration.

1652 / **Epstein, Dena J.** Music publishing in Chicago before 1871; the firm of Root and Cady, 1858–1871. Detroit, Information Coordinators, 1969. 243 p. (Detroit studies in music bibliography, 14.)

Review by Klaus Hortschansky in *Die Musikforschung*, 24 (1971), p. 464–65.

1653 / **Fisher, William A.** 150 years of music publishing in the U.S.; an historical sketch with special reference to the pioneer publisher Oliver Ditson Co., 1783–1933. Boston, Oliver Ditson [1934], 156 p.

A revision and extension of portions of the author's *Notes on music in old Boston*. Boston, Mass. 1918.

1654 / **Fog, Dan.** Dänische Musikverlage und Notendruckerien. Beiträge zur Musikaliendatierung. Kopenhagen, 1972. 27 p.

Basic factual information concerning 60 Danish music printers and publishers. Important events in the history of these firms are given chronologically.

1655 / **Fraenkel, Gottfried S.** Decorative music title pages; 201 examples from 1500 to 1800. Selected, introduced, and annotated by Gottfried S. Fraenkel. New York, Dover, 1968. 230 p.

Introduction, p. 1–15, an historical survey of the items in the collection. 201 plates with historical and descriptive annotations.

1656 / **Gamble, William.** Music engraving and printing; historical and technical treatise. . . . London, New York, Pitman, 1923 [1922], 266 p.

Discusses the technical processes of music printing and engraving, with emphasis on contemporary practices. Illustrated.

1657 / **Gericke, Hannelore.** Der Wiener Musikalienhandel von 1700 bis 1778. Graz. H. Böhlaus Nachf., 1960. 150 p. (Wiener musikwissenschaftliche Beiträge, 5.)

Contents: Wiener Buchhändler als Verkäufer von Musikalien; Privatverkäufer; Kopisten; Kupferstecher; Verzeichnis der Wiener Musikdrucke von 1700–78; Liste der verbotenen Musikbücher; Zusammenfassung; Literaturverzeichnis.

Review by Donald W. Krummel in *Notes*, 18 (1961), p. 229–30.

1658 / **Göhler, Albert.** Verzeichnis der in den Frankfurter und Leipziger Messkatalogen der Jahre 1564 bis 1759 angezeigten Musikalien. . . . Leipzig, C. F. Kahnt Nachf., 1902.

Reprint by Frits A. M. Knuf, Hilversum, 1965.

A major source of information on the activities of early music dealers, printers, and publishers. It lists music entered in the Frankfurt and Leipzig trade catalogs from 1564 to 1759.

This work is also entered under no. 1073.

1659 / **Goovaerts, Alphonse J. M. A.** Histoire et bibliographie de la typographie musicale dans les Pays-Bas. Anvers, P. Kockx, 1880. 608 p. (Extrait des Mémoires de l'Académie Royale de Belgique, Collection in 8; tome XXIX.)

Reprint issued by Frits A. M. Knuf, Hilversum, 1963.

Part I (historical): a chronological discussion of music publishing in the Netherlands from 1539. Part II (bibliographical): chronological list of 1,415 music publications from 1539 to 1841. Full descriptions. Index of personal names, titles, and places.

1660 / **Grand-Carteret, John.** Les titres illustrés et l'image au service de la musique. Turin, Bocca, 1904. 269 p.

Première partie (p. 3–120): Le titre de musique sous la Révolution, le Consulat et le premier Empire (1500–1800). Duxième partie: Le titre de musique et la lithographie, 1. 1817–30; 2. 1830–50.

Abundantly illustrated with facsimiles of title pages, printers' devices, and pages of music.

1661 / **Hase, Oskar Von.** Breitkopf & Härtel. Gedenkschrift und Arbeitsbericht. 5. Aufl. Wiesbaden, Breitkopf u. Härtel, 1968. 2 v. in 3. Bd. 1. 1542–1827. Bd. 2. 1828–1918. Bd. 3. 1918–1968.

Thorough documentation of the activities of the great Leipzig publishing house of Breitkopf & Härtel. Reviews the history of the firm, its business relationships, its dealings with the great composers of the late 18th and 19th centuries; editorial work on the *Denkmäler* and *Gesamtausgaben*. Bd. 3, by Hellmuth von Hase, reviews the history of the firm through World War II to its establishment in Wiesbaden.

1662 / **Heartz, Daniel.** "La chronologie des recueils imprimés par Pierre Attaingnant." In *Revue de musicologie*, 44 (1959), p. 178–92.

Brief survey of Attaingnant's activity as a music printer, followed by a chronological tabulation of all collections published by him from 1528 to 1537.

1663 / **Heartz, Daniel.** Pierre Attaingnant, royal printer of music: a historical study and bibliographical catalogue. Berkeley and Los Angeles, University of California Press, 1969. 451 p.

P. 1–204: Historical study treating the founding of the Attaingnant press, new techniques of music printing, commercial and artistic relationships, together with selected documents, dedications, and privileges.

P. 207–377: Bibliographical catalog of 174 works issued by the press, with precise bibliographical descriptions, listings of contents, and location of surviving copies. 16 black-and-white plates, with a frontispiece in color. An outstanding work in book design and subject coverage. Chronological and alphabetical short-title lists. Index of Latin and French first lines, and of composers.

Review by Nicolas Barker in *The Book Collector* (Summer 1971), p. 261–70; by Samuel Pogue in *Notes*, 27 (1970), p. 258–60; by G. Dottin in *Revue de musicologie*, 57 (1971), p. 87–88; by Howard M. Brown in *JAMS*, 24 (1971), p. 125–26. By Frank Dobbins in *Music & letters*, 51 (1970), p. 447–49.

1664 / **Hill, Richard S.** "The plate numbers of C. F. Peters' predecessors." In *Papers . . . of the American Musicological Society . . .* Dec. 29 and 30, 1938. [c. 1940], p. 113–34.

Surveys the publishing activities of F. A. Hofmeister and A. Kühnel, 1784–1814, with a detailed analysis of their production in 1801–1802, plate numbers 1–102.

1665 / **Hopkinson, Cecil.** A dictionary of Parisian music publishers, 1700–1950. London, printed for the author, 1954.

Describes some 550 publishers, tabulating their name forms and addresses where they were active during specific periods. A useful tool for determining date of undated French publications.

Review by Inger M. Christensen in *Notes*, 11 (1954), p. 550–51; by Vincent Duckles in *JAMS*, 8 (1955), p. 62–64.

See no. 1669 for another approach to the dating of 18th-century French music publications.

1666 / **Hopkinson, Cecil.** Notes on Russian music publishers. Printed for the author for private distribution to the Members of the I.A.M.L. at the Fifth International Congress, Cambridge, June 29th–July 4th, 1959. 10 p.

"This edition limited to 125 numbered copies of which this is no. 60."

1667 / **Humphries, Charles, and William C. Smith.** Music publishing in the British Isles, from the beginning until the middle of the nineteenth century; a dictionary of engravers, printers, publishers, and music sellers, with a historical introduction. 2nd ed. with suppl. New York, Barnes and Noble; Oxford, B. Blackwell, 1970. 392 p.

First published in 1954 by Cassell and Co., London. The 2nd edition differs only in the addition of a 36-page supplement.

This work supersedes the Kidson volume (no. 1672). It covers more than 2,000 persons and firms associated with British music printing and publishing. An introductory essay gives an excellent survey of the field. Indexes of firms outside London and of makers and repairers of musical instruments. 25 plates.

Review of the first edition by J. M. Coopersmith in *Notes*, 11 (1954), p. 549–50; of the second edition by William Lichtenwanger in *Notes*, 27 (1971), p. 489–90.

1668 / **Imbault, Jéan-Jerôme.** Catalogue thématique des ouvrages de musique. Avec un index des compositeurs cités. [Réimpression de l'édition de Paris, c. 1792.] Genève, Minkoff Reprint, 1972. 284 p.

Classified thematic catalog of works published by Imbault. Each section has its own pagination.

1669 / **Johansson, Cari.** French music publishers' catalogues of the second half of the eighteenth century. Uppsala, Almquist & Wiksell, 1955. 2 v.

Vol. 1 (octavo): Textband. 228 p. Vol. 2 (folio): Tafeln. 145 facsimiles of catalogs by French music publishing houses.

The first volume analyzes and describes the contents of the catalogs and their use for dating purposes. Compare Johansson's method with that of Hopkinson, no. 1665, above. Index of names, of titles, and of catalogs chronologically under name of firm.

Review by Donald W. Krummel in *Notes*, 17 (1960), p. 234–35; by A. Hyatt King in *Music and letters*, 37 (1956), p. 376–77; by Wolfgang Schmieder in *Die Musikforschung*, 10 (1957), p. 180–82.

1670 / **Johansson, Cari.** J. J. & B. Hummel. Music-publishing and thematic catalogues. Stockholm, Almqvist and Wiksell, 1972. 3 v. (Publications of the Library of the Royal Swedish Academy of Music, 3.)

Vol. 1: Text, containing essays on the life and work of the brothers J. J. and B. Hummel; "Aids to the dating of Hummel prints," transcription of the Hummel catalogs 1762–1814; list of plate numbers; index of names and titles; index of catalogs. vol. 2: music-publishing catalogs in facsimile; vol. 3: thematic catalog 1768–74 in facsimile.

1671 / **Kast, Paul.** "Die Musikdrucke des Kataloges Giunta von 1604." In *Analecta musicologica, Veröffentlichungen der Musikabteilung des Deutschen Historischen Instituts in Rom*, Band 2 (1965), p. 41–47.

Transcribes the music portion of a general catalog issued by the Florentine music dealer and publisher Giunta in 1604. Contains masses, motets, and secular works of the late 16th century as well as a small selection of instrumental and theory works.

1672 / **Kidson, Frank.** British music publishers, printers and engravers . . . from Queen Elizabeth's reign to George IV, with select bibliographical lists of musical works printed and published within that period. London, W. E. Hill & Sons, 1900. 231 p.

Unaltered reprint by Benjamin Blom, Inc., New York, 1967.

The pioneer work on English music publishing. Not as comprehensive as the Humphries and Smith, no. 1655 above, but many of Kidson's entries are fuller and are accompanied by lists of publications. Entries arranged alphabetically by place. No index.

1673 / **King, A. Hyatt.** "English pictorial music title-pages, 1820–1885, their style, evolution and importance." In *The Library*, ser. 5:4 (1949–50), p. 262–72.

1674 / **King, A. Hyatt.** Four hundred years of music printing. London, published by the Trustees of the British Museum, 1964. 48 p.

A short, well-written account of the history of music printing, with a selected bibliography of 29 items on the subject. Illustrated with facsimile pages of early music printing.

2nd edition, 1968, incorporating a few changes in the text and additions to the bibliography.

Review of the first edition by Harry Carter in *The Library*, ser. 5:20 (June 1965), p. 154–57. By Donald W. Krummel in *Notes*, 22 (1965–66), p. 902–03.

1675 / **Kinkeldey, Otto.** "Music and music printing in incunabula." In *Bibliographical Society of America, Papers*, v. 26 (1932), p. 89–118.

For other discussions of music incunabula, see nos. 1691 and 1733.

1676 / **Kinsky, Georg.** "Beethoven-Erstdrucke bis zum Jahre 1800." In *Philobiblon*, 3 (1930), p. 329–36.

1677 / **Kinsky, Georg.** "Erstlingsdrucke der deutschen Tonmeister der Klassik und Romantik." In *Philobiblon*, 7 (1934), p. 347–64.

Also printed separately by H. Reichner, Vienna, 1934.

1678 / **Kinsky, Georg.** Die Originalausgaben der Werke Johann Sebastian Bachs; ein Beitrag zur Musikbibliographie. Wien, H. Reichner [1937], 134 p.

This and the two preceding items are contributions by one of the leading specialists in music printing of the 18th and 19th centuries.

1679 / Krohn, Ernst Christopher. Music publishing in the Middle Western States before the Civil War. Detroit, Information Coordinators, 1972. 44 p. (Detroit studies in music bibliography, 23.)

1680 / Krummel, Donald W. "Graphic analysis, its application to early American engraved music." In *Notes*, 16 (1959), p. 213–33.

Discussion of the history of early American music publishing in terms of the printing processes used, with special reference to the work of Blake and Willig. Seven plates.

1681 / Layer, Adolf. Katalog des Augsburger Verlagers Lotter von 1753. Kassel, Bärenreiter, 1964. 44 p. (Catalogus musicus, 2.)

Facsimile edition of the 1753 catalog of the music publications of the firm of Johann Jacob Lotter in Augsburg. Lists some 370 titles by 170 composers of the late 17th and early 18th centuries. Index and "Nachwort" provided by the editor.

1682 / Lenz, Hans U. Der Berliner Musikdruck von seinen Anfängen bis zur Mitte des 18. Jahrhunderts . . . Lippstadt, Westf., Buchdruckerei Thiele, 1932. 116 p.

Also issued as a dissertation, Rostock, 1932.

Discussion of the Berlin music printers, their output, their techniques. P. 27–35: chronological listing of 126 prints.

1683 / Lesure, François. Bibliographie des éditions musicales publiées par Estienne Roger et Michel-Charles Le Cène (Amsterdam, 1696–1743). Paris, Heugen, 1969. 173 p. (Publications de la Société Française de Musicologie. Sér. 2, Tome 12.)

Documents the production of one of the most active music publishers of the early 18th century, some 700 volumes of vocal and instrumental music for French and Italian musicians.

Contains a transcription of the catalog by Roger published in 1716 and a facsimile of a Le Cene catalog printed in Amsterdam in 1737.

1684 / Lesure, François et G. Thibault. Bibliographie des éditions d'Adrian le Roy et Robert Ballard (1551–98). Paris, Société française de musicologie, Heugel et Cie., 1955. 304 p. (Publications de la Société française de musicologie. 2 sér., t. 9.)

An exemplary bibliography of 319 musical editions issued by the Le Roy-Ballard press, cited chronologically with full bibliographical descriptions, lists of contents, and locations in public and private collections. Brief historical introduction, and an anthology of the most important prefaces, dedications, and other documents. First-line index of texts, index of titles and personal names. Nine facsimile plates.

Review by Kenneth Levy in *JAMS*, 8 (1955), p. 221–23; by Vincent Duckles in *Notes*, 15 (1957), p. 102–03.

1685 / **Lesure, François et G. Thibault.** "Bibliographie des éditions musicales publiées par Nicolas Du Chemin (1549–1576)." In *Annales musicologiques*, 1 (1953), p. 269–373.

Bibliography similar in scope and format to the preceding work. Covers 100 editions published by Du Chemin, with full descriptions, listings of contents, and locations of copies. Numerous facsimiles of title pages. First-line index of Latin and of French texts, and of titles and names.

1686 / **Littleton, Alfred H.** A catalog of one hundred works illustrating the history of music printing from the 15th to the end of the 17th century, in the library of Alfred H. Littleton. . . . London, Novello, 1911. 38 p., 12 facsimile plates.

Includes both musical and theoretical works grouped by nationality, with annotations directing attention to their interest as examples of music printing.

1687 / **Marco, Guy A.** The earliest music printers of continental Europe, a checklist of facsimiles illustrating their work. The Bibliographical Society of the University of Virginia, 1962. 20 p.

An index of facsimile plates of the work of early music printers to be found in a variety of music histories, monographs, and other reference works. 101 printers from the late 15th century to 1599 are included.

1688 / **Meissner, Ute.** Der antwerpener Notendrucker Tylman Susato. Eine bibliographische Studie zur niederländischen Chansonpublikation in der ersten Hälfte des 16. Jahrhunderts. Berlin, Merseburger, 1967. 2 v. (Berliner Studien zur Musikwissenschaft, 11.)

Vol. 1 contains biographical information and an analysis of Susato's activity as a music printer. Vol. 2 is a chronological bibliography of all of Susato's publications, with indexes of composers and a first-line index of compositions.

Review by Winfried Kirsch in *Die Musikforschung*, 22 (1969), p. 237–38. By Donald W. Krummel in *Notes*, 25 (1969), p. 500–01.

1689 / **Meyer, Kathi and Inger M. Christensen.** "Artaria plate numbers." In *Notes*, 15 (1942), p. 1–22.

1690 / **Meyer, Kathi, and Eva J. O'Meara.** "The printing of music, 1473–1934." In *The Dolphin*, 2 (1935), p. 171–207.
A well-illustrated sketch of the history of music printing. Includes a bibliography of works on the subject.

1691 / **Meyer-Baer, Kathi.** Liturgical music incunabula, a descriptive catalog. London, The Bibliographical Society, 1962. 63 p.
257 entries, arranged alphabetically by title, treating of some 800 items. References made to the standard bibliographies of incunabula and to locations of copies in major libraries. 12 plates illustrating types of notation. Chronological index, and index of printers and places.
See also the author's preliminary study, "Liturgical music incunabula in the British Museum," in *The Library*, 4th ser., 20 (1939), p. 272–94.
Review, anon., in *The Times literary supplement*, Nov. 16, 1962, p. 880, and by Donald W. Krummel in *Notes*, 21 (1964), p. 366–68.

1692 / **Molitor, P. Raphael.** "Italienische Choralnotendrucke." In his *Die Nach-Tridentinische Coral-Reform zu Rom*, v. 1, p. 94–119. Leipzig, 1901.
A general discussion of Italian printers of liturgical books of the later 15th and 16th centuries.

1693 / **Neighbour, Oliver, and Alan Tyson.** English music publisher's plate numbers in the first half of the 19th century. London, Faber, 1965. 48 p.
Review by Klaus Hortschansky in *Die Musikforschung*, 21 (1968), p. 102.

1694 / **Novello (Firm, Music Publishers, London).** A century and a half in Soho; a short history of the firm of Novello, publishers and printers of music, 1811–1961. London, Novello [1961], 85 p.
A popular history of the music publishing house that has exercised

a wide influence on public taste in England through the printing of inexpensive editions of the classics.

Review by Donald W. Krummel in *Notes*, 19 (1961), p. 60–61; by Richard Schaal in *Die Musikforschung*, 17 (1964), p. 183–84.

1695 / **Oldman, Cecil B.** Collecting musical first editions. London, Constable, 1938. 29 p. (Aspects of book collecting.)

Reprinted from *New Paths in book collecting*, ed. by John Carter, London, 1934. p. 95–124.

An informal and inviting discussion of the pleasures of collecting early music. Bibliography, p. 120–24.

1696 / **Pattison, Bruce.** "Notes on early music printing." In *The library*, ser. 4, 19:4 (1939), p. 239–421.

1697 / **Plesske, Hans-Martin.** "Bibliographie des Schrifttums zur Geschichte deutscher und österreichischer Musikverlage," in *Beiträge zur Geschichte des Buchwesens*, Band III (1968), p. 135–222.

A bibliography of 755 items listed alphabetically under the names of the firms. The first section is devoted to information in general reference works, the second to histories of music publishing.

1698 / **Pogue, Samuel F.** Jacques Moderne, Lyons music printer of the sixteenth century. Genève, Librairie Droz, 1969. 412 p. (Travaux d'humanisme et renaissance, 101.)

The book includes an extensive bibliography of all of Moderne's output, with full bibliographical descriptions of the non-musical books, and contents with concordances of the music books – a total of 149 entries, of which 59 are for books of music.

Includes music.

Review by Albert Dunning in *Notes*, 29 (1972), p. 46–47; by Frank Dobbins in *JAMS*, 24 (1971), p. 126–31. By Charles Cudworth in *Music & letters*, 51 (1970), p. 85–86.

1699 / **Poole, Edmund.** "New music types: invention in the eighteenth century." In *Journal of the printing historical society*, 1 (1965), p. 21–38.

Reviews the history of music printing, with special emphasis on the contribution of Breitkopf.

1700 / **Przywecke-Samecka, Maria.** Drukarstwo muzyczne w Polsce do kónca XVIII wieku. Kraków, Polskie Wydawnictwo Muzyczne, 1968. 263 p. 40 plates.

A study of music printing and publishing in Poland from the 16th through the 18th centuries.

Bibliography of early printers' works, arranged under location (p. 181–240). Bibliography of literature on music printing.

1701 / **Redway, Virginia L.** Music directory of early New York City; a file of musicians, music publishers and musical instrument makers listed in N.Y. directories from 1786 through 1835, together with the most important New York music publishers from 1836 through 1875. . . . New York, The New York Public Library, 1941. 102 p.

Three main sections: (1) musicians and teachers; (2) publishers, printers, lithographers, and dealers, with names and addresses as they appeared in successive years; (3) instrument makers and dealers. Appendices include chronological list of firms and individuals, 1786–1811, and a list of musical societies, 1789–99.

1702 / **Ricordi (Firm, Music Publishers, Milan).** Casa Ricordi, 1808–1958; profilo storico a cura di Claudio Sartori. . . . Milano, G. Ricordi, 1958. 116 p. 48 plates.

16 of the plates are facsimile pages of composers' autographs; the remainder are chiefly reproductions, in color, of cover designs for noteworthy Ricordi music publications.

Review by Donald W. Krummel in *Notes*, 17 (1960), p. 400–401.

1703 / **Robert, Henri.** Traité de gravure de musique sur planches d'étain et des divers procédés de simili gravùre de musique . . . précédé de l'historique du signe, de l'impression et de la gravure de musique. 2nd éd. Paris, Chez l'auteur, 1926. 151 p.

First published in 1902.

A rather sketchy historical survey of music writing, printing, and engraving, followed by a description of the technical processes involved in preparing engraved plates.

1704 / **Ross, Ted.** The art of music engraving and processing; a complete manual, reference and text book on preparing music for reproduction and print. Miami, Hansen Books (1970). 278 p.

Subtitle: "A complete manual, reference and text book on preparing music for reproduction and print."

Full of historical and technical information. Well illustrated.

1705 / **Sartori, Claudio.** Bibliografia delle opere musicali stampate de Ottaviano Petrucci. Firenze, Olschki, 1948. 217 p. (Biblioteca di bibliografia italiana, 18.)

Chronological bibliography of Petrucci's work, with full descriptions, contents of each publication. Index of titles, lists of libraries and their holdings of Petrucci prints. Bibliography.

1706 / **Sartori, Claudio.** Dizionario degli editori musicali italiani (tipografi, incisori, librai-editori). Firenze, Olschki, 1958. 215 p. (Biblioteca di bibliografia italiana, 32.)

Italian music printers, editors, and publishers from the 16th century to the present. Some bibliographical references given. The principal issues of the publishers are noted but no complete catalogs given. Index of names, but no chronology. Eight plates of early title pages.

Review by Dragan Plamenac in *Notes*, 16 (1959), p. 242–43; by Gerhard Croll in *Die Musikforschung*, 12 (1959), p. 255–56.

1707 / **Schmid, Anton.** Ottaviano dei Petrucci da Fossombrone, erste Erfinder des Musiknotendruckes mit beweglichen Metalltypen, und seine Nachfolger im sechzehnten Jahrhunderte . . . . Wien, P. Rohrmann, 1845. 342 p.

Reprint by Amsterdam, B. R. Grüner, 1968. 356 p. with 4 fold. 1.

One of the first scholarly studies of early music printing. Contains important information about Petrucci's contemporaries in other European centers of music printing.

1708 / **Smith, William C.** A bibliography of the musical works published by John Walsh during the years 1695–1720. London, The Bibliographical Society, 1948. 215 p. 38 plates.

622 Walsh publications cited for the period under consideration, with numerous descriptive annotations. Index of titles and works and general index.

Review by J. Coopersmith in *Notes*, 7 (1949), p. 104–06; by A. Hyatt King in *Music and letters*, 30 (1949), p. 273–76.

1709 / Smith, William C., and Charles Humphries. A bibliography of the musical works published by the firm of John Walsh during the years 1721–1766. London, The Bibliographical Society, 1968. 351 p.

Review by J. Merrill Knapp in *Notes*, 26 (1969), p. 274–75, and by Lenore Coral in *JAMS*, 23 (1970), p. 141–43. Review by Charles Cudworth in *Music & letters*, 50 (1969), p. 416–17.

1710 / Steele, Robert. The earliest English music printing; a description and bibliography of English printed music to the close of the 16th century. London, printed for The Bibliographical Society, 1903. 102 p. (Illustrated monographs, 11.)

Brief introduction covers methods of printing, and the book includes a chapter on early English printers of music. The bibliography of 197 items is arranged chronologically from 1495 to 1600, giving full title and collation, library locations, and notes on typography. Bibliography of 34 items on music printing.

Reprinted London, 1965, with a new appendix of *addenda* and *corrigenda*.

1711 / Stellfeld, J. A. Bibliographie des éditions musicales plantiniennes. [Bruxelles, Palais des Académies, 1949.] 248 p. (Academie royale de Belgique. Classe des beaux-arts. Memoires in 8°, T. 5, fasc. 3.)

Brief historical account of the Plantin press, with detailed bibliographical description and discussion of the 21 music items printed by the press at Antwerp and at Leiden. 21 plates.

Toledo (Ohio). Museum of Art. The printed note. . . . See no. 1490.

1712 / Tyson, Alan. The authentic English editions of Beethoven. London, Faber and Faber, 1963. 152 p.

An important work, one of the first to apply detailed bibliographical analysis to early-19th-century music printing. The author is able to make significant revisions in the chronology of Beehoven's works.

Review by Dagmar von Busch-Weise in *Die Musikforschung*, 17

(1964), p. 443–44; by Albi Rosenthal in *Music and letters*, 45 (1964), p. 256–58; by Donald W. MacArdle in *Notes*, 22 (1965–66), p. 920.

1713 / **Vernarecci, D. Augusto.** Ottaviano dei Petrucci da Fossombrone, inventore dei tipi mobili metallici fusi della musica nel secolo XV. Seconda Edizione. Bologna, Romagnoli, 1882. 288 p.

1714 / **Vol'man, B.** Russkie pechatnye noty XVIII veka. Leningrad, Gosudarstvennoe muzykal'noe izdatel'stvo, 1957. 293 p.
Russian printed music of the 18th century.

1715 / **Weinmann, Alexander.** Beiträge zur Geschichte des Alt-Wiener Musikverlages, 1948– .
A series of studies related to Viennese music publishing of the late 18th and early 19th centuries. They appear under varied imprints and in two subseries: Reihe 1, *Komponisten*; Reihe 2, *Verleger*. The volumes are listed below in series order.

1716 / Reihe 1, Folge 1: Verzeichnis der im Druck erschienenen Werke von Joseph Lanner, sowie Listen der Plattennummern der Originalausgaben für alle Besetzungen. . . . Wien, Leuen [1948], 31 p.
Tables listing the work of Lanner (1801–43) in opus number order, with plate numbers of the first editions. Alphabetical index of works by title.

1717 / Reihe 1, Folge 3: Verzeichnis sämtlicher Werke von Josef und Eduard Strauss. Wien, Ludwig Krenn, 1967. 104 p.

1718 / Reihe 2, Folge 1: Verzeichnis der Verlagswerke des Musikalischen Magazins in Wien, 1784–1802. "Leopold Kozeluch." Ein bibliographischer Behelf. Wien, Österreichischer Bundesverlag [1950], 31 p.
Works without plate numbers, and with questionable plate numbers, in chronological order; works with plate number in numerical order, followed by an alphabetical list by composer, of Kozeluch's catalog, 1800.

1719 / Reihe 2, Folge 2: Vollständiges Verlagsverzeichnis Artaria & Comp. Wien, Ludwig Krenn [1952], 179 p.
A history of the Artaria firm, with a classified list, chronological

within classifications, of its publications, giving in most cases exact dates of publication. Index by composers.

Review by Richard S. Hill in *Notes*, 10 (1953), p. 449–50.

1720 / Reihe 2, Folge 3: "Volständiges Verlagsverzeichnis des Musikalien des Kunst- und Industrie Comptoirs in Wien, 1801–1819." *In Studien zur Musikwissenschaft; Beihefte der DTOe*, 22 (1955), p. 217–52.

Contains a listing of 802 plate numbers in numerical order, with composer, title, and date of publication of the corresponding works. Composer index.

Review by William Klenz in *Notes*, 14 (1956), p. 117.

1721 / Reihe 2, Folge 4: "Verzeichnis der Musikalien des Verlages Johann Traeg in Wien, 1794–1818." In *Studien zur Musikwissenschaft; Beihefte der DTOe*, 23 (1956), p. 135–83.

Lists all works published by the firm, in chronological order.

1722 / Reihe 2, Folge 5: Wiener Musikverleger und Musikalienhändler von Mozarts Zeit bis gegen 1860; ein firmengeschichtlicher und topographischer Behelf. Wien, Rohrer, 1956. 72 p. (Österreichische Akademie der Wissenschaft . . . Veröff. der Kommission für Musikforschung, 2.)

Lists and discusses 38 music dealers and publishers and 19 related general book dealers and publishers. Tables showing early and existing addresses of the firm. Useful in dating Viennese musical imprints.

Review by Richard S. Hill in *Notes*, 15 (1958), p. 396–97.

1723 / Reihe 2, Folge 6: Verzeichnis der Musikalien aus dem K. K. Hoftheater-Musik-Verlag. Wien, Universal [1961], 130 p. (Wiener Urtext Ausgabe.)

Brief history of the firm and biographical notes on the men associated with it. List of publications from 1796 to *c.* 1820, with plate numbers and dates of issue if known.

Review by Donald W. Krummel in *Notes*, 19 (1961), p. 76.

1724 / Reihe 2, Folge 7: Kataloge Anton Huberty (Wien) und Christoph Torricella. Wien, Universal, 1962. 135 p.

Brief histories of the firms, followed by detailed listings of their

publications, giving composer, title, date of publication if known, location of copies in European libraries.
Review by Richard Schaal in *Die Musikforschung*, 18 (1965), p. 83.

1725 / Reihe 2, Folge 8: Die wiener Verlagswerke von Franz Anton Hofmeister. Wien, Universal, 1964. 252 p.
Contains a biography of Hofmeister; a dated list of plate numbers; entries, largely thematic, for all of the firm's publications; brief historical discussions of aspects of the firm's history.

1726 / Reihe 2, Folge 9: Verlagsverzeichnis Traquillo Mollo (mit und ohne Co.). Wien, Universal, 1964. 111 p.
Biography of the Mollo family and history of the firm. Transcriptions of catalogs, with plate numbers. Alphabetical indices by composers. The firm was a successor to Artaria.

1727 /Reihe 2, Folge 10: Verlagsverzeichnis Pietro Mechetti quondam Carlo (Mit Portraits). Wien, Universal Edition, 1966. 205 p.
Review by Harald Heckmann in *Die Musikforschung*, 21 (1968), p. 507–08.

1728 / Reihe 2, Folge II: Verlagsverzeichnis Giovanni Cappi bis A. O. Witzendorf. Wien, Universal Edition, 1967. 210 p.
Review by Imogen Fellinger in *Die Musikforschung*, 25 (1972), p. 371.

1729 / Reihe 2, Folge 12: Verzeichnis der Musikalien des Verlages Joseph Eder–Jeremias Bermann. Wien, Universal Edition, 1968. 78 p.

1730 / Reihe 2, Folge 13: Wiener Musikverlag "Am Rande." Ein lückenfüllender Beitrag zur Geschichte des Alt-Wiener Musikverlages. Wien, Universal Edition, 1970. 155 p.

1731 / Reihe 2, Folge 14: Verzeichnis der Musikalien des Verlages Maisch-Sprenger-Artaris. Mit 2 Supplementen: I. Die Firma Matthias Artarias Witwe u. Compagnie. II. Supplement zum Verlagsverzeichnis des Musikalischen Magazins in Wien (Kozeluch). Wien, Universal Edition, 1970. 95 p.

1732 / Reihe 2, Folge 15: Verlagsverzeichnis Ignaz Sauer (Kunstverlag zu den Sieben Schwestern), Sauer und Leidesdorf und Anton Berka & Comp. Wien, Universal Edition, 1972. 100 p.

1733 / **Wolf, Johannes.** "Verzeichnis der musiktheoretischen Inkunabeln mit Fundorten." In Caza, Francesco, *Tractato vulgare de canto figurato.* . . . (Veröffentlichungen der Musikbibliothek Paul Hirsch, 1.) Berlin, M. Breslauer, 1922. p. 64–92.

Wolf lists 104 incunabula in the field of music theory, with locations where copies are preserved, as a supplement to his edition of Caza's treatise.

1734 / **Zur Westen, Walter von.** Musiktitel aus vier Jahrhunderten; Festschrift anlässlich der 57 jährigen Bestehens der Firma C. G. Röder. Leipzig [1921], 116 p.

A study of musical title pages from the Renaissance to the end of the 19th century, with 96 facsimile illustrations.

Discographies

WITHIN THE LAST few decades the field of recorded sound has given rise to an abundance of documentation of interest to librarians, teachers, research scholars, and private collectors. One effort to bring these diverse interests together has resulted in an Association for Recorded Sound Collections, which issued in 1967 *A preliminary directory of sound recording collections in the U.S. and Canada*, New York, New York Public Library, 157 p. (Also entered as no. 1817.) It is an area that has a particular attraction for the collector, whether his interests lie in early vocal discs or cylinders or in jazz recordings. There has been a proliferation of record reviews, listeners' guides, manufacturers' catalogs and numerical lists, and journals devoted almost exclusively to discography. Some indication of the scope and variety of the bibliographical coverage is suggested by "A bibliography of discographies," by Carl L. Brunn and John Gray, in *Recorded sound*, *Journal of the British Institute of Recorded Sound* (Summer 1962, p. 206–13). A field of this kind requires its own guide to reference materials. No effort has been made here to list more than a few representative examples of the major types of reference tools available to the specialist in recorded sound.

In the organization following, "Encyclopedias of recorded music" have been distinguished from "Collectors' guides." The distinction is perhaps an arbitrary one, but it is intended to separate the few comprehensive discographies from those directed toward the interests of collectors of classical music, jazz records, or early discs.

ENCYCLOPEDIAS OF RECORDED MUSIC

1735 / **Clough, Francis F., and G. J. Cuming.** The world's encyclopedia of recorded music. London, Sidgwick & Jackson, 1952. 890 p.

First supplement (April 1950 to May–June 1951) bound with the main volume.

Second supplement (1951–52) London, 1952. 262 p.

Third supplement (1953–55) London, 1957. 564 p. Reprint by Greenwood Press, Westport, Conn., 1970.

The world's encyclopedia is an indispensable reference tool for record specialists. Arrangement is alphabetical by composer, with a subclassification of works under prolific composers. Full information given as to content and labels. Special section for anthologies.

Review by Philip Miller in *Notes*, 10 (1952), p. 94–95; of the *Third supplement* by Richard S. Hill in *Notes*, 14 (1957), p. 357–59.

1736 / **Gramophone Shop, Inc., New York.** The Gramophone Shop encyclopedia of recorded music. New York, The Gramophone Shop, Inc., 1936. 574 p.

Reprint of the 3rd edition (1948) by Greenwood, Westport, 1970.

Compiled by R. D. Darrell. 2nd ed., New York, Simon & Schuster, 1942; George C. Leslie, supervising editor. 558 p. 3rd ed., rev. and enl., New York, Crown, 1948; Robert H. Reid, supervising editor. 639 p.

The prototype for all encyclopedias of recorded music in its organization and coverage. Works arranged alphabetically under composer and partially classified. Brief biographical accounts of composers. All three volumes must be consulted, since the later editions are not fully cumulative. Coverage restricted to 78 rpm discs.

1737 / **Johnson, William W.** The gramophone book, a complete guide for all lovers of recorded music. London, Hinrichsen [1954], 169 p.

A compendium of miscellaneous information useful to record collectors. British emphasis. Lacks an index.

1738 / Myers, Kurtz, and Richard S. Hill. Record ratings, the Music Library Association's index of record reviews. New York, Crown Publishers, 1956. 440 p.

> *Record ratings* is essentially a guidebook pointing the way to a tremendous body of critical writing about recordings. [*Preface*]

Two main sections: (1) composer and subject list; (2) composite releases. By means of a system of symbols, the user is given a summary of critical opinion concerning the discs. Full descriptions of each recording, including composer, title, label, number, and price. Contents list for composite recordings. The editors have taken great pains to clarify and verify information about the discs and their contents. This is a major reference work in the field of discography. See also the current listings which appear in each issue of *Notes* under the heading, "Index of record reviews."

COLLECTORS' GUIDES TO CLASSICAL MUSIC

Books of this kind, of which there are an increasing number, can be described as compilations of brief record reviews in which observations on the technical quality of the recordings are combined with comments on the work recorded and on its performance. The listings below are confined to the more comprehensive English-language works in this category. Specialized collectors' guides are available in abundance. See, for example, the useful set of paperback editions published by J. B. Lippincott in the series *Keystone books in Music*, including: Cornelius G. Burke, *The collector's Haydn* [1959], 316 p.; John Briggs, *The collector's Tchaikowsky and the five* [1959]; Harold C. Schonberg, *The collector's Chopin and Schumann* [1959], 256 p., etc.

1739 / Coover, James B. and Richard Colvig. Medieval and Renaissance music on long-playing records. [Detroit, Information Service, Inc.] 1964. 122 p. (Detroit studies in music bibliography, 6.)

Supplement, 1962–71. (1973) 258 p. Issued as *Detroit studies in music bibliography,* no. 26.

A well-organized guide to the recorded resources in Medieval and Renaissance music. Part I of the *Supplement* analyzes 901 antologies, as compared with the 322 analyzed in the 1964 edition. Part II: index to anthologies and individual discographies by composer. Part III: performer index.

Review of the 1964 edition by George F. DeVine in *Journal of research in music education,* 13 (1965), p. 260; by Ludwig Finscher in *Die Musikforschung,* 20 (1967), p. 84–85.

1740 / **Discography Series.** Nos. 1–7. Utica, New York, 1970? Editors: no. 1–4, J. F. Weber; no. 5–7, Peter Morse.

Discographies of some of the major song composers of the romantic period. Contents as follows:

1. Schubert Lieder. 49 p.
2. Hugo Wolf complete works. 34 p.
3. Schumann Lieder. 20 p.
4. Brahms Lieder. 20 p.
5. Schubert, Schumann, Brahms, choral music. 26 p.
6. Mendelssohn vocal music. 11 p.
7. Strauss Lieder. 13 p.

Each number is preceded by an informative introduction, including reference to bibliographical sources.

1741 / **The Guide to Long Playing Records.** New York, Knopf, 1955. 3 v.

Vol. 1: Irving Kolodin. *Orchestral music.* 268 p. Vol. 2: Philip L. Miller. *Vocal music.* 381 p. Vol 3: Harold C. Schonberg. *Chamber and solo instrument music.* 280 p.

1742 / **Hall, David.** The record book, a music lover's guide to the world of the phonograph. New York, Smith & Durrell, 1940. 771 p.

Supplement. 1941. (Continuing pagination, 777–886.)

Second supplement. 1943. (Continuing pagination, 887–1013.)

Complete edition. New York, Citadel Press, 1946. 1,063 p. Incorporates the two preceding supplements.

410

1743 / **Hall, David.** The record book. International edition. New York, Durrell, 1648. 1,394 p.

1744 / **Hall, David.** Records: 1950 edition. New York, Knopf. 524 p.

Hall's books are addressed to the private collector with an interest in serious music. In the earlier editions the material is classified by medium. Beginning with the *International edition* (above) the arrangement is alphabetical by composer. Much general information for the record collector is included. The 1950 edition is the first to direct attention to long-playing discs.

1745 / **Kolodin, Irving.** A guide to recorded music. Garden City, N.Y., Doubleday, 1941. 495 p.

1746 / **Kolodin, Irving.** New guide to recorded music. Rev. ed. Garden City, N.Y., Doubleday, 1947. 512 p.

1747 / **Kolodin, Irving.** International edition. Garden City, N.Y., Doubleday, 1950.

Kolodin has adhered to an alphabetical arrangement by composer, with classification by form and medium under composer. Index of performers and performing groups.

1748 / **Records in Review.** The seventeenth High Fidelity annual. 1972 edition. Great Barrington, Mass., The Wyeth Press—New York, Scribner's Sons, 1972. 512 p.

Compiled and edited by Clifford F. Gilmore.

The set through volume 12 (1972) has been reprinted by the AMS Press, Inc., 1972– .

An annual anthology of reviews printed in *High fidelity* magazine. The main listing is by composer, followed by nine categories of collections: vocal, piano, organ and harpsichord, strings, woodwinds and brass, guitar, orchestra, medieval and Renaissance, miscellaneous. Index of performers.

1749 / **Russcol, Herbert.** Guide to low-priced classical records. New York, Hart (1969), 831 p.

411

Over 300 composers covered; over 1,500 works appraised; over 3,000 records evaluated; a wealth of solid information. [Quoted from the book jacket]

1750 / Sackville-West, Edward, and D. Shawe-Taylor. The record guide. London, Collins, 1951. 763 p.

1751 / Sackville-West Edward, and D. Shawe-Taylor. The record guide . . . with Andrew Porter and William Mann. Rev. ed. London, Collins [1955], 957 p.
Supplement [1956], 191 p.

1752 / Sackville-West, Edward, and D. Shawe-Taylor. The record year, a guide to the year's gramophone records, including a complete guide to long playing records. Assisted by Andrew Porter. London, Collins [1952], 383 p.

The Sackville-West guides are designed for British record collectors. The commentary is literate and well informed. The discs are arranged by composer, with special sections devoted to collections and a performer index.

1753 / Stahl, Dorothy. A selected discography of solo song. Detroit, Information Coordinators, Inc., 1968. 90 p. (Detroit Studies in Music Bibliography, 13.)
Supplement, 1968–1969, 95 p. Detroit, 1970.

Review of the 1968 edition by Ruth Hilton in *Notes*, 26 (1969), p. 281, and of the *Supplement* in *Notes*, 29 (1972), p. 257–58.

1754 / The Stereo Record Guide. By Edward Greenfield, Ivan March, and Denis Stevens. London, The Long Playing Record Library, Ltd., 1960– . 8 v. to 1972.

The main arrangement for each volume is by composer, followed by special sections devoted to concerts, recitals, light music, etc. Vol. 1 contains a selection of 50 outstanding records for 1958/59; vol. 2, a selection of 100 outstanding records for 1960/61. The third volume supplements the two preceding, but it relists the important recordings from the earlier books, with page references to earlier commentary. The guide is distinguished by its intelligent, highly readable annotations.

1755 / **Wilson, William John.** The stereo index: a complete catalogue of every recommended stereo disc. 3rd ed. London, Wilson Stereo Library [1967], 174 p.

COLLECTORS' GUIDES TO EARLY RECORDINGS

The field of discs and cylinder recordings of the period from 1898 to 1925 has long been the province of private collectors. Emphasis is usually placed on the performer, particularly the vocalist, rather than on the composer. Recently the importance of collecting in this area has been recognized on a large scale by libraries and research institutions throughout the world, as, for example, the New York Public Library, The Library of Congress, The British Institute of Recorded Sound, The Stanford University Archive of Recorded Sound, etc.

1756 / **Bauer, Robert.** The new catalogue of historical records, 1898–1908/09. London, Sidgwick and Jackson [1947], 494 p.
   Reprinted, 1970.
   Recordings listed under performer, grouped under label and year of pressing. Serial numbers given. Brief entries for composer and title of work.

1757 / **Bescoby-Chambers, John.** The archives of sound, including a selective catalogue of historical violin, piano, spoken, documentary, orchestral, and composer's own recordings. Oakwood Press, 1964. 153 p.

   Vocal recordings are fairly well documented today. . . . Violin, Piano, and orchestral recordings are rarely written about, and there is a vast, almost uncharted sea of piano roll recordings that are almost forgotten today.

A valuable contribution to the discography and player piano resources for instrumental music. Brief biographies of performers, and listings of their recordings. Some chapter headings: "The violin on record," "Historical piano recordings," "Orchestral recordings," and "The composer's own interpretation."

1758 / **Deakins, Duane D.** Cylinder records; a description of the numbering systems, physical appearance, and other aspects of cylinder records made by the major American companies, with brief remarks about the earliest American companies and the foreign record manufacturers [2nd ed.] Stockton, Calif. [1958], 35 p.

1759 / **Deakins, Duane D., Elizabeth Deakins, and Thomas Grattelo.** Comprehensive cylinder record index. Stockton, Calif., 1966– .

Pt. 1. Edison amberol records.
Pt. 2. Edison standard records.
Pt. 3. Edison blue amberol records.
Pt. 4. Indestructible records.
Pt. 5. U.S. everlasting records.

1760 / **Girard, Victor, and Harold M. Barnes.** Vertical-cut cylinders and discs; a catalogue of all "hill-and-dale" recordings of serious worth made and issued between 1897–1932 *circa*. London, British Institute of Recorded Sound, 1971. 196 p.

Facsimile reprint (corrected) of the original 1964 edition.

A major contribution to the discography of early recordings. Arranged in three major categories: (1) vocal recordings; (2) speech recordings; (3) instrumental and orchestral recordings; with appendices devoted to complete operas and to anonymous Pathé discs. The approach is mainly by performer.

1761 / **Hurst, P. G.** The golden age recorded. New and revised edition. The Oakwood Press, 1963. 187 p.

First published by Sidgwick and Jackson, London, 1946.

A manual for private collectors. General discussions of record collecting followed by biographical notices of the major artists classified by voice. Appendix, p. 147–87: a selected list, by performer, of important early recordings.

1762 / **Karlin, Fred J.** Edison Diamond Discs 80001–52651. Santa Monica, Calif., Bona Fide Publishing Co. [n.d.], 160 p.

414

A numerical listing of every Edison Diamond Disc issued in the 50,000 series from 1912–1929. Cities 5,200 titles as well as the performing artists, composers, and lyricists.

1763 / **Koenigsberg, Allen.** Edison cylinder records, 1889–1912, with an illustrated history of the phonograph. New York, Stellar Productions, 1969. 159 p.
Review by Edward Colby in *Notes*, 27 (1971), p. 499–500.

1764 / **Moses, Julian M.** Collector's guide to American recordings, 1895–1925; foreword by Giuseppe de Luca. New York, American Record Collectors' Exchange [1949], 199 p.
Discs arranged under performers by serial or matrix number. P. 172–95: numerical guide, Columbia and other labels. Index of operas and instrumental index.

1765 / **Moses, Julian M.** Price guide to collectors' records, including revised value chart. New York, American Record Collectors' Exchange, 1967.
First published in 1952.
Discs identified by matric number under performer, with estimates of value on the current market. Designed to accompany the author's *Collector's guide*, above.

1766 / **Voices of the Past.** v. 1– [Lingfield, Surrey, The Oakwood Press, 1955–].
Vol. 1: A catalogue of vocal recordings from the English catalogues of the Gramophone Company, 1898–1899; the Gramophone Company Limited, 1899–1900; the Gramophone & Typewriter Company Limited, 1901–1907; and the Gramophone Company Limited, 1907–1925; by John R. Bennett. [1955]
Vol. 2: A catalogue of the vocal recordings from the Italian catalogues of the Gramophone Company Limited, 1899–1900. The Gramophone Company (Italy) Limited, 1899–1909; the Gramophone Company Limited, 1909; Compagnia del Grammofono 1912–1925; by John R. Bennett. [1957]
Vol. 3: Dischi Fonotipia, including supplement (1958) and addenda (1964), by John R. Bennett. [1964?]
Vol. 4: The international red label catalogue of "DB" & "DA" His

Master's Voice recordings, 1924–1956; book I: "DB" (12-inch), by John R. Bennett and Eric Hughes. [1961]

Vol. 5: The catalogue of "D" & "E" His Master's Voice recordings, by Michael Smith. [1961]

Vol. 6: The international red label catalogue of "DB" & "DA" His Master's Voice recordings, 1924–1956; book 2: "DA", by John R. Bennett and Eric Hughes. [1967?]

Vol. 7: A catalogue of vocal recordings from the 1898–1925 German catalogues of the Gramphone Company Limited, Deutsche Grammophon A.-G., by John R. Bennett and Wilhelm Wimmer. [1967]

Vol. 8: Columbia Gramophone Company, Ltd.; English celebrity issues: D and LB series, L and LX series. (By Michael Smith.) [1968?]

Vol. 9: A catalogue of vocal recordings from the 1898–1925 French catalogues of The Gramophone Company Limited, Compagnie française du gramophone, by John R. Bennett. [1971?]

These catalogs list the early recordings, chiefly vocal, in numerical order under their respective labels. Most of the volumes also provide an artist index. These are invaluable tools for organizing and identifying early vocal discs.

COLLECTORS' GUIDES TO POPULAR RECORDINGS

The jazz record collector lives in a world of his own and is well equipped with reference tools designed to meet his needs. The impetus toward documentation has come from European rather than American enthusiasts: see Delaunay and Panassié, below. Most of the periodicals devoted to popular music include jazz record reviews and print occasional discographies of jazz musicians.

1767 / **Allen, Walter C.** Studies in jazz discography I– . Intro. by William M. Weinberg. New Brunswick, N.J., Institute of jazz studies, Rutgers University, 1971. 112 p.

Review by James Patrick in *Notes*, 29 (1972), p. 236–39.

1768 / **Carey, David A., and Albert J. McCarthy.** The directory of recorded jazz and swing music. London, Cassel, 1950– .

Cover title: *Jazz directory*. Vols. 2–4 have appeared in 2nd editions, 1955–57.

An alphabetical listing of performers and ensembles, with detailed information as to their recorded output. Informative annotations.

The work has progressed through six volumes (as of 1957), paged continuously through p. 1112, as far as the entry "Longshaw."

Vols. 1–4 published by the Delphic Press, Fordingbridge, Hants. The 2nd editions of vols. 2–4 and vols. 5 and 6 are published by Cassel, London.

Continued in Jepsen (no. 1775) and McCarthy (no. 1778).

1769 / **Delaunay, Charles.** New hot discography, the standard dictionary of recorded jazz. Edited by Walter E. Schaap and George Avakian. New York, Criterion, 1948. 608 p.

First published in France in 1936.

Separates the "pioneers of jazz" from "post-1930 jazz." Subdivided by region. An elaborate classification system groups recordings by major jazz personalities. Complete index of names.

1770 / **Dimmick, Mary L.** The Rolling Stones: an annotated bibliography. Pittsburgh, Pa., University of Pittsburgh, Graduate School of Library and Information Sciences, 1972. 73 p. (Pittsburgh studies in library and information sciences.)

Liberal annotations, some critical, some descriptive. As a collection of documents and commentary, this is a model of its kind.

1771 / **Godrich, J., and R. M. W. Dixon.** Blues and gospel records, 1902–1942. 2nd ed., revised. London, Storyville Publications, 1969.

First published by Brian Rust.

Review by Frank M. Gillis in *Ethnomusicology*, 14 (1970), p. 499–500.

1772 / **Harris, Rex, and Brian Rust.** Recorded jazz. [Harmondsworth, Middlesex.] Penguin Books, 1958. 256 p. (Pelican Books A417.)

It must not be regarded as a comprehensive discography, but nevertheless the authors have presented a reasonable cross-section of real jazz, together with biographical notes of performers and a critical assessment of the records listed. [*Preface*]

1773 / **Jay, Dave,** *pseud.* The Irving Berlin songography; 1907–1966. New Rochelle, N.Y., Arlington House [1969], 172 p.

1774 / **Jazz on Record: A Critical Guide to the First 50 Years: 1917–1967.** [By] Albert McCarthy, Alun Morgan, Paul Oliver, Max Harrison. London, Hanover Books, 1968. New York, Oak Publications, 1968. 416 p.

> *Jazz on record* is not a gramophone catalogue but a reference book to the best, the most significant, or occasionally simply the most typical recorded works of the leading jazz and blues artists to come to prominence during the last half century. [Author's *Introduction*]

Much biographical and critical commentary. Arranged mainly by jazz artists, with additional sections devoted to styles and traditions.

Supersedes a work published under the same title by C. Fox, P. Gammond, and A. Morgan, London, Hutchinson, 1960.

Review by Frank Tirro in *Notes*, 26 (1970), p. 756–58.

1775 / **Jepsen, J. G.** Jazz records: a discography. Holte, Denmark, Knudsen, 1966– . 8 in 11 v., pub. irregularly.

A major reference work covering recorded jazz from 1942 to 1969. Vols. 5 and 6 published by Nordisk Tidskrift Forlag, Copenhagen.

Further volumes projected.

1776 / **Lange, Horst H.** Die deutsche Jazz-Discographie. Eine Geschichte des Jazz auf Schallplatten von 1902 bis 1955. Berlin, Bote & Bock, 1955. 652 p.

One of several recent European compilations of jazz records. Includes a number of English and Continental performers.

1777 / **Leadbitter, Mike, and Neil Slaven.** Blues records, January 1943 to December 1966. London, Hanover Books, Ltd., 1968. 381 p.

A listing by artist and ensembles with discographies as complete as the compilers could make them. Gives instrumentation for the groups and dates of recording where known.

Review by Frank Tirro in *Notes*, 26 (1970), p. 756–58.

1778 / **McCarthy, Albert J.** Jazz discography 1: an international discography of recorded jazz, including blues, gospel, and rhythm-and-blues for the year January–December 1958. London, Cassell, 1960. 271 p.

The first volume of a projected yearbook to cover all jazz recordings issued throughout the world. New releases are listed alphabetically by country. Full contents of each disc listed, with personnel, place, and date of recording if known.

This volume was an attempt to carry on the work started by Carey and McCarthy in their *Directory of recorded jazz* (no. 1768). Only one volume was published but supplements appeared in McCarthy's periodical *Jazz monthly*.

1779 / **Panassié, Hughes.** Discographie critique des meilleurs disques de jazz. Paris, Robert Laffont [1958] 621 p.

An earlier edition, Paris, Corrêa, 1951. 371 p.

The author is a prolific writer on jazz and one of the first important discographers in the field. Arrangement is by performer, with an analytical index by medium and an index of names.

1780 / **Rohde, H. Kandy,** ed. The gold of rock & roll, 1955–1967. New York, Arbor House, 1970. 352 p.

A discography listing the ten most popular rock and roll recordings for each week during the years covered. "The top fifty" for each individual year are extracted. Brief commentary for each year's activity. Indexed by song titles and artists.

1781 / **Rust, Brian.** Jazz records, 1897–1942. London, Storyville Publications, 1970. 2 v.

Vol. 1: A–Kar. Vol. 2: Kar–Z.

This work supersedes an earlier edition issued under the title *Jazz records A–Z* (1961–65).

> This set of two books covers in the fullest possible detail all known records made in the years between 1897 and 1942 in the ragtime, jazz and swing idioms. . . . Only records made by American and British musicians are listed. [Compiler's *Introduction*]

Performers and groups are listed alphabetically with their records identified by matrix numbers and titles. Introduction and index of abbreviations for musical terms and record labels. Artists' index compiled by Mary Rust. A rich source of information on jazz history and recording activity for the period specified.

1782 / **Smith, Charles E.** The jazz record book . . . with Frederic Ramsey, Jr., Charles Payne Rogers and William Russell. New York, Smith and Durrell, 1942. 515 p.

P. 1–125: a survey of the history of jazz in its various regional styles. P. 130–508: record listings by major performers and ensembles, with critical and descriptive commentary. Selected bibliography of jazz; index of bands.

1783 / **Smolian, Steven.** A handbook of film, theater, and television music on record, 1948–1969. New York, The Record Undertaker, 1970. 64 p. alphabetical listing and 64-p. index.

A handbook for collectors of show and soundtrack recordings.

This book should assist the reader in two basic ways—to outline what has been issued: what can be bought through regular record shops, and when he will either have to do some "bin hunting" or call on the services of a specialist dealer in cut-outs, and also to identify the records in his collection and tell him something about them. [Compiler's *Introduction*]

1784 / **Whitburn, Joel.** Top pop records, 1955–1970. Facts about 9,800 recordings listed in *Billboard's* "Hot 100" charts grouped under the names of the 2,500 recording artists. Detroit, Gale Research Company, 1972.

This publication is a complete factual record of the most successful popular music in the United States for the past 16 years. [Editor's note]

ETHNIC AND FOLK MUSIC ON RECORDS

The use of recorded materials is basic to the techniques of modern ethnomusicology. Here the scholar is concerned less with commercially recorded discs and tapes than he is with recordings made in the field by research institutions and by individual collectors. The problem of bringing these diverse materials under "bibliographical control" is a difficult one. A good start has been made with the cooperation of UNESCO in two series published under the general title *Archives of recorded music*. Series B is concerned with Oriental music; Series C, with ethnographical and folk music. (*Series A*, not under consideration here, is devoted to Occidental music and has produced a general discography of the works of Frederic Chopin.)

1785 / **Archives of Recorded Music (Archives de la Musique Enregistrée). Series B: Oriental Music.** A catalogue of recorded classical and traditional Indian music. General discography and introduction by Alain Danielou. Paris, UNESCO [1952], 236 p.

The main organization is by region, subdivided by instrumental and vocal music, and listed under the performing artists. Chapter V is devoted to the songs of Rabindranath Tagore. Index of names. Bilingual (English–French).

1786 / **Archives of Recorded Music. . . . Series C: Ethnographical and Folk Music.** 1. Collection Phonothèque Nationale (Paris). Catalogue prepared by the International Commission on Folk Arts and Folklore. Paris, UNESCO [1952], 254 p.

Lists 4,564 discs in groups as acquired by the Phonothèque. Recordings for any particular national group are scattered throughout the volume. There is an index of countries, however. Bilingual (French–English).

1787 / **Archives of Recorded Music. . . . Series C: Ethnographical and Folk Music.** 2. Collection Musée de l'Homme (Paris). Catalogue prepared by the International Commission on Folk Arts and Folklore. Paris, UNESCO [1952], 74 p.

Catalog of a collection of 1,007 recordings, chiefly made in the field in various parts of Asia and Africa. Grouped under the name of the collector or expedition.

1788 / **Archives of Recorded Music. . . . Series C. Ethnographical and Folk Music.** 3. Katalog der europäischen Volksmusik im Schallarchiv des Instituts für Musikforschung Regensburg . . . Bearbeitet von Felix Hoerburger. Regensburg, Gustav Bosse [1952], 189 p.

Material grouped by country and province.

1789 / **Archives of Recorded Music. . . . Series C: Ethnographical and Folk Music.** 4. International catalogue of recorded folk music. . . . Edited by Norman Fraser, with a preface by R. Vaughan Williams and introduction by Maud Karpeles. Prepared and published for

UNESCO by the International Folk Music Council in association with Oxford Univ. Press, 1954. 201 p.

Part I: "Commercial records," a listing of the commercially recorded discs of ethnic and folk music, arranged by continent and by country. Part II: "Recordings held by institutions," a survey of the major collections of ethnic and folk music in libraries and research institutions throughout the world. Statistical summary of their holdings; addresses, names of chief administrators.

1790 / **Briegleb, Ann,** ed. Directory of ethnomusicological sound recording collections in the U.S. and Canada. Ann Arbor, Mich., Society for Ethnomusicology, 1971. 46 p. (Special series, 2.)

Surveys the resources of 124 collections, public and private. Arranged alphabetically by state. Includes a list of institutions with "no holdings in ethnomusicology."

1791 / **Hickmann, Hans et Charles Grégoire, Duc de Mecklenbourg.** Catalogue d'enregistrements de musique folklorique égyptienne. Strasbourg, Heitz, 1958. 78 p. (Collection d'études musicologiques, 37.)

Description and analysis of the contents of a recorded collection of Egyptian folk music assembled in 1955. 211 items. Preceded by a discussion of the music and instruments employed.

1792 / **Lumpkin, Ben G., and N. L. McNeil.** Folksongs on records. . . . Issue three, cumulative, including essential material in issues one and two. Boulder, Colorado, Folksongs on Records, 1950. 98 p.

Lists 700 commercially recorded discs and albums of folksong and folk music, chiefly American. Contents of discs given, with informal annotations. Useful indexes to English and Scottish ballads, spirituals, work songs, Irish songs, Mexican and Latin-American songs; numerical list of albums.

1793 / **Merriam, Alan P.** African music on L.P. An annotated discography. Evanston, Illinois, Northwestern University Press, 1970. 200 p.

Describes and inventories the contents of some 389 recordings of African music, excluding the Hugh Tracy "Sound of Africa" series since it has been documented elsewhere. Entries are grouped by record labels. 18 indexes permit a wide variety of approaches to the information.

1794 / **Museum für Volkerkunde.** Katalog der Tonbandaufnahmen M1–M2000 der Musikethnologischen Abteilung des Museums für Völkerkunde Berlin. Hrsg. von Dieter Christensen unter Mitarbeit von Hans-Jürgen Jordan. Berlin, Museum für Völkerkunde, 1970. 355 p.

1795 / **U.S. Library of Congress. Division of Music. Archive of American Folk Song.** Checklist of recorded songs in the English language in the Archive . . . to July 1940. Washington, D.C., Library of Congress, Division of Music, 1942. 3 v. in 1.

A guide to the holdings of one of the world's great folk song collections. Songs listed by title, with name of singer, collector, and date of recording. The third volume is a geographical index.

1796 / **U.S. Library of Congress. Music Division. Recording Laboratory.** Folk music: a catalog of folk songs, ballads, dances, instrumental pieces, and folk tales of the United States and Latin-America on phonograph records. Washington, D.C., Library of Congress [1964], 107 p.

Earlier listings of the same nature appeared in 1948, 1953, and 1959.

A catalog of recordings available for purchase from the Archive of American Folk Song at the Library of Congress. Presents a sampling of American folk music and tales recorded for the most part of their native environment.

1797 / **Waterhouse, David.** "Hogaku preserved: a select list of long-playing records issued by Japanese record companies of the national music of Japan." In *Recorded sound*, no. 33 (Jan. 1969), p. 383–402.

CURRENT OR ANNUAL DISCOGRAPHIES

Current listings and record review are in abundant supply. There are periodicals, such as *High fidelity*, the *American record guide*, and *The gramophone*, devoted exclusively to the interests of record collectors. Other literary or professional journals such as *The Saturday review*, *The nation*, and the *Library journal* have regular departments of record reviews and comment. For a description of some 30 foreign periodicals devoted to recordings, see no. 616.

1798 / **Gramophone Shop, Inc., Record Supplement.** V. 1: 1 (Jan. 1938)—v. 17: 2 (Feb. 1954).

Title varies: 1939, *Record reviews.* (Cover title: *Record supplement.*)

Extensively annotated listing of the major releases in the field of serious music. Confined chiefly to 78 rpm discs. A monthly publication.

1799 / **High Fidelity Record Annual.** 1955– . Edited by Roland Gelatt. Philadelphia, J.B. Lippincott, 1955– .

Title varies: from 1957, *Records in review.* Great Barrington, Mass.. The Wyeth Press. Editor, 1957: Joan Griffiths. Editor, 1958–60: Frances Newbury.

A yearly compilation of reviews from *High fidelity* magazine. Recordings arranged alphabetically by composer, with a section on "Collections and miscellany." Signed reviews by *High fidelity* contributors.

1800 / **"Index of Record Reviews,** with symbols indicating opinions of reviewers." In *Notes,* 5 (March, 1948)– , p. 211– .

Since its inception, in the March, 1948 issue of *Notes,* this index has been a regular feature. Compiled chiefly by Kurtz Myers with the assistance of various specialists from time to time. A valuable guide to record selection for libraries and for private collectors.

1801 / **Polart Index to Record Reviews.** Detroit, Polart, 1960– .
An annual publication indexing all record and tape reviews published in the major journals. No evaluations, but the length of the review is indicated. Main entries under composer, with separate sections for collections and for "pop and jazz" recordings.

1802 / **Schwann Long Playing Record Catalog,** monthly guide to mono and stereo records. [Boston, Mass., W. Schwann, Inc.] 1949– .

The standard guide to long playing records currently available for retail purchase. The May issue of each year is an "Artist's issue" in which the entries are under performers; otherwise the entries are under composer, with special sections devoted to collections, spoken and miscellaneous, musical shows, folk music, popular music, etc.

SPECIALIZED DISCOGRAPHIES

1803 / **American Music on Records.** A catalogue of recorded American music currently available. Prepared in cooperation with the Committee on Recordings of American Music of the National Music Council. New York, Amercian Music Center [1956], 39 p.

A composer listing in alphabetical order, with references to published scores and parts if available.

1804 / **American Society of Composers, Authors and Publishers.** 40 years of show tunes, the big Broadway hits from 1917–57. New York, ASCAP [1958], 149 p.

Chronological list of recorded show tunes arranged alphabetically under year of production. Composer, publisher, performing artist, and record number given. Title index.

1805 / **American Society of Composers, Authors and Publishers.** 30 years of motion picture music, the big Hollywood hits from 1928–1958. New York, ASCAP (1959?), 122 p.

1806 / **Band Record Guide.** Alphabetical listing of band records by title of composition, composer, performing group, and record title. 1969 edition. Evanston, Illinois, The Instrumentalist Co. (*c.* 1969), 102 p.

Indexes 1,480 works by title; 574 composers, 170 bands. There is also a listing of record manufacturers and distributors.

1807 / **Cohn, Arthur.** The collector's twentieth-century music in the Western Hemisphere. Philadelphia, Lippincott [1961], 256 p. (Keystone books in music, KB–23.)

One of the best discographies of contemporary music. Well annotated; full coverage for American composers.

1808 / **Cohn, Arthur.** Twentieth-century music in Western Europe, the compositions and the recordings. Philadelphia and New York, J. B. Lippincott [1956], 510 p.

Part I, p. 3–345: discussion of the compositions of 30 contemporary

European composers. Part II, p. 349–510: entries for the recordings of the works discussed in the preceding section. The records are graded from "poor" to "exceptional" in performance quality. The annotations in this section are devoted almost entirely to observations on performance.

1809 / **Davies, Hugh.** "A discography of electronic music and musique concrète." In *Recorded sound, journal of the British Institute of Recorded sound,* no. 14 (April, 1964), p. 205–24.

Fully annotated listings of records and tapes; addresses of distributors and index of compositions.

1810 / **International Roman Catholic Association for Radiodiffusion and Television.** Catalogue du disque de musique religieuse. Préf. de J. Schneuwly; introd. de Jean-Michel Hayoz. Edité par UNDA, Association catholique internationale pour la radiodiffusion et la télévision. Fribourg [1956], 300 p.

1811 / **Maleady, Antoinette A.,** comp.   Record and tape reviews index—1971. Metuchen, N.J., Scarecrow Press, 1972. 234 p.

16 periodicals indexed. Section I: a listing of reviews by composer. Section II: reviews of music in collections, listed under record labels. Section III: spoken recordings.

1812 / **Smart, James R.** The Sousa band: a discography. Washington, D.C., U.S. Library of Congress, 1970. 123 p.

Yearbooks and Directories

PUBLICATIONS APPEARING under the title "Yearbook" can take a variety of forms. They may be annual volumes issued by learned societies, as, for example, the Spanish *Anuario musical*, the British *Proceedings of the Royal Musical Association*, the Swiss *Schweizerisches Jahrbuch für Musikwissenschaft*, or the *Jahrbuch für Liturgik und hymnologie*. They may be annual volumes issued by music publishing houses such as C. F. Peters, Simrock, or Breitkopf & Härtel; or they may be publications of societies devoted to the work of a particular composer, as, for example, *Bach Jahrbuch*, *Handel Jahrbuch*, *Mozart Jahrbuch*, or *Haydn Jahrbuch*. Finally, they may be directories or compilations of factual information covering a specific year. Works of this kind have emphasized in the following, highly selective list. Yearbooks in this sense are often useful for reference purposes, since they provide data on current musical activities and personalities difficult to find elsewhere.

1813 / **Annuaire du Spectacle, 1971.** Paris, Éditions Roault, 1972. 937 p.

With 704 pages of photos and indexes.

A yearbook of the French world of entertainment, emphasizing the commercial aspects. All areas are treated, including theater, cinema, music, radio, and television.

1814 / Annuaire National de la Musique, 1967–1968. Paris, Annuaire National de la Musique (1970), 677 p.

Classified listings of names, with addresses, of people associated with musical activities, including performers of all kinds, editors, printers, societies and associations.

1815 / Annuaire OGM, 1970. Industries et commerces de radio, télévision, electronique, electroacoustique, musique. Paris, Horizons de France. 61e année, 1970. 532. 880 p.

An annual directory of the French audio-television industries. Includes listings of dealers and manufacturers of musical instruments.

1816 / Annuario del Teatro Lirico Italiano, 1940– . Pubblicazione ufficiale della Federazione Nazionale Fascista dei Lavatori dello Spettacolo. Milano, Edizioni Corbaccio, 1940– . (737 p)

A compendium of facts related to the Italian lyric theater, including opera companies, legal aspects, theaters, artists (with portraits), index of interpreters for the standard repertory, instrumentalists, statistics on performances.

1817 / Annuario Generale della Musica Italiano. Rassegna delle attività lirico-concertistiche in Italia. Prima Edizione 1968–69. Direttore: Tito Chelazzi. Condirettare: Alberto Calcagno. Roma, 1970– . 174 p.

1818 / Association for Recorded Sound Collections. A preliminary directory of sound recordings collections in the United States and Canada. Prepared by a committee of the Association for Recorded Sound Collections. New York, The New York Public Library, 1967. 157 p.

Preface written "for the Committee" by Jean Bowen.

Collections listed alphabetically by state. Addresses given; brief information as to content of collections. Many private collectors listed.

The College Music Society. Directory of music faculties in American colleges and universities. . . .
See no. 178.

1819 / "Directory of National Music Centers." Compiled by Keith MacMillan. Introduction by André Jurres. In *Notes*, 27 (1971), p. 680–693.

Describes the history, organization, and services of 19 music information centers: Australia, Austria, Belgium, Canada, Czechoslovakia, Denmark, Finland, France, Federal Republic of Germany, Iceland, Israel, The Netherlands, Norway, Poland, Portugal, Sweden, Switzerland, United Kingdom, and United States.

1820 / Goertz, Harald. Österreichisches Musikhandbuch. In Zusammenarbeit mit Christa Flamm und Rudolf Klein. Hrsg. von der Österreichischen Gesellschaft für Musik. München, Jugend und Volk Verlag, 1971. 349 p.

A directory of Austrian music organizations and institutions and their personnel. Information includes archives and libraries, theaters, radio and television organizations, societies, periodicals, etc.

1821 / Hinrichsen's Musical Year Book, 1944– . London, Hinrichsen Edition, Ltd., 1944– . 11 vols. to 1961.

A series of volumes edited by Max Hinrichsen, issued at irregular intervals, remarkably varied in content. The articles range from trivia to substantial contributions by recognized authorities. Most of the volumes contain bibliographies of current music publications as well as numerous lists, illustrations, chronologies. More recent volumes have been organized about some central theme, i.e., vol. 8, "The organ of Bach and matters related to this subject" (1956); vol. 9, "John Gay and the Ballad Opera" (1956); vol. 10, "Organ and choral aspects and prospects" (1958). vol. 11 (1961) contains the papers read at the Joint Congress of the International Association of Music Libraries and the Galpin Society, Cambridge, 1959.

1822 / International Directory of Music Education Institutions. Paris, UNESCO, 1968. 115 p.

A source book of information compiled by the International Society for Music Education for UNESCO. Covers 10 categories:

1. Conservatories and academies of music
2. Music and music education schools or faculties in universities
3. Other music institutions
4. International music and music education workshops, summer courses, teacher-training courses
5. International competitions
6. International music festivals
7. Music libraries, archives and documentation centers of international standing

429

8. Collections of musical instruments
9. Organizations, societies and institutions of music and music education
10. National and international music periodicals

1823 / Jacobs, Arthur. The music yearbook, 1972–73. Houndmills, Basingstoke, Hampshire, The Macmillan Press, 1972. 750 p.

A survey of musical activities in 1971 in articles and statistics; a directory of the musical profession, institutions, and the music industry. Chiefly British in orientation, but with some international. coverage.

New York publisher, St. Martin's Press.

1824 / Jahrbuch der Musikwelt. The yearbook of the music world. Annuaire du monde musical. 1. Jahrgang, 1949–50. Bayreuth, Verlag Julius Steeger, 1949. 696 p.

Only one volume published. Contains a vast amount of information regarding musicians and musical institutions throughout the world. Contents include a classified listing of German music dissertations, 1885–1948; a chronology of music dictionaries and encyclopedias; a list of European music periodicals, 1945–48; a bibliography of German music and writings on music, etc.

1825 / The Music Magazine/Musical Courier. The annual directory of the concert world. 1963– . Evanston, Ill., Summy-Birchard Co.

Editions for 1957–61 published as the mid-January issue of *Musical courier*, with title: *Directory issue of the musical arts and artists.*

The 1963 issue, edited by Max D. Jones, contains pertinent information on American and foreign music organizations, artist and concert managers, artist availability, current series and associations, orchestras, opera booking organizations, festizals, foundations, schools of music, publishers, periodicals, recording firms, and music dealers.

1826 / Musical America. [Annual directory or annual booking edition.] New York, Music Publications, Ltd.

A special annual issue devoted chiefly to advertising performing artists, but editions in recent years contain many special articles and lists.

430

1827 / **The Musician's Guide:** the directory of the world of music. 1972 ed. Editor-in-chief, Gladys S. Field. New York, Music Information Service, Inc., 1972. 1,013 p.

First issued in 1955. 3rd ed., 1957; 4th ed., 1968.

A classified directory of names connected with all phases of commercial music activity. Contains more than 50 rosters of persons, organizations, activities, and businesses concerned with the musical profession.

Review of the 1957 edition by Richard S. Hill in *Notes,* 14 (1957) p. 111–13; of the 1968 edition by Thor Wood and Neil Ratliff in *Notes,* 25 (1969), p. 736–37. Also reviewed in *The Booklist and subscription books bulletin,* Dec. 1, 1972. p. 307–08.

1828 / **Opera Annual.** Edited by Harold Rosenthal. No. 1– . London, Jahn Calder, 1953/54– .

Articles on aspects of the opera world during the current year. Attention focused on developments in Great Britain.

1829 / **Pavlakis, Christopher.** The American music handbook, a guide to organized musical activity in the United States. An inventory of musical resources: the people, places, and organizations. New York, The Free Press, 1974.

A directory focused on professional musicianship in the United States: organizations, vocal and instrumental ensembles, performers, composers, festivals and awards, education, radio and television, music industries, periodicals, and management. A foreign supplement treats international festivals and contests, music publishers.

1830 / **Pierre Key's Music Year Book,** the standard music annual, 1924–38. New York, Pierre Key, Inc., 1925-38. 6 v.

A directory of musical organizations and musicians, chiefly performers; issued irregularly over a period of 13 years. The earlier volumes are international in scope, the later are restricted to U.S. coverage.

1831 / **The Purchaser's Guide to the Music Industries.** Annual edition, 1897– . New York, The Music Trades, 1897– .

Title varies: after 1958, *Directory issue.* . . .

Annual classified directory of instrument manufacturers, music publishers, engravers and printers, retail music stories, dealers in music merchandise, etc. Excludes performers and performing groups.

1832 / The Year in American Music, 1946/47–1947/48. New York, Allen, Towne & Heath [1947–48], 2 v.

1946/47 edited by Julius Bloom; 1947/48, by David Ewen.

The first part of each volume is a chronological survey of the important musical events of the year; this is followed by a miscellany of factual information, biographical and bibliographical.

1833 / The Year's Work in Music, 1947/48–1950/51. Edited by Alan Frank. London, New York, published for the British Council by Longmans, Green & Co., 1948–51. 3 v.

Each volume contains a series of essays by various specialists on aspects of British musical life during the year: musical research, the making and playing of instruments, the British Broadcasting Corporation and contemporary music, etc. Contains an annual bibliography of published music and musical literature compiled by A. Hyatt King.

Miscellaneous Bibliographical Tools

IN THIS SECTION the few existing bibliographies of music bibliography are listed, together with a selected group of statements concerning the nature and current status of the field of music bibliography. The principal codes for cataloging music have been included, as well as the major guides to music library practice. Among the remaining miscellany will be found several works concerned with the vexing problem of music copyright. See nos. 1915 and 1917.

1834 / **Allen, Warren D.** "Bibliography of literature concerning the general history of music in chronological order." In his *Philosophies of music history.* New York, American Book Co., 1939. P. 343-65. Also issued in paperback. New York, Dover, 1962.

317 titles arranged chronologically from 1600 to 1939. Not all can be described as histories in the modern sense, but they have bearing on the development of music historiography.

1835 / **Berner, A., J. H. van der Meer, & G. Thibault.** . . . Preservation and restoration of musical instruments. Provisional recommendations. The International Council of Museums, 1967. 76 p.

Not a full-scale treatise on its subject, but suggests the problems to be encountered in the restoration and preservation of instruments. Illustrated with plates from early treatises on musical instruments. P. 23–29: bibliography.

1836 / **Bobillier, Marie** (Michel Brenet, *pseud.*) "Bibliographie des bibliographies musicales." In *L'Année musicale*, 3 (1913), p. 1–152.
    Reprint by Da Capo Press, 1971. 152 p.
    One of the first, and still one of the few, specialized bibliographies of music bibliography. Outdated but still useful. Lists general works, including periodical articles, by author; individual bibliographies; catalogs of libraries; catalogs of dealers and publishers.

1837 / **Bradley, Carol June.** The Dickinson classification; a cataloguing and classification manual for music. Including a reprint of the George Sherman Dickinson Classification of musical compositions. Carlisle, Pa., Carlisle Books, 1968. 176 p.
    A classification system developed by George Sherman Dickinson, music librarian at Vassar College, 1927–1953. This volume contains a reprint of the Dickinson *Classification*, originally published in 1938, together with a discussion of cataloging procedures based on it.
    For a description of the classification and a demonstration of its applications, see Carol Bradley's article "The Dickinson classification for music" in *Fontes artis musicae*, 19 (1972), p. 13–22.

1838 / **The British Catalogue of Music Classification.** Compiled for the Council of the British National Bibliography, Ltd., by E. J. Coates. Published by the Council of the British National Bibliography, Ltd., British Museum, London, 1960. 56 p.
    The classification scheme developed for use in *The British Catalogue of Music.* See no 823.

1839 / **Brook, Barry S.** Thematic catalogues in music, an annotated bibliography, including printed, manuscript, and in-preparation catalogues; related literature and reviews; an essay on the definitions, history, functions, historiography, and future of the thematic catalogue. Hillsdale, N.Y., Pendragon Press, 1972. 347 p.
    Published under the joint sponsorship of the Music Library Association and *RILM abstracts of music literature.* This work supersedes *A*

check-list of thematic catalogues edited by an MLA Committee on Thematic Indexes (1954) and its *Supplement* issued by Queens College (1966).

Indexes some 1,500 entries, including a number of 18th-century manuscript catalogs, a great many unpublished catalogs, and some large-scale national projects currently in progress.

1840 / **Brown, Howard Mayer, and Joan Lascelle.** Musical iconography; a manual for cataloguing musical subjects in Western art before 1800. Cambridge, Mass., Harvard University Press, 1972. 220 p.

Includes bibliographical references.

1841 / **Bryant, Eric Thomas.** Music librarianship; a practical guide. London, James Clarke [1959], 503 p.

Reprint by Stechert-Hafner, 1963.

Part I, p. 3–285; discussion of the administration, services, and technical processes of music libraries. Part II, p. 289–450: a series of annotated bibliographies of basic materials, chiefly scores, for a public library collection. The emphasis is on British practices.

Review by Alfons Ott in *Fontes artis musicae,* 7 (1960), p. 72–73; by Rita Benton in *Notes,* 17 (1960), p. 397–98.

1842 / **Code International de Catalogage de la Musique.** I. Der Autorenkatalog der Musikdrucke. The author catalog of published music. [By] Franz Grasberger. Trans. by Virginia Cunningham. Frankfurt/London, C. F. Peters, 1961. 53 p.

This and the two following volumes are the result of the work of the Commission on Music Cataloging of the International Association of Music Libraries. Later volumes projected include a code for the cataloging of music manuscripts and sound recordings.

Review by Richard S. Angell in *Notes,* 15 (1957), p. 110–11.

1843 / **Code International de Catalogage de la Musique.** II. Code restreint. Rédigé par Yvette Fédoroff. . . . Kurzgefasste Anleitung— Limited code. Übersetzung von Simone Wallon. Trans. by Virginia Cunningham. Frankfurt/London, C. F. Peters, 1961. 53 p.

Review by Minnie Elmer in *Notes,* 19 (1961), p. 247–49; by Richard Schaal in *Die Musikforschung,* 17 (1964), p. 295–96.

1844 / Code International de Catalogage de la Musique. III. Rules for full cataloging—Règles de catalogage détaillé—Regeln für die vollständige Titelaufnahme, compiled by Virginia Cunningham. . . . Frankfurt, C. F. Peters, 1971. 116 p.

1845 / Coover, James B. "The current status of music bibliography." In *Notes*, 13 (1956), p. 581–93.

A survey of the accomplishments, progress, and lacunae in the field of music bibliography as of 1956. The paper takes its point of departure from A. Hyatt King's statement in *The library* (1945). See no. 1882, below.

1846 / Coover, James B. Music lexicography, including a study of lacunae in music lexicography and a bibliography of music dictionaries. Third edition, revised and enlarged. Carlisle, Pa., Carlisle Books, 1971. 175 p.

First issued as *A bibliography of music dictionaries*, Denver, Bibliographical Center for Research, 1952. Second edition, Denver, 1958.

The most comprehensive bibliography available of music dictionaries. 1,801 items arranged alphabetically, including all known editions of the works cited. Preceded by a general discussion of the history of music lexicography and of existing lacunae. Index to personal names, index to topics and types, and an index, by date of publication, to dictionaries before 1900.

Review of the 2nd edition by Irene Millen in *Notes*, 16 (1959), p. 383–84.

1847 / Currall, Henry F. J. Gramophone record libraries, their organization and practice. . . . With a preface by A. Hyatt King. 2nd ed. Published for the International Association of Music Libraries, United Kingdom Branch. London, Crosby Lockwood and Son, 1970. 303 p.

The work was first published in 1963.

A manual for the administration of a record library, with contributions by British librarians and sound recording experts. P. 131–46: "A basic stock list"; p. 171–76: "Gramophone librarianship: a bibliography." Illustrated.

1848 / Dadelsen, Georg von. Editionsrichtlinien musikalischer Denkmäler und Gesamtausgaben. Im Auftrag der Gesellschaft für

Musikforschung. . . . Kassel, Basel, Bärenreiter, 1967. 143 p. (Musik-wissenschaftliche Arbeiten, 22.)

Presents standards and techniques for editorial practice as employed in the German critical editions.

Review by Robert L. Marshall in *Notes*, 25 (1969), p. 733–35.

1849 / **Davies, John H.** Musicalia: sources of information in music. Second edition, revised and enlarged. Oxford, Pergamon Press, 1969. 184 p. 48 facsim.

First published in 1966.

A practical guide to music reference materials, illustrated with fac-simile pages of the major reference works.

Review by François Lesure in *Fontes artis musicae*, 17 (Jan.–Aug. 1970), p. 55.

1850 / **Detroit Studies in Music Bibliography.** No. 1– . Detroit, Information Coordinators, Inc., 1961– .

A series of manuals, diverse in character and content, but each con-cerned with some aspect or area of music bibliography.

1851 / (1) *Reference materials in ethnomusicology*, by Bruno Nettl. Second edition, revised, 1967.

First published in 1961. Also entered as no. 690.

1852 / (2) *Sir Arthur Sullivan: an index to the texts of his vocal works*, by Sirvart Poladian, 1961.

1853 / (3) *An index to Beethoven's conversation books*, by Donald W. MacArdle. 1961. 46 p.

Review by Fred Blum in *Notes*, 20 (1963), p. 225–27.

1854 / (4) *General bibliography for music research*, by Keith E. Mixter. 1962. 38 p.

Surveys the nonmusical aids to musical research, with emphasis on such reference works as general bibliographies of bibliography, national and trade bibliographies, general dictionaries, encyclopedias, union lists, and library catalogs.

Review by Fred Blum in *Notes*, 20 (1963), p. 225–27.

1855 / (5) *A Handbook of American operatic premieres, 1731–1963*, by Julius Mattfeld. 1963. 142 p.
Also entered as no 356.

1856 / (6) *Medieval and Renaissance music on long-playing records*, by James B. Coover and Richard Colvig. 1964. 122 p.
Also entered as no 1739. 2nd ed. 1973.

1857 / (7) *Rhode Island music and musicians, 1733–1850*, by Joyce Ellen Mangler. 1965. 90 p.
Also entered as no. 182.

1858 / (8) *Jean Sibelius, an international bibliography on the occasion of the centennial celebrations, 1965*, by Fred Blum. 1965. 114 p.
P. 1–11: Books and dissertations devoted to Sibelius; p. 13–45: books partially devoted to Sibelius; p. 47–71: music journals; p. 73–94: nonmusic journals. Index of names.
Also entered as no. 792.

1859 / (9) *Bibliography of theses and dissertations in sacred music*, by Kenneth R. Hartley. (1967). 127 p.
Also entered under no. 655.

1860 / (10) *Checklist of vocal chamber works by Benedetto Marcello*, by Caroline S. Fruchtman. (1967). 37 p.
Also entered under no. 999.

1861 / (11) *An annotated bibliography of woodwind instruction books, 1600–1830*, by Thomas E. Warner. (1967). 138 p.
Also entered under no. 784.

1862 / (12) *Works for solo voice of Johann Adolf Hasse (1699–1783)* by Sven Hostrup Hansell. (1968). 110 p.
Also entered under no. 995.

1863 / (13) *A selected discography of solo song*, by Dorothy Stahl. (1968). 95 p.
Supplement, 1968–1969. (1970). 95 p.
Also entered under no. 1753.

1864 / (14) *Music publishing in Chicago before 1871: the firm of Root and Cady, 1858–1871,* by Dena J. Epstein. (1969). 243 p.
Also entered under no. 1652.

1865 / (15) *An introduction to certain Mexican musical archives,* by Lincoln Spiess and Thomas Stanford. (1969). 184 p.
Also entered under no. 1370.

1866 / (16) *A checklist of American music periodicals, 1850–1900,* by William J. Weichlein. (1970). 103 p.
Also entered as no. 641.

1867 / (17) *A checklist of 20th-century choral music for male voices,* by Kenneth Roberts. (1970). 32 p.
Also entered as no. 935.

1868 / (18) *Published music for the viola da gamba and other viols,* by Robin de Smet. (1971). 105 p.
Also entered as no. 941.

1869 / (19) *The works of Christoph Nichelmann: a thematic index,* by Douglas A. Lee. (1971). 100 p.
Also entered as no. 1003.

1870 / (20) *The reed trio: an annotated bibliography of original published works,* by James E. Gillespie, Jr. (1971). 84 p.
Also entered as no. 896.

1871 / (21) *An index to the vocal works of Thomas Augustine Arne and Michael Arne,* by John A. Parkinson. (1972). 82 p.
Also entered under no. 982.

1872 / (22) *Bibliotheca Bouduaniana: a Renaissance music bibliography,* by D. W. Krummel. (1972). 191 p.

1873 / (23) *Music publishing in the Middle Western States before the Civil War,* by Ernst C. Krohn. (1972). 44 p.
Also entered under no. 1679.

1874 / **Duckles, Vincent,** ed. Music libraries and librarianship.

Library Trends, 8 (April, 1960) p. 495–617. [Published by the University of Illinois, School of Librarianship.]

15 specialists discuss various aspects of music librarianship, covering the areas of training for the profession, bibliography and selection, cataloging, services, and administration.

Review by Vladimir Fédorov in *Fontes artis musicae*, 8 (1961), p. 30–31.

1875 / **Duckles, Vincent.** "Music literature, music, and sound recordings," in *Bibliography, current state and future trends*, edited by Robert B. Downs and Frances B. Jenkins. Urbana, University of Illinois Press, 1967. p. 158–183.

First published in *Library Trends*. January, 1967.

1876 / **Duckles, Vincent.** Music reference and research materials, an annotated bibliography. 2nd ed. New York, Free Press; London, Collier-Macmillan, 1967, 385 p. 3rd ed. New York, Free Press; London, Collier Macmillan Publishers, 1974, 526 p.

First published in 1964.

Review of the first edition by Jan LaRue in *JAMS*, 19 (1966), p. 257–61; of the 2nd edition by William S. Newman in *Notes*, 24 (1967), p. 265–66. Review of the first ed. by Klaus Speer in *Notes*, 21 (1964), p. 375.

1877 / **Fischer, Wilhelm.** "Verzeichnis von bibliographischen Hilfswerken für musikhistorische Arbeiten." In Adler, Guido, *Methode der Musikgeschichte*. Leipzig, Breitkopf & Härtel, 1919. P. 200–222.

Classified list, including general bibliographical works, general musical works, and bibliographies of single aspects of music history. Some inaccurate dates and incomplete titles for French and English works, which are less well covered.

1878 / **Hoboken, Anthony van.** "Probleme der musikbibliographischen Terminologie." In *Fontes artis musicae*, 1958: 1. p. 6–15.

A discussion centered in the difficulties of establishing music bibliography as an "exact science" in view of the variety and complexity of the materials with which it is concerned.

1879 / **Hopkinson, Cecil.** "The fundamentals of music bibliography." In *Fontes artis musicae*, 1955: 2. p. 122–31.

An attempt to stimulate discussion of some basic points as to the nature, content, and procedures of music bibliography as it serves the needs of collectors, musicians, and historians.

1880 / **International Association of Music Libraries. Deutsche Gruppe.** Systematik der Musikliteratur und der Musikalien für öffentliche Musikbüchereien. Erarbeitet von der Kommission für Musiksystematik bei der Arbeitsgemeinschaft für Musikbüchereien in der Deutschen Gruppe der Association Internationale des Bibliothèques Musicales (AIBM) [Reutlingen] Bücherei und Bildung, 1963. 39 p.

A system of music classification devised for German public library practice.

1881 / **Keys to Music Bibliography.** v. 1– . Kent, Ohio, The Kent State University Press, 1970– .

1. Vorhees, Anna Tipton. Index to symphonic program notes in books. 1970.

1882 / **King, A. Hyatt.** "Recent work in music bibliography." In *The library*, 26: 2 (Sept.–Dec. 1945), p. 99–148.

Surveys the accomplishments in music bibliography during the period just prior to and during World War II.

1883 / **King, A. Hyatt.** Some British collectors of music. Cambridge, Cambridge Univ. Press, 1963. 178 p. (The Sandars Lectures for 1961.)

A pioneer study of the activity of private collectors of music in England, with an appendix containing classified lists of collectors from the mid-17th century to the present.

Review by Albi Rosenthal in *Music and letters*, 45 (1964), p. 258–59; by Irving Lowens in *Notes*, 22 (1965–66), p. 906–07.

1884 / **Koltypina, Galina Borisovna,** ed. Bibliografia muzykalnoi bibliografii. [Bibliography of musical bibliography.] Moscow, 1963. 226 p.

An annotated bibliography of Russian music bibliographies. The work cites bibliographies of literature on music separately published, lists books, articles, and reviews. Designed for bibliographers and scholars.

1885 / **Koltypina, Galina Borisovna, ed.** Spravochnaia literatura po muzyke [Reference literature on music . . . 1773–1962] Moscow, 1964. 249 p.

A publication of the Moscow State Library.

Annotated bibliography of Russian reference literature on music, including dictionaries, collected biography, calendars, etc., published in Russia from 1773 to 1962. Cites reviews in Russian periodical literature.

1886 / **Krohn, Ernest C.** "The bibliography of music." In *MQ*, 5 (1919), p. 231–54.

One of the first surveys of the state of music bibliography by an American scholar. Useful as a statement of the accomplishments in the field at the time of writing. Incomplete citations. Narrative style.

1887 / **Krummel, Donald W., and James B. Coover.** "Current national bibliographies, their music coverage." In *Notes*, 17 (1960), p. 375–88.

Surveys the music coverage in the national bibliographies in the Western Hemisphere, Western and Eastern Europe, Africa, Asia, and Oceania.

1888 / **Laforte, Conrad.** Le catalogue de la chanson folklorique française. Québec, Les Presses Universitaires Laval, 1958. 397 p. (Publications des archives de folklore, Université Laval.)

Demonstrates a method for establishing an alphabetical catalog, by title, of French folk songs, with appropriate cross-references to permit the grouping of variants under a common title. Based on material in Canadian archives and collections.

1889 / **Luther, Wilhelm Martin.** "Bibliographie . . . Literatur." In *MGG*. Kassel, Bärenreiter, 1949– . V. 1, col. 1837–39.

Recounts the history and surveys the concepts of music bibliography, with an extensive listing of titles pertaining to the field.

1890 / **McColvin, Lionel R., and Harold Reeves.** Music libraries, including a comprehensive bibliography of music literature and a select bibliography of music scores published since 1957. . . . Completely rewritten, revised, and extended by Jack Dove. London, Andre Deutsch, 1965. 2 v.

First published in 1937–38.

Vol. 1 is made up of a series of chapters on various aspects of music library administration and practice: staff, binding, classification, cataloguing, etc. There are chapters devoted to British public libraries, British university and special libraries, overseas libraries, etc.

Vol. 2 consists of bibliographies and indexes of music literature and scores which are cited elsewhere. See nos. 556, 813.

Reviews by Harold Spivacke and by K. H. Anderson in *Notes*, 22 (1965–66), p. 872–77.

1891 / **Mixter, Keith E.** An introduction to library resources for music research. Columbus, Ohio, School of Music, College of Education, Ohio State University, 1963. 61 p.

A practical list of music books and editions for use in courses in music bibliography at the college or university level. Selective. A minimum of annotations.

Review by Richard Schaal in *Die Musikforschung*, 17 (1964), p. 295.

1892 / **Music Indexes and Bibliographies.** George R. Hill, general editor. No. 1– . Hackensack, N.J., Joseph Boonin, 1970– .

1893 / (1) *A thematic locator for Mozart's works, as listed in Koechel's Chronologisch-thematisches Verzeichnis*, 6th ed. . . . By George R. Hill, *et al.* (1970), 76 p.

1894 / (2) *A preliminary checklist of research on the classic symphony and concerto to the time of Beethoven (excluding Haydn and Mozart).* By George R. Hill. (1970), 58 p.

1895 / (3) *A checklist of writings on 18th-century French and Italian opera (excluding Mozart).* By Elvidio Surian. (1970) 121 p.

1896 / (4) *An index to the solo songs of Robert Franz*, by Joseph M. Boonin. (1970) 19 p.

1897 / **Music Librarianship and Documentation.** Report of the Adelaide Seminar, May 1970. Published by the Department of Adult Education, University of Adelaide, Adelaide, S.A. 145 p.

A stimulating series of papers reporting on various aspects and problems of music librarianship and documentation in a part of the world where these disciplines have recently become established.

1898 / **Music Library Association.** Code for cataloging music and phonorecords. Prepared by a Joint Committee of the Music Library Association and the American Library Association, Division of Cataloging and Classification. Chicago, American Library Association, 1958. 88 p.

The five major divisions of the code are entry, description, phonorecords, simplified rules, and filing rules for conventional titles. Glossary and index.

1899 / **Music Library Association. Committee on Information and Organization.** Manual of music librarianship. Ed. by Carol June Bradley. Ann Arbor, Michigan, Music Library Association Executive Office, 1966. 150 p.

1900 / **Music Library Association.** *MLA* index series. No. 1– . Ann Arbor, Michigan, Music Library Association Executive Office, 1963– .

A series of short, self-contained bibliographies or indexes prepared under the supervision of the Publications Committee of the Music Library Association. The volumes published to date are as follows:

1901 / (1) An alphabetical index to Claudio Monteverdi *Tutti le Opere*. Edited by the Bibliography Committee of the New York Chapter MLA (1963).

1902 / (2) An alphabetical index to Hector Berlioz *Werke*; edited by the Bibliography Committee of the New York Chapter MLA (1963).

1903 / (3) A checklist of music bibliographies (in progress and unpublished); compiled by the Publications Committee MLA [n.d.]. 2nd, revised ed. compiled by James Pruett, 1969.

1904 / (4) A concordance of the thematic indexes to the instrumental works of Antonio Vivaldi, by Lenore Coral. (1965).

1905 / (5) An alphabetical index to Tomás Luis de Victoria *Opera Omnia*. Edited by the Bibliography Committee of the New York Chapter MLA (1966).

1906 / (6) Schumann index, part I. An alphabetical index to Robert Schumann: *Werke*, comp. by Michael Ochs (1967).

1907 / (7) Schumann index, part II. An alphabetical index to the solo songs of Robert Schumann, comp. by William Weichlein (1967).

1908 / (8) An index to Maurice Frost's *English and Scottish psalm and hymn tunes*, compiled by Kirby Rogers (1967).

1909 / (9) *Speculum*: an index of musically related articles and book reviews, compiled by Arthur S. Wolf (1970).

1910 / (10) An index to *Das Chorwerk*, vols. 1–110, compiled by Michael Ochs (1970).

1911 / (11) Bach aria index, compiled by Miriam K. Whaples (1971).

1912 / **New York Public Library. Reference Department.** Music subject headings, authorized for use in the catalogs of the Music Division. Boston, G. K. Hall, 1959. 512 p.
Reproduced from cards in the subject heading file of The New York Public Library. An important tool for music catalogers, since it represents the practice of one of the great American music libraries.

1913 / **Ott, Alfons.** "Die Musikbibliotheken," in Fritz Milkau's *Handbuch der Bibliothekswissenschaft*. 2nd ed. vol. 2, p. 222–42.
Also printed as a separate by Harrassowitz, Wiesbaden, 1959.
Review by C. B. Oldman in *Fontes artis musicae*, 7 (1960), p. 71–72.

1914 / **Pethes, Iván.** A flexible classification system of music and literature on music. Translated by Mihaly Sandory. Budapest, Centre of Library Science and Methodology, 1968. 49 p.
In Hungarian and English.

1915 / **Pohlmann, Hansjörg.** Die Frühgeschichte des musikalischen Urheberrechts (*ca.* 1400–1800). Neue Materialien zur Entwicklung des Urheberrechtsbewusstseins der Komponisten. Kassel, Bärenreiter, 1962. 315 p. (Musikwissenschaftliche Arbeiten. Hrsg. von der Gesellschaft für Musikforschung, 20.)

One of the few studies in the history of music copyright practice treating the sociological and psychological aspects of composers' rights, plagiarism, the history of honoraria for composers. An appendix gives 31 original documents in transcription.

Review by Werner Braun in *Die Musikforschung*, 17 (1964), p. 298–99.

1916 / Regeln zur Katalogisierung der in der Deutschen Bücherei eingehenden Musikalien. Entwurf. Leipzig, Deutsche Bücherei, 1959. 35 p.

Cataloging rules developed for German libraries.

Review by Virginia Cunningham in *Notes*, 16 (1959), p. 567.

1917 / Rothenberg, Stanley. Copyright and public performance of music. The Hague, Martinus Nijhoff, 1954. 188 p.

A survey of the current status of music copyright and performers' rights in the United States and in Europe.

1918 / Schulze, Erich. Urheberrecht in der Musik. Dritte, neubearbeitete Auflage. Berlin, Walter De Gruyter, 1965. 474 p.

First published in 1951, 4th revised edition, 1972.

A source book of information on music copyright practice. European orientation. 37 appendices of codes and other documents related to copyright. The bibliography, p. xii–xxiv, provides an international listing of performer's rights organizations.

1919 / U.S. Library of Congress. Subject Cataloging Division. Classification. Class M: music and books on music. 2nd ed., with supplementary pages. Washington, 1963. 157, 101 p.

First issued in 1904, revised 1917.

Largely the work of O. G. T. Sonneck, this classification schedule has been accepted, with various modifications, in a great many American music libraries, chiefly in colleges and universities.

"Additions and changes to July 1962" occupy the last 101 pages.

1920 / U.S. Library of Congress. Subject Cataloging Division. Music subject headings used on printed catalog cards of the Library of Congress. Washington, D.C., Govt. Printing Office, 1952. 133 p.

1921 / **Wallon, Simone.** "Musicologie," in L. N. Malclés, *Les sources du travail bibliographique.* Tome II: Bibliographies spécialisées (Sciences humaines). Genève, E. Droz, 1952. p. 536–52.

Basic but highly selective list of music reference works, classified and well annotated.

1922 / **Winchell, Constance M.** "Music." In her *Guide to reference books.* 7th ed. Chicago, American Library Association, 1951. p. 346–56.

See also the appropriate sections in later supplements.

Index of Authors, Editors, and Reviewers

449

459

Index of Subjects

Index of Titles

Index of Titles

484

Index of Titles

Index of Titles

Index of Titles

500

Index of Titles

Index of Titles

506

Index of Titles

Index of Titles

Index of Titles

Index of Titles

DATE DUE

DEMCO 38-297